The Future:
Opportunity
Not Destiny

Edited by
Howard F. Didsbury, Jr.

World Future Society
Bethesda, Maryland
U.S.A.

Editor: Howard F. Didsbury, Jr.

Editorial Review Committee: Deirdre H. Banks, James J. Crider, Howard F. Didsbury, Jr. (Chairman), Charles H. Little, Theodore J. Maziarski, Andrew A. Spekke

Staff Editor: Edward Cornish

Administrative Coordinator: Susan Echard

Editorial Consultants: Sally Cornish, James J. Crider, Frances Segraves

Editorial Assistant: Patty McNally

Production Manager: Jefferson Cornish

Cover: Michael Hill

Published by: World Future Society
4916 Saint Elmo Avenue
Bethesda, Maryland 20814
USA

© 1989 World Future Society

Library of Congress Catalog Card Number: 89-051059

International Standard Book Number: 0-930242-36-X

Printed in the United States of America

Contents

Applying Futures Research

New Mental Attitudes

Humanist Views of the Future

NOTE

The Future: Opportunity Not Destiny was prepared in conjunction with the World Future Society's Sixth General Assembly, "Future View: The 1990s & Beyond," held in Washington, DC, July 16-20, 1989. The Chairman of the Conference was Kenneth W. Hunter. Susan Echard served as staff director. Robert M. Schley was program coordinator and Tracy L. Nathan served as assistant program coordinator.

The papers presented here were selected from a very large number submitted to the Editorial Review Committee. A number of distinguished papers whose subject matter did not lie within the limits of the volume could not be included.

Footnotes and other academic paraphernalia have been minimized to avoid disrupting the flow of the author's ideas and insights.

PREFACE

THE GREAT TRANSFORMATION

Over two centuries ago the great transformation of the world began with the advent of the Industrial Revolution in England. Though the rise of modern science and the coming of the Industrial Revolution were essentially unrelated though parallel developments, by the late 19th century they were wed and proceeded to produce—and continue to produce—a prodigious number of scientific and technological innovations which affect human life immensely.

Until recently the impact of the great transformation was not experienced by all peoples. This is no longer the case as a result of the revolution in electronic communication media. The media today serve as the nerve cells of humanity. In such a world we all can know the promises and problems of the worldwide transformation.

The contemporary interest in futures studies stems from the need to give greater attention to "foresight," "anticipation" and consideration of the likely effects of scientific and technological innovations. The challenges and opportunities arising out of such innovations transcend politics and political ideology. The quest for "wholly political and ideological approaches [to the future]," futurist John McHale observed some years ago, "are now patently bankrupt." We must strive to create a vision of the future and what it may promise by a variety of means (i.e., the methodologies of futures studies) and never overlook the importance of creative imagination in attempts to visualize the future or futures.

In the standard "Gee-Whiz" technological view of the future, the mind is sent spinning in a whorl of statistical data, geometric projections of information accumulation and a list of fantastic potential developments such as automation and robotics. We should rather focus on likely ecological, economic, political and social effects of the present and emerging scientific and technological innovations. How may they effect human beings, singly and collectively?

A sense of history helps us anticipate the future. Gaining such a sense in an age of information overload and the communication media's tendency to concentrate on the "present"—the latest, the "new," the sensational—makes this difficult. Much speculation about the future in the 1960s did not measure up to the actual unfolding of the future. Two examples come to mind. On the one hand, the 1960s were characterized by an unalloyed optimism vis a vis the whole process and results of the modernization of "undeveloped countries" (the term then in vogue). Decades later the majority of these countries are still undeveloped and, for many, the prospects are gloomy. There was also great enthusiasm for the theory of "convergence," that is, the belief that as countries develop, modernize, and avail themselves of all of the trappings of industrial civilization and utilize modern science and technology a world community would occur. During the 60s many were enthralled with a global future enhanced by evermore dramatic scientific and technological achievements and economic development. Political ideologies would wane as East and West converge. Instead we had Vietnam and East-West tensions seemingly refuting the convergence view of the future.

As we enter the last decade of the 20th century however, we may be witnessing the "re-birth" of the convergence theory, with emphasis placed on the common global ecological threats to the survival of humanity. For without concerted global action and continued concern for maintaining a habitable planet, humanity is endangered. This ecological concern has been added to the recognition of the evident limitations of all absolute, "pure" political-economic philosophies be they capitalist, communist or socialist. Dogmatism notwithstanding, there is a universal push for creating a "mixed economy"—one providing for both "private interest" and "public interest."

How to encourage individual initiative and ingenuity (in the old-fashioned phrase "enlightened self-interest") in economic life and, at the same time, see to it that the general welfare of society is advanced? Individual self-interest can easily degenerate into selfish disregard for the common good; an injudicious concern for the welfare of society can lead to an unimaginative, oppressive bureaucratic frame of mind which stifles initiative and creativity. Both extremes do disservice to their citizens.

The great question: How to create an arrangement which circumvents these dangers? There may be no "perfect" solution. A willingness to accept tentative, pragmatic policies which are always subject to modification depending upon changing economic and social conditions as the great transformation continues may be the best solution.

The United States is now in a political and economic milieu which embraces "deregulation." However, as the great transformation advances, this period of deregulation may be but a brief, passing phase. If, as Oliver Wendell Holmes observed, "Taxes are the price we pay for civilization," regulation and indicative planning may be the price we must pay for survival in a society and world of complexity, interrelatedness and—if unplanned and unregulated—mutually destructive competition and overproduction. We can anticipate a dramatic reversal of the present emphasis upon deregulation and an abhorrence of planning. Ingenuity and skill are required to solve the real problem: *regulating the regulators*. Planning, that is, indicative planning which involves voluntary, cooperative encompassing various segments of society may become an integral feature of the much-talked about Information Society. Prudence dictates that the preservation of a wholesome environment, clean water and air, reduction of pollution and responsible resource utilization require imaginative regulation and enforcement on a grand scale.

In the not-too-distant future, it will become clear that regulation and indicative planning are necessary in order to prevent environment degradation and economic anarchy, national and global.

In the exuberance of scientific and technological achievements, it is easy to forget the hard fact that regardless of the information/ automated society and the information flood we see rising around us, we are still dealing with essentially the same type of human being that existed millennia ago. We must always be aware of the fact that we are dealing with a being filled with passions, fears and hopes. This being now finds himself in a world of ever-accelerating change, increasing complexity and a deluge of information. More and more he finds himself living in an artificial environment. No wonder he is frequently ill at ease and apprehensive. It should never be forgotten that amid all the clamor for gadgetry and technological fixes, human beings have a thin veneer of civilization covering a comparatively primitive psyche.

It becomes evident that "unless there is the right mixture of common sense and science and technology," as Nobel laureate Norman E. Borlaug noted, "the world is doomed." Mindful of the nature of human nature, decision-makers need to try to know what may happen in the future in order to take judicious and timely action in the present.

Organization of the Book

The title of the present volume, *The Future: Opportunity Not Destiny*, was inspired by a sentence in H. G. Wells' 1928 book entitled *The Open Conspiracy: Blue Prints for a World Revolution*. (London: Victor Gollancz, Ltd., p. 8). Viewing the immense challenges confronting humanity in the contemporary world, Wells was not pessimistic about the future. He confidently asserted: "It is opportunity and not destiny we face."

The papers in this volume are grouped into six sections:

A Historical Retrospective;
Economics, Development and the Future;
Meeting Challenges;
Applying Futures Research;
New Mental Attitudes; and
Humanist Views of the Future.

A Historical Retrospective

Where America Was a Century Ago
Dan Walker and John Center

As we speculate on what lies before us in the 21st century with a mixture of hope and anxiety it may be instructive to get a glimpse into what life was like in the United States as the 19th century drew to a close. This paper provides a fine insight into that period. "America . . . spent 25 years rising from the ashes of the Civil War and the trauma of Reconstruction. It would be years before the terrible trauma of World War I . . . " Our authors ask and answer important, probing questions: "Where was America when it was internationally innocent, brash, and expectant with the 20th century about to dawn? What were its thoughts about the present and the future?" After reading this brief historical retrospective the thought that "Today's society was yesterday's utopia" may cause one to pause—and wonder.

Economics, Development and the Future

Biotechnology: Agriculture's Last Hurrah?
Clifton Anderson

"Agricultural production and processing will be revolutionized by biotechnology in the 1990s. Through biological manipulation, new forms and functions will be given to microbes, plants and animals. As new life-forms enter agriculture, many farmers will be leaving—casualties of the biotechnology revolution. The new processes of biotechnology will hasten the industrialization of agriculture. Serious environmental problems may follow. When farmers fail to exercise their traditional custodianship over the land, who will watch over the countryside's environmental health?"

Perestroika in America
Steven M. Clark

"Socialism in the USSR and capitalism in the US are two advanced industrial systems, each facing adaptation as it moves toward a post-industrial economy and social system. Western leaders may be too smug—the Soviets at least acknowledge the necessity of structural change in this historic transition. Socialism needs to foster democracy and build a market; its strengths lay in its concentrated assets and tradition of planning for overall social development. In contrast, capitalism has a perfected market and strong democratic and entrepreneurial tradition; capitalism, however, lacks mechanisms for planning and cooperation in the overall social interest. Fortunately, a new mechanism is beginning to emerge to address this gap in US society: the public interest partnership. The public interest partnership has a particular character, and its emergence is bolstered by four specific trends characteristic of post-industrial transition in the US. Americans need to appreciate and promote the public interest partnership as the cornerstone of our own *perestroika*."

One World: The Coming Union of a New Capitalism and a New Socialism
William E. Halal
"The long conflict between the 'Old Capitalism' and the 'Old Socialism' may soon be resolved as the revolutionary force of information technology transforms both systems into a roughly similar blend of democracy and free enterprise. All nations have unique cultural differences, which should produce wide variations on this generic model of political economy for the information age—Democratic Free Enterprise. But the coming union of a 'New Capitalism' and 'New Socialism' promises to unify this rich diversity into a single coherent, manageable, and compatible global system that works—One World."

Why US Industry Should Be Looking at Soviet Technology
John W. Kiser
"Unlike American universities, Soviet research institutes are not uncomfortable with issues relating to confidentiality, proprietary rights and other issues which may appear to conflict with Western universities' concerns with academic freedom and openness." "There is a tremendous amount of technology for sale in the USSR, and not only in research laboratories. In many cases technologies in full commercial production have been acquired by US firms. Revolutionary surgical stapling technology was introduced in the 1970s by a new venture formed specifically to exploit the Soviet patents." "About one-third of all the world's knowledge today is generated in Eastern Europe and the Soviet Union, though much is poorly utilized. Greater familiarity with that knowledge base in both its scientific and technical dimensions can produce tangible benefits for the United States . . . "

'Factories of the Future' Today
Albert Madwed
"The building and operation of computerized automatic factories is beginning to change the method of producing products in the industrialized nations of the world. A description and analysis of one Swedish, two Japanese and one United States factory are presented . . . " "These four futuristic factories produce completely different products. The Swedish factory produces Volvo trucks and automobiles. The two Japanese factories produce motors and machinery. The United States factory produces many different models of electric motor starters. The components and systems used in these four factories" as well as "basic principles for engineering an automatic futuristic factory" are described and discussed.

Effective Food Marketing as a Tool of Socio-Economic Development in the Third World
Frank Meissner

"Since the end of World War II the Green Revolution has helped produce an abundance of inexpensive food. Yet, in many parts of the world, including such industrialized and wealthy countries as the USA, malnutrition is getting worse. In 1988 at least 800 million people—or 15% of the world's population of 5.3 billion—were on diets that fall short of essential nutrients needed for survival, growth, reproduction as well as for capacity to work, learn, and effectively function in society. Evidently the technology of marketing, which includes all functions performed in getting food from producers into consumers' stomachs, has been subjected to benign neglect." The author quantifies "the extent and reason for this neglect . . . " and explores some remedial actions for the 1990s and beyond.

The Labor Movement and the Redesign of the Workplace"
Arthur B. Shostak

"American trade unionism remains one of the most strategic components of the world of work, a social movement significant far beyond its 16% membership of all workers. Scenarios exploring tomorrow's workplace culture, productivity prospects, and the American standard of living must include sensitive attention to labor's varied prospects. A good case can be made for the likely persistence and revival of labor's strength, provided that more unions merge, more union resources are put into organizing campaigns, and more attention is paid by unions to afterwork stressors."

Meeting Challenges

The Enterprising Community: Leading America into the 21st Century
Gregg Edwards and David Pearce Snyder

" . . . The experience of the 1980s raises a fundamental question: 'If our national political leaders *can't* lead the nation, and our national business leaders *won't* lead the nation, how can we expect American enterprise to make the necessary innovations to remain competitive in the 21st Century?' By the process of elimination, the Eighties have shown us that there can be only one answer to that question. It is *we* —the people who will have to demonstrate the personal commitment *and* intellectual integrity needed to make truly innovative and purposeful uses of our new knowledge and technology." "To mobilize the citizens and institutions of a single community to purposefully adopt 'best practice' in all their productive activities would draw on the two traditional sources of economic growth in America: savvy and hard work. The opportunity to be exploited by the Enterprising Community is perfectly straight forward: on the average, it takes about 10 years for current 'best practice' to become 'common practice,' because of the slow diffusion of innovation and change in the general marketplace. But, in a *supportive* environment, new best practice can become common practice in a matter of weeks or months. Thus, the logic behind the Enterprising Community is clear: 'Sooner or later, best practice becomes common practice; why not here and now?'"

Manifesto for an Information Age
T.M. Grundner

"In many ways the development of mankind can be described and at least partially explained in terms of technological innovation. This is no less true now as we enter a computer-driven 'Information Age.' If there is one thing we have learned, however, it is that technology almost never arrives in a value-free context. There will be principles and priorities that will shape this Information Age whether we like it or not. Without dialogue, however, those decisions will be made by default—and surely a more thoughtful approach than that is in order. What is needed at this point is a 'manifesto,' a statement of principles and intentions, around which an emerging Citizen of an Information Age can frame his or her actions and beliefs. In an effort to help begin the dialogue necessary to frame those principles, six initial statements of belief are presented and defended."

Future Talk: Coping With Our Electronic Technologies
Joseph N. Pelton

"The 21st century will be the time of humankind's greatest challenge. Telepower, as represented by the technologies of telecommunications, computers, robotics and artificial intelligence will alter almost everybody and everything in basic and lasting ways. Some of these changes will include new jobs and new patterns of work. This will mean lifelong education and training, as well as telecommunicating to and from work, sometimes half way around the world. This will serve to foster 'electronic immigrants' who invisibly and even secretly cross national boundaries. In time this could serve to redefine national boundaries and allegiance as electronically spawned telecolonies come into being." "In general Telepower technologies will propel us forward toward a new world of global consciousness and interaction known for now as the world of Future Talk." "With global consciousness may come increased global cooperation, empathy among all cultures, a global language, and in time perhaps the ultimate Telepower breakthrough—a new species designed for the world of Future Talk, *Homo Electronicus.*"

The Global Challenge: Changing Habits or Changing Climates
Claudine Schneider

"Global climate change caused by the unchecked growth in greenhouse gas emissions poses the threat of unprecedented changes to the earth's ecosystems and societies. Our future, however, is not fated. There are viable options for preventing the worst changes from happening, if we but take advantage of these choices. The widespread application of energy efficient technologies and designs is an excellent example of what can be done. Detailed studies show that using energy more efficiently could prevent a tripling of carbon-dioxide emissions, despite a doubling of the world population and a quadrupling of Gross World Product. To achieve this goal will require removal of various institutional barriers and market imperfections that currently inhibit the timely use of energy-saving measures."

Offworld Diversity: The Branching of Life in Space
Brent Sherwood

The author examines reasons why space colonies are and should be the focus of public interest. "Some inescapable fact about space that will constrain space colony society" and ways in which these constraints will "affect, and effect, human societal evolution" are examined. "By setting forth some boundaries and opportunities deriving from the hard reality of space and its necessary technology, we can seed a more mature, contemporary and evolving outlook on the dream of space colonies. That broader view includes possible futures which harbor striking capacities for expanding the domain, and the variety, of all Earth life."

Learning From One Level Lower
Jan Tinbergen

A contribution "to some of the measures necessary to arrive at a sound management of the Globe." The author suggests this can be greatly facilitated "by learning from the organization of well-governed nations, which constitute 'management at one level lower' if one aims at a well-managed planet Earth." This is based on the "principle of the optimum level of decision making." This "level of decision making to solve a given problem must be as low as possible, but a level where all whose welfare is affected are represented."

Applying Futures Research

The Rise of Futures Thinking in the New States: The Decisions of Nationhood
Wendell Bell

"Among the factors that encouraged the rise of futures thinking after World War II was the formation of the new states from the former colonial territories of European countries and the United States. Over 100 new states have now been created, increasing the number of states about 250 percent with the last 45 years. The international system is still rocking from the impact of this growth. In Africa, Asia, the Middle East, the Caribbean, and later the Pacific, emergent nationalist leaders grasped, sometimes after bloody struggle, the reins of national power. The transition to independence fostered futures thinking by opening to question political, economic, social, and cultural beliefs, attitudes, and institutions, both of colonial and traditional societies. It opened up real possibilities for change, raised the consciousness of the people to the opportunities for change, brought the goals of development into play as yardsticks of critical judgment of various aspects of society, and required decision-making aimed at taking action which in itself is an inherently future-oriented process. The decisions of nationhood involved a wide range of issues from setting the geographical boundaries of each new state to the nature of its polity, economy, society, culture, and even the national character of its people. As they faced such decisions, new nationalist leaders helped to prepare the way for a futures-oriented action science."

Explaining and Implementing Futures Research
O.W. Markley
"This is a two part methodological position paper which addresses two issues:

1. How to explain the futures field to those who are unfamiliar with its unique outlook, assumptions and methods; and

2. How to achieve successful implementation of forecasts other futures research results, especially in organizational cultures in which decision-making based on credible foresight is not readily supported, and in environmental settings too turbulent to permit reliable predictive forecasting.

Part I briefly traces the development of modern futures research, describing: a) how it aims at much more than the achievement of predictive foresight; b) why resistance by organizational leaders frequently prevents its results from being implemented successfully; and c) how methods and tools from a parallel field, organization development, can be used to promote successful implementation of anticipatory management methods and results in spite of resistance.

Using the concept of "2nd order change," Part II introduces several "process architectures" for systematizing anticipatory management in turbulent settings. Although they assume a more proactive management culture than now exists in most organizations, these designs may nevertheless point the way toward the next generation state of the art in applied futures research."

New Mental Attitudes

Creativity and Innovation in the High-Technology Era
S.C. Kitsopoulos

Drawing from personal experiences as well as social events and psychological concepts, we begin by describing several attributes of the creative process: the role of the unconscious; the importance of feelings, moods, ambiguities, paradoxes and the tension of opposites; openness toward the unexpected and chance events; looking for the positive in adversity; complementing the familiar with the unfamiliar; interdisciplinary cross-fertilization between the scientific/technological and the humanistic/artistic cultures.

Creativity, especially in the world of science and technology which characterize our era, obtains social meaning through the process of innovation. While creativity is the hallmark of individuals, innovation is the process by which creativity is channeled into socially useful constructs such as products and services. Innovation is usually brought about through teamwork. It is fostered by a sense of vision and mission; clear goals, open communication, enlightened leadership; respect for the individual and his or her freedom within the team; adaptation to the changing needs of the society at large or culture within which the team is embedded.

While prolonged political struggles to gain democracy in many countries are likely to persist into the 90s and beyond, established democracies struggle to keep democratic tenets alive as they apply in the work lives of individuals. The old hierarchical styles of institutions have become less appropriate and productive. As participants in the struggle to maintain America's reputation for creativity and innovation we offer fresh observations illuminating the need for members of C. P. Snow's two cultures to appreciate each other. Though psychological differences foster instinctive mistrust of "others", knowledge of the creative process suggests we must find ways to close the gap within ourselves and between others.

Computer Partners in Our Future
Ted Slovin and Beverly Woolf

Artificial Intelligence (AI) techniques are already being used to build computer systems that act like partners and colleagues. In this paper, the computer is described as a "trusted consultant," "benevolent mentor", "cognizant tool", and "problem-solving partner". Examples of existing systems which operate at this level are described, along with applications to education, training, and consulting. Predictions are made about how additional systems might be built and guidelines presented for future development in the fields of instruction and communication technology.

The paper also discusses current barriers that make building these systems difficult and defines a need for breakthroughs in psychology, education and computer science to achieve truly partner-like computer systems. Ethical and moral issues related to the impact of technology on daily life are acknowledged which will play an increasingly important role in the responsible design, implementation and use of computer power.

Theology, Science and Management: Past, Present, Future
Frederick C. Thayer

"Management principles and practices have been the same throughout the few thousand years of civilization, as long as written language has been available to spell them out. The legitimate authority to issue orders is based upon the assumption that a boss has knowledge (derived from God or Science) that subordinates do not have, i.e., what values (objectives) are to be pursued and how. Religion and management, therefore, are a single theory, and the only change in thousands of years has been from *certain knowledge* (God) to *uncertain knowledge* (Science). Unfortunately, we have not used 'uncertainty' as a management principle. Hierarchy and Obedience remain the global theory of religion and management, and also of knowledge (objectivity), economics (competition and 'consumer' sovereignty) and politics (winners and losers). There can be no viable planetary future so long as we believe this single theory of religion, management science and values can be retained. Only the creation of yet another civilization holds out any hope, but some optimism is possible."

Humanist Views of the Future

Endtime and Beyond
Bruce Brander

As we reel through more changes in our culture than any society since the Renaissance or the fall of ancient Rome, social thinkers are led to ask what these massive changes mean. A remarkable number of them believe that the transformations we are witnessing—in ethics, the arts, philosophical thought and other aspects of culture—signify the terminal decline of Western civilization.

The thinkers who see the culture coming to its end are remarkably diverse. They include historians, sociologists, literary figures, religious thinkers, and political analysts from America, Britain, France, Germany, and Russia.

Chief among them are three intellectual titans of the 20th century: the German social philosopher Oswald Spengler (*The Decline of the West*), the English historian Arnold Toynbee (*A Study of History*) and the Russian-American sociologist Pitirim Sorokin (*Social and Cultural Dynamics*).

Taking the works of these three social thinkers and many others together, we observe a panorama of more than two dozen civilizations rising and growing then declining and collapsing. Their historic lives all follow similar patterns. As we detect this, we see our own Western civilization moving along the same course and already into the decline phase.

The pattern also can suggest the future: continued social disintegration, possibly another great war of annihilation, dictatorship, world government, a universal church, total cultural collapse, a reign of barbarism and the birth of a new civilization from the ashes of the old.

The only major point on which the social thinkers disagree is the matter of time. The grand transformation from death to new life, from one high culture to another, could unfold within centuries or within decades.

Faith and the Future: The Role of Belief in Shaping Events
Michael J. G. Gray-Fow
"This is a historian's response to the question 'What is the role of belief and/or religion in creating the future?'. It rests on a number of simple premises: 1) there is little evidence to suggest that the nature of humanity (whatever that means) is likely to change dramatically in the near future, 2) given the last premise we can reasonably assume that the way in which belief and/or religion has helped to create the future in the past will probably continue to operate *mutatis mutandis* in the future, and 3) while we are not prisoners of our past, nor condemned to repeat its mistakes, we have a cautionary interest in knowing how belief and/or religion has in fact influenced the shaping of the future."

Histories of the Future
W. Warren Wagar
"The quintessentially modern utopian vision is that of a world order in process of continuous improving change, set in the future of humankind. Such visions may be purveyed in novels, in works of social philosophy, or, rarest of all, in imaginary histories of the future, which occupy a literary no-man's-land between fiction and non-fiction. This paper discusses histories of the future from H. G. Wells's *The World Set Free* (1914) to *The Third Millennium: A History of the World, AD 2000-3000* (1985), and concludes with a preview of my own *Short History of the Future*, to be published in October, 1989 by the University of Chicago Press."

Howard F. Didsbury, Jr.

A Historical Retrospective

WHERE AMERICA WAS A CENTURY AGO

by

Dan Walker and John Center

INTRODUCTION

Where was America in 1890? Where was America in 1900? The Gay Nineties were the halcyon days for American society. America had just spent 25 years rising from the ashes of the Civil War and the trauma of Reconstruction. America was poised and happy. It would be many years before American society would see the terrible trauma of World War I, the Great Depression, the global conflict of World War II, the Atomic Age, and the Vietnam War. Where was America when it was internationally innocent, brash, and expectant with the 20th Century about to dawn? What were its thoughts about the present and the future?

The contemporaneous accounts of the 1890s, upon which this article largely relies, had one very striking characteristic. In great part they ignored the lives led by the less prosperous people. Most of the accounts relate to the middle and upper classes. To that extent they are misleading. With that caveat, let us look at the America of a century ago.

American Life

American society of the 1890s saw that it was in a very good position indeed. It was both optimistic and realistic. The nation was very conscious that it had fully settled down from the Civil War and Reconstruction years. The population of almost eighty million had a firmly-founded system of self-government. The gun-slinging West was moving from reality into fiction. National pride was high.

The nation, particularly in the South and West, was largely rural. While many of the amenities of life were becoming commonplace in the cities, they were still absent in most of the farming and ranching areas. The South had a real resurgence with substantial growth of business, trade, and prosperity. Interestingly, this was at the same time that the "dry" wave swept the South, closing thousands of saloons. The farm economy was strong in the Midwest. The frontier was not yet closed; the West was still filling with people. A severe recession occurred from 1894 to 1896, but the

Dan Walker *is a former governor of Illinois, an author, and a corporate executive.*
John Center *is principal consultant, Center Associates, St. Paul, Minnesota.*

nation was again prosperous at the turn of the Century and the mood was one of optimism.

Leisure time was limited for the working man, so were savings deposits. Working days were long, and the six-day week of ten-hour or twelve-hour days was prevalent. Trade and craft guilds were well-established, but industrial unionism was an issue for the next century. "Sweat shops" still abounded. Strikes were just coming onto the scene as a labor negotiation tactic. Attempts to win wage increases were frequently met by management with, "They'd only drink up what they get." Leisure for working men, both in the cities and on the farms, was mostly Sunday at home with the family. Attempts to change that were met with such responses as, "Shorter hours means that time will be spent in idleness and drunkenness."

In fashion and attire, the times were going through major change. The age of whiskers had gone by; it would not return for several decades. Clothing styles were still uncomfortable. An editorial commented on, "the plight of the man who swelters in the summer in coat and vest . . . the only people who look cool in hot weather are women." Some things never change!

Concern about conservation was just starting. The phrase "the air we breathe and the water we drink" was just coming into use. Only in rural areas and in the West was the "out of doors" treasured.

International Affairs

America had grown up. As it reached adulthood, America became fully aware of the world beyond its shores. The late 1890s saw the Spanish American War and the creation of an American "empire". Before the 1890s, America spanned the continent, from the Atlantic to the Pacific plus Alaska. After the 1890s, America's empire included Cuba, Puerto Rico, Guam, and the Philippine Islands. In the flush of imperialism, Hawaii, Wake, and a portion of the Samoan Islands also joined the empire. America was astride the Pacific Ocean. Only three years after the turn of the century, President Theodore Roosevelt capitalized on the spirit of the 1890s and, to use his words, "took the Canal." That act joined the Atlantic and Pacific Oceans. America had become a world power.

The turn of the century also represents the beginning of the end of the Victorian Era. Queen Victoria had built one of the greatest empires in the history of the world. With Victoria gone, voices in Europe spoke of a fear of a "yellow peril" on the one hand and the "Yankee peril" on the other. But at home, the "new boy" on the international block was not at all apprehensive about the prospects for the future. Most of America was actually agog at the novelty of the outside world. However, some were deeply troubled at this rapid assumption of responsibility over strange peoples in strange lands spread over thousands of miles of two oceans.

The predictions of the day for international affairs were many. Some were dismal failures; some were remarkably accurate. One author saw a world a hundred years in the future where the British Isles would be a dependency of the United States, and Russia would dominate a "Slavonic" area including Eastern Europe. Already some talked of an "inevitable revolution" in Russia. It was proposed that the US and Russia would be the two greatest world powers, with a German Empire running a poor third. After the United States helped crush the Boxer Rebellion in China, China was referred to as a "plague spot among the nations" which would "remain suspicious, semi-barbarous, tricky, isolated and unchanging." Japan, on the other hand, was freely predicted to become "industrially affluent as well as politically powerful."

Some saw a bright future, even if marred by war. John Habberton had this view:

> World-conquering after the old fashion is a dead business; nothing can bring it to life again. Nations may continue to fight, but very few and small are they that will disappear in the maw of their victors. The real conquests of the future will be made by the traders, the teachers and the missionaries who follow new flags into old lands. The United States are setting the example in Cuba, Puerto Rico and the Philippines, and the robber-nations of Europe are too wise not to profit by it.

And some commentators of the times foresaw the peril of war even worse than that seen in the 19th Century as described in the article "Promise of Peace in the Horrors of War":

> Many lurid pictures have been drawn of airships flying over forts and dropping high explosives. The idea is by no means an exaggeration, and it must be left to the imagination to appreciate what awful havoc in life and property would result.
>
> Almost as terrible would be the work of those submarine boats creeping under the naval monsters and blowing the great machines and their hundreds of men to destruction and death.
>
> Indeed, war may yet be made so horrible that the world will have the peace for which it prays.

Economics and Business

The abiding spirit of the 1890s revolved around money, good times, and hard work. The rich were greatly admired and the general feeling was that, as the saying goes, America was "on a roll". At the same time, society was very moralistic and religious beliefs were very strong. In a sense, it is hard to reconcile a set of strong moral and religious values with the fact that in the 1890s the rich were very rich and the poor were largely ignored.

The American middle-class was firmly in place by the 1890s. Exalting money and belittling culture and higher education were badges of the times. In the arena of money making, the heroes were Jay Gould, Russell Sage, Andrew Mellon, John D. Rockefeller, James J. Hill, William Waldorf Astor, and other business tycoons of the day. They were even household names, much like Trump, Icahn, Boesky, and Iacocca are today.

Men who did work had long hours and leisure time was limited. Married women did not work. "Bachelor girls" worked mostly in offices or factories. Living expenses appear to be very low. However, one must consider the weekly or daily pay of 1890 when reading this editorial entitled "Where the Money Goes":

> A young couple, after living along for nearly a year at the rate of $30 a week on an income of $25, reached the place where a sober, serious, heart-to-heart talk was imperative—a situation of the greatest delicacy, with the breakers upon the reefs of matrimonial disaster roaring in their ears. But they remained cool-headed and learned, among other things, that during the preceding week they had spent $3.15 on just nothing at all, $7.40 by paying too high prices for necessities when a little thought and care would have prevented it, $2.25 for things they could have very well done without, $2 for which they could not account at all; total, $14.80. They had spent in all during that week $34.50.
>
> Subtract what was "fooled away" from what was spent, and you have $19.70—that is, they spent for value received $5.30 less than their income. The hint in this incident is as valuable to the single as to the married.

Child labor was at its peak in that decade. In the cities it was common for children under 12 to work long hours. For $2 to $5 a week, they worked as factory piece-workers, messengers, janitors, "tail-end" boys on wagons, or if lucky as a "tyer", a high-hat livery boy in a carriage. Job titles also included "buttons", boys who attended people in the hallways of the higher class apartment buildings, and the "fronts", our present day bellboys. In those days, young boys and many young girls were driven by the inordinate desire for wealth or by the poverty of their parents, many of whom were first-generation immigrants who themselves were only a step or two above slave labor.

Race

The only race problem really bothersome to the Gay Nineties society was the Negro. The Chinese were only a minor difficulty in California. The Indians had been brutally controlled by the end of the 1880s. And the troublesome Irish had been largely absorbed. In Boston where they were most numerous, they even ran the city and elected the mayor.

Blacks remained outside the mainstream. Plessy v. Ferguson, the landmark Supreme Court decision, proclaimed in 1896 that "separate but equal" was constitutional in all public facilities. The sham that separate could be, or really ever was, equal continued for over another half century. Booker T. Washington taught that Negroes could advance by learning to be farmers or mechanics. However, when Theodore Roosevelt invited him to the White House as a dinner guest, there was a national uproar. A writer professed great surprise that "one man, coal black, illiterate, 'stole the rate' of a carpenter" and "a jet-black boy of twenty-two managed a small hotel." Vicious articles described the Negro as "childlike and helpless, lazy and shiftless"—but also "savage and bestial."

Race stereotypes abounded. They were freely used in advertisements and cartoons. Blacks were openly portrayed as animals, particularly monkeys. Perhaps one of the worst prophecies made at the turn of the century was that of Thomas Dixon, Jr., a widely-published author, in his article "Booker T. Washington and the Negro", published in the *Saturday Evening Post*. The article is subtitled "Some Dangerous Aspects of the Work of Tuskegee" referring to the now famous Tuskegee Institute. In his opening statement, Dixon attempts to prove lack of prejudice by stating, "My household servants are all Negroes," and calling himself, "one of their best friends." Dixon then forecasts:

> If allowed to remain here the Negro race in the United States will number 60,000 at the end of this century by their present rate of increase. Think of what this means for a moment and you face the gravest problem which ever puzzled the brain of stateman or philosopher. No such problem ever before confronted the white man in his recorded history. It cannot be whistled down by opportunities, politicians, weak-minded optimists or female men. It must be squarely met and fought to a finish.

The status of the Black in the large city, where integration was still an unknown word, was characterized by Dr. DuBois of the University of Pennsylvania in a widely reprinted study:

> The great deficiency of the Negro is his small knowledge of the art of organized social life—that last expression of human culture. His development in group life was abruptly broken off by the slave-ship, directed into abnormal channels and dwarfed by the Black Codes, and suddenly wrenched anew by the Emancipation Proclamation. He finds himself, therefore, peculiarly weak in the nice adaptation of individual life to the life of the group which is the essence of civilization. This is shown in the grosser forms of sexual immorality, disease, and crime, and also in the difficulty of race organization for common ends in economic or in intellectual lines.

The Chinese did not totally escape from race prejudice. The Mayor of San Francisco in "The Case Against the Chinaman," referred to them as opium dealers and addicts, disease-spreaders, and enslavers of women. Stories were told, and verified, of Chinese coolies being buried alive as a means to avoid paying wages when their work on a section of the transcontinental railroad was completed.

By 1890, the Indian tribes had been conquered. A few Americans were beginning to be troubled at what the conquest of the West had wrought. However, this editorial shows how far America had yet to go:

> If we take into account what has been done within the past few years—conveniently forgetting what went before—we have many pleasant facts. Two years ago a new policy went into effect: able-bodied Indians were given work instead of pensions. Result, 12,000 Indians dropped from the ration rolls and earning livings for themselves and their families. The old Indian agency system was honeycombed with evil. This year there are only twenty-three agencies compared with forty-three two years ago, and these are under educators instead of politicians. Schools are being greatly improved, and they show over 25,000 pupils—an increase of a thousand in a year. Much was done to deprive the red man of cheap whisky; as an alternative he took to patent medicines, which proved more devastating than the whisky; now the patent-medicine evil will be removed. Even the bad Indian is being sobered. So, after all, isn't the showing calculated to inspire optimism even in the Indian problem?

Some commentators did see past part of the phony racial "menaces" such as the one featured by the Hearst press, the "Yellow Peril". This is one reply to the views of the Hearst organization:

> All our truly great journalists, statesmen and volunteer thinkers agree upon the existence of the "yellow peril"; but they radically disagree as to what the yellow peril is. Some hold that the triumphant Japanese will set the teeming millions of the Orient at work manufacturing cheap goods with which they will flood the Occident. Others hold that the yellow peril is military—the Japanese arming the teeming millions aforesaid and flinging them upon the Occident in such wars as those that submerged ancient Rome. Happily, both perils cannot coexist. If the teeming Orient millions are at home manufacturing cheap goods they cannot be away from home making war. Further to allay fear, if the Orient sends forth floods of cheap goods the millions of buyers of those goods will, at least, survive the inundation—else, how could goods be sold?

Urban Life

In the 20th Century, technology created modern big-city America. Before 1850, cities were not materially different from the Rome of fifteen hundred years before. Animals provided land motive power; wind and oars did it on water. Candles and oil lamps provided light; stoves or fireplaces provided warmth. Person-to-person contact provided most communications. Buildings were low, 2 to 4 stories. By the end of the 19th Century, much of that had changed. Trains, trolleys, and subways forever altered cross-country and urban transportation. The engine, steam and otherwise, was of age. The industrial revolution was a fact. The telephone was no longer a curiosity, but it was still hardly commonplace. Telegraphs were revolutionizing communications. The elevator, the real driving factor behind the skyscraper, had been invented; cityscapes would never be the same. The days of suburbs and commuters had arrived. (350,000 people came into New York City daily.) In short, most of the physical problems of the 20th Century metropolis were foreshadowed during the 1890s.

Some predictions for urban life were exaggerated comments on the times. John Jacob Astor foresaw huge cities where pedestrians would stroll far above the movements of goods and people for trade and commerce. Edward Everett Hale, of "The Man Without a Country" fame, imagined people being shot from city to city through tubes. In perhaps the best wrong prediction, a magazine writer concluded that the new vehicle, the automobile, would produce streets "as quiet as a country lane—all the crash of horses' hoofs and the number of steel tires will be gone, and since vehicles will be fewer and shorter than the present truck and span, streets will appear less crowded."

In 1901, H.G. Wells very accurately predicted the future of the megalopolis:

> We are on the eve of a great development of centrifugal possibilities. And since it has been shown that a city of pedestrians is inexorably limited by a radius of about four miles, and that a horse-using city may grow out to seven or eight, it follows that the available area of a city which can offer a cheap suburban journey of thirty miles an hour is a circle with a radius of thirty miles . . . But thirty miles is only a very moderate estimate of speed, and the available area for the social equivalent of the favored season-ticket holders of today will have a radius of over one hundred miles, and be almost equal to the area of Ireland. The radius that will sweep the area available for such as now live in the outer suburbs will include a still vaster area. Indeed, it is not too much to say that the vast stretch of country from Washington to Albany will be all of it "available" to the active citizen of New York and Philadelphia.

Americans were thronging to the cities. In 1800, no city in America had over 100,000 people. By 1900, almost one hundred cities were that size or larger. Those large cities held about one-third of the American population.

Women

Before 1900, only four states had granted to women the right to vote. All four were in the West. It was not until 1865 that a woman could get a college education—if she could afford to attend Vassar. Women were entering relatively new fields in great numbers— teachers, artists, stenographers, nurses. The first woman practiced law in 1869. By 1900, women doctors and lawyers were becoming accepted for "women" situations, but still faced extreme hostility from the dominant males. They faced hostility as well from social commentators who were widely critical of the failure of "modern women" to live up to the "true ideals of womanhood."

Their dress included upswept hair, shirtwaist dresses, sweeping decorated hats, wasp-waists with pushed-up buses, long skirts flirting with ankles. This was the so-called Gay Nineties. Romanticism was everywhere and female beauty was widely and openly admired. The Victorian lady was passe—the nation was ready for active flirtatious women. Those who trained secretaries tried to stem the tide of romanticism with instructions like these given in an article entitled "Why Flirting Stenographers Fail":

> The stenographer who, in the mildest and most harmless way flirts with her employer, her fellow clerks, or callers at the office, who is called to the telephone on an average of five times a day by some one to whom she talks in a honeyed voice, and whose giggle is a well known sound in the office, need not be surprised if she is pushed to one side and a man preferred when a responsible duty is to be performed.
>
> Feminine graces will be rewarded with candy and compliments, never with promotion or confidence.
>
> The stenographer who goes into an office expecting to win recognition and compensation on an equality with men must remember first and distinctly that she is not a woman, but a stenographer.
>
> It is all well to talk about a woman's presence inculcating gentleness and courtesy in an office, but a busy man has not time for an extra word; he has not time for the effort to make that word a pleasant one when he does not feel pleasant.

Education

Discontent with public school education is not a phenomenon peculiar to the end of the 20th Century. It was also present in the Gay Nineties decade. E. Benjamin Andrews, the Chancellor of the University of Nebraska, argued in the early 1900s that recent experience with public education was grounds for denying financial support, thus killing it.

One of the major complaints of that time about the education process was non-participation. One year in Chicago, 16,791 children were enrolled in school, but truant officers reported that 31,593 cases of non-attendance were investigated. Criticism was also common about undue concentration on the 3 Rs to the exclusion of all else. E. Benjamin Andrews described it this way in "The Public School of the Twentieth Century":

> All the common virtues need to be inculcated in the school as well as at home. This is a work that the school of the twentieth century is going to undertake and successfully carry out. A most useful code of morals will be taught in the school, which will fasten upon the child at the very beginning of his mental life the principles that tend

to produce good citizenship, the end and aim of the public school system.

Instead of Japan, Germany was America's trade opponent in 1890. Many complaints were related to the feelings that German schools gave better commercial training. Founding of practical commercial schools to provide "special training in every department of trade and commerce" was supported. Dr. G. Stanley Hall and Dr. Edward Brooks give an interesting report about the lack of practical education in their article entitled "Public Occurrences":

> Not one-half of Boston school children knew what sheep was; only one in ten knew growing wheat; three fourths of them did not know an oak tree and nine out of ten did not know where their own ribs and hearts were, but the most astonishing thing was that in Boston seven out of ten did not know beans.

Some men were in college, and a few women too. Even then, enlightened families were encouraging their daughters to go to college. In 1890, the "necessary expenses" for one year at Harvard were about $500. Today's undergraduate will be surprised to learn that college rooms were typically suites of 2 or 3 rooms; bedrooms were furnished by the student with bed, bureau, washstand, chairs, rug and curtains for $50.

College life was constantly criticized. The criticism was accepted with acclaim by many ordinary Americans, particularly Westerners, who continually decried colleges as hot-beds of corruption and decay. The prevalent attitude of the general population toward higher education at the turn of the Century is summed up in this editorial:

> The plain fact is that three-fourths of these children will be tradesmen, mechanics, laborers, cooks and shop-women. They have but four short years to master the training which will enable them to earn a living by these trades and to live with intelligence and dignity. Why rob them of this chance to better and widen their lives by cramming them with scraps of knowledge which by no possibility can be of any service to them hereafter? What use can Joe Pratt, who means to be a plumber, make of Homer? Or why should his sister, who is to be a trained nurse, go to a woman's college to study the Semitic tongues?

Science and Technology

The working man was told he had an unlimited future. The *Saturday Evening Post* hailed the coming of the "Reign of the Mechanic":

> The time was foreseen when the land would be overrun by half-starved lawyers and doctors, and left destitute of mechanics. The industrial revolution now underway has changed all that . . . As every soldier in Napoleon's Army carried a Marshal's baton in his knapsak, so every workman in a modern factory carried potentially

the presidency of a trust.

In the area of science and technology, many prophecies were failures and some were successes. Snow on the Moon, and "men" and canals on Mars were all off the mark. A little off the mark were the predictions that "drudgery will be a thing of the past for the cook" and there would be "roses the size of cabbages." But on the mark were predictions of "a cheap and practical storage battery"; "actual portrait transmitted by telegraph", which we now call television; non-refillable bottles; and "that it will be as easy to telephone from New York to Peking as from New York to Brooklyn." Hudson Maxim, writing for the *Woman's Home Companion* in 1900, had some winners—taking nitrogen from the air to make fertilizer (it happened in the 1920s), the "wireless telephone" (we now call it radio), color photography, and the sun-engine.

The marvels of electricity were just beginning to be appreciated by great numbers of people—as were the gramophone, the X-ray, the telephone, the camera. The concepts and principles that would lead to the aeroplane were just beginning to be understood. The automobile was further along, horse-less carriages were beginning to be produced. In short, the fantastic explosion of science and technology was just commencing.

Housing and Housework

The typical single-family home of the 1890s was a white framed "colonial" with a usable front porch. The "bungalow" became widely popular in the cities. It was a one-storied house with wide eaves and had a large front porch also. Planned kitchens became the rage, complete with ice boxes, cupboards, and sinks. The large cast-iron cooking range was prevalent. It was fueled with wood in rural areas, with gas or coal in the cities. Open fires for warmth and looks were commonplace but central heating was available by 1900. Lighting was largely by gas or oil, but electricity was becoming available. Telephones were limited to the upper and middle classes, and not too many of the latter. Labor-saving devices like improved washing machines, sewing machines, and stove heated flat-irons were available, even if not yet in widespread use. Some phonographs were in use, but they were far from being commonplace. The same was true for fully-equipped bathrooms. Many had them; most did not.

An editorial view on "Housework and Machinery" presented some interesting views:

> If the men of the United States should be compelled by the statute to do, themselves, all the housework of the country for ten years there would be such a shaking up of methods as twenty centuries have not brought about. When the women came to their own again, they would find that for the first time in history there were really adequate tools for carrying on the conduct of home life.

We would like to see it tried—after we are dead. If housework were put on to the men, heat would be turned on by pressing a button, suction-pumps would draw all the dust out of the house, and a lot of methods and devices would be perfected for the relief of that large group of families in our society which can afford only one servant. The house of 2005, says our contemporary, ought to be no more like the house of 1905 than a motor-car is like an ox-cart.

For our part we are not so sanguine that invention is going to help so prodigiously in housekeeping. When the women got back to housework after their ten years' release they would promptly let the men's more intricate machines get out of order, and presently throw them out.

The chief things that houseworkers do are to keep houses clean, to cook and serve meals, to wash and mend clothes, and to keep things in order. There is a machine that comes to sweep by suction. Four or five men bring it on a dray. Only rich people can afford to have it come. There is no prospect that houses ever will be kept clean by machinery. Nothing but human hands deals successfully with daily dust in such a city as New York.

As for cooking, there are breakfast foods that come cooked or are guaranteed to be good to eat raw, and a vast line of nourishments come in cans, but household cooking requires brains as well as hands. There is no hope that it will ever be done by machinery. It is an art. You cannot get art results by pressing a button.

As for clothes-washing, there are laundries and laundry machinery a'plenty. But to wash clothes properly, so that they retain their proper hues, dimensions, qualities, and shapes, requires an intelligence so nearly human that it is easier come by in a human being.

No, there is not much more to hope for from labor-saving household appliances. The reasons are good why more has not been done to make homes self-regulating and automatic. If servants are to be scarcer and dearer the relief must come by the simplification of living: by elimination of household possessions, and not by increase of household machinery.

Transportation

By 1900, the American automobile age had begun—12 companies produced a total of over 4,000 cars. A decade later, that had grown to almost 200,000 vehicles. In 1900, *Collier's Weekly* was already calling for a "national highway". H. G. Wells, in the *North American Review*, hit the nail right on the head with this futuristic description of highways:

> These special roads will be very different from macadamized roads they will be used only by soft-tired conveyances; the battering horseshoes, the perpetual filth of horse traffic, and the clumsy wheels of laden carts will never wear them . . . Their traffic in opposite directions will probably be strictly separated. The promoters will doubtless have a hint from suburban railway traffic, and where their ways branch the streams of traffic will not cross at a level but by bridges.

Automobiles could not yet go very fast; top speed was about 20 MPH. However, "speed mania" became a concern. That was the name given to a new medical condition described by William Lee Howard, M.D. in his work *Speed Mania:*

> The facts we have to seriously consider are not those dealing with accidents or risks to lives, nor with the effects on the adult of middle life, but the harmful effects on the very young who are being literally whirled through the world at an age when their nervous systems need quiet and normal development.

Highly customized cars quickly appeared in the automobile world. The following is a 1900 account of such vehicles:

> So long ago as the French Automobile Show of 1900 there was exhibited, in the grand Palais des Champs Elysees, an enormous touring-car, with a dinner table completely set for eight persons. At the time it seemed a fantastic affair, and, in all probability, "for exhibition purposes only." Yet now it is known that the King of Belgians already has such an auto-car, only on a scale even more elaborate—a car with a state-room, saloon, kitchen, and office. It is likely to be the only one of its kind, for an appreciable time at least. As the builder said, his Majesty is not desirous, in the first year of possession, to meet others on the road, no doubt filled with Americans. Therefore, up to this time, the plans, even the appearance, of the King's car have been kept secret.

The impact of the automobile in making large scale changes to our society was not yet appreciated in the 1890s. Just 15 years before motorized warfare struck Europe in 1914, Brigadier-General A. W. Greely, Chief Signal Officer of the US Army, made this myopic prediction:

> It is unquestioned that automobiles will play important parts in future wars, but it will be many years before they constitute the major transportation of an army. Motors can not replace mounted couriers or the military telegraph. For special uses, however, they are indispensable to every modern army, although the evolution of the types must be necessarily slow and tedious, especially in the United States.

The passing of the steam locomotive was freely predicted by 1900, long before its final demise. The urban electric railway was highly popular in the 1890s and in the first part of this century. It began to lose out to automobiles, and it also became extinct by mid-20th Century. Within the cities, bicycling became the rage. That finally led one editorial writer to say, "Almost everything that it is possible to say about 'what the bicycle has done' would seem to have been said." The "cheap bicycle" was used by working men, as well as those of moderate means, for home-to-work trips as well as "their sole chance of reaching the country and of knowing nature's beauties."

A 1900 vision of transportation was voiced by Professor A. C.

Albertson, an electrical engineer at Copenhagen University. He patented the widely publicized Albertson Magnetic Train. He saw a train equipped with powerful electric magnets that would slide along under narrow rails and move from New York to San Francisco in 10 hours at 300 MPH. Today, just such a train is on the horizon of practicality as a result of recent developments in superconductivity.

Sports, Health, and Fitness

Today's sport fans may be interested to know that the evils of college athletics were widely attacked in 1890. Many of the complaints were on the grounds of health and moral behavior. The charges went all the way from "slugging" to attracting athletic students with inducements. One of the biggest complaints was against the use of "outsiders" on college teams. It seems that the practice of hiring players who did not attend the college was widespread in Eastern colleges. Both college deans and newspaper editorial writers decried a new college development—using athletic team success as a "method of advertising". It was discovered, to the dismay of these purists, that winning teams were attracting students. College sports of the 20th Century had truly begun to arrive.

Not much was written about health and fitness in the 1890s. Little appears about disease and surgery, except the multitude of advertisements for products that could cure anything and everything. Perhaps members of the medical profession, or editors, were not interested in publicizing new developments in the field of medicine. There were some exceptions. The successful use of vaccination to stem the scourge of smallpox was publicized. It was in 1900 that Walter Reed conducted the experiments proving that mosquitoes carried the deadly yellow fever, and the results got good coverage.

Sanitation was discussed in the press. Society began to make changes in what it perceived as "satisfactory" living conditions. Milk cleanliness and water sanitation were just beginning to be recognized as important to health. Feature stories and editorials began to link health, sanitation, and living conditions. Consider the following story on the living conditions and health of servants:

> Many people who try to live healthfully fail because they neglect the two chief sources of disease—what comes in from the streets and what comes down from the servants' rooms which the mistress of the house never visits, never even thinks of. The mistress of the house says that she gives "the girl" or "the servants as good as they have been used to at home," and is content with herself. Putting wholly aside the moral question of having a slum or a near-slum under one's roof, there remains the cold fact of the dangerous unhealthfulness of it. The servants should, for prudence's sake, have not "as good as they've been used to," but as good as the laws of

health dictate—and that is very good indeed.

Everybody was, of course, worried about their own health. Publications of the day were full of ads for all kinds of nostrums. We find much of it humorous today but not so the editorial writers of the day:

> Far more important and encouraging as "signs of the times" than any developments in politics or industry are the advertisements of physical culture systems and health foods and other means for promoting a sound body. The enormous increase in this kind of advertising within the past five years means a sudden enormous increase in intelligent public interest in health. And that means oncoming generations with purer, stronger blood and therefore with clearer, more active, more courageous brains. And that, in turn, means that all the problem of living, personal, social, political, will be met and taken care of.

Even Pabst Beer, which was to later earn a Blue Ribbon and include that fact in its name, *seriously* advertised itself as the "best tonic." It was supposed to, "set every spring of health in action." One ad pointed out that it was particularly good for the convalescent "to fight his way back to perfect health and full recovery." Such was the nature of truth in advertising in the 1890s.

Conclusion

Within America's borders, people argued about when the 20th Century began. Mathematically, 1900 was the *last* year of the 19th Century. "New Century Day" was officially January 1, 1901. However, the public and the press would have none of it. In the waning days of 1899, newspapers throughout America heralded an unlimited, almost utopian future. On the last day of 1899, the *New York Times* concluded: "We step upon the threshold of 1900 which leads to the new century facing a still brighter dawn of civilization."

This was the 1890s. It was a different world, a different nation from today. We could say this about the decade of the 1890s, "It is much better to be living now than then. And I am glad that American society was well prepared to achieve all the great things that were about to happen during the upcoming century."

In terms of perceptions and expectations, it was a nation sure of itself, optimistic. From today's perspective, American society of 1890 seems to have been more optimistic than we are a century later. Members of the 1890 middle class seemed to be satisfied; those in the lower class knew of the Horatio Alger route to the top. Members of the 1990 middle class are worried about being able to maintain their "quality" of life; those in the "underclass" see no way out. Yet there is still optimism in our society. We are optimistic about the good things that will soon take place—a cure for cancer, freedom from fossil fuels, complete disarmament, and so on.

Let us now go forward during the last decade of the 20th Century and prepare ourselves and our society to achieve great things during the 21st Century. Let us hope that some author in 2090 can look back at today and see our optimism, respect our realism, appreciate our dreams, laugh gently at our follies. Let us hope that author can say some of the same positive things about 1990 that we can say about 1890.

Economics,
Development and
the Future

BIOTECHNOLOGY: AGRICULTURE'S LAST HURRAH?

by

Clifton Anderson

Farming is an essential activity, according to conventional wisdom. A much-repeated maxim says farmers will be indispensable as long as city people require nourishing food. This truism now seems out of date, in view of ongoing technological developments in the food industry. Thanks to the versatility of modern science, food technologists are gaining the ability to duplicate most of the foodstuffs which are currently being grown down on the farm.

In the future, biotechnology may move from the laboratory to the factory, equipping industry with processes for producing in vats, towers and conduits a great variety of foods—red meat, vegetables and fruits, plus ersatz grain and other synthetic products carefully compounded to have distinctive tastes and textures.

During the 1990s and the early part of the 21st century, there will be extensive research and development which should equip industrial firms for large-scale off-the-farm production of food. At the same time, science will be making available to farmers new, highly sophisticated technologies for producing food and fiber. The age of high-tech farming will have arrived. If farmers employ the new technologies successfully, they may be able to avoid being supplanted by industrialized food production facilities.

Just because automated food factories could produce basic agricultural commodities, it does not necessarily follow that they will do so. By 2010, the economics of the situation may still dictate a two-stage production system—with the raising of crops and livestock occurring primarily on farms and ranches, and the factories attending to the processing of natural foods and the fabrication of a great array of synthetic food products. Nevertheless, the integration of agriculture and industry into a single food production system will be more complete than ever before.

Throughout the 20th century, agriculture and industry have been closely allied. A trend which could be labelled "the industrialization of agriculture" has been marked by two major developments: 1) the mechanization of agriculture, which began in the 1800s and has continued apace since the 1920s; 2) the widespread and intensive use of agricultural chemicals, which has resulted in far-reaching changes in farming practices in the decades after World War II. Now, a third development—the advent of agricultural biotechnol-

---

Clifton Anderson *is extension editor, University of Idaho, Moscow, Idaho.*

ogy—is pushing agriculture and industry closer together. When industry can copy all agricultural products—matching them molecule for molecule—the uniqueness of agriculture may be at an end. Biotechnology could be agriculture's last hurrah—signalling industrial know-how's triumph over an older production system and its traditional rural values. If agriculture ceases to address environmental issues from its down-to-earth point of view, the ecological consequences could be very serious.

Farmers are a singular class of people. Although individual scientists and soil conservation technicians would qualify as "practicing ecologists," the occupational group most intimately linked to ecology has to be farmers. Can a way be found to conserve this human resource? Can biotechnology be introduced into agriculture in a manner that will contribute to social stability and environmental well-being? Can the environmentally hazardous elements of biotechnology be suppressed or otherwise prevented from harming the countryside? These are the kind of questions I want to interject into current discussions that concentrate on technical and economic aspects of biotechnology.

Agriculture and the Environment

Culture is an important component of agriculture. Wendell Berry, philosopher and poet, insists that the cultural component is being fragmented as farmers fail to take a firm stand against their cooptation by industry. For other observers, the distinctive culture of farmers still persists, despite the inroads which industry and urbanism have made into rural regions. During my long association with agriculture, many changes have occurred, but I find that farmers still consider their work to be meaningful and satisfying if it takes place in a cultural context. The farmer's accomplishments are not his alone but are made possible by the cooperative efforts of family members and neighbors. The farmer supports the rural community—and is sustained by it. The farmer is linked to the soil. His farming decisions are environmental decisions. If he takes any action that may harm the environment, he is in danger of damaging the land in which his life and his self-esteem are anchored. Moreover, since the land is the living legacy which one farming generation lovingly passes on to the next generation, environmental protection is a time-honored rural value.

When community bonds disintegrate in a rural area, environmental degradation is likely to occur. Any weakening in the farmer's feeling of attachment to the land may have undesirable ecological consequences. Farm operators and migrant laborers who move from one farm job to another without forming permanent ties may be inclined to misuse or abuse the land. Farmers who seek short-term profits are likely to "mine" the soil's nutrients, use tillage methods that invite erosion and attempt to push yields by applying excessively large doses of agricultural chemicals. In these scenarios, environmental problems are linked to destruction of rural culture.

Rural values notwithstanding, environmental difficulties do occur in the country. Non-point pollution—the contamination of rivers and streams by sediment and wastes issuing from large acreages of land—is in large part an agricultural problem. Caught in a severe cost-price squeeze, farmers sometimes risk long-term environmental losses as they try to obtain short-term economic gains. Protection of the environment can be encouraged by government, by means of financial inducements for soil conservation improvements. Science can help also. Science-induced technological changes in agriculture can tip the balance either toward ecological disruption or environmental harmony. As biotechnology is introduced into agricultural systems, it is extremely important that farmers be encouraged to use new products and procedures in environmenally sound ways.

Agricultural Biotechnology Today

Biotechnology—the use of biological processes to produce goods and services—has the potential for solving many troublesome problems which agricultural producers face. Knowledge of molecular genetics has progressed rapidly in the 1980s, leading to the initiation of promising research projects in genetic engineering. From this research will come new, improved strains of crops and livestock.

Developments now in prospect include crops with the built-in ability to tolerate a host of diversities—destructive insects, disease-causing organisms, arid and salty soils, extreme summer heat and untimely frosts. Production of meat, milk, wool and eggs may become more efficient as superior livestock are produced through genetic manipulation. Using genetic engineering techniques, researchers can transfer genes from one organism to another, thereby transforming crops and livestock in ways that could not be accomplished in traditional breeding programs.

Genetically engineered crops and livestock will be available in the 1990s. A wide variety of livestock medicines, drugs and growth enhancers will be on the market. At present, pharmaceuticals for humans are the biotechnology firms' most profitable product lines. Health products for the livestock industry rank in second place. Major livestock diseases are being controlled by genetically engineered vaccines. These vaccines are extremely safe to use because they are derived from microorganisms which have been genetically altered so they do not cause disease. Since they do provoke an immune response in livestock, the new vaccines combine effectiveness with safety.

Working with bacteria, fungi and viruses, researchers use gene-splicing and other techniques of genetic engineering to develop biopesticides. Since each pesticide is targeted at a specific insect or

23

weed pest, beneficial insects and non-targeted plants are not harmed. In field tests, biopesticides are kind to the environment. Unlike chemical pesticides, they do not pollute groundwater, and they pose no threat to humans or livestock.

Genetically engineered bacteria have been used to extend the growing season of frost-susceptible crops. Researchers developed a strain of bacteria incapable of forming the type of protein which ordinarily serves as a nucleus for ice to form on the surface of plants. Sprayed on crops in large amounts, the "ice-minus" bacteria replace the ice-forming wild bacteria which normally live on plant surfaces. During chilly nights, the ice-minus bacteria will protect the host plants from frost damage.

In this age of molecular biology, researchers may discover ways to attack problems which previously had been considered to be insoluble. In the past, there was no way to get around the fact that legume crops can benefit from free nitrogen in the atmosphere while non-legume crops cannot. The difference is due to beneficial nitrogen-fixing bacteria which colonize on the roots of beans, clover and other legumes. They extract free nitrogen from the air and make it available to their host plants. The nitrogen-fixing bacteria will not form a symbiotic bond with crops such as wheat, corn or potatoes, and the nitrogen needs of these non-legume crops must be supplied in other ways—principally by the application of commercial fertilizers.

Agricultural researchers hope to change this situation. One possible approach is to introduce into non-legume plants the traits which make legume plants attractive to nitrogen-fixing bacteria. Theoretically, this could be done by transferring genes from legumes to non-legumes. Another possibility is to transfer genes from one species of bacteria to another. Colonies of soil bacteria frequently take up residence on and around the roots of non-legume crops. These are not nitrogen-fixing bacteria, but in theory it should be possible to endow them with this ability. Through gene manipulation, researchers may be able to develop new types of bacteria that will help us reduce the economic and ecological costs of nitrogen fertilizer applications on non-legume crops.

In agricultural production and food processing, improved strains of micro-organisms are being put to work. On the farm, genetically altered bacteria produce better corn silage. Bakeries, breweries and cheese factories benefit from new developments in microbiology. In order to reduce livestock feeding costs, scientists are trying to upgrade the nutritional quality of inexpensive roughages. Their task is being accomplished with the aid of bacteria that produce cellulose-digesting enzymes. Micro-organisms also are involved in research that shows promise of improving the yield of fuel alcohol from grain crops.

Biotechnology and the Environment

Agricultural biotechnology projects now in progress envision the release into the environment of a variety of organisms altered or recreated by means of genetic engineering. In these pioneering ventures, science cannot be certain what the outcome will be. An element of risk is unavoidable. As seen by ecologists and other concerned citizens, the environmental threats posed by biotechnology are of five types:

1) Catastrophic disruptions
2) Pervasive changes, not of catastrophic proportions
3) Limited, containable changes
4) Subtle changes, difficult to assess
5) Snafus (misdirected effort and unrealized opportunities)

Catastrophic biological events, as pictured in science-fiction films, should not be in agricultural biotechnology's script. Regulations and review processes should be comprehensive in scope, conscientiously enforced, and undeviatingly supportive of a safe, clean environment. The uncontrollable monster—whether it be microbe, mammal or insect—should be stopped at the outset, before the horror begins.

Pervasive disruptions of the environment—if they occur—are likely to be troublesome rather than catastrophic. When novel organisms are introduced into the environment, unforeseen problems may result. Introduced into the US as forage crops, kudzu and Johnson grass are now invasive pests in some areas. Bee-breeding experiments in Brazil produce the "killer bees" that have set up colonies throughout Latin America and are now invading the US. Notoriety also has been earned by the starling, the gypsy moth, Dutch elm disease fungus and countless weeds and other pests that have made themselves at home in alien environments. Many biologists do not foresee serious difficulties, but biologically engineered bacteria, plants and animals could become annoying pests in the future.

Limited and containable problems are likely to recur fairly frequently as novel organisms are released into the environment. In the 1990s, when farmers begin using biopesticides and other new biotech products, there could be a series of surprises. Researchers may, for example, develop toxic-producing micro-organisms which will do a good job of controlling an insect pest that attacks corn plants. Although the corn plants tolerate the microbes' toxin, it may become apparent that desirable plants of other species do not. Again, the targeted insect may develop the ability to tolerate the microbes' toxin. Also, the introduced micro-organisms might disrupt the ecological balance of bacteria and other organisms residing in the soil. Extreme care must be taken in monitoring environmental changes. Problems which are limited and containable one season may later develop into major environmental disruptions.

Subtle changes in the environment, difficult to measure or assess, present a challenge to plant physiologists and agricultural ecologists. In recent years, researchers have become aware of slight changes in the metabolic processes of various plants that have been exposed to agricultural chemicals. Generation by generation, the changes appear to grow more pronounced. To trace the long-term development of subtle changes in the environment, capable researchers and adequate funding are required. Monitoring is essential in order to identify environmental changes that may be triggered by biotechnology. Since biotechnology is brand-new, there is much we need to learn about its possible impacts on the environment.

Misdirected effort is a problem in science, as well as in other pursuits. The remedy—as every scientist knows—is to subject goals and methodologies to rigorous ongoing scrutiny. Time and again, the question has to be asked: "Why are we doing this?" In some quarters, biotechnology projects are considered worthwhile if they have the potential to generate good profits. For scientists, curiosity—the need to know—may be sufficient justification. Somewhere in the decision-making process, socio-environmental considerations should be weighed. Is a project environmentally sound? What would be the social and cultural consequences? Would a biotechnology project prejudice the survivability of farm owner-operators who now serve as custodians of the rural environment? Would the project be likely either to facilitate or discourage environmentally sound courses of action on the part of farmers? Questions such as these should come to mind as projects are planned and prioritized. Consider the range of choices involved in the following projects:

● New varieties of farm crops now under development by biotech firms reportedly are tolerant of the chemicals contained in widely used weed-killers. The chemical-tolerant crops could be grown in fields that receive heavy treatments of herbicide. This would boost herbicide sales—and it could have deleterious effects on the environment if the herbicides involved were of the type that breaks down slowly in the soil. Long-lasting herbicides can contaminate groundwater and cause damage to any herbicide-sensitive crop which is planted in treated soil the following season.

● In the future, there may be genetically engineered crops which will enable farmers to reduce their use of herbicides and other agricultural chemicals. Some crops may be equipped with built-in insecticides. In others, plant roots may secrete toxins that will keep various weed species under control. Some crops may utilize soil nutrients very efficiently, producing high yields but not requiring the heavy applications of commercial fertilizers which are commonly used at present.

● Impressive in many ways is research aimed at incorporating into important crops the genes that permit drought-resistant wild plants to survive in dry, salty soil. This research might change the agricultural geography of the world, enabling farmers to grow crops on vast acreages of waste land which have been retired from crop production due to excessive salinity.

- Energy-efficient agricultural production methods are urgently needed. Using an energy-in/energy-out set of calculations, analysts can demonstrate that most farming enterprises on modern farms are losing propositions. The amount of energy being used (in the form of fuel, fertilizer, feed, electric power and other inputs) exceeds the amount being marketed (in products such as meat, milk and grain). Agricultural biotechnology, by encouraging the use of fertilizer and herbicide, could make agriculture more energy-wasteful than it is at present. On the other hand, research that leads to the development of crops with improved processes of photosynthesis would increase food harvests tremendously—with no pollution problems. Free, clean solar energy is everywhere, ready to be tapped by genetically improved plants. Our entire society would benefit if agricultural production were to become more energy-efficient. Nevertheless, the projects that biotech firms will develop initially are likely to encourage farmers to continue their high-input, energy-deficit modes of production. A low-input, energy-efficient, sustainable system of agriculture may develop later, but high-input habits are difficult to change.

Choices—how should they be made and by whom? The choices our global society must make regarding biotechnology are not confined to the realm of science. These choices concern economic development, social change, cultural values and the health of the environment. The choices will impact everyone.

Agriculture's Third Major Revolution

Agriculture has survived two major technological transformations—a revolution in mechanization and a chemical revolution. In the 1990s, the biotechnology revolution will exert far-reaching changes on all facets of agricultural production, all fields of biological science and all aspects of environmental protection. The world community is not prepared to deal with this revolution, and planning at the national level is still sketchy and poorly organized.

In the US, many leading figures in government and science subscribe to the myth that no immediate revolution is in prospect. As if to downplay the importance of biotechnology, the national government has fragmented its machinery for biotech regulation and policy planning. No central agency has overall responsibility for regulating biotechnology. Regulatory functions are divided between a number of agencies, notably the Environment Protection Agency, the Food and Drug Administration, the US Department of Agriculture and the National Institute of Health. Policy planning takes place within various agencies, but national goals have not been articulated clearly. More should be done to involve individual citizens and public interest organizations in biotechnology conferences, task forces and advisory groups. It may be necessary for citizen groups, acting on their own initiative, to take the lead in informing the public about biotechnology's potentialities and also to explain the policy options which might be used to direct biotechnology along environmentally sound, socially constructive lines.

Biotech installations, small in size and difficult to detect, could manufacture horrendous weapons for biological warfare. Biologically altered microbes and special toxins could be implements of mass destruction or tools of localized terrorist attacks. The world community has to face up to this threat. Also of grave dimensions is the economic threat which biotechnology poses to Third World countries. Agriculture in the Third World may not be able to participate in the biotechnology revolution's first round. The price of super-seeds, animal growth enhancers and bioinsecticides may be too high for poor countries to pay. Moreover, high-value agricultural products which now help sustain the economies of developing nations may be targets of the modern-day alchemists in biotech laboratories. American investigators are presently seeking ways in which a product identical to cocoa might be produced in this country. Vanilla, coffee and tea also are likely candidates for genetic engineering and industrial production. Since these developments would place in jeopardy the livelihood of many Third World rural people, treaties or other international understandings may be needed to deal with the problem. Possible displacement by biotechnology is a threat hanging over all agricultural producers— the Wisconsin diary farmer no less than the Colombian coffee producer.

At a minimum, society's investment in biotechnology must include extensive problem-solving research, unrelenting monitoring of the environment and continued involvement of informed citizen activists. Keeping in mind missteps technology has taken before— shattering the ozone layer, suffocating our cities, dumping toxic wastes on land and sea—we must resolve to have biotechnology develop in an environmentally responsible manner. For this task, we will need the help of farmers and all other good people who respect the environment.

References

Berry, Wendell. *The Unsettling of America: Culture & Agriculture* (San Francisco, 1977).

"Biotechnology," *The Economist*, Vol. 305 (April 30, 1988), pp. 3-18.

Calder, Nigel. *The Green Machines* (New York, 1986)

Crick, Francis. "The Challenge of Biotechnology," *The Humanist*, Vol. 46 (August 1986)

Chamberland, Dennis. "Genetic Engineering: Promise and

Threat," *Christianity Today*, Vol. 30 (February 7, 1986) pp. 22-28.

"David Baltimore: Setting the Record Straight on Biotechnology," *Technology Review*, Vol. 89 (October 1986) pp. 38-46.

Dibner, Mark D. "Biotechnology's Human Resources: What Lies Ahead?" *Biotechnology Progress*, Vol. 4 (December 1988) p. D3.

Eppley, David and Kristen Muller. "Biotech's Promise: Panacea or Pie in the Sky?" *Agrichemical Age*, Vol. 33 (April 1989), p. 14 and following.

Pimentel, David. "Down on the Farm: Genetic Engineering Meets Ecology," *Technology Review*, Vol. 90 (January 1987), pp. 24-30.

Sylvester, Edward J. and Lynn C. Klotz, *The Gene Age: Genetic Engineering and the New Industrial Revolution* (New York, 1987).

Thompson, Susan. "Biotechnology—Shape of Things to Come or False Promise," *Futures*, Vol. 18 (August 1986), pp. 515-525.

Vergopoulos, Kostas. "The End of Agribusiness or the Emergence of Biotechnology?" *International Social Sciences Journal*, Vol. 37 (1985), pp. 285-289.

Wald, Salomon. "The Biotechnological Revolution," *The OECD Observer*, No. 156 (February-March 1989), pp. 16-20.

PERESTROIKA IN AMERICA

by

Steven M. Clark

Mikhail Gorbachev's bold effort to restructure Soviet society has western leaders saying, "It's about time. We told you so. You've got to deal with democracy and the marketplace."

Certainly, the Soviet problems—now even more glaringly exposed under *glasnost*—lend credence to this western summation. But can we be too smug? Are we not facing the same problems, but from an opposite vantage?

Our problems, too, are quite significant. We have a similarly declining rate of growth. Our debt is unprecedented. Social, racial and economic polarization is at new extremes. Public education is in decline. Social security is in jeopardy. Housing is inadequate. Accustomed to unrivaled dominance in international trade, we are now a debtor nation facing superior competition in the industrial and agricultural arenas.

Moreover, despite years of acknowledgement of these growing concerns, we have been unable to develop any systematic effort to address them. The executive and legislative branches of our government remain divided; Congress is a political gridlock.

A look at our nation from this perspective raises the issue of our own *perestroika*—our own political and economic restructuring. How can it happen?

The USSR and the USA

It is well known that the Soviet Union is a top-down, highly centralized economic and political system. For most of the last 70 years the country has tried to ignore market forces and plan the entire national economy. This has created a massive bureaucracy, stifled initiative, fomented corruption and, most importantly—after the initial leap into the industrial age—strangled economic growth in the post war era.

The only way to crack this system is from the top, and finally the Soviets have found someone to do it. Naturally, this is a most dramatic episode in world history.

In contrast to the Soviet Union, the economic and political system of the United States is highly decentralized and marked by near total domination of the profit motive achieved through participation in the marketplace. Our expertise in planning is concentrated in

---

Steven M. Clark *is a free lance writer and editor of a quarterly journal on issues of public affairs.*

individual enterprises, contained to serve the interest of that entity alone. Political forces generally serve specific economic interests, and given the decentralized, democratic nature of our society, the more powerful economic interests tend to dominate the political system to their benefit.

Our system cannot be cracked from the top; no one force has such power. Our system must change in a much more evolutionary way, based on bottom-up, market-driven forces. Naturally, our changes will appear—at first, at least—much less dramatic.

American Restructuring Already in Progress

In fact, the forces of restructuring are already well in motion in the United States. They involve no grand plans to reconfigure Congress, to change the nature of our current system of checks and balances, to modify the separation of powers, to establish proportionate representation or to abolish the electoral college.

While, no doubt, the revolution in the mode of production embodied in the transition to post-industrialism will eventually transform much of the political superstructure of American society, the process has not begun by tinkering with these mechanisms. Rather, it is developing outside (albeit, in conjunction with) our present, "normal" political decision-making system. It is in the *augmentation* of our present system with new mechanisms of planning and cooperation that the initial *perestroika* of America is occurring.

We speak of the "public-private partnership" (more accurately, the "tripartite partnership").

Tripartite Partnership

The tripartite partnership is a three-sided effort to size-up, plan and implement solutions to specific social and economic problems. The three partners are 1) the government, 2) the corporate sector and 3) the professional expertise grounded in the affected constituencies (often embodied in non-profit organizations).

In its ideal operation, the government is the senior partner, serving to identify key problems/opportunities and to bring the other partners into the process. The corporate sector provides expertise and major financial resources. Authority (authorization from and respect among the affected constituencies) and competency (knowledge of the particulars) are provided by professionals directly connected with and, perhaps, part of the affected constituencies.

Initiative may come from any source, and a role is developing for professionals whose principal task is to facilitate the process of partnership formation and the development of widespread public support and participation (a public relations and marketing function).

No perfected models of the full tripartite partnership currently exist, but many partial models are operational and developing. A big shortcoming is the failure of government at all levels to appreciate the full role it can and should play in the process. Our society is just awakening to the potential of these new forms, and we are about to enter a long period of creative development in which a multitude of varieties and strains of partnership will be tried and perfected.

Partnerships in Transition

Actually, public-private partnerships are nothing new. An old example is the cooperation after the Civil War between the government and the surging railroad industry in the building of the first railroads linking the two coasts. The government basically gave the land to the railroads to encourage their efforts. A more recent example is the UDAG (Urban Development Block Grant) program of the 1970s. Local development agencies were able to access government grants to leverage private money to finance major community redevelopment projects. Often, these were downtown revitalization efforts designed to stimulate the general business and tourist climate of dying industrial centers.

Generally, it is safe to say that the main beneficiary of the public-private partnerships has been the private sector. Successful partnerships simply have not been formed unless it was in the direct financial interest of the corporate sector. In some circles, this fact has tarnished the image of these partnerships and is a factor restricting their widespread support and development.

However, a number of new economic, political and social trends have emerged which not only encourage widespread creation of new partnerships, they demand it. Moreover, they promise to build the public consensus which will broaden support for these partnerships. What are these trends?

Demands of Post-Industrial Capital Formation

First and foremost is the transition to the post-industrial mode of production—otherwise called the Third Wave or the Information Age. The demands and opportunity of this transition are as monumental as that of the Industrial Revolution, except that the present transformation is happening at a far greater rate of change.

Post-industrial production requires unprecedented capital investment. For example, the next level of computer generation is impossible by any single American corporation. A collective effort is demanded.

Even more fundamental, post-industrial production requires a highly educated, motivated and socially skilled workforce. America's is sadly lagging and falling further behind the demand. The problems with drugs, teenage pregnancy, structured unemployment, rising illiteracy, increasing suicide and decreasing fitness not only are vivid demonstrations of unpreparedness, they are the direct result of it.

Those with illusions that the great potential of post-industrialism can be sustained on the creativity and ingenuity of a small portion of our population are sadly mistaken. Not only will the weight of poverty and mediocrity drag us down, it will limit our collective creativity and emasculate our best efforts. There is no choice but open opportunity based on efforts to unleash the full potential, participation and empowerment of our entire society.

The demands of post-industrial capital formation—both for research and development and for investment in human capital—require a level of cooperation and planning as yet undeveloped in US society. Everything is interconnected and interdependent. So much must be done. Cooperation is vital. Yet, not everything can be done at once. Priorities must be set; plans must be made.

Thus, the emergence and development of post-industrial society, itself demands the creation of new mechanisms of planning and cooperation.

Corporate Outlook Is Changing

Second, the nature of ownership in our society has changed substantially in the past century, and, now, corporate consciousness is beginning to catch up with the new realities.

Today's modern Fortune 500 companies were founded and owned by private individuals. When they died, their ownership was transferred to their more numerous heirs. Not only was ownership diffused, the heirs were not necessarily capable of effective management. Very quickly, it became indispensible in all but the exceptional case that corporations hire professional management to lead the enterprise.

Over the ensuing decades the professional management strata came to dominate the corporate system, subordinating the interests of owners to their own. Management ideology, however, remains—to this day—steeped in the goal of profit maximization for the owners.

The corporate critique which was launched in the 1960s struck a nerve among many Americans who could see that there is a lot more utility to corporate enterprise than mere profit. There are jobs for the community. There is air and water quality. There is civic and social responsibility. These, in total, are at least as important as profit maximization, and in a variety of ways Americans have made this clear to business over the last two decades.

The most advanced and farsighted corporate managers now understand that their enterprise's strategic interest in continuity and growth is intrinsically linked to that of the community, nation and society of which they are a part. Moreover, these managers have found that ownership is so dispersed that no owners can exercise effective control over management's decisions. In this context managers have begun to redefine the corporate agenda, not to eliminate profit, but to relieve demands for profit maximization and to recognize the need to ensure other important social and civic responsibilities.

Proof of this trend is the growth of corporate giving and cause-related marketing. It is further evidenced in the variety of partnerships between business and local school systems.

While examples of philanthropy go back to the beginning of corporate enterprise, the trend of direct corporate efforts to participate in and influence community growth and development began a sharp rise following the critique and challenge of the 60s. The progress is encouraging, but the opportunity is only beginning to be appreciated. The decades ahead will foster many significant new developments along this line.

Public Interest Sector Growing

Third, the complexity of demand in modern consumer society has created a vast array of non-profit organizations designed to meet specialized civic and social needs, usually in conjunction with business forces and traditionally with critical support from government. These range from hospitals to universities to social service agencies to community development corporations to advocacy groups to self-help associations and more.

The last decade's cuts in federal assistance has freed these organizations to find self-sufficient ways to earn their keep. Essentially, they have moved from a "do good" orientation to a business orientation. They have gone into business themselves, filling gaps in the local service economy and, in some cases, competing directly with the for-profit sector.

However, the managers of this sector are not primarily profit-oriented. Even the profits from their profitable enterprises are reinvested in the service mission of the organization. This non-profit sector is the fastest growing part of the US economy. It is tuned to the problems and opportunities of community economic and social development.

Post-War Generations Bring Fresh Perspective

Fourth, a new generation is beginning to assume civic leadership in our society. Born in the post war era, this generation is the first raised entirely in the post-industrial epoch. Its perspective is decidedly different.

Inspired in part by John F. Kennedy's great call to "ask not what your country can do for you, but what you can do for your country," this generation launched the social critique of the narrow, self-interested posture and outlook of 1950s corporate America. Idealistic, yet riding the prosperity of the post war era, this generation rebelled against the complacency of the times and fought, sometimes literally, to make itself heard.

The pressing reality of life's necessities (work and family), along with the seemingly deaf ear of the establishment, eventually drove this youthful generation back into the American mainstream. Fifteen years have passed, and the natural evolution of civic power has brought this generation to the brink of social leadership throughout the country. While the top echelons of power have yet to fall, the middle level positions of authority in corporate circles have begun to swing. Outside the corporate circle, in the private, non-profit sector and at the lower levels of local political power, the tide has turned.

This generation, like its predecessors, brings new values and fresh perspective to civic leadership. It is two generations removed from the special interest, constituency politics of the New Deal coalition, and it is a generation removed from the Cold War, Pax Americana outlook of the 50s. Its values and vision were forged by the necessity to overcome antagonism and build cooperation—the imperatives of the post-industrial era—at home and abroad.

Partnership Potential Unappreciated

These four trends—post-industrialism, ownership changes, the growing non-profit sector and a new generation of civic leadership—bode well for the emergence and development of tripartite partnerships as a vital, new element for planning and cooperation in our society; yet, still, as a society, we have little systematic consciousness of their purpose and potential.

Thus, the tasks ahead are clear. First, we must raise widespread consciousness of where our society is in its process of social development. We must talk about the obstacles and opportunities in post-industrialism, discuss the critical need for increased cooperation and planning.

Second, we must create the mechanisms which will allow such cooperation and planning to become real. We must foster restructuring through the encouragement of the tripartite partnership.

These partnerships are the cornerstone of *perestroika* in America. Our restructuring is in progress, and it promises to be every bit as exciting and revolutionary as that of the Soviet Union.

ONE WORLD: THE UNION OF A NEW CAPITALISM AND A NEW SOCIALISM

by

William E. Halal

After decades of bitter conflict between capitalism and socialism have polarized the Earth into warring camps, today a technological revolution is driving these two major systems of political economy toward a unified but diverse global order—One World that works.

It has become increasingly clear in recent years that nations are rapidly coalescing into some sort of global system. International trade is growing at twice the rate of domestic trade, competition across national borders is now intense, and telecommunication networks encircle the Earth. This newly emerging reality was dramatically illustrated when the 1987 crash on Wall Street reverberated almost instantaneously throughout the financial centers of the entire world, and in 1988 the leader of the Soviet Union, Mikhail Gorbachev, told the UN that the world is becoming a "single global organism."

However, there remains deep confusion over how the old conflict between capitalism and socialism will be resolved. Many scholars claim the two systems have been moving toward a "convergence" for years,[1] and this trend became more striking recently when China and the USSR began adopting market mechanisms. Although many believe this means socialism has failed and that the socialist bloc will soon be practicing capitalism, socialist states are unlikely to adopt the West's version of free markets because it clashes with their cultures. It is hard to believe, for instance, that the Soviets will permit their carefully planned state enterprises to be dismembered by the type of brutal corporate takeovers now flourishing in the US. A Chinese official noted: "Capitalism doesn't have a patent right over markets. We're trying to establish an unprecedented form of market economy based on public ownership."

And in the USA, that bastion of capitalism, employee directors have gained seats on the boards of about a dozen major corporations in recent years, which indicates a trend toward more democratic labor relations, or what some would call "socialism." At the same time, however, America's faith in the efficacy of unfettered free enterprise has been rejuvenated under Reaganomics to deregulate industries, curtail government programs, and encourage neo-

William E. Halal *is professor of management, George Washington University, Washington, DC and, the author of* The New Capitalism *(Wiley, 1986). He is working with a Soviet scholar on a book with the same title as this article.*

robber barons like today's corporate raiders. This is hardly socialism.

Thus, there seems to be convergence in some areas and divergence in others. In a major study that summarized the evidence on nine dimensions of economic structure for 28 nations, Clark Kerr found that six dimensions show "substantial convergence," while three dimensions indicate "little or no convergence."[2] Many provocative questions are raised by such conflicting trends. What underlying forces can explain why capitalism and socialism seem to be following similar yet distinctively different paths of development? How will nations from incompatible systems coexist in a unified world, if at all? Is it possible to predict the outlines of the coming global order?

This paper presents a conceptual framework based on the complementary principles of convergence and divergence to help answer such questions. A few prominent examples will then be used to establish key trends and to forecast where these changes should lead. My main conclusion is that keen differences will always persist among nations, but that a "New Capitalism" and a "New Socialism" are evolving that may in time embody roughly similar blends of democracy and free enterprise. In a decade or two, this resolution of the old conflict between the two dominant forms of political economy should then lead to a unified global community.

A Framework of Political Economy

A conceptual framework is outlined in Figure 1 consisting of two dimensions that distinguish different types of political economy.[3] The horizontal dimension of "structure" defines the degree to which the system is organized as a single monolithic hierarchy—"centralized planning"—versus a dispersed network of independent business units—"free enterprise." The vertical "process" dimension describes whether decision-making is conducted in an "autocratic" or "democratic" manner.

Four ideal systems, or archetypes, can be located at each corner of Figure 1 to illustrate the scales in meaningful terms. "Laissez-Faire Capitalism"—which I will sometimes abbreviate as "capitalism"—appears at the lower-right corner since it stresses free markets. "Democratic Socialism"—or simply "socialism"—is at the opposite corner since it shifts the focus to government control of the economy. The lower-left corner could be called "Dictatorial Socialism," as practiced in the USSR under Stalin. At the upper-right corner, the combination of both democracy and free enterprise forms another, but as yet unrealized, ideal type—"Democratic Free Enterprise"—which is discussed more fully later.

The positions shown for individual nations are my own rough estimates and are provided mainly to illustrate the framework. Most nations are scattered somewhere about the middle of Figure

1, as shown. Various "capitalist" nations tend to be located toward the Laissez-Faire Capitalism corner, "socialist" nations gravitate toward the opposite corner, and "mixed economies" are found in the center moving toward the Democratic Free Enterprise model. The following examples of the two superpowers will help clarify these estimates.

The USA is positioned nearer the Laissez-Faire Capitalism model since its system of political economy is strong on free enterprise but weak on democracy. The *political* system of the USA may exemplify democratic ideals, but this is not generally true of the *economic* system. Apart from the legal rights of shareholders, most industries are not directly controlled to a significant degree by labor, consumers, local government, or other interest groups. The only exception is bargaining with labor, but union membership only

Figure 1
DISTRIBUTION OF VARIOUS ECONOMIC SYSTEMS ALONG DIMENSIONS OF STRUCTURE AND PROCESS

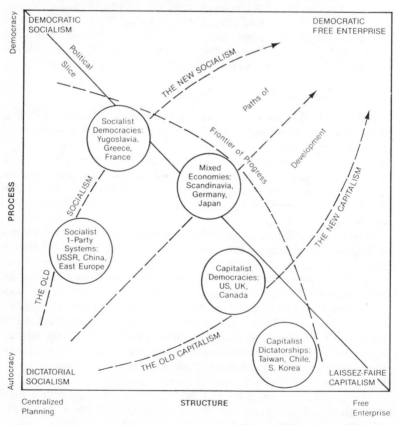

covers a fifth or so of the economy and may be in further decline. As a result, the interests of these groups are not generally considered in decisions unless regulated by the federal government. The USSR, in contrast, is located near the Dictatorial Socialism corner for obvious reasons.

This framework allows us to define two principles describing how systems of political economy are evolving into a unified but diverse global order. The first describes how the approaching information age seems to be encouraging a strong tendency toward *convergence*, and the second notes that cultural differences simultaneously exert an opposing tendency toward *divergence*.

Convergence: The Imperative of Information Technology

History suggests that nations generally tend to move toward democratic governance and free markets since these ideals are usually preferred to dictatorship and bureaucratic controls. This tendency is accelerating now because the onset of an information age is causing a crucial shift in the technological foundation of business and economics. The central fact of our time is that the computer is beginning to harness the power of information, just as the invention of the mass-production assembly line harnessed the power of machinery to begin an industrial age. But where the Industrial Revolution shifted the critical factor of production from labor to capital equipment, now the shift is from capital to *knowledge*.

A "knowledge-based economy" is a poorly understood recent phenomenon, but it seems to exert a fundamentally different imperative. The industrial era fostered conflict basically because physical resources are finite, forming a zero-sum game in which economic actors struggle over a limited supply of material wealth. Information *increases* when shared, however, thereby urging positive-sum games of collaborative problem-solving and creative enterprise. This explains why the rapid proliferation of information technology seems to be creating a more sophisticated type of political economy now, one in which democracy and enterprise are being extended into new economic areas and united into an unusual synthesis of cooperation and competition.

This is not simply theory since examples abound. A good example is the move toward collaborative labor-management relations during the 1980s. Forced to survive under growing competition, the auto, steel, and airline industries signed historic contracts in which unions gave up work restrictions and pay increases in return for profit-sharing and a say in management decisions from the shop to the boardroom. As a result of unyielding economic pressure, then, no-nonsense executives who abhor any whiff of lofty ideals are almost unwittingly moving toward the democratization of the workplace simply because it is *efficient*. Employee directors are now seated on the boards of Chrysler, Pan Am, Kaiser Aluminum, and about a dozen other major companies, while the auto industry paid its workers a $400 million share of profit in 1986. *Business Week* noted: "Worker representation is spreading faster than anticipated . . . it has probably become a permanent part of industrial life."

Even competitors are collaborating. About 50 collaborative research consortia have been formed recently in the US alone, such as the Microelectronics and Computer Technology Corporation (MCC)—a joint venture of 20 competing firms to advance information technology for their mutual benefit. The advent of cooperative R&D has been called "the most significant step forward since the computer chip."

These trends are restricted to a small avant-garde of progressive companies, but they show that a "New Capitalism" involving an unusual blend of democracy and enterprise seems to be emerging— not because of devotion to ideals—but because the information age demands it. The advantage of combining these two principles is nicely illustrated by the "strategic alliances" that auto makers have formed with their counterparts abroad. While GM, Ford, and Chrysler compete more fiercely against Toyota, Fiat, and Renault— they are also cooperating with these same adversaries by jointly making and selling autos in each others markets.

The socialist bloc also seems to be moving in this direction. It is often thought that planned economies are inherently antagonistic to computerization because central controls block the free flow of information. But the freewheeling power of information technology seems to be running through socialist economies as well. Undaunted by government restrictions, an underground information network is proliferating in the Soviet bloc through the illicit use of video tapes, VCRs, photocopiers, journals, and PCs. In Hungary the new spirit of *glasnost* has permitted an information starved, critical citizenry to create socialist versions of the TV talk show that would make Phil Donahue blush. One show culls 20,000 letters to select 66 people who quiz a government official on the air until the audience is satisfied with his answers. And part of Gorbachev's policy of *perestroika* is to launch a major effort to upgrade computerization and communication capabilities throughout the Soviet Union. Loren Graham summed up the consequence in the *Washington Post:* [4]

> It is becoming increasingly clear that [information technology] is challenging basic principles of the Soviet state—control over information and secrecy about vital data . . . The question is not whether the Soviets will accept this technology—external competition will force them to.

The result has been an astonishing flood of experimentation throughout the socialist bloc. These various forms of "market socialism" typically permit small business ownership, incentive systems for workers, and greater freedom for state enterprises. The Soviet Union recently required managers of 48,000 plants controlling 60% of the economy to achieve "economic accountability" by planning their own operations and retaining profits; meanwhile the state bureaucracy has been slashed from 80 to 20 ministries. Hungary now permits the sale of company stock to finance private enterprises and free market pricing. In China, the private sector now employs more than 20 million workers, and state factories producing half of the nation's goods are being turned loose to operate as profit centers.

The move to democracy also seems inevitable. Hungary and Poland are now adopting multiparty political systems similar to the parliamentary governments of their neighbors in Western Europe, and the Soviet Union is reforming its one-party system to include contested elections among multiple candidates. Some socialist states, like Hungary, are also creating a democratic form of enterprise governed by councils composed of management, labor, and party officials. The crisis over the Solidarity Union in Poland indicates that the fierce determination behind this type of economic democracy is likely to persist until reforms are made. Gorbachev told his nation: "It is either democracy or social inertia. There is no third way, comrades."

Naturally, the question remains as to how socialist nations will accept the plant closings, unemployment, citizen unrest, and other disorders that are an inevitable consequence of these new freedoms. However, Franz Loeser, a former official in the Communist Party, thinks change is unavoidable:[5]

> The communist countries are losing the economic race with the West. People feel it and the party membership know it. What we are likely to witness is the painful dying out of an outmoded model of socialism and a fierce struggle for new, diversified and more democratic forms.

The fact that the unusual power of information may drive the socialist bloc to a "New Socialism" emphasizes the strength of this underlying dynamic that is now moving the world toward different economic principles. Information technology exerts a novel force, as revolutionary as industrial technology was two centuries ago, that seems to be uniting nations into some sort of global order based on both collaboration and competition. Thus, there appears to be a long-range tendency for nations to evolve in the general direction of the "Paths of Development" noted in Figure 1, thereby gradually converging toward the Democratic Free Enterprise model of political economy.

Divergence: The Imperative of Cultural Differences

Despite this tendency toward convergence, all nations have unique histories, political movements, subjective beliefs and other

41

cultural attributes which encourage different paths to fostering the national welfare, thereby also creating an opposing tendency toward *divergence*. This can be illustrated by taking a "Political Slice" through Figure 1, as indicated, to show the dispersion of economies across a political spectrum ranging from Social Democracy in the upper-left corner to Laissez-Faire Capitalism in the lower-right corner. Nations at the left of the political slice favor "social" values of security, public welfare, and equity, while those to the right favor "enterprise" values of freedom, growth, and innovation.

Table 1
COMPARISION BETWEEN CAPITALISM AND SOCIALISM

	Capitalism (USA)	Socialism (USSR)
Strengths	Economic Freedom	Economic Security
	Productivity & Growth	Social Welfare
	Innovation	Reasonable Equity
Weaknesses	Risk & Competition	Loss of Freedom
	Social Costs	Poor Productivity
	Wide Inequalities	Bureaucracy
Polititcal System	Two-Party	One-Party
Economic Institutions	Profit-Driven Corporation	State-Controlled Bureaucracy
Stage of Development	Services (Tertiary)	Manufacturing (Secondary)

The drawbacks of socialism are dwelled on at great length in capitalist nations, but less is understood about the advantages Soviet citizens see in their system. True, their freedom to start a business, buy a home, and travel abroad is limited, but polls and knowledgeable observers indicate that the Soviets are proud of the way their system assures them of basic needs like education, employment, housing, health care, and pensions, which are often precarious in capitalist nations. Russians may envy America's sophisticated consumer goods, however, the USSR has achieved considerable economic progress from a feudal society composed largely of impoverished, illiterate peasants just a few decades ago. Soviet GNP per capita approximately quadrupled between 1950 and 1980, and growth rates generally matched those of the US. Socialist economies have been stagnating lately, but this is largely part of the economic crisis that struck all industrialized nations during the 80s, including the US.

The Soviet political system also has a different rationale. The USSR may be a "totalitarian" society in that the Communist Party controls most aspects of life in a paternalistic way, however, that does not mean it is a brutal form of repression without a legitimacy of its own. A one-party system is not a dictatorship of the type found in nations like Chile under Pinochet since the party uses some processes of representative government and its members are drawn from throughout Soviet society. In other words, it is a form of government that channels the conflict of political opinion *within* the party to arrive at a consensus needed to establish legitimate rule. As a result, Soviet politics do make needed reforms. Khrushchev was ousted when he lost the confidence of the nation in 1964, and Gorbachev was elected in 1985 to provide the precise blend of affability and pragmatism needed to rejuvenate their nation. Instead of the conflict and change that multiple-party systems stress, a one-party system has other advantages that emphasize stable, central control, rather like capitalist corporations. These features are attractive to some Western nations, which is why Italy, Mexico, and other countries with multiple-party systems have been dominated by a single party for decades.

In short, life in the USSR may be less exciting and comfortable, but it is more secure and orderly. Many Soviets who have immigrated to the US say Americans have "too much freedom" while "the Russian is secure;" that the "anonymity and stress of competitive life" are "in many ways even worse than the USSR." Michael Kernan's studies of Russian emigres led him to conclude:[6]

> The price we [Americans] pay for our freedom from authority [is] that nobody is responsible for you . . . in the all embracing way the Soviet state takes care of its own . . . Emigres speak of the indifference, the coldness of people absorbed in getting ahead, the status based on money.

In contrast, capitalism provides other advantages. The productivity of free enterprise has produced a luxurious standard of living in the US, whereas in the Soviet Union only a privileged elite can afford the material comfort most Americans take for granted. These gains are mainly the result of a cultural heritage of economic freedom that has allowed the US to become widely admired as one of the most vital, creative nations in the world.

But the unavoidable price for this freedom is that serious social disorders are allowed to go unchecked. Bankruptcies, layoffs, recessions, and other forms of economic hardship abound in the US because of the sheer uncertainty, risk, and constant change produced by a competitive economy. A wide range of social costs are also endemic since the system focuses attention on economic rather than social values: poverty and homelessness, worker accidents, consumer fraud and injuries, pollution, and other public maladies that are often very severe. That explains why capitalism's vaunted superior productivity of material goods does not necessarily translate into better life styles. Studies consistently show that the USA may have the highest GNP per capita in the world, yet it ranks below many other nations in overall quality of life. A recent survey rated the US 27th out of 124 nations.[7]

One of the most troublesome drawbacks is the social inequality that capitalism produces. Inequalities persist under socialism, despite the claim of a "classless society," but they seem less severe. The average American earns an annual income of about $17,000 that only provides a marginal existence and about one fifth of the nation lives in poverty—while the economic system glorifies multi-million dollar incomes of paper entrepreneurs, rock musicians, TV announcers, athletes, and movie stars. The big winners in the capitalist sweepstakes earn so much beyond their most extravagant needs that money ceases to have any meaning, and one can only wonder what purpose such gross wealth may serve. The top .5 percent of Americans owns 35 percent of all wealth, and the top 10 percent owns 70 percent of all wealth. Although many applaud these differences as proof that capitalism offers opportunity, polls show that the majority feels they are excessive and unjust. One American put it this way:[8]

> Now let me see if I have my values straight . . . An executive is worth over $7 million a year. A baseball player is worth $2 million . . . But a teacher for our children is worth about $18,000 a year . . . It certainly makes one proud to be part of such an intelligent species.

Thus, the differences between capitalism and socialism are largely due to cultural preferences, rather than a question of which system is superior. The superpowers have somehow arrived at bipolar solutions to the common problems of industrialization, with opposing strengths and weaknesses, thereby unwittingly creating a symmetrical, symbiotic relationship between the two dominant ideologies. Many nations are committed to socialism because of the flaws they see in capitalism, and, conversely, capitalism is attractive to many others because of the problems in socialism.

Because the two superpowers serve as archetypes of capitalism and socialism, this comparison illustrates the underlying forces that create divergence in political economies. Cultural differences among nations seem to divide such that roughly half of the world gravitates toward values favoring economic security, public welfare, and social equity, while the other half favors economic freedom, productivity, and innovation. The resulting bipolar division in this rich cultural ecology forms a "symmetric structure" of the present industrial order, a sort of dynamic tension that gives the world balance as a system in its own right—like the two poles of a magnet. In fact, from this larger systems view the bipolarity of the globe has been functional. The mutual antagonism of the superpowers served to drive both nations to develop their technological skills quickly, to draw together into cohesive societies united against an external enemy, and other such purposes.

Although this seems to contradict the tendency toward convergence, the situation is more subtle since nations tend to favor either the left or right as they converge. As Figure 1 shows, those holding social values develop along a path in which the Old Socialism yields to a New Socialism, while those favoring enterprise will move from the Old Capitalism to a New Capitalism.

Analysis and Forecast

Naturally, the trends described here are speculative in many respects, they are only supported by selected examples, and there is no assurance that they will continue. The following analysis evaluates the significance of these trends and offers a forecast of where the world seems likely to be heading over the next decade or so.

The main conclusion of this paper is that a proliferation of economic experiments seem to be producing a New Capitalism and a New Socialism that may in time converge. All nations have distinctive cultural differences, so it is not that the *USA* and the *USSR* are converging; rather, it is that the ideological *systems* of *capitalism* and *socialism* seem to be moving along a common path leading toward some new combination of enterprise and democracy.

As noted, both sets of nations are infusing their economies with market principles. The US, England, and other Western nations are deregulating industries, privatizing government functions, and breaking up corporate bureaucracies to unleash the creativity of enterprise that has often been a distant ideal in capitalism. China and the Soviet bloc are starting to do the same to overcome the bureaucratic inefficiencies that have plagued their economies, albeit without relinquishing some form of state control. Thus, both systems seem to be moving toward some roughly similar type of free enterprise to avoid the drawbacks of regulated, oligopolistic capitalism on one hand and centrally planned socialism on the other.

Similar trends are also moving both systems toward democratic forms of governance. Europe, Japan, and more recently the US are all incorporating various forms of "participative management," which fosters the social goals advocated by socialism, although they are doing so using democratic principles rather than the control of the state. Likewise, socialist nations are beginning to create democratic institutions, as in Hungary, Russia, and China. The proportion of the world's population living under democracy reached an all-time high of almost 40% in 1988.

It should be noted, however, that these changes present sensitive political obstacles because they disturb fundamental beliefs in both ideologies, with each system being challenged in opposite directions. While capitalist nations are fearful that social control of the economic system will infringe on entrepreneurial freedom and productive efficiency—socialist states are reluctant to *yield* social control over their economy for fear of releasing destructive market forces of profiteering and individualism.

These "symbolic" issues could be resolved by interpreting the required changes in terms that are palatable for each "mythology." Capitalist nations tend to think of these concepts as a "broader" or "modern" version of "free enterprise" incorporating "democratic" or "human" values that is justified by being more "productive." Socialist nations, on the other hand, may see the same practices as an extension of "socialist principles" that enable "the proletariat" to directly control the "means of production" using "decentralized planning" to create an "advanced" form of "market socialism" that improves the "social welfare." So both ideologies may evolve toward a similar set of operational policies, although this common system would probably continue to be viewed differently through the lens of each culture.

However, it would be misleading to believe that some "optimum" system may become universal because the opposite tendency toward divergence can also be seen in the above examples. The world is growing far too complex for any monolithic approach, so it is more likely that diverse forms of political economy should flourish during the next few decades to suit the unique cultural backgrounds of various nations. The center of this spectrum may be popular in Scandinavian states, West Germany, Yugoslavia, France, Japan, Greece and other moderate nations with mixed economies. Countries like the USA, England, Canada, Taiwan, South Korea, and the South American states that prefer laissez-faire systems should tend toward the capitalist end, while China, Hungary, Poland, the USSR and other nations favoring collectivist regimes will probably lean toward the socialist end. Thus, it seems that the coming world order should be characterized by wide diversity, but—rather than being polarized between the opposite extremes of the Old Capitalism and the Old Socialism—this diversity should be viewed as variations of the same universal principles of political economy: democracy and free enterprise.

Although individual nations should develop a single variation that suits their unique culture, the role of multinational corporations (MNCs), seems destined to be more complex. They face the challenge of developing sophisticated networks of economic and technical systems to form the infrastructure of a global economy, thereby becoming the central institutions uniting this enormous diversity. So MNCs will have to use a wide range of institutional styles to accommodate different cultures. They will have to endure some state control in more socialist countries, form cooperative alliances in mixed economies, and enjoy greater freedom in capitalist nations.

Of course, it may be that the historic challenge of redefining the two pivotal systems of capitalism and socialism is so great that it may fail. Attempts to change the economic system in the USSR have thus far largely produced chaos, and a leading Soviet economist predicted that the current reforms will not yield tangible results until 1995. In 1988 *Pravda* announced that state enterprises are flatly refusing to fulfill their production targets but they are not yet able to work effectively with clients as in a market. The new demand for holding all enterprises accountable for performance has also resulted in identifying 50 major manufacturers that are failing and should be declared bankrupt. And it has now been discovered that the state is running a deficit of approximately $163 billion per year, roughly the same size as the US budget deficit. In Yugoslavia, 700 strikes broke out during 1986 involving 60,000 workers, and the number is rising rapidly. China has experienced a burst of inflation, 60,000 workers have been fired, and it is estimated that another 1-2 million may soon lose their jobs.

The capitalist world is more advanced since it has well-developed markets, but the "Great Crash of 87" may be an ominous signal that the USA has serious problems as well. The "twin deficits" show no signs of abating; per capita income, productivity, and capital investment remain stagnant; raiders hold major corporations hostage to the threat of a hostile takeover; and Big Business is paralyzed with the same debilitating bureaucracy once condemned in Big Government. John Akers, the CEO of IBM, one of the most successful corporations in the world, acknowledged recently that the firm is strangling in its own bureaucracy. Thus, the Crash of 87 may mark a loss of faith in that old "magic of the market" that underlies America's tight ideological grip on laissez-faire capitalism. The idea that a brutal struggle among a dominant elite of predatory, authoritarian business people would somehow be sublimated into healthy progress can now be seen as an outmoded myth out of touch with the realities of a more complex global economy. Unless Americans face this issue squarely, the locus of power will continue to shift toward rising Pacific nations like Japan that are leading the way to a new form of capitalism based not only on competition but cooperation as well.

These are enormous obstacles to change that may not be resolved, so it is useful to envision three alternative scenarios that could develop over the next few years. The first could be called the "Global Decline" scenario in which resistance among critical political centers in the USA and the USSR prevents altering their present systems, leading to continued economic and political stagnation. A "Global War" scenario is also possible if this deadlock leads to renewed antagonism between the ideologies of capitalism and socialism, eventually erupting into some sort of violent conflict. The most optimistic scenario, "Global Order," could result if progressive leaders in both superpowers can recognize the limitations of their own systems and strive to remedy them, as noted above, thereby creating a coherent system of global economy based on common principles.

It is impossible to predict which of these alternatives may actually occur, of course, especially over the short-term of about five years when almost anything is possible. It may turn out, for instance, that the intense political pressures surrounding Gorbachev are too great for even his charismatic leadership. A Soviet colleague confided to me that he does not want to even think about what may happen if Gorbachev falls from power. The forces now driving an historic shift to a new era based on information technology, however, are so profound that I am more deeply impressed by the almost inexorable logic they compel over the long-term of 10-20 years.

An unprecedented global economy is evolving among a diverse mix of nations, all of which are modernizing rapidly to create roughly a ten-fold increase in economic production and consumption as the planet's population grows to 10-12 billion people living at an industrial level, thereby inexorably posing unimagined new problems of resource scarcity, economic development, manufacturing sophistication, competition for world markets, and ecological decay that will require some far different type of global order. And as the unusual power of information technology spreads to form a "central nervous system" for the planet, this historic challenge seems to be slowly but unavoidably forcing the world toward a new era based on the two central imperatives of a knowledge-based economy noted earlier.

Such massive levels of complexity can only be handled with economic systems that permit innovation, flexibility, and local control, moving the world relentlessly toward decentralized market structures—free enterprise.

Yet there is an equal need for collaborative institutions that integrate communities, enterprises, nations, and the entire globe into a loosely organized whole, thereby also driving the world toward various types of legitimate, cooperative decision-making—democracy.

These two imperatives of a new era, therefore, should eventually make some combination of democracy and free enterprise the central focus of a diverse global order—not because of good intentions, altruism, or even sound planning—but because a more productive new blend of cooperation and competition is essential to survive under these difficult new conditions and so it is rapidly becoming one of the most powerful new forces in the world today. Nations around the world are moving in this direction for the same reason all life changes: evolution forces us to make adaptations that are functional. The evidence summarized here shows that capitalism and socialism may offer special advantages, but they also suffer severe disadvantages because of structural limits in both ideologies: economic freedom is creative but socially disruptive while government controls are orderly but stifling.

The key solution that now seems to be emerging to this dilemma focuses on redefining the very nature of the enterprise so as to directly incorporate social controls at the grassroots. The result would produce a different form of economy that inherently serves the public welfare while simultaneously permitting entrepreneurial freedom—Democratic Free Enterprise. Because this model unifies both ends of the political spectrum, it could prove to be an especially powerful combination of both economic and social values.

Creating this more sophisticated form of political economy is still largely uncharted territory, but progress seems to be moving in this direction. As the examples described above and many others show,[9] progressive corporations and governments in America, Europe, and Japan are developing economic prototypes combining various forms of democracy and free enterprise: worker participation, client-driven marketing, democratic governance, entrepreneurial organizational structures, deregulated industries, privatization of government functions, business-government partnerships, and other innovations. In fact, if a "Developmental Slice" is taken through Exhibit 1, running from the most primitive model—Dictatorial Socialism—to the most advanced—Democratic Free Enterprise—the resulting dispersion explains why some nations outperform others economically. Mixed economies that are developing such innovations at the "Frontier of Progress" tend to perform best while both planned and laissez-faire economies usually perform worse because they lag behind. It is no coincidence that the highest overall living standards in the world are generally found in about a half-dozen nations which have carefully cultivated mixed economic systems for decades: the Scandinavian states, West Germany, Switzerland, and Japan. (Kuttner, 1984)

A major challenge posed by the revolutionary nature of the information age, it seems to me, is to synthesize the ideologies of the Old Capitalism and the Old Socialism into a common conceptual framework upon which to construct a unified global order. The two major systems of political economy that dominate the world may never be the same, but they could then be *compatible*. Vadim Medvedev, an historian and the chief theoretician of the Soviet Union, recently acknowledged that the two systems "will inevitably intersect."

We should caution, however, that this union of a New Capitalism and a New Socialism will not be a panacea for all the world's many ills: the North-South conflict between developed and developing nations, the Third World debt crisis, stifling economic protectionism, wildly accelerating money flows and fluctuating exchange rates, and continuing damage to the fragile global ecosystem we all depend on for life itself. It should, however, allow the world to direct its undivided attention to these problems more effectively by finally resolving the central conflict over capitalism and socialism that has plagued almost the entire century of the industrial age.

This conflict has been such a central issue because it embodies not only a clash between philosophical ideologies and systems of political economy, it also marks major differences in the way power is used, cultural values, and even personal conflicts within each individual. All of us struggle with the opposing needs for freedom to grow versus the need for security; the flip side is the fear of striking out alone to realize one's talents versus the struggle to get along with others. This old conflict between capitalism and socialism is, at once, a syndrome of the divisions that polarize the globe and also of the psychological traumas that torture each individual soul, it is the universal dilemma of individuality versus community.

From a deeper perspective, the coming synthesis of capitalism and socialism represents the healing of this ageless dilemma, a union of free enterprise and democracy, of competition and cooperation, individual freedom and collective obligations, of right- and left-wing values—all of which are part of the broader unification of the planet as it grows toward a more mature phase in what I have called the "Life Cycle of Evolution."[10]

Sometime over the next decade or two, about the turn of this century, I estimate that some form of world governance is likely to emerge out of today's turbulent change, opening the way for a truly global community. Naturally, there will remain local pockets of conflict, as in any community, and there always exists the possibility of a serious setback. But the remarkable events of our time seem to indicate that the long evolution of civilization may be rapidly leading toward a climatic turning point.

The struggle of organized societies shows a steady but tortuous trend toward aggregation into ever larger social systems: from cave dwellers, to tribes, to cities, to nations, to superpowers. This unmistakable trajectory now seems headed toward the next logical level of a unified global order. Who would have believed just a few years ago, for instance, that the superpowers would agree on major arms reductions (the Intermediate Nuclear Force Treaty) to begin winding down the cold war? Today, Americans and Soviets seem in a rush to get to know one another and to work together. Recently, a half-dozen major US corporations concluded agreements to form joint ventures with Soviet enterprises, and more are following this lead. Hazel Henderson predicts that the old global "game" of "Mutually Assured Destruction" is now yielding to a new game of "Mutually Assured *Development* ."[11]

Thus, the coming union of a New Capitalism and a New Socialism should provide a conceptual and political basis for resolving the antagonism between the superpowers, it should encourage international arrangements for managing a far more complex global economy, and permit major arms reductions by providing common security in a global community. Even now, global enterprises from major nations like the USA, the USSR, Europe, Japan, and China are starting joint ventures in each other's nations, and this trend should soon cause national economies to intermesh into a single, indivisible system. Before too long, I think we may see the present growth of economic trading blocs like the European Common Market and Pacific Rim Common Market merge into a unified global economy of unrestricted free trade. An explosion of international communications, TV, publications, and travel is rapidly weaving the world's diverse cultures together into a rich tapestry of different people, all working together fairly harmoniously. A common global currency, banking system, and some form of world government should finally put an end to the arbitrary political boundaries that separate all of us.

I realize there is a lot of cynicism about such prospects, and events will undoubtedly work out somewhat differently from today's confident forecasts. But I think we may soon be surprised to see the globe unified into fairly coherent, manageable, cohesive system that works—One World.

Notes

1. See, Paul R. Gregory and Robert C. Stuart. *Comparative Economic Systems*. Boston: Houghton-Mifflin, 1980; Thorkil Kristensen, *Development in Rich and Poor Countries*. New York: Praeger, 1974; and Stephen Jay Kobrin, *Foreign Direct Investment, Industrialization, and Social Change*. University of Michigan, 1975.

2. Clark Kerr, *The Future of Industrial Societies*. Cambridge, MA: Harvard University Press, 1983.

3. William E. Halal, "Political Economy in the Information Age." *Research in Corporate Social Performance and Policy*. Greenwich, CT: JAI Press, 1988.

4. Loren Graham, "The Soviet Union is Missing Out on the Computer Revolution." *The Washington Post*. March 11, 1984.

5. Franz Loeser, "Communism Won't Change Until the Party Machine Goes." *The Washington Post*. August 19, 1984.

6. Michael Kernan, "The Russians are Here." *The Washington Post*. June 13, 1983.

7. Richard Estes, paper presented at the Global Development Conference. College Park, Pennsylvania: University of Pennsylvania. September 15, 1986.

8. Forest Miller, "Letters to the Editor." *The Washington Post*. April 15, 1984.

9. William E. Halal, *The New Capitalism*. New York: Wiley, 1986.

10. William E. Halal, "The Life Cycle of Evolution: A Study in MacroTechnological Forecasting." *Technological Forecasting & Social Change*. Forthcoming.

11. Hazel Henderson, *Mutually Assured Development*. Plowshare Press. Autumn, 1987.

WHY US INDUSTRY SHOULD BE LOOKING AT SOVIET TECHNOLOGY

by

John W. Kiser

In the aftermath of the recent summit in Moscow, policymakers, businessmen, and Soviet-watchers continue to be intrigued by the implications and opportunities attending the changes taking place under Gorbachev's leadership.

Among the opportunities much talked about these days are joint ventures. These typically conjure up images of multimillion dollar deals and massive transfers of US technology. In contrast to these mega-deals, there is a multitude of smaller high technology ventures and related activities that draw instead on Soviet science and technology.

More attention to the Soviet knowledge base and awareness of their technical capabilities might save the US government the embarrassment caused by underestimating them, as occurred in the case of Soviet penetration of the new US embassy as well as the old one. Soviet passive sensors embedded in the walls of the new embassy were far more sophisticated than anyone could have imagined. To this day the US doesn't have the capability to duplicate their ability to bug IBM Selectrics for real time remote transmission of a message as it is being typed.

For several years Kiser Research Inc., and other companies (National Patent Development, Diversified Technology, Considar Varian, Perkin Elmer) have had regular access to Soviet and East European research centers and been engaged in the transfer of technical know how and patent rights to the US. Technology transfer need not be a one way street, but it certainly will be as long as firms are unaware of the opportunities that exist for acquiring Soviet know-how. Developing ways to utilize the huge undervalued knowledge base in the Soviet Union to benefit the US economy requires recognizing that there is a big difference between what the Soviets know how to do and what the system actually does. This is the disjunction between brainpower and implementation power that Gorbachev is trying to address. Recently William Norris, former chairman of Control Data Corporation, has been advocating the creation of a large scale effort to match up innovative Soviet R&D languishing in their institutes and small entrepreneurial US companies that can

John W. Kiser *is president and founder of Kiser Research, Inc., business to transfer proprietary technology to the United States from Eastern Europe and the USSR.*

commercialize and market new technology.

Joint ventures, task research and aggressive use of open literature sources—all activities drawing down on Soviet knowledge—can produce a variety of benefits for the US government and private industry. The information that will be generated from more intensive knowledge of commercially available Soviet technology can have an impact on several important public policy issues:

Competitive Brain Picking

Japanese firms spend as much as 20% of their R&D budgets acquiring information about foreign technology. It is a way of life for them. As any good football coach knows, games are won by the offensive team. We need to take the offensive in using our competitors' knowledge. The US has no monopoly on brains. Some US research teams know this already. We need to encourage much more exploitation of foreign sources of knowledge.

The Soviet Union is traditionally viewed in only one way—as a market for selling. It can also be viewed as a market with a surplus of brains seeking commercial outlets. There is a relationship between a buying mentality when approaching the Soviet market and the deteriorating US competitive position in the world today. A "buying" mentality implies a readiness to recognize that others may have something of interest. This can translate into an ability to learn.

This relates not simply to products, but to the broader art of using foreign ideas and technology to stay competitive. If a company or a nation wants to remain scientifically competitive, it must be plugged in to the best brains all around the world. The US is not used to paying much attention to foreign technology, because until recently Americans assumed the US was the best in everything. We forget that prior to World War II, US industry routinely looked to the European market for new ideas. It had good reason: the Europeans pioneered everything from jet engines and computers to steel making and beer brewing.

About one-third of all the world's knowledge today is generated in Eastern Europe and the Soviet Union, though much is poorly utilized. Greater familiarity with that knowledge base in both its scientific and technical dimensions can produce tangible benefits for the United States as the examples below demonstrate.

• *Dupont* in the 1960s changed its production techniques for making vinyl acetate based on alternative Soviet methods described in open literature.

• *AT&T* researchers first got the idea to use lasers for annealing semi-conductor chips from Soviet literature, and hearing Soviet scientists present papers in Albany, New York, in 1977.

• *Varian Associates'* 1983 annual report credited Soviet research that helped break the bottleneck on the development of ultra high frequency gyrotrons-millimeter wavelength generators used for communications and initiating nuclear fusion reactions.

• *Los Alamos:* US government researchers utilized Soviet literature to design more effective technology for neutral particle beam weapons—based on RFQ or radio frequency quadropole.

These are only a few examples of how awareness of foreign work and Soviet research specifically, can help US research efforts. A more systematic approach to tapping the Eastern bloc technology base will yield even more benefits. This generic need is exemplified by the bill recently passed by Congress that was drafted by the Commerce Department calling for the regular translation of Japanese technological literature. A similar effort should be made with Soviet bloc open source literature as well. Sadly, the country's main efforts in this direction, such as those at Battelle Institute, are not readily available to industry for commercial exploitation even though the source material itself is mostly unclassified.

For obvious reasons, the Department of Defense spends more time tracking Soviet bloc technology than does industry. The US needs to establish a mechanism to transfer the potential benefits of this technical knowledge source to industry when good dual use possibilities are identified. This requires looking at the Soviet bloc technical literature for its "opportunity potential" as well as its "threat potential".

Several US corporations are now tapping into high quality, low cost R&D centers in Eastern Europe and the USSR. These R&D centers bill out a fully supported Ph.D. at one-fifth to one-tenth the US cost. Tremendous opportunity for leveraging R&D dollars exists. East Germany, Czechoslovakia, and Hungary are particularly well organized and accustomed to provide task oriented R&D services on a contract basis. These agreements provide US and foreign companies with an inside track to gain access to new technology from R&D centers which have a surplus of good brains and a shortage of means and incentives to commercialize results.

Unlike American universities, Soviet research institutes are not uncomfortable with issues relating to confidentiality, proprietary rights and other issues which may appear to conflict with Western universities' concerns with academic freedom and openness.

Trade and Export Control

National security has many faces. Export controls are intended to keep the enemy a few steps behind technologically, though in some cases controls have clearly been a creative stimulus to advances that leapfrog US art. There is little doubt however, that controls complicate life for the Eastern bloc nations, in the short term.

Controls also severely complicate the competitive environment for US industry, whose strength is vital to US national security. It

is essential that controls take into account current levels of technological development in the USSR and Eastern bloc countries. Controls have the negative effect of reducing the very interaction that
is necessary to develop useful technological assessments based on
current knowledge. For example:

- *Gallium Arsenide*, for use in ultra high speed computing, was
to be put on the weapons list, yet the USSR is a major producer
of gallium arsenide. ITT purchased ultra high purity material from
the Soviets in the 1960s. The Soviets were the first to grow gallium
arsenide crystals in the 1940s.

- *Artificial Intelligence or Expert Systems* are export control sensitive
subjects, yet some of the most advanced expert systems for predictive chemistry are being developed in Hungary. The EPA is having
such a system developed by a Hungarian team to predict potential
toxic effects in plants and animals. The Hungarian software is designed for IBM AT and is ahead of the current US state of the art.

- Advanced Ceramics Manufacturing using state of the art low
cost technology has been developed in the USSR and is available
for licensing.

While such information does not necessarily indicate that the
controls on equivalent US technology are without basis, it does
provide cause to look more closely at the information being used
to make initial judgments. In addition, Eastern Europe is frequently
overlooked as an alternative source of advanced technology for the
USSR.

Business Opportunities

It is frequently stated that US industry must become more internationally minded. The sentiment still bears repeating. Reading
and observing is not always enough in order to take full advantage
of others "brainware". Rights must be purchased to practice a technology efficiently. Why reinvent the wheel as the US government
did ten years ago when it spent millions on in situ coal gasification
technology already developed in the USSR?

There is a tremendous amount of technology for sale in the USSR,
and not only in research laboratories. In many cases technologies
in full commercial production have been acquired by US firms.
Revolutionary surgical stapling technology was introduced in the
1970s by a new venture formed specifically to exploit the Soviet
patents. The stapling technique had been long in use in the Soviet
market, but unknown in the West because of lack of contact. People
are now stapled together more often than stitched, saving time and
money and giving better results on patients. US companies are
investigating technologies in the fields of food processing,
medicine, ceramics, and semiconductor fabrication that are over
ten years old in the Soviet Union.

For US companies wishing to sell to the USSR, simultaneous

investigation of opportunities to acquire Soviet technology might be advisable. Such interest will help to sell US products and may represent a consolation prize in the event a company's efforts fail. Investigating collateral Soviet technology can also provide US companies with information necessary to confront outdated information, or assumptions by the Commerce or Defense Department when seeking an export license.

Unfortunately for US interests, the excessive attention devoted to Soviet espionage and the defense of US technology can blind the business and government community to opportunities. America's perestroika must include the shedding of smug attitudes, especially towards its competitors. This includes learning to understand more fully the strengths of the Soviets and the opportunities they provide as well as the threats they pose.

"FACTORIES OF THE FUTURE" TODAY

by

Albert Madwed

The building and operation of computerized automatic factories is beginning to change the method of producing products in the industrialized nations of the world. A description and analysis of one Swedish, two Japanese and one United States factory are presented in this paper. These four futuristic factories produce completely different products. The Swedish factory produces Volvo trucks and automobiles. The two Japanese factories produce motors and machinery. The United States factory produces many different models of electric motor starters. The components and systems used in these four factories are described and discussed. The conclusions of this study are basic principles for engineering an automatic futuristic factory. A first law of a manufacturing business for the future is presented and a new definition of a futuristic factory is developed. These principles, laws and definition can serve as a guide for planning and analyzing "Factories of the Future."

Swedish Factory for Volvo Automobiles and Trucks[1]

Project work on Kalmar, AB Volvo's newest Swedish automotive manufacturing plant, began in August 1971. One of the main objectives influencing Kalmar's development was to aim to create a workplace that met the needs for an individual's motivation and satisfaction in his daily work, without a reduction in efficiency. The management of Volvo promoted this objective with the belief that a product made by people who found meaning in their work would be a product of high quality.

This innovative step toward the world of flexible manufacturing began with a combination of technology and sociology in mind. A committee of foremen, architects, technicians, union representatives, safety experts, and medical doctors was responsible for formulating the plans for this Swedish industrial masterpiece. Many new, highly technological ideas were incorporated into this production scheme.

The most unique aspect of the Kalmar plant is its method of Automated Guided Vehicle System (AGVS). Cars are assembled on wire-guided platforms referred to as carriers. These carriers are computer-controlled and battery powered. At Kalmar there are two different models of carriers: "high" and "low". The names refer to the carriers' appearances and use of fixturing. Because each of the

Albert Madwed *is president of A. Madwed Co., designers and manufacturers of robotics systems.*

the 260 carriers are controlled independently, production is able to be organized in both parallel and straight-line configurations.

At Kalmar employees are able to influence their working environment through a variety of means. Working in teams of five or six people, members are able to rotate jobs and vary their pace of work. This working arrangement is possible through use of the wire-guided carriers.

The elimination of the traditional conveyor assembly line, whereby workers are assigned only a limited number of tasks, and the introduction of an AGVS have afforded Kalmar employees the opportunity to become experts in a complete system of the car. Workers are aware of their responsibility toward the system quality that their team assembles. This is because they do not merely assemble a "portion" of that system, instead, their work entails from start to finish details as well as any repairs the quality control stations advise after each system inspection. Team members are also permitted to determine their job rotation length. They may agree to rotate their jobs on a daily, weekly, or monthly basis.

Implementation of the AGVS has not only helped to improve the work environment for employees, but has also helped to increase the quality of Volvo's product. Assembly of cars on carriers allows the team members to perform their tasks in physical positions conducive to quality. For example, the "low" carriers used at Kalmar are able to tilt a car body 90 degrees, and the "high" carriers are able to suspend the car at a height whereby workers can access the underside from a standing position. Because 15% of a car's assembly must be performed from its underside, this 90 degree tilt and overhead suspension enables employees to execute their tasks from the plant floor, eliminating the need for factory floor pits.

The independent control of wireguided carriers, as opposed to a synchronous conveyor line, promotes the use of buffer zones at the start and finish of each team area. These buffers permit a balance in production to be achieved. Also, buffer zones and parallel assembly configurations help to avoid costly manufacturing "bottlenecks" so common in traditional, serial assembly lines. Production is no longer halted by a disfunction in one assembly work station. Instead, independent carriers can be routed around the problem area in order not to affect planned production requirements.

The key to this highly technological manufacturing endeavor is the magnitude of Kalmar's computerized control system. The central computer system monitors: receiving and inspection data of incoming components, inventory control system, assembly flow of each production level, quality control inspections and report compilations, dispatch of maintenance crews, and shipping processes.

One of the advantages of this computer-controlled inventory system is that inventory turnover time has increased by 57% since implementation.

The results of all quality control inspections are input into the computer which records and analyzes the outcome. If repairs are needed, the computer routes the appropriate carrier back to the team area which made the error and records the new sequence of that car. The computer randomly chooses 3% of all cars produced that day to have one last quality control inspection before the car is shipped.

For every quality control inspection performed on a car, a quality level is assigned to each system. This quality level (100 points if there are no mistakes, faults, damage, etc.) is input into the central computer system and compiled into a bi-monthly report for each team.

Twice a month there is a discussion with each team regarding the quality level results of the prvious two weeks. The results of these reports are important because the higher the quality levels, the greater the individual bonuses paid to each team member. The bonuses referred to are paid every six months in order to motivate the employees to attain higher levels of quality.

Since Kalmar implemented the AGVS into its manufacturing scheme, many advantages have become evident. Total assembly time using this flexible manufacturing system (FMS) has been reduced in contrast to the assembly time of traditional assembly lines. In fact, the man hours required to complete the assembly process have been reduced by 25% since the introduction of the AGVS. Although the initial investment was approximately 10% higher than that of traditional manufacturing systems, fewer supervisors and increased efficiency have justified the investment. Quality errors per car have been reduced by 39% since 1978.

There is improved production flow, elimination of "bottlenecks," and reduced assembly downtime. In addition there is a 57% reduction in inventory turnover time and improved management of work-in-process (WIP). Also, improved management of material inventories, system maintenance, quality control, production planning, and shipping resulted from this system. This system greatly improved flexibility for assembly process changes, intermittent and short production runs, expansions, and general rearrangements.

Over 900 driverless, wire-guided carriers have been used in manufacturing facilities for over 10 years without a single serious accident reported. This is due to the many safety devices with which the carrier is equipped.

Since the carriers are battery powered, the noise level of the plant remains low enough for employees to communicate in a normal voice. Even in areas of the facility near primary sources of noise, measures of sound absorption have been taken to avoid the need for hearing protection. Another advantage of the battery powered carriers is the elimination of exhaust fumes. The design of Kalmar encourages team organization and cooperation. Consequently, turnover and absenteeism of employees have decreased.

The Yamazaki Japanese Factory for Machine Production[2]

Most FMS installations involve 2 to 10 machines, but at Yamazaki's new factory at Minokamo, near Nagoya in southern Japan, there are 43 machines. In addition, there are 17 robots and there is a separate FMS for sheet metal parts.

Not that FMS is new to Yamazaki. Two years ago it unveiled its first two systems (consisting of 18 machines), at the headquarters plant at Oguchi. Since then, it has built systems with 28 machines at Yamazaki Seiko, and with 15 machines at its US subsidiary at Florence, Kentucky.

Significant though those plants are, they are overshadowed by the sheer boldness and breadth of the operation at Minokamo. Built on a levelled hillside on the outskirts of the town, the plant covers $49,000m^2$ of a $330,000m^2$ site. There the FMS produces flanges, spindles and small parts which are turned, milled, drilled and tapped; gearboxes and large frames are machined, flame-hardened and ground; and sheet metal parts are punched, formed and welded.

All these operations are under computer control, with unmanned trolleys transporting parts. In addition, there are some interesting developments in auxiliary equipment, such as one robot to clear chips, and another to load workpieces on to pallets. Yamazaki has further developed its principle of demountable automatic tool changers (ATCs), to provide a huge variety of tools.

Yamazaki talks of an investment of Yen 14 billion (£40 million) for the plant, excluding the land. With a staff of 240 people, it has a potential monthly output on three shifts of 120 lathes and machining centers. Altogether, there are 60 CNC (computer numerical control) machine tools, 28 universal machines, 12 AGVs, and six computers in the plant. Yamazaki calls this "System 21" after the twenty-first century, and tried to give the building a modern look to reflect that idea.

Because Yamazaki is in the business of selling machine tools there is a good deal of showmanship at Minokamo which gives the place a slightly unreal air. It hopes to be able to sell turnkey large-scale FMS. So the factory was opened to visitors to inspect the system at Oguchi.

On arrival, visitors are supposed to press a button on a small computer to find out where they should go. In fact, one of those girls that are everywhere in reception areas in Japanese companies, soon rushes out and presses the button for you, which makes the machine unnecessary. Then, there is an unmanned trolley on which visitors can go around the plant. Also visitors can walk around the gallery, stopping to be told by cassette recorder what is happening at various stations.

The rectangular plant is laid out in three bays, all served by six automated guided vehicles (AGVs), with one rail guided trolley serving each line. The first two sections of the first bay are empty, and are due to be used for assembly soon. The FMS at the other end of the bay are those for flanges and spindles. These are laid out in one long row, separated by a common area for the control computer terminals. On the other side of the first bay are some surface grinders, a small automatic storage and retrieval (ASR) warehouse, and the robot loading station for the "box" machining line. The box line itself is in the middle bay, which it shares with the frame line. Between these two lines, which are back-to-back, is a track for the special trolley to transport tool drums to and from the tool room. In the third bay are a large CNC machining center, which can operate on five faces, and a bed grinder, together forming the cell for large bases, columns of beds in the 5-25 ton range, and the flame hardening machine. Also in this bay is the assembly area. On the first floor there is the unit assembly area, where modules are assembled manually. Automatic lifts are used to transfer machined components from the ground to the first floor and back. There is a main aisle for the delivery of workpieces across the plant, with spurs running longitudinally to the various areas. The six AGVs follow wires buried in the floor as they transfer workpieces, unmachined and machined, between different lines and the lifts. However, these AGVs do not serve the machines themselves. The flange line consists of seven Slant Turn 40N Mill Centers and three machining centers—two horizontal and one vertical. At the end of the line is the control area, with two computers, and a station to which workpieces can be delivered. At the other end of the control area is the spindle line of five Slant Turn 40N Mill Centers, one vertical machining center, and a CNC cylindrical grinder.

Yamazaki says that the average process time on the two lines is 20 minutes, with the spindles taking longest—75 minutes, including 25 minutes handling. The two lines can process 435 different parts—spindles, rings, housings and flanges—monthly, the potential output being 9,000 units/month. This includes 1,600 spindles of 35 types.

There are 12 horizontal machining centers in the box line, and a small ASR warehouse with capacity for 228 pallets—equivalent to 248 hours on average for the gearboxes, headstock housings, turrets, carriages and sundry housings machined there. The average process time is put at 6 hours. Potential output is 1,200/month of 85 different parts. This line, and the frame line next to it, follow the plan of the original Yamazaki FMS at Oguchi, but it has some variations. Thus, there is a rail guided trolley for each line—chosen as elsewhere, for example, at Minokamo, for their speed—and these run between the pallet stockers and the APCs at the machines, transferring as necessary.

In the tool room the operator uses a Sony instrument to measure the tools, which are reground as necessary. Before a tool is used again, the offset is measured and is fed into the control computer in preparation for use on any machine. In fact, this is one area where theory and practice have not matched up.

When machining is complete, workpieces are transferred to a turnover device which turns them 180 degrees and back again to ensure that all swarf and chips are removed. However, for the larger frames, such a procedure is impractical, so Yamazaki has installed its "cleaning robot." This robot is suspended from a beam carried on a four-post structure and carries a suction pipe. Since the robot can be programmed to move in the x, y and z axes, it can traverse the periphery of the frame, sucking up the swarf from the flanges and faces as it goes. There is a central swarf disposal system which draws swarf from all the lines, removal generally being automatic.

In addition to this large FMS shop, there is a small metal working shop, where two CNC punch presses, three CNC press brakes, and two welding robots are arranged to produce fabrications. Then there are the subassembly and assembly areas, and a paint shop. Yamazaki also produces ball screws in temperature controlled shops at Minokamo.

Yamazaki plans to put the whole system under the control of a computer at the head office, with connections by modems and the telephone lines—but no indication is given of when this will happen. Currently, each of the five computers at the Minomako plant is operated independently, with the necessary data input locally by operators, so that the system is really a collection of small FMS. The large CNC machines and the flame hardener seem to be controlled indirectly only by the transport computer arranging for deliveries to be made. Although purists may turn up their noses, in practice, such a system is adequate and has the merit of simplicity.

There is one computer to control the frame and the box line; a small computer for the flange line, and another for the spindle line; there is also one computer to control the transport system, and another to control the air conditioning and energy use. Yamazaki claims that as far as the operators are concerned, these are simple to control, since they use conversational languages—just like the CNC themselves. Since the systems are independent, a breakdown in one system has no effect on the others.

Currently, the plant is being operated 15 hours a day, with 240 people, and Yamazaki claims that this is solely due to the slack market. Only 39 people are needed to run the FMS, with three men/shift on the spindle line, three men/shift on the flange line, five on the box line, and four on the frame line. Three people are needed to load workpieces on to the AGVs outside the ship, there is an operator in the computer room, and another in the tool room.

The system would be virtually unmanned on the third shift and clearly has the potential for an unmanned second shift. About 80 people work on assembly.

In several ways, this FMS breaks new ground. First, there is the extensive use of lathe/mills, which reduce setting up time while usefully extending the cycle, so that too much time is not lost in loading/unloading. Secondly, because these machines are robot loaded, they are virtually unmanned. Then the process of marking out workpieces and machining location pads or holes has been eliminated completely. The use of a robot to set workpieces on the pallets is an innovation, as is the vacuum cleaning robot, although utilization of both robots seems to be low. Also of significance are the integration of flame hardening and surface grinding. On top of that, there is the sheer scale. It expects to get it £40 million investment back in three and a half years—as long as it can operate on three shifts—and claims that the plant will break even at 33% of capacity, which is equivalent to one-shift operation.

A comparison of this plant with a conventional plant shows the number of machine tools at 48% and the number of employees at 20%, the machining time at 9%, and total processing time including assembly at 33%. Also the floor space for this operation is only 40% of a conventional factory.

In addition, the total process time for a lathe is now put at four weeks, against 12 weeks previously. What's more, Yamazaki reckons it can pull this down to seven days in due course. Quite a lot of ballyhoo surrounds the plant, but it is working, and on balance it must be well on the way to being a success. If that's not an argument for FMS, what is?

Japanese Factory for Fanuc Motor Production[3]

Fanuc, whose principal products are CNC units, ac and dc servo motors, small CNC machining centers, EDM wire-cut machines and robots, established its Motor Manufacturing Division next to its first FMS near Mount Fuji to produce ac and dc servo motors. The range of dc servo motors ran from 0.3 to 22 kW output, ac servo motors from 0.02 to 2.8 kW output, and there are also spindle motors. When the plant was established, demand was principally for dc servo motors, but the move towards ac motors, which require less maintenance, had started. Of course, Fanuc did not know how fast this change would take place, nor the likely balance between output of ac and dc motors after three or five years. Thus flexible manufacture was an attractive proposition.

The new factory is a compact two-story building, 200x60m, with a machine shop on the ground floor and an assembly shop on the first floor. The cost of the plant was £17 million, a little less than was invested in the first Fuji factory. It is controlled by computer which also dictates the production schedule in response to orders from the head office. Capacity on three shifts is put at 10,000 motors of 40 models monthly, and 900 different parts are machined in lot sizes from 20 to 1,000.

In the machine shop are 60 CNC machines, and 52 of these are loaded and unloaded by robot. The other eight machines—these are large machining centers—have multiple pallet carriers with a capacity of 12 pallets each. On the first floor there are 49 robots arranged in 25 cells in a linear pattern to carry out most of assembly.

An important feature of the handling system is a large warehouse which extends from the ground floor up through to the first floor. This is used to store unmachined workpieces, parts from suppliers, partly machined and fully machined parts, and eliminated the need for lifts. Thus, parts are frequently being shuttled between the warehouse and the pallet stations at the machining and assembly cells.

There are five rows of machines in the machine shop, the end row consisting of the larger CNC machining centers which have automatic pallet changers. These are loaded manually, as at the first Fuji factory, but the pallet changers are big enough to carry workpieces for 16 hour operation. The other four rows consist of 44 CNC lathes and eight CNC cylindrical grinders, each with its own monitor and tool wear compensation system.

Fanuc has placed its faith in wire-guided AGVs, two working on the ground floor, and five on the first floor for handling. They transfer standard pallets, usually carrying 20-50 workpieces—enough for a few hours work—to the stations adjacent to the robots. There are standard pallet stations at each cell, the monitor and control units being mounted at the end of the station.

In practice, there are often pallets at two stations only, these being shuffled along one station when the robot has finished processing the first pallet. Generally, the robot transfers the workpiece directly from the pallet to the machine, but a few robots have extra grippers. In that case the robot has its normal gripper, but for part of the operation it picks up a secondary gripper which handles the workpieces. This part of the plant works smoothly enough, although since it is manned during one shift only, the men seem to be kept busy adjusting and maintaining machines. It operates for 24 hours a day.

On the first floor, there are four assembly lines consisting of 25 cells incorporating 49 robots—a mixture of M-Models (material handling robot) for handling, and A-Models (precision assembly robot) for precise work. Workpieces are transferred between cells by conveyor. Surprisingly, the assembly shop is operated for only eight hours a day. The reason for this is that some of the assembly is done manually, and that demand was not as high as had been hoped when the plant was opened. The level of automated assembly is put at 65% and the aim is to completely eliminate the need for manual assembly. In fact although the machine shop is geared up to produce 10,000 sets/month, the assembly shop can currently produce 6,000 units/month.

The actual operations performed by the assembly robots differ according to the size. There are three "cells" in the line for the spindle motors, and in each of the other lines there are an average of eight. At the beginning of the line, the rotor/shaft assembly is balanced, then the ball bearings are pressed on to the shaft at each end of the rotor. An oil seal is pressed into a flange, and sealant is applied. Then, the flange is mounted flat on a fixture, and the rotor is lowered vertically into it. Next the shell is lowered over the rotor on the flange. Subsequently, the end bell is assembled to the shell and pressed in position. Four tie-bolts are then inserted, washers and nuts are lowered into position, and the nuts are tightened. Afterwards, the motor is passed to the manual line for adjustment. Currently there are a few major jobs that are done manually. Firstly, the rotary encoders must be adjusted to the correct datum by hand. Then the flange is adjusted so that equal current is fed to both coils, and some wires are fitted by hand. Then the flange is adjusted so that equal current is fed to both coils, and some wires are fitted by hand.

Five AGVs carry parts on standard pallets along four aisles between the warehouse and the various cells. The capacity of each pallet is 20-50 parts, according to size of the part. The arrangement of the pallet stations is similar to that in the machine shop, with space for three standard pallets, and the control unit adjacent to the pallet station.

In the complete plant, there are 60 employees, including 21 in the machine shop—on one shift—and 19 direct workers in the assembly shop. There is just one man in the control room on the unmanned shifts. To give him a fair indication of what is happening, there are 21 cameras in the machine shop, and he can switch from camera to camera on his three monitors.

In the early stages, the robots worked very slowly, and downtime was high. The priority was not to stop the robots, and then to gradually increase speed. As Fanuc's president, Seiuemon Inaba, explained "We have high variety and low volumes, so we need robots. All the Japanese electrical companies are trying to increase productivity, and in theory, our new plant increases productivity three-fold. We used to have 32 robots and 108 men to produce 6,000 motors; we now have 60 men and 101 robots producing 10,000 motors."

Certainly, the motor plant is very flexible in that a wide variety of components can be machined unmanned for two shifts, while 65% of assembly is done by robots—that certainly gives low labor costs and much more flexibility than a conventional plant. In addition, the components being machined and assembled are much smaller than those produced by other FMS, so consequently cycle times are short. Inaba asserts that the manufacturing cost of the servo motor will be cut by 30% including depreciation by the adoption of the new manufacturing methods. The value of the output when the plant is in full swing will be more than £36 million a year, or more than twice the capital investment.

In addition, of course, Fanuc will be able to gradually switch from dc to ac servo motors as demand changes; it will not need to make a sudden switch, as would have been needed with hard automation. Since the assembly robots are operating for only one shift, any faults can be eliminated outside normal production hours.

This is the typical Japanese long-term approach. If the plant produces only 3,300 motors/month, its level of productivity per man will be the same as in the old plant, yet it will have the potential to operate with broadly similar manning levels with much higher output. As with many FMS for small parts, it requires a large number of parts as work-in-progress to prevent excessive movement of the trolleys—but since this is all under control, the total amount is far less than in a normal factory.

If the market for servo motors were to dry up overnight, Fanuc could convert it very easily to produce some other products of the same size and type, such as pneumatic motors, pumps or compressors. So, this is a true FMS in that it can process families of motors, and in the way that it could be switched to completely different products without loss in productivity. Of course, it will not be the ultimate in low manning until all assembly is automated flexibly. But it is well on the way to the goal.

However, with 240 people, over 10,000 components are being machined and assembled monthly. Altogether over 560 different workpieces, from a small collar about 100mm diameter by 50mm long to huge castings over 3m long and weighing about 20 tons are produced, in reasonable batches. That is a wide range of products on a small range of machines. Like the Fanuc plant, Yamazaki's is most suitable for in-house manufacture—and the main limitation is that fundamental one of capacity, which is easier to match to output with in-house manufacture than is jobbing machining.

In any case, the FMS could be converted to the manufacture of a different product, such as diesel engine cylinder blocks and components, but that misses the point. The object with these and other FMS is to give the manufacturer an advantage in costs so that he can increase market share. Of course, as products in general become more software oriented, so manufacturers will need to change their products. But as these large scale FMS show, Fanuc and Yamazaki will be much better placed to make that change than others; indeed, in switching from dc to ac servo motors, Fanuc is following such a trend.

In addition, although completely integrated computer control is the ultimate aim, the top priority is to get the system cutting metal in a cost efficient manner. Complete integration will give a further quantum jump, but the starting point is the hardware.

Overall, these are practical systems, operating economically with very low manning levels on a large scale. Moreover, they can operate economically with relatively low utilization—and there would be no question of anyone being laid off.

Allen-Bradley's New Automated Assembly Facility for Electric Motor Starters [4]

Allen-Bradley Company has implemented an automated assembly line to produce motor starters in 125 variations for the international market. Computer-integrated, the flexible manufacturing system can produce 600 units an hour—including lot sizes of one—with consistent quality. The new factory-within-a-factory eliminates work-in-progress and finished goods inventory and direct labor. Allen-Bradley said the facility is thought to be the most advanced in the electrical controls industry, and its control and communications technology can be applied to industries as diverse as automobiles and computers. The basic automation control technology remains the same.

Only a few attendants oversee operations in the $15 million factory in the company's Milwaukee headquarters location. The system took two years to design and build. Design of the product was coordinated concurrently with the design of the 45,000 sq. ft. production facility. The facility produces the electromechanical motor contactor in two sizes and many variations. It permits a one-day production lead time, order to shipment, utilizing a stockless production approach.

The company said development of the facility focused on lowered production costs through reduction of materials, direct and indirect labor, scrap and rework; higher production rates; improved asset utilization through minimized inventory and capital investment for production changeover; lessened warranty expense through enhanced product quality; and improved marketability through shortened lead times, consistant quality and flexibility in production product mix.

The products meet standards set by the International Electrotechnical Commission, which are observed throughout most of the world. Products built for the US market meet standards set by the National Electrical Manufacturers Association. IEC products are highly application specific, relatively smaller than NEMA products, and can economically be replaced after a given period of usage. NEMA standard products are built for great durability and worn-out parts can be easily replaced, rather than the entire control. Allen-Bradley said it developed its new products and new CIM facility both to protect one of its core businesses from foreign competition and to allow it to compete worldwide in markets for these products.

Designing the product and the production process together, said Allen-Bradley, was the key to developing a well-functioning CIM (computer integrated manufacturing) factory. Marketing, development, quality, manufacturing, management information systems, cost and finance functions all were involved in writing the specifications. Objectives included the ability to compete with both domestic and foreign competitors; a favorable gross margin; superior design features, and conformity to Allen-Bradley quality standards. To help achieve competitive costs, the company moved to automatic assembly, eliminating direct labor. An alternative would have been to move offshore but the need for skilled craftsmen to install, design and maintain the line was critical. Flexibility also was recognized as a primary need. So product and assembly operations were designed not to disrupt the manufacturing process when changing from one product variation to another.

Equally important was the need to enhance product quality while reducing the cost of achieving it. Said a spokesman, "We want to give better wear for the dollar than our competitors can." Another key need was to provide the product quickly. So quick turn-around was built into the system. Another important means of cost reduction was to minimize handling and warehousing. Allen-Bradley mimimized inventory, both in raw materials and finished product. Utilizing stockless production, the factory-in-a-factory receives orders one day and the product is manufactured, tested, packaged and shipped the next. When a special order of, for example, one variation of product is inserted into the system, it can be manufactured and sorted right along with the others; the master controller will instruct each machine to change over automatically and back again as required. The "lot size of one" concept in this instance totally eliminates set-up and changeover time.

A high level of quality can be maintained under these tightly controlled conditions, which implement the company's Total Quality Management System. The goal of TQMS is zero defects. The system utilizes statistical quality control methods to maintain tolerance levels. It rejects any component outside those parameters, to provide complete uniformity of quality. In addition, 100 percent automated testing within each manufacturing process virtually assures optimum quality, the company stated. Automated quality control gives a superior quality consistency and saves expensive inspection costs and time, the company noted. Testing of the product takes place progressively as the assembly moves from station to station—with some 3,500 data collection and 350 assembly test points in all.

The factory-in-a-factory is located on a site 150 by 300 feet on the eighth floor of Allen-Bradley's main plant in Milwaukee. The facility has two doors. Materials such as brass, steel, silver, molding powder, coils and springs enter through one door and the finished products exit through the other. Initially, machines mold raw materials into workable contactor parts: plastic molding machines produce housings for the contactors; other machines make terminals and spanners for the contactors. In all, 26 machines, including assembly, subassembly, testing and packaging, are needed to manufacture the contactor. The machines are synchronized to take a variety of parts, some of them extremely small, and turn out a completely manufactured and packaged product without a human hand touching them. More than 60 percent of the machinery and equipment used was designed and built by Allen-Bradley and the remainder was supplied to Allen-Bradley design specifications.

The system begins operating when a distributor enters an order through his terminal direct to Allen-Bradley's mainframe computer. This computer receives incoming orders and integrates them with manufacturing, sales and accounting. The mainframe at 5 a.m. each day downloads all orders received the previous day for the new contractor to the Area Controller within the new facility. The Area Controller translates the orders into specific production requirements. Once the information is broken down into production language, it is downloaded to the cell level and the Allen-Bradley PLC-3 master controller. The PLC-3 serves as the master controller, giving instructions to each machine and informing each of its appropriate tasks. The hierarchy of control and communications linking the plant floor with the mainframe computer provides a working example of Allen-Bradley's "Productivity Pyramid" concept of industrial automation control. The product actually instructs production. Each product base carries its own bar-code identification. This bar-code instructs each station as to the work to be performed. As the work is completed, constant reports are provided to the PLC-3 cell controller.

To maintain minimum downtime, a variety of multi-level production diagnostics are built into the system. These keep attendants aware of operations throughout the 45,000 sq. ft. facility. At the floor level, a three-light system is in place. If a blue light comes on, the attendant is notified that a parts feeder is running low. A yellow light indicates a part jam or malfunction. A red light states that a machine malfunction has resulted in an automatic shut-down. An operator display gives an attendant approaching the machine a readout of the condition requiring attention.

As the starter proceeds through the assembly line, many of the automatic inspections are tied into a CRT vision system and the computer-aided statistical process control system. If a component fails an inspection, the reject automatically causes the computer to order a replacement made. If the part is repaired and returned to the line, it is immediately identified by the computer. Extras or leftovers accumulate in a special line to be automatically reviewed against the next day's schedule.

The systems operator in the control room can monitor diagnostics via a color graphics terminal. At the same time, the supervisory unit also accumulates information on all faults. Answers are instantly available to such questions as what were the last 10 faults on the line or which fault occurred most often in the last shift or the last month.

A final control highlight is the personnel control used in the CIM facility. Magnetic ID badges permit access to the plant floor. The same badges are used to log all maintenance activity. Records are accumulated on how long it took attendants to respond as well as how long it took a service to be completed.

Allen-Bradley noted that effective application of CIM technology requires a new way of thinking of both management and operating personnel. A spokesman commented, "Perhaps the most profound change is the shift to a longer-term solution. CIM is not a quick fix, but requires a tremendous amount of up-front planning on the part of many individuals representing different disciplines." The company stressed both the tangible and intangible benefits of CIM.

Among the tangibles: reduced labor, both direct and indirect, and thus less supervision; lower inventory costs, as there is no work in progress and no finished goods inventory; significant reductions in cost accompanying realization of high quality; and efficient operating results with respect to reduced energy consumption. And intangible: Flexibility for the future, with respect to increased product variations as the market dictates, without additional machinery; the removal of direct labor and resulting gains in consistency of product quality; reduction of downtime, and gain in productive uptime, related to advanced diagnostics; and faster turnaround, in terms of greater customer satisfaction and savings in inventory.

Significantly, the company stated, its future capacity for an important product line is already in place. As market demand grows, capacity can be increased simply by running the facility for additional hours. "In effect," a spokesman said, "we can respond instantly to increased demand. And, because of all these things, we expect capital expenditures to be lower than they otherwise would be in years to come. CIM really does represent a new way of thinking."

Conclusion of this Study

Based on the description of these four showcase modern futuristic factories and their similarities, we can develop a new definition of a factory and a series of basic principles for engineering a futuristic factory.

According to Webster, a factory is defined as "a building or group of buildings with facilities for the maufacture of goods, usually from raw material." This definition is satisfactory for the past but for the future 21st-century factory a more explicit definition is required if it is to be a guide for planning a factory. A possible good definition is: "A 21st-century factory is a building or space or a collection of buildings and spaces called a system (not necessarily located in the same city or country) across whose boundaries enter energy, data, capital, people, raw material, components, orders, production intelligence, market and financial intelligence, sales income, and customer feedback and across whose boundaries exit payroll money, profit, taxes, financing money, people, production intelligence, orders to subcontractors, energy both usable and wasted, solid waste, liquid waste, gaseous waste, data and, most important, quality products."

The First Law of a Manufacturing Business

"The factory must function to maximize profit, quality product output and manufacturing intelligence for the society while minimizing payroll, financing money, workers hours, energy consumed and solid, liquid, gaseous and energy waste."

The direction of the factory system's activities shall be by a data base central control with the capacity to make modifications of the factories activities by utilizing machine intelligence commonly called artificial intelligence in order to strive for a goal of 100 percent efficiency. A schematic diagram of the factory of the 21st century is presented in Figure 1.

Because of our ability to electrically communicate almost instantaneously by sight, sound, printed word or data interchange, the requirement of having departments of a factory in close proximity is not applicable any more.

In this paper a factory building is just another component in the total manufacturing system. The conversion of our manufacturing industries to this format will usher in the Third Industrial Revolution and result in the Future Post Industrial Age when only a small percentage of our population will be involved in manufacturing.

This Industrial Revolution is gaining momentum now. The new High Tech Manufacturing Systems will make possible the application of automation to practically all manufactured products.

The key word in this new High Tech Era of manufacturing is *flexibility*. Therefore it is only logical that the design of futuristic factories should be designed so that present as well as future manufacturing systems can be installed with a minimum of effort and physical changes in the factory.

Some of the important departments for the future factory which are listed in the following diagram demand that the factory design principles must accommodate flexibility.

1) Data Base Department
2) Design & Engineering & Manufacturing Engineering Depart-

ment
3) Manufacturing Machinery Department for parts and assembly
4) Production and Quality Control Department
5) Operations Management Department
6) Warehousing and Retrievel System
7) Education Department
8) Research and Development Department

Figure 1
SCHEMATIC OF THE FACTORY OF THE 21st CENTURY

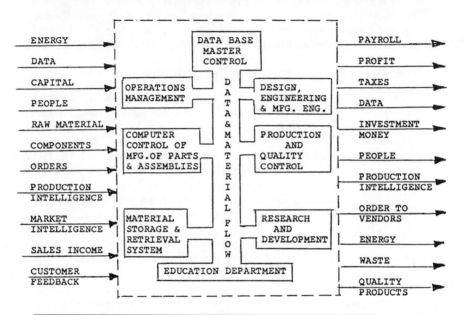

The flexibility of these departments is made possible because of the family of computing equipment and computer-directed equipment now entering the manufacturing industries such as robots, programmable controllers, computer-aided drafting and designing equipment, computer-directed manufacturing machinery, computer-aided engineering calculation equipment, computer-controlled transportation equipment and warehousing equipment, inexpensive personal computer, computer-controlled inspection equipment, sensors of all types and etc. It seems that every day new equipment or improved equipment becomes available for the automated factory.

All these elements of a manufacturing enterprise will be interconnected into some network such as shown in Figure 2. The brains or intelligence of the enterprise will be the data base and will be connected to all departments so that data can flow out to each department and data can flow back into the data bank for storage and processing. In addition there will also be an interconnecting data bus connecting each department and sections of each department for interchange of data that does not necessarily have to return to the central data bank. The present day factory was usually designed about the assembly line, hard automation concept. In the assembly line concept from Adam Smith through Babbage to Ford to the present day which was the idea of dividing the manufacturing process into discrete departments or work stations where only one manufacturing step at a time was accomplished prevailed such as the automobile industries assembly line. This concept resulted in the investment in huge inventories of parts to make sure the assembly line did not have to stop because of shortages. With the cost of money increasing, the financing of huge inventories became an important problem. It is important to break out our thinking from the shackles of past manufacturing constraints and think of the "ideal" way to incorporate this computerized manufacturing concept into the factories of the 21st century.

Figure 2
DATA BUS SYSTEM FOR THE FACTORY OF THE 21st CENTURY

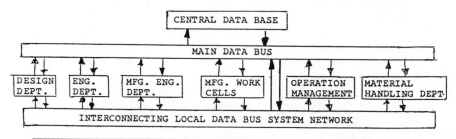

A Brief Summary of the Design Principles for the Automatic Factory of the Future

1) A data base system should be used as the directing instrument making decisions for all equipment in the factory using computer-aided drafting, designing, engineering, material handling, process control, manufacturing control and artificial intelligence or machine intelligence control.

2) All equipment or process systems should be module design with provisions to be updated when new controls are possible or in order to make communication between equipment systems possible.

3) Tooling should also be modular and designed so that tool changing and measurement and quality control can be easily maintained and executed.

4) Material, raw parts, and finished parts storage can be integrated into the system without difficulty or complication and can utilize

up to date AI concepts of the transportation problem in order to minimize work in storage, work in processing and work in buffer storage areas throughout the factory.

5) A comprehensive inspection system should be installed so that any deviation from the quality norm can be detected instantly in order to have a near 100% acceptable quality output.

6) Careful consideration must be given to the placement of sensory feedback systems in order to keep the total system operating efficiently and to give the AI section of the Data Base Control Computer System time to make necessary corrections in system control in real time. For example it takes time to change tools, to switch machines or material routing in a factory.

7) The central control should have a problem anticipation capability which should monitor all inputs or potential inputs such as raw material or subcontractor deliveries and make necessary changes in control based on the input intelligence.

8) Every step taken or planned should not be executed until its ability to have complete communication with central control is designed into the installed step.

9) The success of the future automatic factory will depend on the development of automation techniques for assembly. This will require a change in engineering thinking from the concept and design stages of manufacturing in order to make flexible automatic assembly practical.

These design principles can serve as a guide for The Factory of the Future. More principles can be added to this list in particular cases, but always the principle of *flexibility* should be the guide.

References

1. Literature from Volvo of America Corporation Automated Systems Division, Sterling Heights, Michigan, 1985.

2. "Flexible Automation in Japan," John Hartley, IFS (publication) Ltd., UK, 1984, p. 210-214. *The Design and Operation of FMS* by Paul Ranky, IFS Ltd., UK, 1983.

3. *FMS at Work* by John Hartley, IFS Ltd., UK and North Holland, Elsevier Science Publishers B.U., 1984, *The Design and Operation of FMS* by Paul Ranky, IFS, Ltd., UK 1983.

4. Allen Bradley Literature on "Factory Within a Factory" 1985-1986, Allen-Bradley, Milwaukee, Wisconsin.

5. "Design and Planning of Futuristic Factories" by Albert Madwed, December, 1984. Paper presented at University of North Carolina at Charlotte for the International Conference "The Factory of the Future."

EFFECTIVE FOOD MARKETING AS A TOOL OF SOCIO-ECONOMIC DEVELOPMENT IN THE THIRD WORLD

by

Frank Meissner

The causes of hunger in the world today are different from those of a decade ago. Agricultural technology has advanced, allowing food production to outpace demand in many regions, but hunger persists because of poverty . . .

The ability to produce a sufficient food supply does not mean a nation will eliminate hunger. In the United States surpluses are so large that farmers are paid to produce less. Yet the government must provide food stamps each month to more than 19 million people so they can obtain food. A more important factor than food production in determining vulnerability to hunger is the extent of popular *access* to gainful employment, to arable land, to suitable technologies and to other productive resources.

Effective marketing facilitates physical access of the poor to affordable quality food. Peter Hendry, former editor of CERES UN Food and Agricultural Organization (FAO)[1]

1. The Challenge

The number of people living in cities increased more than three-fold from 600 million in 1950 to over 2.2 billion in 1988. By the year 2000, more than half of humanity will be urbanites.

Latin America, with 65% of its population in urban areas, has some of the biggest cities in the world: Mexico City 18 million, Sao Paulo 14 million, Buenos Aires 12 million. By the year 2000, 77% or some 465 million Latin Americans are likely to be living in cities.

The recent speed of urbanization in LDCs is without precedent. It took Greater London 110 years to increase its population from 1.1 million in 1800 to 7.3 million in 1910. Many Third World cities achieved that magnitude of growth within one generation. Consequently, in the next decade or two most cities with populations of 15 million will be in LDCs.

The rapid urbanization of the world is among the major causes for steadily increasing marketing margins, i.e. costs of getting food from producers into consumer stomachs. Subsistence farmers, who consume what they produce, do little marketing. The further consumers live from food production areas, the more important mar-

Frank Meissner *retired in 1988 as a marketing economist in the agriculture and forestry development division of the Inter-American Development Bank (IDB) Washington, DC.*

keting gets to be. This is because the distance between food producers and consumers increases geographically, in form and in time.

"The technology to produce enough food for all the world's population is known and largely in practice in both developed and developing countries."[2] Paradoxically enough malnutrition is growing in the midst of plenty.

In 1988 an estimated 0.8 billion people, or 15% of the 5.3 billion world population[3] were on diets that fall short of essential nutrients needed for survival, growth, reproduction as well as for capacity to work, learn and effectively function in society.

Among major causes of hunger are poverty and ineffective marketing systems. In this essay I will focus attention on food marketing, a subject that has inadvertently been neglected by the development profession.

In the first section I review available data on food marketing margins, and derive some clues about tentative goals for what should be "reasonable" investments in food marketing hardware and software.

I then compare these goals with reality, and try to explain why investment in food marketing has lagged behind food production. Finally I will suggest that, in order to bridge the food production-consumption gap the marketing profession should emulate the successful strategies pursued by the Green Revolutionaries who are helping to boost agricultural production and productivity.

2. Investment Implications of Marketing Margins for Staple Foods

Since World War II the absolute and relative cost of getting food from producers to consumers has been growing in the Third World as well as in industrial countries. By the late 1980s, US farmers have been getting only 25 cents of the average dollar spent by consumers on food at retail.[4] Peasants in Less Developed Countries (LDCs) were getting about 50% of the retail value of food.[5]

The huge and growing food marketing bill in the United States is primarily caused by two factors: a) the country is highly urbanized, with farm workers representing only about to 2.5% of total employment; and b) in order to get staple foods from producers to consumers the US uses highly *capital intensive* mass marketing and processing technologies.

In contrast, Third World countries: a) are less developed, and b) tend to use traditional *labor intensive* marketing technologies.[6] Rapid urbanization of LDCs is causing food marketing margins to increase in absolute as well as relative terms, although at levels substantially below those of the US (Figure 1). With half the food retail value currently represented by the traditional labor intensive food processing and distribution technologies in the Third World "adequate" long-term marketing investments would probably rep-

Figure 1

Marketing Margins for Staple Foods, USA and LDCs

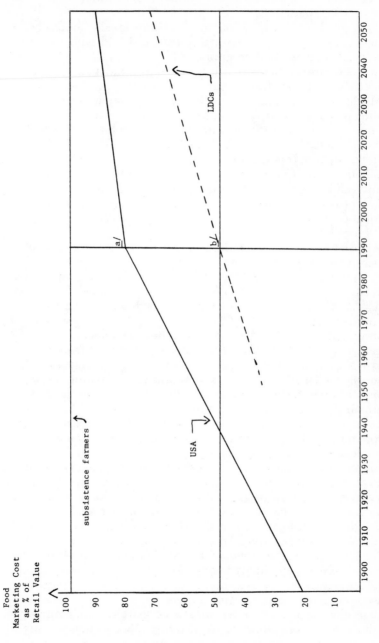

Food
Marketing Cost
as % of
Retail Value

a/ US Department of Agriculture 1988 Chart Book, p. 63.
b/ Mittendorf and Hartog, 1983

89/SEC16

resent much less than half the funds channeled towards the agricultural sectors of LDCs.

I know of no published figure and no rule-of-thumb that would provide a ball park indicator of what the "ideal" ratio of investment in food production and marketing functions ideally should be.

Let us assume that a reasonably balanced mid- and long-term food system investment program in LDCs should have at least 25% of the total funds channeled into marketing functions, including all software and hardware related to assembly, processing, transport, distribution, finance, and information activities involved in getting staple foods from producers into consumer stomachs.

How does reality compare with this 25% benchmark? To the best of my knowledge no systematic quantitative study has been made to help answer this question. I have therefore assembled some qualitative indicators of software work, while obtaining some quantitative clues about investments made by major donors. The data are to provide preliminary clues about orders of magnitude; substantial refinements will be required in years to come.

2.1 Marketing Software

At least 5 measures of the relative importance of marketing software are being presented and commented on.

a) Examination of *publications* from ten (10) leading multilateral and bilateral development agencies—including Elsevier Publishers, Inter-American Development Bank (IDB), International Development Research Center (IRCD), International Food Policy Research Institute (IFPRI), Inter-American Institute of Cooperation on Agriculture (IICA), United Nations reports and studies from UNIDO and UNCTAD, Winrock Agri-bookstore, Overseas Development Council (OCD), World Bank and Worldwatch Institute (WWI)—shows a total of 1,593 titles. Only 107, or 4% of the total, were marketing related. With the honorable exception of IFPRI—27 market and marketing related items out of a total of 57 publications—development agencies and researchers demonstrate an underwhelming interest in marketing topics.

b) In *vocational training* activities the situation appears even more dismal. In 1987 the International Training Program of the US Department of Agriculture (ITP/USDA) had 2,330 participants; only 56 or 2.4% of the total, were studying marketing and agroindustries.

c) Still more disheartening is the *fellowship* program administered by the Winrock International Institute for Agricultural Development (WIIAD). None, repeat none, of the 681 M.S. and Ph.D. scholarship holders were to major in marketing. It is likely that majors in agricultural economics would take some marketing courses and write their dissertations on marketing related topics.

d) In 1986 the San Jose (Costa Rica) headquartered Inter-American Institute for Cooperation on Agriculture (IICA)—which aims to provide agricultural software assistance to its member countries in the Western Hemisphere—had 110 ongoing projects. The activities of IICA were concentrated in 5 major program areas: (i) agricultural policy analysis and planning, (ii) technology generation and transfer, (iii) organization and management of rural development, (iv) marketing and agroindustry, and (v) animal health and plant protection.

In 1986 some 17 projects, 15.5% of the total of 110 projects, were marketing and agroindustry related; some $2.3 million of external resources were earmarked for these projects, or 10.3% of the total budget of $22.3 million.

Although total funding has gone up from $22.3 million in 1986 to $23.8 million in 1987 marketing activities of IICA have declined in absolute as well as relative terms: number of projects decreased from 15.5% to 9.7% while *funding went down* from 10.3% to 5.4%. Furthermore, of the 248 documents listed in the IICA Annual Report for 1987, only 26, or 10.5% were marketing related (Table 1).

e) At the end of the journey through the wasteland of marketing software, I have examined a sample of 16 English book-length publications on Marketing in LDCs. The selected readings, monographs and conference proceedings, contain individual papers written by some 425 authors. Only 173 authors, or 41% of the total, came from Third World Countries. The data in Table 2 shows that since the January 1974 International Conference on Marketing Systems in Developing Countries (INCOMAS), the number of authors from LDCs has been increasing. This might provide an indication of the rate at which the profession is getting to be de-Westernized. In fact, it does not. This is simply because: a) most authors from LDCs have been trained in the West, b) an increasing number from part of the "brain drain" towards West European and North Amer-

Table 1
MARKETING RELATED ACTIVITIES OF THE INTER-AMERICAN INSTITUTE FOR COOPERATION ON AGRICULTURE, IICA, 1986 and 1987

	Number of Projects		Total Funds (in $1,000)		Number of Publications
	1986	1987	1986	1987	1987
Marketing and Agroindustry	17	11	$2,298	$1,291	26
Other	93	102	19,962	22,551	212
Total	110	113	22,260	23,842	248
Marketing and Agro-Industry as a % of Total	15.5%	9.7%	10.3%	5.4%	10.5%

Source: IICA Annual Reports for 1986 and 1987.

Table 2
SELECTED BOOK-LENGTH PUBLICATIONS ON MARKETING IN LDCs, 1976-88

Name of Publication a/	Year of Publication	Origin of Authors b/				LDC as % of Total
		IC	NIC	LDC	Total	
1. Marketing Systems in Developing Countries	1976	22	17	5	44	11%
2. Urban Food Marketing and Third World Development	1982	1	-	-	1	-
3. Marketing Systems in Developing Countries	1984	3		14	17	82
4. Markets Myth and Middlemen	1984	1	-	-	1	100
5. Internal Marketing of Food in Latin America	1985	5	-	7	12	58
6. No Free Lunch: Food for Revolution in Cuba	1985	3	-	3	-	
7. World Food Marketing Systems	1986	21	1	10	32	31
8. Role of Marketing in Development	1986	31	4	41	76	54
9. Marketing and Economic Development	1986	-	-	1	1	100
10. Marketing Perspectives of Public Enterprises in Developing Countries	1986	1	1	11	13	85
11. Applied Research and Technical Assistance in Agricultural Marketing	1986	6	-	1	7	13
12. Agricultural Marketing Strategy and Pricing Policy	1986	10	-	2	12	17
13. Agricultural Marketing Enterprises in the Developing World	1987	7	2	6	15	40
14. Agricultural Marketing: Selected Training Materials from Asian and African Countries	1988	16	5	17	39	45
15. Marketing and Economic Development: Issues and Opinions	1988	77	8	45	130	35
16. Marketing and Development: Toward Broader Dimensions	1988	8	2	13	23	57
Total		212	40	173	425	41%

a/ Authors and editors as well as name of publishers are listed on the following page.

b/ IC = Industrialized Country

NIC = Newly Industrialized Country

LDC = Less Developed Country

Annex to Table 2
AUTHORS, EDITORS, AND PUBLISHERS OF
BOOKS ON MARKETING IN DEVELOPMENT

1. Proceedings of *First International Conference on Marketing Systems in Developing Countries* (INCOMAS) held January 6-12, 1974, in Tel Aviv (Israel). Edited by Dov Izraeli, Dafna N. Izraeli, and Frank Meissner, John Wiley & Sons (New York) and Israel University Press (Jerusalem), 1976.
2. T. Scarlett Epstein, London: Croom Helm, 1982 pp.260.
3. Edited by Guprit S. Kindra with Foreword by Phillip Kotler, New York: St. Martin's Press, 1984, pp. 259.
4. Gregory J. Scott, Lima (Peru): International Potato Center (ICP), 1984, pp. 196.
5. Edited by Gregory J. Scott and M. Gary Costello, Ottawa (Canada): International Development Research Center (IDRC), 1985, pp. 253.
6. Medea Benjamin, Joseph Collins, and Michael Scott, San Francisco (CA): Food First, 1985 pp. 240.
7. Edited by Erdener Kaynak, London: Buttersworth, 1986, pp. 333.
8. Edited by Erdogan Kumcu and A. Fuat Firat, Istanbul University (Turkey), 1986, pp.480.
9. Erdener Kaynak, New York: Praeger, 1986. pp. 201.
10. Edited by K.L.K. Rao, Ljubljana (Yugoslavia): International Center for Public Enterprise in Developing Countries (ICPE), 1986, pp. 211.
11. Edited by Sigma One, Washington, D.C.: AID Workshop held during November 18-19, 1986 at Foreign Service Institute (FSI), Rosslyn (VA).
12. Edited by Dieter Elz, Washington, D.C.: Economic Development Institute (EDI) of the World Bank, 1986, pp. 140.
13. John C. Abbott, Cambridge University Press, 1986, pp. 214.
14. Anonymous, Washington, D.C.: Economic Development Institute (EDI) of the World Bank, Volumes I, II, III, and IV, forthcoming. Blacksburg: Virginia Polytechnic Institute, 1988, pp. 336.
15. Proceedings of the Second International Conference on Marketing and Development, held at Karl Marx University of Economic Science, Budapest (Hungary), July 10-13, 1988, Edited by James E. Littlefield, and Magdolna Csath, Blacksburg: Virginia Polytechnic Institute, 1988, pp. 1988.
16. Edited by Erdogan Kumcu and A. Fuat Firat, JAI Press: 55 Old Post Road, No. 2, Greenwich, CT, 1988.

ican institutions of higher learning, and c) for one reason or another, over half the marketing professionals from LDCs are of Indian and Turkish origin.

The quality and relevance of these writings, an essential ingredient in appraising the status of the marketing craft, is somewhat more difficult to establish. A useful guide is the *Mittendorf Criterion*, which "measures the relevance of documents by their usefulness as conceptual framework for formulation of development strategies adaptable to differing sets of conditions."[7] In this respect most of the writings turn out to be diffused, inconclusive, non-commital and therefore of little direct use to policy makers, implementors and professional staff of bilateral and multilateral development agencies.

A review of the substance of theoretical, conceptual as well as pragmatic case studies shows that the profession has not been able to: (i) systematically sort out the enormous backlog of experience; (ii) systematically translate it into operationally useful recommendations for marketing policy markers, and (iii) help implementors put these marketing policies into practice.

2.2 Marketing Hardware

The benign neglect of marketing should not be merely judged by training in agricultural marketing or by what academicians of the profession do research on and write about, but also by what practitioners do. In this respect the picture is less gloomy.

a) During 1960-85 the 8.2% of the agricultural portfolio of IDB was earmarked for marketing, while during 1972-83 the World Bank channeled 16.1% into marketing (Table 3).

Table 3
FOOD MARKETING RELATED PROJECTS IN THE AGRICULTURAL PORTFOLIO OF IBRD AND IDB

Type of Project	World Bank 1972-83 (a)		IDB, 1960-85 (b)	
	Millions	% of total	Millions	% of total
Agroindustries	$2,156	48%	$462	66%
Storage facilities	$1,572	36%	$123	18%
Other	$748	16%	$112	26%
Total Marketing	$4,476	100%	$697	100%
Total Agriculture	$27,900	–	$8,500	–
Marketing as a % of Total Agricultural Portfolio	16.1%	–	8.2%	–

(a) James G. Brown, *Post-Harvest Considerations for Diversification,* Washington, D.C.: World Bank, Symposium on Sustainability Issues in Agricultural Development, January 8-9, 1987.
(b) Frank Meissner, "Micro and Macro-Marketing Activities of IDB: 25 Year Track Record and Roads Ahead," *Quarterly Journal of International Agriculture,* Vol. 25, July-September 1986, p. 272.

b) During 1980-86 major bilateral and multilateral technical and financial assistance agencies—including EEC countries, IDB, IFAD, OPEC, World Bank, USAID, and others—made capital commitments to agriculture amounting to $12.5 billion, of which IDB and the World Bank accounted for $10.4 billion, or 94%. Marketing related functions—i.e., agricultural services and agroindustries—accounted for $1.5 billion or 8.2% of total commitments. There was a wide variety of emphases on marketing ranging all the way from zero for IFAD to a high of 16% for USAID.

c) In addition to funding of explicit marketing functions, many non-marketing projects do contain marketing components. This data is usually not available in adequate detail to permit quantification of the amounts. A typical case in point is the Inter-American Foundation (IAF). Vignettes, describing projects approved by IAF in its 1987 Annual Report, indicate that about one-fourth of the grant amounts as having some marketing content indicated by use of such words as agroindustry, marketing, marketability, markets, product design, retail or wholesale outlets, storage, store, warehouse, street vendors, commercial intermediation, bulk purchasing, distribution, export, and buying. Without a laborious examination of line-item budgets, presented in individual grant applications, it is impossible to determine what proportion of total dollar amounts these marketing components represented—perhaps as little as 5 to 10%. Still, it is reassuring to note that the grass root applicants for IAF grants were conscious of the need to incorporate some marketing functions into rural and urban community development projects and programs.

The above reviewed selected indicators of marketing related software and hardware activities in Third World countries are summarized in Table 4, warts and all. Assuming that within a reasonably balanced set of agricultural sector activities marketing represents roughly 25%, the track record of the included agencies and institutions is bleak. Only FAO projections for years 1983-2000, suggesting that marketing investments should represent 32% of agricultural investments in Latin America, come within ballpark range of the 25% target, and indeed exceed it slightly. The very fact that this projection has been made and published indicates a keen awareness, at least among FAO planners, of the importance of smoothing the way for more effectively moving food from farm gates to consumers.

Since the early 1980s, when the "FAO at 2000" projections were made, the debt crisis has virtually dried out the flow of new private agricultural investments to LDCs. Net contributions from bilateral and multilateral development agencies have also shrunk substantially. The recent decline in IICA marketing activities as well as looming cut-backs in marketing related lending of IDB and the World Bank indicates that the FAO optimism has so far been unwarranted.

Table 4
SUMMARY OF SELECTED INDICATORS OF MARKETING RELATED SOFTWARE AND HARDWARE ACTIVITIES AIMED AT LDCs

Software (numbers)

Indicator	Total	Marketing	Marketing as % of Total
Titles in 1987 Catalogues of Major Development Agencies	1,482	104	7.0
International Trainees of the US Department of Agriculture (USDA), 1987	2,330	56	2.4
Winrock International Institute for Agricultural Development (WIIAD, 1987)			
(a) Projects	79	5	6.3
(b) Fellowships for MS and PhD degrees	2,330	0	0.0
Inter-American Institute for Cooperation on Agriculture (IICA)			
(a) Projects, 1986	110	17	15.5
(b) Projects, 1987	113	11	9.7
(c) Publications, 1987	248	26	10.5

Hardware/Software Funding (US$ millions)

Indicator	Total	Marketing	Marketing as % of Total
Agriculture Portfolio of Inter-American Development Bank (IDB) 1960-85	8,500	697	8.2
Agriculture Portfolio of World Bank, 1972-83	27,900	4,476	16.1
Agriculture Related Capital Assistance Commitments of Major Donors, 1980-86	12,494	1,525	8.2
Inter-American Institute for Cooperation on Agriculture (IICA)			
(a) 1986	22.3	2.3	10.5
(b) 1987	23.8	1.3	5.4
FAO Projections of Investment in Agriculture, Latin America and Caribbean, 1983-2000	425.5	134.9	31.7

In short the data on hand, such as they are, indicate clearly that unless some major catalyst appears on the scene, food marketing is most likely to retain its Cinderella status in the development processes of Third World countries. This forecast will hold for at least the rest of the 20th Century. Let us now turn to the causes of this seemingly inherent neglect of marketing.

3. Causes of Benign Neglect of Food Marketing

There are hypotheses galore about the reasons for the apparent benign neglect of marketing as a tool of agricultural and rural development. Let me mention just a few. Many political leaders in LDCs refer disdain fully to marketing as a wasteful, parasitic and socially irrelevant activity.

a) The merchant class in many LDCs belong to foreign minorities, which are accused to be "exploiting" the indigenous populations. Political leaders therefore tend to assign marketing improvement activities a very low priority, while actively consciously putting up barriers to their effective performance.

b) Most of the professionals engaged in agriculture development related activities have traditionally been agronomists, with prime concern for increasing physical on-farm production.

c) Project analysts in development agencies, who need to quantify economic feasibility by such indexes as internal rates of return (IRR), find that incremental on-farm production is easier to measure than benefits generated by improvements in marketing functions.

d) Policy makers tend to believe that marketing institutions spring up spontaneously to bring agricultural commodities to market and production inputs to farms.

e) Hunger in the midst of plenty is primarily caused by inequitable income distribution, a matter outside the scope of marketing.

f) Last, but certainly not least, the marketing profession has been incredibly inept at *marketing marketing* to policy decision makers and implementors in LDCs.[8]

4. Food Production Revolution vs. Marketing Stagnation

David Hopper, senior vice president of the World Bank, recently appraised the outlook for continued satisfactory food production performance of farmers around the globe:

> Technology is knowledge. It is built into tools and other capital equipment, it is embodied in manufactured products and it is part of the skills farmers, farm suppliers and agricultural products processors bring to their professions and enterprises. But knowledge unused adds nothing to the output of goods and services people consume . . .
>
> The classical paradox of food supply and demand was sketched by the Rev. Thomas Malthus in the 18th century. He noticed that food supplies tended to increase arithmetically while population

grew exponentially—a classic case for a longer term disequilibrium. Malthus argued that balance was maintained between these separate phenomena only by periodic calamities that brought death rates into line with fertility. But he reckoned without a knowledge of the impact of science and science-derived agricultural technologies, an impact that has given food production an exponential rate of growth and enabled it to remain ahead of population expansion.

Short of climatic change, I see no threat that would alter the prospect for a continued exponential growth of agricultural output based on an expansion of farm technologies.[9]

Not everybody agrees with Hopper's optimism. Among the pathological pessimists is Lester R. Brown, president of the Worldwatch Institute (WWI) in Washington, DC. In the wake of the 1988 drought in North America and China, Brown sees a "loss of momentum in the growth of world food output, (which) is reducing food security everywhere . . . It's particularly pronounced in the low income countries. They are being asked to tighten their belts when they don't have any notches left."[10]

The reader can take a pick. I happen to be inclined toward Hopper's appreciation of the situation, and firmly believe that: a) benefits of genetic engineering still remain largely untapped, and b) the Green Revolution has barely gotten under way. I therefore suggest that the Green Revolutionaries have been so successful because leaders of adaptive production research have clearly established their work priorities, and stuck to them. Thus the Consultative Group on International Agricultural Research Centers (CGIAR), which helps mobilize and allocate resources to the worldwide network of 13 International Agricultural Research Centers (IARCs), was able to concentrate its work in commodities that represent about 3/4 of the nutrition intake of mid- and low-income populations in LDCs. There are no secrets in CGIAR's approach. A former senior vice president of the World Bank, describes how CGIAR started, how it governs itself, how it operates by common consent, how it has forged an effective partnership of scientists and aid administrators from industrial and Third World countries, what impact on agricultural development it has had, and what potential for replication and/or adaptation to other fields of endeavor the CGIAR precedent might have.[11]

In stark contrast to the target oriented CGIAR guidance of food production work, the marketing profession has not been able to "put its act together." So far no priorities have been assigned to identified issues. Consequently there is no systematic way for filling the "black holes" in knowledge via an internationally coordinated marketing research effort similar to the one used by CGIAR. As a result, the marketing profession has lots of data, much of it of anecdotal nature, but little operationally useful information.

Consequently, little progress has been made during the last three decades in systematically translating gained marketing experience into a coherent body of knowledge usable by food policy makers and practitioners in LDCs.

The lag between production and marketing of food is often referred to as Second Generation of Green Revolution problems. In the words of Montague Yudelman, former director of agricultural development at the World Bank: "The price paid by Third World farmers and consumers for this benign neglect of marketing has been high: skyrocketing food imports, large post-harvest losses, increasing malnutrition among the poor in LDCs. In the upsurge of agricultural production, which occurred in the last 35 years or so, it turned out that even if there is enough food in the world it does not reach all those who need it."[12]

5. Roads Ahead

It is my contention that what CGIAR accomplished in food production can also be done in marketing, the function that gets commodities from farmers to consumers in the process, doubling or tripling value added to the raw products that leaves the farmgate.

The relentless concentration of CGIAR efforts on crucial commodities evidently helped to avoid spreading thin the scarce resources at hand and to make an impact where it really mattered. This is precisely what the marketing profession needs to do. In short, there is a clear need to set up a Technical Advisory Committee on Agricultural Marketing (TACAM), which would establish criteria for establishing work priorities. It might be advisable to confine work in the developing countries to one region, say the Western Hemisphere, so as to make the initial effort more manageable. A number of circumstances favor this approach.

CGIAR has gradually succeeded to achieve international coordination of an increasing volume of high priority biological and genetic research projects. In the course of time awareness grew among members of the CGIAR of need to extend activities beyond on-farm production. Consequently, coordination mechanisms have been established for planning, execution and dissemination of basic and applied research in such off-farm activities as rural industries and food technology.

This broadening of CGIAR's terms of reference opens up an opportunity for expanding food marketing work within its existing framework. That idea is not new. Ever since it was first formulated at the International Conference on Marketing Systems in Development Countries (INCOMAS) (Izraeli, Izraeli and Meissner, 1976), the idea has been repeatedly recycled.

Participants of INCOMAS then suggested establishment of an International Consultative Marketing Research Group (ICMRG), aimed at facilitating coordinated generation, analysis and dissemination of policy-oriented research on marketing systems in developing countries.

ICMRG was to perform at least the following five (5) specific functions:

a) continuously review existing national, regional and international research activities, with the purpose of identifying marketing research related to technical and socio-economic problems of developing countries;

b) recommend feasibility studies designed to explore how to organize and conduct marketing research on priority problems, particularly those calling for international or regional effort;

c) examine results of these or other feasibility studies and prepare recommendations action to guide ICMRG activities;

d) advise ICMRG on effectiveness of specific existing international marketing research programs; and

e) further creation of an international network of marketing institutions with an effective mechanism for interchange of information and coordination of research (Izraeli, Izraeli and Meissner, 1976).

The idea came up again at the Marketing in Development Workshop held in conjunction with the Tenth Conference of the Society of International Development (SID) held in Baltimore during July 1983. The concept also popped up at the International Conference on Marketing and Development held in Istanbul during September 1-4, 1986 (Kumcu and Firat, 1986).

Yet, 15 years after the INCOMAS meetings, there is still a need to establish an international network of marketing research centers aimed at pulling together existing knowledge, defining missing links, developing a research agenda, and transferring it into policy and project preparation guidelines and implementation measures. An International Technical Advisory Committee on Agricultural Marketing (TACAM) is needed to assign responsibility for research and implementation as well as to mobilize required funds.

In early 1987, Renee Mathieu—international economist of the US Department of Commerce and co-chair of the Marketing Work Group, Washington Chapter of the Society for International Development (SID)—went much further. She noted that "The International Food Policy Research Institute (IFPRI) is already doing marketing-related trade and food policy research and would be a natural home for such an organization. All that is needed is to broaden IFPRI's scope of work by including (into its agenda) some well-defined (high priority) macro- and micro-marketing topics."[13]

That proposal seems tempting in its simplicity. After all, IFPRI, which was created in 1975, focuses its research work on such topics as food production and consumption projections, impact of food subsidies, food distribution systems, international stockholding and food security, investment in agricultural research, and international foodgrain markets. Substantial work on pricing policies has been undertaken.

In view of this precedent IFPRI might conceivably be able to provide a home to intensified marketing research as well as related dissemination and outreach towards other CGIAR centers. To hook up with an existing organization is obviously a conceptually attractive proposition. The late 1980s are simply not a time for starting a new international marketing research institution. The bilateral and multinational development agencies are belt tightening, while private foundations are reluctant to engage in brand new pioneering ventures.

6. Suggested Follow-Up Action

"Imitation is the most creative form of originality." Jean-Baptiste Voltaire

No matter what the conceptual attractiveness of IFPRI—or whatever other agency might provide a suitable home for the proposed marketing work—they should not be approached "cold" with an extensive "laundry list" of important marketing research topics. Rather, a modest, but very specific initial research program focusing on high priority food marketing issues, should be prepared.

This means that a mechanism needs to be promptly established for: a) drafting criteria by which to assign priority to policy oriented food marketing research, b) apply those criteria to an updated "laundry list" of challenges, and c) suggest alternative strategies for getting the work under way.

By whom and where can this job be done? Washington, DC seems a good place to take the initial steps. An ad-hoc Technical Advisory Committee on Agricultural Marketing (TACAM) can readily be created with individuals selected from: local consulting firms; staffs of locally headquartered bilateral (USAID) and multilateral (IBRD, IDB, OAS) agencies; think tanks (ODC, IFPRI); universities as well as from Private Voluntary Organizations (PVOs). This paper can serve as background for the first meeting. The Marketing Work Group of the Washington, DC Chapter, Society of International Development (MWG/SID) can provide a neutral ground on which an ad-hoc TACAM could hold its initial meetings aimed at accomplishing the above 3 crucial tasks. The output would be an exploratory draft plan of operation to be submitted for consideration by funding agencies.

In short, professionals concerned with improvement of food marketing in LDCs, should follow the successful CGIAR precedent, remembering that imitation is the most creative form of originality. This modest action seems a realistic point of departure for making marketing a powerful tool of socio-economic development, rather than continue subjecting it to benign neglect.

The proposed plan might, of course, not sound sophisticated enough. Let me therefore close with reminding the more ambitious colleagues of an ancient Chinese maxim: "Even a journey of a thousand miles has to start with a first step."[14]

Author's Note: Based on a paper read at the 14th World Congress of the Czechoslovak Society for Arts and Sciences, held at the National 4H Center in Chevy Chase, Maryland, September 15-18, 1988.

For stimulating comments I am indebted to: a) Messrs. Cesar Cainelli and Claudio Meira, colleagues with whom I have enjoyed intellectual crosspollination over long years of our joint tenure at IDB, and b) anonymous referees of an earlier version of this paper.

Full responsibility for the text is mine. Interpretations of past events and suggested agenda for future actions do not necessarily reflect policies of any associations, agencies, and enterprises that are being mentioned. No commitment to action is implied in any proposals.

Notes

1. "Food and Population," Washington, DC: *Population Bulletin,* April 1988.

2. Martin Kriesberg, Politics, Poverty and Hunger, New Delhi: World Conference of the Society for International Development (SID), March 1988.

3. Maurice Williams, "Technology Surplus Food, Changing Farm and Trade Policies," *Development,* 1987, 4, p. 4.

4. Denis Durham, *Food Costs Review 1987,* Washington, DC. Economic Research Service, US Department of Agriculture (ERS/USDA), September 1988, p. 33.

5. Anon, *Food Margins Analysis: Aims, Methods and Uses,* Paris: Organization for Economic Cooperation and Development (OECD), 1981, p. 89; and J. Mittendorf and O. Hertag, *Marketing Costs and Margins for Major Food Items in Developing Countries,* Rome: Food and Agricultural Organization of the United Nations (FAO), 1982, p. 9.

6. See: "In Search of Appropriate Marketing Technology for the Third World," by Frank Meissner in *Economic Analysis and Agricultural Policy,* edited by Richard Day, Ames: Iowa State University Press, pp. 320-333, issued in 1983 as Inter-American Development Bank (IDB) Reprint No. 116; and "Agricultural Marketing Policies and Activities of the Inter-American Development Bank," by Frank Meissner, *Food Policy,* Vol. 12, No. 3. August 1987, issued as Inter-American Development Bank Reprint No. 167.

7. Hans Mittendorf, former Chief of Marketing and Credit Services, Food and Agriculture Organization of the United Nations (FAO, Rome) in the Introduction to *World Food Marketing Systems,* E. Kaynak, editor, London: Buttersworth, 1986, p. xviii.

8. The low repute of marketing is not confined to LDCs. In a series on Marketing Nursing Services, the authors ruefully note that " . . . until recently, many health care professionals felt that

marketing was the sole purview of certain *mendacious businessmen* who competed solely for profit, and *completely without moral conviction*. However, our view of marketing and profits no longer is equated with consciousless greed. A healthy profit now means survival—especially in not-for-profit organizations . . . healthcare administrators (now) see marketing as an *honorable discipline* which utilizes scientific tools, but also as an optimal management system which can help sustain their organization.

"Nurses, too, are taking a second look at what marketing can contribute to (helping resolve such issues as): an increasingly aging population, escalating healthcare costs, an oversupply of physicians, technological advances, continued emphasis on health promotion and self care."

See: Gregory A. Adams, Marianne L. Hockema and Laurie Wood, "Integrating Marketing into Nursing Service," *Nursing Management*, September 1988, p. 30. My emphasis.

9. David Hopper, "Toward an Agro-Industrial Future," *The Bank's World*, September 1988, p. 13.

10. Quoted by Keith Schneider in "The Green Revolution: How Much Further Can It Go?" *New York Times*, August 21, 1988. See also Brown's op. ed. article "Bring on the Family Planner: Gains in World Food Output May Not Come Fast Enough," *Washington Post*, September 8, 1988, A21.

Brown is in good company. In 1986 Robert Herdt, senior economist at the Rockefeller Foundation, presented the following future scenarios: "In the absence of technical change, agriculture in most developing countries will grow too slowly to permit adequate economic growth, which, in turn, will make it impossible for developing countries to import food for domestic consumption . . . if their agricultural sectors and incomes grow 3-4 percent per year, their food demand will probably outpace economic growth rates, making food imports necessary and feasible." See: "Technological Potential for Increasing Crop Productivity in Developing Countries" in Matthew Shane, editor of *Trade and Development Proceedings* of the Winter 1986 Meeting of the International Agricultural Trade Research Consortium, Washington, DC: US Department of Agriculture Economic Research Service Staff Report AGES 70928, July 1988, p. 65.

11. Warren Baum, *Partners Against Hunger*, Washington, DC: World Bank, 1986, p. 337. See also: Jock R. Anderson, Robert W. Herdt and Grant M. Scobie, *Science and Food: The CGIAR and Its Partners*, Washington, DC: World Bank, 1988, p. 134.

12. Address to the first session of the Work Group on Marketing, held in December 1980 at the Brookings Institute by the Washington, DC Chapter of the Society of International Development (SID).

13. "Marketing as a Tool of Socio-Economic Development," *Development Connections* (Newsletter of the Washington Chapter of

the Society for International Development - SID), March 1987, p. 7.

14. To my surprise and delight the word processor has hardly cooled down from typing a draft of this paper, before MWG/SID has taken action. At its initial September 23 and October 21, 1988 meetings, it decided to pursue the above proposal: a) a new list of issues was prepared, b) some highly sui generis priorities tentatively agreed on, and c) the problem of street foods selected for a pilot exercise.

It is too early to tell how this pioneering experiment will go. Members of MWG/SID therefore: a) intend to keep the profession informed about the progress of its work; and b) look for volunteers, who would be willing and able to intellectually stimulate and materially support the effort.

THE LABOR MOVEMENT AND THE REDESIGN OF THE WORKPLACE

by

Arthur B. Shostak

> No group has more to lose or gain from the process of technological change than the labor movement . . . unions are challenged to affect the course of technological development, not merely react to managerial initiatives . . . Ultimately, the issues transcend collective bargaining and their political character becomes apparent. At stake is a more democratic structure of economic as well as political decision-making.
> Harley Shaiken, *Work Transformed*, (1985), pp. 269, 277

If we are soon to bolster our global competitive position, enhance our export position, and substantially improve the quality of life (both on and off the job), we had best expand and improve our understanding of labor's part in recasting the American way of work.

Five aspects of this overlooked matter warrant special attention, as each appears an especially promising source of rewarding gains . . . provided, that is, that researchers merit and earn the hard-to-win trust of skeptical, wary trade unionists.

The situation here pivots on four critical assumptions, each of which must be clearly understood before we can go on to discuss priority candidates for research:

First, while its scope and impact tend to overwhelm us, technology is *not* a natural immutable force with its own inner dynamic. There is *no* one "correct" way to automate, or to mechanize any industry. Instead there is a *range* of options from which to choose.[1]

Second, new technology and the redesign of work, "particularly in today's virulent anti-labor climate, should be included in a list of the current corporate battles against labor . . . new technology brought on line in offices and factories is loaded with social choices—management's choices on how to create greater profitability, not how to fulfill human potential."[2]

Third, it is "entirely logical and reasonable, since workers and their unions have a vital interest, that they should have a voice in determining how technology is introduced in the workplace and in society. Unions must make sure workers and ordinary citizens are not scrapped, ignored, and tossed aside, that equity is given the same attention as efficiency, and that human values prevail in the new workplace."[3]

Finally, while most attention is paid to union setbacks from plant

---

Arthur B. Shostak *is a professor of sociology, Drexel University, Philadelphia, Pennsylvania.*

closings or from a shift to non-union types of employment, it is premature to write off labor's prospects: " . . . the most revolutionary effect of the new technology may not be enhanced speed or productivity. Instead, it may well be the long overdue introduction of organized labor on a wide scale into the 'office of the future.'"[4]

With these four assumptions (the malleability of technology, its historic anti-labor employ, its strategic worth to unions, and its pro-labor potential) now on the record, I focus below on priority matters for academic examination (each of which, of course, gives rise itself to numerous intriguing subsidiary concerns).

1) *Unions and Technology at the Shop Level.* Especially where a far-flying international union has a tradition of local autonomy and responsibility, the locus for making union strategy is often the shop floor. Not surprisingly, however, as researchers are often more comfortable dealing with headquarters types, very little research exists—in the public domain, at least—that illuminates this strategic process.[5]

We do not know, for example, how local union officers and activists:

a) interpret the firm's history of technological change;

b) analyze the industry's technological trends and prospects;

c) assess the positive and negative impacts of recent technological changes at work;

d) draw on advice received here from the *AFL-CIO News,* the publications of the relevant international union; and most especially, the personal counsel of a union business agent or international representative; and

e) take a pro-active stance concerning prospective technological changes. As these are consequential matters, academic researchers should expect to encounter initial resistance, and must be prepared to make a case for local union *gains* before barriers are lowered.

Helpful as a model worth emulating is a rare 1982 study of local union experiences with the introduction of new technologies, a study that illuminates how the International Association of Machinists and Aerospace Workers (IAM) meets this challenge— and the complexity here in front of hardy researchers. The study's author, operating from inside (Staff Assistant to the President), explains how IAM locals use "informal information networks, contract language defining the bargaining unity, job descriptions, and their own intrinsic skills and knowledge of the work process and the grievance procedure, as levers to insure the technological change was not an unrestricted prerogative of management."[6]

2) *Unions and Technology at the Bargaining Table.* Historically, union leaders after World War II "welcomed rapid technological advance since it could produce a bigger pie from which to cut their slice . . . Most unions remained passive as their industries were trans-

formed through new technology . . . "[7] In the 60s and 70s, many unions actually viewed change favorably, provided they could offer "protection to displaced members and play a role in determining work procedures under the new technology. In the 1980s, as well as earlier, some unions pressed management to modernize their plants with new investments, as they realized failure to do so means ultimate loss of jobs."[8]

Nowadays, however, the situation appears far more complex, and labor's options at the bargaining table are greater than ever. In the past, bargaining took place around a set of "defined rules and procedures governing wage determination, work practices, discipline, and job assignments, all linked to a clearly defined and carefully specified set of jobs, unambiguously assigned to particular workers . . . All of this, however, was only really possible when there was a well-defined production process with a clear set of work tasks and responsibilities that could be identified in advance . . . "[9] As little of this is true any longer, bargaining has an indeterminancy now in scope, depth, and drama beyond anything seen before.

Accordingly, we need fresh and discerning research on such bargaining table issues as:

a) the emphasis labor is placing on *employment guarantees* (as in the recent UAW national contracts with Ford, GM, etc.);

b) the willingness of labor to trade concessions for *retraining provisions* and *job re-classifications* ;

c) the interest locals show in winning *advance notice* of workplace change; and

d) the effort locals make to *preserve skill and craft levels,* or extract compensatory earnings should skill dilution be unavoidable. Above all, research is overdue on the fundamental question of labor's *power* in bargaining effectively to address *any* aspect of technological change! With the "withering away" of the strike's effectiveness, and the erosion of NLRB support for labor, there is considerable reason to doubt whether labor is presently capable of winning through collective bargaining more than a bare shadow of its goals.

3. *Unions, Technology, and QWL Programs.* Thanks to a thorough-going 1982 labor-sponsored study of quality of working life (QWL) programs,[10] researchers are in a strong position to advance our understanding of this strategic option, one initially condemned by labor as "simply another in the long list of efforts of American employers to weaken the labor movement."[11]

In the late 1980s there is a wide diversity of views within labor concerning the desirability and viability of quality circles, employee involvement schemes, labor-management participation schemes, socio-technical work systems, and so on.

Militants, for example, have rallied behind a hard-boiled co-op-tation strategy advanced by Mike Parker in his best-selling 1985 manual, *Inside the Circle: A Union Guide to QWL.* [12] Parker urges feisty suspicion of all QWL efforts, especially those that threaten to sap traditional union militancy. He reminds rank-and-filers:

> The primary job of the union is to project and advance the conditions of its members and those of other workers—not to protect and increase company profits, market share, or reputation. [13]

Careful to agree QWL has "some genuinely positive features," Parker indicates how unions might put some QWL techniques to good use—especially in meeting the challenge of technological change. Overall, however, he worries that most of the QWL-type programs currently in place "are taking away our only real power by undermining our unions." [14]

Quite different is that tact taken by labor consultant Peter Lazes, who helps unions and companies alike use QWL to "take full advantage of employees' skills and their desire to help their companies remain competitive." [15] Lazes has recently helped Local 14-A of the Amalgamated Clothing and Textile Workers, Local 1097 of the UAW, and others, make better use of available technologies; for example:

> Redesigning work flow and floor layout, reducing scrap, involving employees in purchasing new equipment and in determining appropriate uses for automated equipment, and identifying and solving problems at the shop-floor level were among the recommendations of the [union-employer ACTWU] team. [16]

Lazes has also pioneered in linking QWL workplace committees with nearby academic resources:

> By September, 1983, students and faculty from the University of Alabama (helped by hourly employees, engineers, and managers) found ways to reduce the operating budget by over $645,000 per year . . . and saved 225 jobs." [17]

Overall, Lazes is optimistic that labor has much to gain from careful, upbeat use of QWL options, especially if guided by astute, objective consultants.

Plainly, with the subject as volatile as indicated above, we cannot get enough good research soon enough. Attention, for example, might be paid to:

a) labor press treatment of QWL;

b) labor education material on QWL; and

c) labor leader speeches about QWL. Of greatest value, however, would be the study of a scientific sample of actual QWL projects in unionized workplaces, for only then could strategic light be shed on such QWL vexations as:

d) the hostility of workplace nonparticipants, and their use of rumors, competition, and internal political conflicts;

e) the reduction of the "common rule" strategy unions have relied on to limit competition and standardize conditions; and

f) the abandonment of detailed rules governing specific, narrowly defined jobs. Research is overdue, in short, on labor's ability to manage variability and flexibility *without* falling victim to increasing divisiveness and competition.[18]

4. *Unions, Technology, and Union Staffers.* Exceedingly sensitive, and therefore possibly impossible to study—though no less strategic for all that—is the question of union staff adequacy where technological change is concerned.

Union participants are often full-time district officials "who are usually quite removed from new technological impacts and their impacts on the shop floor."[19] Their efforts here are just one small part of their overall responsibilities, and not one especially high on a list of tasks to attend to, a list that has technological change often relegated to the back burner of union (and managerial) priorities:

> In general, the unions have barely begun to think through what it would take to make concrete their hopes for a substantial role in the development of new technology. They have not committed the necessary resources—in terms of personnel, training, time, or money—in order to effectively influence the technological change process.[20]

Not surprisingly, therefore, union staffers *may* not always measure up to the task here—a weakness, alas, commonly matched by managerial ineptitude with similar roots.

If the necessary trust were somehow earned, a research agenda here might explore:

a) the nature of union education for staffers where workplace technological change is concerned;

b) the staff assessment of this schooling; and

c) the staff "wish list" in this regard.

Above all, attention might usefully be focused on outstanding on-going projects here, the better to highlight lessons transferable to other unions.

5. *Unions, Technology, and Mismanagement.* As contentious as are all the preceding matters, this topic outdoes them all—and raises hackles in every direction: Employers insist there is nothing to explore here! Union officialdom hesitates to get involved. And feisty grass-roots militants contend that nothing else is half as important! The effort to carve out a new frontier in this matter for the American labor movement is a small, but exceedingly promising one—predicated as it is on the awesome notion that "management is too important to be left to the managers."[21]

Proponents want unions to learn how to detect both the obvious and the "invisible" brands of mismanagement, which they define as "anything which endangers the long-term viability of a workplace, whether by omission or by commission."[22] Examples include disinvestment, antagonistic labor-management relations, contracting out, irregular attention to quality control, nepotism and cronyism, and failure to pursue new technology.

This last "screw up" is represented as a common experience:

> Who hasn't seen a boss spend big on new equipment or a system which is expected to produce magic results, only to see it lay idle or never be fully utilized because it was poorly chosen, or because not enough training was included, or because a miscalculation was made about the demand for its use?"[23]

Unions, however, have rarely seized on these errors and turned them into offensive weapons for labor in specific campaigns.

Research into labor's likely use of mismanagement at the shop level might explore:

a) varying attitudes toward this matter held at four levels of labor (rank-and-file; local officers; international staffers; international and AFL-CIO officers);

b) case studies of on-going use (as highlighted in the summer '87 issue of *Labor Research Review*);

c) management views of the pros and cons here; and

d) the perspective of academic and government specialists in labor-management relations. Especially valuable is research to test the contention that workers might be *more* productive than ever if reasonably allowed a chance to diplomatically correct screw-ups: "If labor had more control, many disasters could be averted, and a greater emphasis would always be placed on long-term competitiveness and stability."[24]

Underlying all of this—and therefore, a very high priority for field research—is an ever-longer list of grievances union militants have with corporate errors:

> . . . accounting methods irrationally steer investment away from basic manufacturing . . . low and mid-level supervisors intentionally subvert quality circles because they would make the supervisors unnecessary; . . . managers fail to grasp the potential of computer-aided design or flexible manufacturing systems or are not applying them to appropriate tasks; . . . computerization is used to increase management control and produce more work stress rather than to improve flexibility by complementing worker skills; . . . marketing managers fail to adequately track consumer preferences or shifts in market niches; . . . strategic planning; fails to produce long-term success.[25]

Until unionists gain fresh and substantial confidence in America's business leadership, the nation's labor-management relations will continue to undermine, rather than advance national well-being.

Summary. Unions have essentially responded to the impacts of technological change on workplace conditions in three ways:

legislation at the city, state, and federal levels, generally seeking to limit job losses (as with plant-closing and/or retraining aid);

contract negotiations at the shop and organizational level, addressing both job security and compensation; and *public relations,* addressed to rank-and-filers and non-unionists alike, generally trying to convey an upbeat and accommodationist perspective. Coursing through all of these approaches is keen sensitivity to both short-term (protectionist) and future-oriented issues:

Protectionist Clauses: Advance notice, Attrition Clauses, "Bumping" Clauses, Income Guarantees, Layoff Prohibitions, Layoff Recall Rights, Negotiation of Rights, Preferential Hiring, Seniority Rules, Severance Pay, Special Joint Committees, etc.

Future-Oriented Clauses: Moving Allowances, Outplacement Aid, Training, Transfer to Replacement Facilities, etc. Given this complexity, it is little wonder that a researcher who has thoroughly studied the matter (and authored the itemized lists above) concludes "the time is ripe for new strategies and innovative tactics in labor negotiations."[26]

To better help this along, the research recommendations made earlier in this paper could be extended to also illuminate labor's present and prospective role in:

a) overseas experiments in workplace technology reforms (as in Norway and Sweden);[27]

b) industry-by-industry case studies of workplace technology reforms (as in autos, computers, printing, steel-making, etc.);[28]

c) the case of women workers, handicapped workers, or older workers and workplace technology reforms;[29] and

d) the forecasts of 21st century changes in workplace technology realities.[30] In combination with the five issues discussed earlier in the body of this paper, enough work appears called for to keep an army of researchers busy for decades to come.

Only, however, if such research proves sensitive, trustworthy, and *constructive,* is it likely to win labor's indispensable cooperation—and merit it. Unionists have been far too disappointed by far too much academic work to welcome researchers with open arms—though labor understands the indispensable nature of such endeavors. A case, in sum, can be effectively made with unionists on behalf of the research espoused in this essay—provided such unionists believe they have the full respect of the researchers, and the project's goals are consonant with their own.

Unfortunately, a dark cloud hovers over this prospect, one which challenges would-be researchers to recognize the relevance of prevailing anti-union attitudes and politics:

> . . . how workers and managers control the implementation and outcomes of technological change, whether with increased managerial control or labor participation in managerial decision-making, will depend on their capacities and motivation to redistribute authority in the workplace. The continuation of political conditions which further the decline in unionization is likely to facilitate *increased, unilateral managerial decision-making.* [31](italics added)

Unions that feel ceaselessly under siege, unions that sense their very existence endlessly undermined in both covert and overt ways, are unlikely..understandably . . . to value research on *secondary* matters, like workplace technological issues, when a primary matter, or labor's basic survival, is still problematic: Not until labor has a secure and valued place in the American scene will it be free to fully cooperate, as we academicians would like, in frank and unfettered research of *mutual* reward.

> Workers' actions reflect those created by management. We cannot fault the labor unions. Richard P. Simmonds, CEO, Allegheny Ludlum Steel Corp., in *The New York Times*, Jan. 12, 1988. p. D-1

Notes

1. See in this connection, Noble, David. "Social Choice in Machine Tool Design," in *Case Studies on the Labor Process*, edited by Andrew Zimbalist. New York: Monthly Review Press, 1979.

2. Kohn, George. "Changing Competitive and Technology Environments in Telecommunications," in *Labor and Technology: Union Response to Changing Environments*, edited by Donald Kennedy, *et al.* University Park, PA: Department of Labor Studies, The Pennsylvania State University, 1982, p. 71.

3. Roberts, Markely. "The Impact of Technology on Union Organizing and Collective Bargaining," in *ibid.*, p. 12.

4. Gregory, Judith. "Technological Change in the Office Workplace and Implications for Organizing," in *ibid.*, p. 101.

5. While the public domain contains only research results the unions are comfortable sharing, it is possible to scan proprietary research and even discuss its significance with key union staffers— provided one has earned trust and volunteered safeguards against "leaking" this material. Secrecy here is a grim and fairly serious matter, though over time one *can* win the confidence of top labor researchers and learn how to convey fresh insights without violating a trust.

6. Nulty, Leslie E. "Case Studies of IAM Local Experiences with the Introduction of New Technologies," in *Labor and Technology*, edited by D. Kennedy, *et al., op. cit.*, p. 116.

7. Salpukas, Agis. "Unions: A New Role?," in *The Worker and the Job: Coping with Change*, edited by Jerome M. Rosow. New Jersey: Prentice-Hall, 1974. pp. 104-105.

8. Freeman, Richard B. and Jamee L. Medoff. *What Do Unions Do?* New York: Basic Books, 1984. p. 170.

9. Piore, Michael J. "Computer Technologies, Market Structure, and Strategic Union Choices," in *Challenges and Choice Facing American Labor*, edited by Thomas A. Kochan. Cambridge, MA: MIT Press, 1986. p. 198.

10. Kochan, Thomas A., *et al. Worker Participation and American Unions: Threat or Opportunity?* Kalamazoo, MI: W.E. Upjohn Institute for Employment Research, 1984.

11. *Ibid.,* p. 5.

12. Parker, Mike. *Inside the Circle: A Union Guide to QWL.* Boston, MA: South End Press, 1985.

13. *Ibid.,* p. 1.

14. *Ibid.,* p. 2.

15. Lazes, Peter. "Employee Involvement Activities: Saving Jobs and Money Too." *New Management,* 3, 3, Winter 1986, p. 58.

16. *Ibid.,* p. 59.

17. *Ibid.,*

18. See in this connection, Kochant, T., *et al., Worker Participation . . . , op. cit.*

19. Howard, Robert and Leslie Schneider. "Worker Participation in Technological Change: Interests, Influence, and Scope," in *Worker Participation and the Politics of Reform,* edited by Carmen Sirianni. Philadelphia, PA: Temple University Press, 1987. p. 79.

20. *Ibid.*

21. Anon. "Introduction." *Labor Research Review,* Spring 1987. p. II.

22. LeRoy, Greg. "Mismanagement: Labor's Rightful Cause." *Labor Research Review, ibid.,* p. 3.

23. *Ibid.,* p. 4.

24. *Ibid.,* p. 10.

25. *Ibid.,* p. 6.

26. Solomon, Janet S. "Union Responses to Technological Change: Protecting the Past or Looking to the Future?" *Labor Studies Journal,* 12, 2, Fall, 1987. p. 64.

27. Relevant essays on unions and technology change in Sweden, Italy, Germany, France, Hungary, Yugoslavia, Poland, China, Jamaica, Chile, and Peru, can be found in Sirianni, *Worker Participation and the Politics of Reform, op. cit.*

28. Relevant essays on unions and technology change in agriculture, the newspaper industry, longshoring, the Postal Service, the insurance industry, education, air traffic control, coal mining, the auto industry, the steel industry, the construction equipment industry, the commercial aircraft industry, the sanitation service, and telecommunications, can be found in *Workers, Managers, and Technological Change,* edited by Daniel B. Cornfield. New York: Plenum, 1987.

29. See, for example, *Working Women: Past, Present, Future,* edited by Karen S. Koziara, *et al.* Washington, DC: BNA, 1987.

30. See, for example, Howard, Robert, *Brave New Workplace.* New York: Viking, 1985.

31. Cornfield, Daniel B., ed., *Workers, Managers, and Technological Change, op. cit.,* p. 353.

Meeting Challenges

THE ENTERPRISING COMMUNITY: LEADING AMERICA INTO THE 21ST CENTURY

by

Gregg Edwards and David Pearce Snyder

With the 1980s drawing to a close, we are already beginning to see a flurry of speculative books and articles on the outlook for the 1990s. Early reviews of the coming decade are decidedly mixed, ranging from rosy to rotten.

There is good reason to be uncertain about the 1990s. Current trends and developments give us a contradictory and confusing picture of the near-term future, full of "good news" and "bad news." Overseas, for example, the liberalization of communist political systems appears to offer real hope of reduced global tensions, while the simultaneous rise of ethnic and sectarian militancy throughout the world threatens to plunge us all into an era of growing international terrorism. In the economic arena, the rapid industrialization of many Third World nations will mean improved living standards for their citizens, but it also implies a steadily rising tide of foreign competition for American enterprise—and American workers.

In fact, most economists now agree that, if we expect our prosperity to survive the globalization of the marketplace, we will have to substantially increase our productivity during the 1990s. Fortunately, current forecasts indicate that the coming decade will present us with a veritable cornucopia of new knowledge and technology with which to increase our productivity *and* improve our quality of life. But, we have just passed through a decade of unprecedented technological innovation and, as a society, we appear to have derived very little benefit from the experience.

Although US employers spent hundreds of billions of dollars on new workplace technology during the 1980s, American productivity growth has remained far behind that of our principle industrial competitors, and far below our own levels of 20 to 30 years ago. As a direct result of our diminishing productivity, *both* average corporate profits *and* median household income in the US have been falling for more than a decade. Poor economic performance, in turn, has forced a reduction of our "social safety net," and has sharply curtailed the maintenance of our public infrastructure. Simultaneously, major reforms and increased funding have failed to halt the decline of our educational system, while cost contain-

---

Gregg Edwards *and* David Pearce Snyder *are consulting futurists.*

ment has failed to curtail the spiraling price of health care. And, if all of that weren't enough, recent studies show that 20 years of environmental regulation have failed to protect our air and water from frightening degradation.

The trends of the recent past are the basis of our most reliable forecasts of the future. Thus, America's faltering socio-economic indicators of the 1970s and 1980s underlie a broad array of gloomy predictions for the 1990s. Our ongoing economic restructuring is widely expected to create further regional and occupational waste-lands in America, as old industries decline and old skills are made redundant or obsolete. As a consequence, household income will continue to fall, so that more than 10% of all Americans may be unable to afford decent housing by the year 2000. At the same time, Congressional forecasts estimate that skyrocketing health care costs will *impoverish 1/3 to 1/2 of our elderly*. Meanwhile, educators estimate that it will take at least another 10 years to restore US public schools to world class performance, and ecologists increas-ingly express fears that the nation has *neither* the resources *nor* the resolve to restore our environment.

All of these forecasts are simply extrapolations of past trends. Such forecasts rest on the assumption that nothing will intervene to keep these trends from continuing into the future. This doesn't mean that we *can't* intervene to alter and improve our future—of course, we can. As a democratic society we can—and do—intervene in our future by creating new public institutions, for example, or redistributing our collective income. What's more, if we look across the Atlantic, we can see several working models of mature industrial economies, like our own, that appear to have solved some of the basic problems that we will have to address in the 1990s, such as housing, health care, education and economic productivity.

Today, as America confronts growing numbers of homeless, de-caying public schools, inadequate child and elder care, and soaring costs that threaten to put quality medical treatment and a college education beyond the means of most people, the first class human services and comprehensive social safety nets afforded the citizens of such countries as Holland and Sweden have a distinct appeal. Using basically the same technologies that are available to us, the advanced social democracies of Europe are clearly doing a much more effective job of mobilizing themselves for the general well-being of their citizens than does the United States. Thus, as a means of solving our growing social distress, we could simply choose to make the advanced social democracies our model for the 21st Cen-tury, and spend the 1990s developing an array of high quality human service programs like theirs.

Of course, all of those universal, high quality public services wouldn't be free; the average Dane or Dutchman pays out 1/2 to 2/3 of his or her income in taxes; 2 or 3 times the tax rate of the typical American. What's more, the efficient delivery of high quality housing, health care and education doesn't happen without considerble government planning: social planning; land-use planning; economic planning, etc. It may not be entirely implausible that Americans would double or triple their own taxes to assure the universal availability of first class public services. It seems, however, highly unlikely that Americans would willingly subject themselves to the constraints upon personal and marketplace behavior that such comprehensive government planning would require.

Americans have always distrusted government planning. Indeed, most Americans today are still inclined to agree with Ralph Waldo Emerson who first expressed the view that "the less government, the better." In the American tradition, the principal function of government has been to provide a framework—a supportive environment—within which individuals and enterprises may flourish and prosper to their fullest potential. Thus, even if Americans were willing to pay the financial price of a comprehensive social system, it does not seem probable that they would be willing to turn their destinies over to governmental forecasters and social planners.

Certainly, the past 10 or 20 years have given us little reason for confidence in government foresight planning. Our politicians and bureaucrats have provided us very little practical guidance for dealing with the current forces of innovation and change, or even given much evidence that they understand those forces themselves. But, neither have our mega-corporations, with their short-term, bottom-line avoidance of risk. A new MIT report, "Made In America," places the responsibility for America's slipping economic performance entirely upon the shoulders of business and its unwillingness to innovate or change. Indeed, a review of the 1980s makes it clear that large institutions, both public and private, have made little—if any—truly productive innovations during the past decade, preferring instead to make only incremental changes, and to use powerful new technologies in superficial—even trivial—ways.

Economic history, on the other hand, makes it clear that the greatest increases in productivity come from the use of new technology to accomplish essential tasks and functions in new, more efficient ways: i.e., new productive processes. But, America's executives—and their accountants—have sought mainly to buy "guaranteed," risk-free increases in productivity off the high-tech shelf, without trying to invent new and better ways of organizing, manufacturing, managing, marketing and decision-making. Unfortunately, installing computers and telematics in a traditional, hierarchial, authoritarian, compartmentalized bureaucracy is about as productive as adding spark plugs to a steam engine.

On balance, then, the experience of the 1980s raises a fundamental question: "If our national political leaders *can't* lead the nation, and our national business leaders *won't* lead the nation, how can we expect American enterprise to make the necessary innovations to remain competitive in the 21st Century?" By process of elimination, the Eighties have shown us that there can be only one answer to that question. It is *we* —the people, who will have to demonstrate the personal commitment *and* intellectual integrity needed to make truly innovative and purposeful uses of our new knowledge and technology.

In fact, experience suggests that a multitude of grass-roots, techno-economic innovation programs should work much better than any single nationwide top-down approach to the problem. The principal sources of innovation processes are not large organizations, in spite of their sophistication and their huge R&D budgets. Most truly productive workplace innovations are first developed by small institutions, including sole proprietorships, family businesses, and the self-employed. Moreover, most new jobs are created when successful local enterprises expand to serve regional or national markets.

The foregoing implies that, in their own interests, local communities should take steps to assure that a maximum number of successful local entrepreneurships arise, in order to provide the broadest possible base for long-term economic growth and prosperity. Just as an increasing number of universities are serving as "incubators" for new, high-tech businesses, an "Enterprising Community" could serve as an incubator for all forms of productive innovation, *both* in the marketplace *and* in the public sector. And the most efficient means by which a community might seek to foster productive innovation would be to assist its individual and institutional members in identifying and adopting proven "best practice" in all areas of economic enterprise.

In every field of endeavor—in every trade, industry, profession, or service, there is a body of knowledge describing current "best practice;" i.e. the most effective and efficient proven means of performing basic automation in an office or a factory; the most effective means of improving public school performance; the most effective measures for improving the reliability of medical diagnoses; the most effective steps for assuring the success of a new small business; the most effective techniques for upgrading and reskilling adult workers; the most effective means for introducing a new product or service to the marketplace, etc.

To mobilize the citizens and institutions of a single community to purposefully adopt "best practice" in all their productive activities would draw on the two traditional sources of economic growth in America: savvy and hard work. The opportunity to be exploited by the Enterprising Community is perfectly straight forward: on the average, it takes about 10 years for current "best practice" to become "common practice," because of the slow diffusion of innovation and change in the general marketplace. But, in a *supportive* environment, new best practice can become common practice in a matter of weeks or months. Thus, the logic behind the Enterprising Community is clear: "Sooner or later, best practice becomes common practice; why not here and now?"

To provide such a supportive environment, examples of best practice would be sought out, and descriptions of it made available to the community's businesses and public sector managers. Where the implementation of best practice requires resources that are not available locally, the members and institutions of the Enterprising Community would seek to create or acquire those resources in the common interest. Similarly, where local laws or regulations bar business and/or government from using best practice, the Enterprising Community would undertake the appropriate revision of its own policies and regulations, based—once again—on proven best practice. In the Enterprising Community, public policy should lead to, and encourage the adoption of superior, new, best practice, rather than defend the retention of old practices.

Finally, to foster the adoption of best practice, the Enterprising Community will have to upgrade the abilities of all of its citizens to understand and employ best practice. By definition, an Enterprising Community must be a learning community. To begin with, this means that public schools must provide their graduates with reasoning, problem-solving and learning skills, so that they will be able to bring those abilities into a workplace where all high value jobs will involve continuous innovation and change. To help all students at all levels better understand how to apply their classroom lessons to real-world situations, public education should incorporate practicum, including apprenticeship and internship assignments.

Policy makers and business leaders have always assumed that higher education would play an instrumental role in retooling the US workforce for the trans-industrial workplace. Throughout America today, the nation's colleges and universities are already heavily involved in the re-skilling and upgrading of adult employees in mid-career, both on and off the job. But, in Enterprising Communities, community colleges would do much more than that. They should model themselves after the Land Grant Universities, soliciting funds from local public and private sources for the development and diffusion of information describing productive innovations for business and government.

Community extension agents, like agricultural extension agents, should be made available to work with local entrepreneurs. Like their agricultural counterparts, these community extension services would organize continuing education programs, and would network with each other, sharing the lessons learned by each, to be applied by each as suits their local needs and opportunities. Ultimately, Enterprising Communities could create "cooperative development banks" to underwrite local new ventures and the adoption of productivity-enhancing innovations by local private *and* public sector institutions.

Thomas Jefferson once described local communities as "civic laboratories" for solving the problems that must inevitably accompany progress. Without doubt, the modern-day realization of Jefferson's ideal in the form of Enterprising Communities would be major innovation on the American scene. Major innovations are never easy, and this would be no exception. Pioneering is hard—and risky—by definition. The first American colonists knew that, and so did the families and merchants who settled the West. Colonizing the 21st Century with a new generation of American ideas, American institutions and American goods and services will also be hard. The experience of the 1980s suggests that our national political leadership and our major corporations are either unwilling to work that hard, or unwilling to take the necessary risks. Thus, if America's greatness is to outlast the 20th Century, we will need many "Enterprising Communities" in the 1990s.

MANIFESTO FOR AN INFORMATION AGE

by

T. M. Grundner

In many ways the development of mankind can be described and at least partially explained in terms of technological innovation. The invention of the wheel, the pulley, and the lever allowed man to magnify his natural physical abilities and laid the groundwork for the development of formal civilization. Gunpowder forever ended feudalism as a social institution. The printing press threw open the doors of literacy to the average person, and the steam engine moved western society from an agricultural to an industrial one. Even in our century, the development of radio and television has affected virtually every aspect of our lives from religion, to politics, to business, to the conduct of international affairs.

One thing we have learned from this experience however, is that technology almost never arrives in a value-free context. With each technological advance come decisions that affect the direction that technology will take. We are now at just such a point with regard to "Information Age" technologies spawned by the computer revolution.

It is entirely possible that no invention in our time will have consequences as profound and lasting as the computer. With this machine we have a device that does not simply magnify the power of our physical being—our muscles, or our eyes, or our legs; rather, we have a device that for the first time in history magnifies the power of our minds.

Among the many valuable characteristics of the computer is its almost unbelievable ability to access and deliver information. When these machines are coupled with the telephone system, they present the possibility of delivering vast information resources to unparalleled numbers of people.

But the operative phrase here is " . . . they present the possibility . . . " There is nothing that says they must; nothing that says they will. Those are *choices* that must be made, and they are choices that will eventually shape the development of an "Information Age."

Whether we are all going to be citizens of this Information Age is not an issue. We are. The only question that remains is what we are going to do about it? Where will we place our values and

T. M. Grundner *is director of the Community Telecomputing Laboratory, Case Western Reserve University.*

priorities? What needs to be done to insure that computer-driven information resources are made available to as many people as possible? In short, what does it mean to be a "Citizen of an Information Age?"

Make no mistake. There will be principles and priorities; but without dialogue and decision they will occur by default, and surely a more thoughtful approach than that is in order.

What is needed at this point is a manifesto—a statement of principles and intentions—around which an emerging Citizen of an Information Age can frame his or her actions and beliefs. It will take a great deal of discussion and debate to hammer these principles into a final form; and, indeed, it is possible a universally held final form may never be achieved. But if a dialogue is to occur, it needs to begin now. The following six initial statements of belief are intended to begin that process.

1. As Citizens of an Information Age, we believe that access to information is a fundamental right of every person in a democracy.

We will not attempt to outline the moral, ethical, and legal underpinnings of the word "freedom." Other sources have done so far more eloquently than we can ever hope to achieve. Suffice it to say, however, that freedom of speech and freedom of the press are two, key, basic rights granted to all who reside in a democracy. They are not things that must be requested. They are not special favors granted by some higher authority. They are rights that anyone may exercise and everyone must honor.

Yet freedom of speech and freedom of the press make no sense without open access to information. They have no value if the information necessary to meaningfully exercise them is limited.

Certainly it is not hard to conjure up isolated examples of information whose dissemination would not be in the public interest. Military and state secrets would perhaps head this list. But beyond those limited examples, access to information is a concept that stands at the cornerstone of a free society; and the extent to which a person's ability to access information is diminished, is the extent to which that person is diminished as a citizen.

2. As Citizens of an Information Age, we believe that information equity—the right of all people to benefit from Information Age technology—must be developed as a national priority.

We are extremely fortunate that this country abounds with opportunities for the acquisition of information. We are generally free to print whatever we wish and we are free to speak out on any issue. We have hundreds of television and thousands of radio stations that anyone can listen to or watch. We are blessed with a magnificent public library system; and it is hard to travel even a few miles without coming across a place where additional books, magazines, or newspapers can be obtained.

In each case, however, these opportunities were made possible because technological innovation made them available to the general public at low or no cost. The printing press gave us low-cost printed material. Radio and television services are made available free to the user after a small initial equipment investment; and access to a public library does not require even that.

This century has witnessed the development of computer-driven communications systems as a new and powerful medium for disseminating information. We believe that—as with print, radio, and television—this medium must be made available at the lowest possible cost to as many people as possible. That, however, is something that is not occurring now.

At the moment computerized information services remain largely in the hands of commercial vendors whose users bear a nearly uniform demographic stamp—$50,000 + household incomes, very well educated, overwhelmingly white, overwhelmingly male. Let us be clear. There is nothing wrong with operating a commercial information service, and there is nothing wrong with occupying that particular demographic niche. Indeed, it could well be argued that the development of telecomputing could not have occurred without those pioneers.

What we *are* suggesting is that there can and should be an alternative to these commercial services, an alternative that can be accessed by all people no matter what their socio-economic level. Furthermore, we believe that commercial and public interests do not stand in conflict on this point.

The development of the public library system, for example, did no harm to commercial booksellers. To the contrary, it immeasurably helped them by introducing books and reading to millions of people. So too, we believe that computerized public access information services will similarly co-exist with the commercial information marketplace of the future. The commercial systems will still be there, but alongside them will be public access systems that will introduce Information Age services to millions.

The main point is that if we, as a society, are to enter the Information Age with equity, then Information Age services must be made available to all. As citizens of that Information Age, we are committed to seeing those services provided.

3. We believe information equity requires that basic computerized community information services be developed as universal utilities.

If access to information is a right; and if the opportunity to access information of right ought to be developed for as many people as possible via as many means as possible; and if computer-driven information services now number among those means; then those services must achieve universal availability.

More specifically, we believe that a nationwide network of computerized public access information services should be established so that, eventually, no citizen will be more than a single non-toll telephone call away from one of these systems. Furthermore, we believe these systems should be operated and maintained as public utilities.

To begin to accomplish this objective we would propose the establishment of free, open-access, community computer systems in cities and towns throughout the nation. Running on these machines would be computer programs that would provide its users with everything from electronic mail services, to information about health care, education, technology, government, recreation, or just about anything else the community operators would like to place on the machine. All of it would be free and all of it could be easily accomplished by a first-time user.

Perhaps the best way to illustrate the concept of community computing is by analogy to the development of the public library system in our country. In the middle of the last century there was no such thing as the free public library. Eventually literacy got high enough (and the cost of books cheap enough) that the public library became feasible. In this century we believe we have gotten to the point where computer "literacy" has gotten high enough (and the cost of equipment cheap enough) that a similar demand for free public access community computer systems has formed. We, as a society, need to meet that demand.

It is important to understand that what is being proposed here is not a pie-in-the-sky ideation. The telephone technology necessary to bring it into being is already in place and is being improved daily to help facilitate computerized information transfer. The computer technology is available both in terms of low cost central machines that can easily handle the user load, and in terms of the dissemination of smaller modem equipped machines in the home, school, and work place. The software necessary to operate these systems has been developed and is available to any city in the country on a lease basis for $1 per year, and pilot community computer systems have been successfully operating for several years in northeast Ohio.

What remains is the commitment to do it; and it is that commitment, that leadership, that we, as Citizens of an Information Age, must provide.

4. We believe information equity requires that Information Age skills be universally taught in our secondary schools and colleges.

Professional educators understand that one of their major roles is to prepare students, not only to be good citizens; but to be productive members of the society in which they will live. There is little question that society will be powerfully shaped and influenced by computers and computer technology and, for this reason, in recent years virtually every secondary school and college has acquired at least some computer instructional capability.

But the era these students will be entering will not be known as

114

the "Computer Age," it will be known as the "Information Age." Computers are not the end, they are the means. Information is the end.

Basic computer operation skills are a necessary but insufficient step in the preparation of these students. To function in the Information Age, to be good citizens, they will have to know how to communicate and access information via computers and how to creatively think about that information once it is obtained. Yet it is precisely this type of instruction that is not now occurring in most schools.

The reason for this situation lies in the inability of the schools to access computerized information resources in a cost effective manner. As long as most information services remain commercial, most schools will be effectively prohibited from teaching Information Age skills and technology to their students. The development of community computer systems eliminates this barrier—but eliminating the barrier alone will not be enough.

Schools have traditionally been charged with teaching reading, writing, arithmetic, and hopefully thinking, as they apply to "Second Wave" media—usually print media. Unquestionably the teaching of these skills must continue, but to them should be added the application of these skills to Information Age technology as well.

We believe there should be ongoing curricula in place in secondary schools and colleges to teach all students both basic computer skills and how to use those skills to communicate and access information. Not only do these skills need to be taught, but the ability to think about the information once it is acquired needs to occur.

As Citizens of an Information Age, we are committed to developing, supporting, and maintaining these types of curricular efforts.

5. We believe information equity requires that the technology necessary to access these services be made universally available at the lowest possible cost.

Providing universal access to computerized information services, and teaching Information Age skills in our schools, is not enough if people do not have access to the equipment necessary to use those services and capitalize on those skills.

In France this problem has been solved by the governmentally sponsored distribution of millions of free terminals to its citizens who can then use them to access a national information service called Minitel. In the United States no such action has been taken.

Access to Information Age technology has been driven largely by a competitive workplace which requires its employees to access information and is willing to provide the equipment and training necessary for that to occur. In addition, there are millions of home computer enthusiasts who own personal computers that are modem equipped. Taken together, these two segments cover a substantial portion of our society; but a "substantial portion" is not enough, and more must be done.

We believe terminals that are connected to community computer systems should be made available in public locations throughout the country. Included in these locations would be public libraries, government buildings, shopping centers, post offices, and other similar locations.

We also support the priority development of what we have come to refer to as the "Model T" terminal. This terminal, like the French Minitel machine, would consist of a screen, a keyboard, a built-in modem, built-in modem software and would sell for under $250. The theory behind this terminal is the same one utilized by Henry Ford whose development of the low-cost "Model T" automobile opened up motoring to the average person and thereby placed America on wheels.

We do not call for governmental distribution of equipment as in France. The French way is not ours. But if governmental subsidy is necessary to allow either these public access stations or the "Model T" terminal to come into being, then we would support it. As Citizens of an Information Age we would hope our government would be able to see what other nations have already seen—and acted upon.

6. We believe that ongoing systematic research into the nature of Information Age technology must be of the highest priority.

What has been described so far are some of the initial steps we believe must be taken to help our society make a complete and equitable transition into an Information Age. But it must be emphasized that they are only preliminary in nature. They are preliminary because we are only now beginning to understand the implications of this technology and can see only dimly what future Information Age advances may hold in store. To keep pace with these developments we must begin to look at this technology in a systematic and scientific fashion.

It is critical that research begin immediately to better understand the nature of telecomputing as a new information and communications vehicle, including—especially including—its social and community implications.

It is critical that research begin on harnessing this medium's unique characteristics with regard to education. We need to know much more about the strengths and weaknesses of this medium and how to utilize it most effectively at all educational levels.

It is critical that we develop better ways to interface people with these services so that, eventually, these systems become no more difficult to use than a telephone. Developments with natural language interfaces and the use of artificial intelligence make that a very real possibility, but it can only occur if essential research is begun and supported.

Above all, we need to establish an ongoing research and development agenda so that we are not taken unaware by the future. Homo sapiens, thinking man, is a tool maker. He always was and always will be. It is the thing that, in many ways, defines and shapes us as a species. Because of that fact technological development is not going to stop—not as long as man exists. The goal is to find a way to ensure that technological development is harnessed always for the good of man and its benefits are made available to all. Because there is no end to technology, there is no end to that task.

FUTURE TALK: COPING WITH OUR ELECTRONIC TECHNOLOGIES

by

Joseph N. Pelton

Today's technologies have fostered wealth and individual opportunity. But we have paid a price: loss of community and dependence on impersonal centralized organizations. However, emerging telecommunications technologies could reverse these losses.

Craig Calhoun, *IEEE Spectrum*

The most profound change for future professionals will occur when machines usurp their intellectual skills.

Frederick Hayes-Roth, *IEEE Spectrum*

Artificial Intelligence . . . looks for shortcuts . . . plays on hunches, and uses metaphors and analogies in its reasoning. Sometimes such programs come up with highly innovative and original solutions, and they also learn from experience. Through their 'experience bank' they can develop a limited world view extending their repertoire of problem solving skills and enabling them to apply a strategy learned in one task to quite different problems.

Neil Frude, *The Ultimate Machine*

We may no longer be in control of this exploding technology. But we can still hope to influence the general direction of the blast. There is unfortunately no STOP button for the network-based society we are now building . . . The central issue I am inviting you to explore . . . is a simple one: in a world invaded by machines that dissolve reality to digitize it, how are we going to recognize truth and preserve quality? How are we going to relate to each other?

Jacques Vallee, *The Network Revolution*

There is a great temptation to see the history of the world and of humankind as a broad continuum of progress and development. The evidence is surprisingly to the contrary. If there is a pattern to be found, it is of rapid spurts of progress followed by lethargy or even protracted backsliding. Consider Archytus of Tarentum, an ancient Greek who built a working reaction-jet engine powered by steam. He carved a wooden case in the form of a pigeon and it flew around his house tied to a string. Twenty-three centuries before SPUTNIK, Archytus had mastered the basic principles of

---

Joseph N. Pelton *is director of INTELSAT special studies and projects, Washington, DC.*

rocketry. Centuries before the birth of Christ ancient scientists in Babylonia, Egypt and Greece knew far more about astronomy, chemistry, mathematics and physics than medieval man could hope to know. The 21st Century is in many ways a historical anomaly. It is a time of continuous exponential growth in the human knowledge base. The last 30 years represents about .0006% of humankind's existence since the emergence of the Southern Ape Man, but it also represents a time of enormous discovery and invention. In this twinkling of time against the backdrop of cosmic time, humans have invented electronic computers, lasers, satellites, rockets, television, robots, artificial intelligence, genetic engineering, biochips, and a host of other "Telepower" tools with which to redefine our world and reshape the biosphere. Before this century the "Sky was the limit". Well, no more. Humans have gone to the moon and now aspire to travel to Mars to permanently colonize the moon and "Terra-form" Mars or other bodies for "natural" human habitation. Today the stars are the limit, and we are not sure what the limit will be tomorrow.

The aspiration of the human species at this stage of evolution is indeed great. Yet the problems of ozone depletion, of CO_2 and CH_4 build-up to create a "greenhouse effect," of oil-spill freeze in the polar ice caps altering the albedo (or reflectivity) of the ice surface all give us pause. Likewise we are concerned by massive social and political problems of crime, drugs, illiteracy, and the threat of nuclear war. One could well ask what is the future? Are we on the verge of a true global human breakthrough—a cosmic advance where humankind evolves to a higher level of intelligence and achievement? Or, will humans as they have so often in the past slip on the slippery slope of ignorance, avarice and jingoism that will pull us back from the potential which the 21st Century seems to offer? The stars and the quagmire both seem to be within our potential grasp.

It seems clearer than ever before that the human use of communications contains the key to our species' future. The linking of our opto-electronic technologies together in new and different ways is not only ironically the key to a new golden age but a high risk gamble as well. In a nutshell our new Telepower technologies can make us or break us. The Global Electronic Machine is where it all starts.

The Global Electronic Machine

The world's biggest machine is much bigger than a nuclear aircraft carrier, a C5A Cargo Jetliner or even a continuous process automobile manufacturing plant. The world's biggest machine has become so big that it is invisible. It contains hundreds of millions of tons of coaxial cable buried under ground and beneath the oceans.

It includes electronic switches and exchange equipment with enough gold and silver to fully stock a Tiffany's. Parts of the machine are invisible because they are flying in space—orbiting in circles a tenth of the way out toward the moon. Over a hundred of these space communications devices are relaying billions of messages around and across the earth every year. The machine parts are now so numerous no one can even count them. Billions of telephones, television sets, facsimile devices, telexes, computers, and radios are linked to this massive network. Each year it grows by leaps and bounds as fiber optic cables, new electronic switches and new "ports" are added to accommodate more users around the world.

The Global Electronic Village is becoming a true reality. Soon people in remote Tuvalu and Niue in the South Pacific will be able to call Chicago and Toulouse or Chiang Mai, Thailand. In the last twenty years since the moon landing the number of people able to see global television events has expanded six fold from 500 million to 3.0 billion people. Our ability to share information and knowledge is today creating global trade and culture. Tomorrow it will begin to form a global brain—a global consciousness.

The power of the global electronic machine is already awesome. Just one satellite, the INTELSAT VI to be specific, can send 200 simultaneous television channels, enough to send all episodes of *Dallas* and *Dynasty* ever made all at once. It could also transmit about 1000 three-hundred-page books in the span of one second. In short, this rather remarkable trillion dollar machine is very fast and very smart. Normal people, even exceptionally bright people, have ever increasing problems of keeping up with our electronic servants.

Perhaps just as important, as the global electronic machine has gotten smarter, faster, and more universal, it has also gotten cheaper. Today we are well on the way to being able to operate a computer, a robotic device and a digital communications line of 64 kilobits per second on the order of $5 an hour! These costs are at least three times less than human labor costs, certainly for Tokyo, New York, London or Paris. Less than a decade ago, the differential was five times, but then it was humans who were cheap and the electronic machines which were so very expensive.

This fundamental shift in human versus machine labor economics is remarkable. It is restructuring our world as we know it, yet the nature of this changeover has largely gone unnoted and unreported. Some day this "incredible story" will be noted by the *Financial Times*, *The New York Times*, *The Economist* or *Le Monde*, and then perhaps legislators, Prime Ministers, even Presidents will understand that some serious change is afoot. Anyway in the meantime, there is the advantage of being among the cognoscenti who were among the first to know about the World of Future Talk.

The World of Future Talk

What will the world be like in the 21st Century? In capsule fashion, it will be more global with new political coalitions. The Pacific Ocean rim will become the new focus of global political and economic power. Further the nature of work and economic activity will be greatly changed. New concepts such as Telecolonies, Electronic Immigrants, the 168-hour work week, and Telecities will emerge. High technology consolidation will continue and new Tele-Computer-Energetics enterprises will reshape the corporate balance of power as the force of Anti-Trust wanes in the US and overseas.

The many dimensions of Telepower will bring us the good and the bad. On the debit side it will bring us Tele-war and techno-terrorist techniques. It will also bring technological unemployment and information overload. Yet it will bring hope for high quality schooling, nutritional advice and medical services through Tele-Education and Tele-Health techniques. Well into the 21st Century there can even be hope for the building of a true global consciousness, ultimately the emergence of a "global brain". When this truly happens, the era of Future Talk will begin to unfold. Eventually we may even see the evolution of a new human species. No one today can say what might define the capabilities and intelligence of this new being, but half in jest and half in seriousness it has been suggested that the appropriate name for this "plugged-in" creature would be simply *Homo Electronicus*.

Globalism

Examples of the electronic village are today everywhere. Global television coverage of the 1988 Summer and Winter Olympics reached an estimated global audience of 3 billion or 60% of the world. Close to 100 trillion dollars in electronic fund transfers occur via satellite or cable connection each year. Everything from weather forecasting and scientific data exchange to commodity trading, airline reservations, and global marketing are tied to the global electronic machine. Most machine industries are discovering they can exist only in a global market. Their global competitors can outcompete them if they scale their production to local markets only. As the service industries become more and more predominant the imperative to operate on a global scale becomes even more clearcut regardless of whether one is in retailing, banking, trading, transportation, or management consulting. Low cost communications systems, economies of scale, global marketing systems, deregulation, and corporate consolidation and merger all serve to make the Age of Future Talk the Age of Globalism.

The Age of the Pacific

Just over a century ago US Secretary of State John Hay said rather prophetically: "The Mediterranean is the ocean of the past, the

Atlantic is the ocean of the present and the Pacific is the ocean of the future." The prophecy has been realized. When one combines the Gross National Products of the US, Japan, Canada, and the Newly Industrialized Countries (NICs) of the Asia/Pacific region, the total nearly doubles that of Europe. Based on current trading patterns, strong industrial R&D programs, high technology patents, and entrepreneurial attitudes, it seems not unreasonable to see the emergence of a new super alliance with Japan, Canada and the US at its core. This new JA-CAN-US alliance would draw in the so-called Gang of Four, namely Hong Kong, the Republic of Korea, Singapore and Taiwan. Other countries of the ASEAN group such as the Philippines, Indonesia, Malaysia and Thailand could also join in, as well as Australia, New Zealand or even China or India. The key, however, would be the JACANUS high-technology triad and a Pacific-facing United States and Canada.

By the mid 21st Century, it seems most likely that virtually all aspects of Telepower leadership will reside with this powerful new grouping whether it be in main frame computers, superconductivity, nuclear fusion, fiber optic communications, intelligent satellites with on-board processing, artificial intelligence, robotics, space planes, or advanced space projects. Based on current trends, perhaps 60% of the world's R&D and close to 75% of advanced technology patents may be consolidated within the JACANUS alliance. Although there are many possible outcomes, if the US and the other countries of the Pacific Rim decided to create and encourage a coordinated plan of economic and technical cooperation and development, the result would be the greatest possible economic powerhouse the world has ever seen. Our world would be redefined as dramatically as it was in the time of Columbus.

The New Telepower Economy

The global electronic machine cannot help but redefine work and reshape both the US and the international economy. One of the ways already developing is the 168-hour work week. You may say the 35 to 40 hour work week is bad enough, and if the Koreans can stand to work 54 hours a week (the world's highest average work week) this is already pushing things too far. The trouble is that with a global society the movement of the sun and of our economy just never stops. Airline booking systems, global electronic fund transfer systems, satellite system control systems, and hundreds of computer systems, robotic manufacturing units, and power and telecommunications networks run day and night, seven days a week, 365 days a year. Our electronic help doesn't need to eat or sleep and usually is most productive if left running every hour of the week—namely 168 hours. This means more shift work, more automation, and even more Tele-robotics so that many plants and facilities can be monitored and controlled from remote locations.

The extent to which work of all types can be automated will undoubtedly lead to a reduction in jobs. Between now and the 21st Century the biggest impact will clearly be in manufacturing, and laid-off workers will be largely re-trained for new jobs in the service industries. The only trouble is that many of these new service jobs will not be challenging, high-tech occupations but low paying activities such as fast food work, retail clerking or become a teaching or nursing aide, etc. More significantly, economic studies by M.I.T. economist, Dr. Charles Jonescher, projects that artificial intelligence and expert systems will be replacing highly skilled service jobs by around 2005. Instead of automating manufacturing jobs on the assembly line we will soon be talking about replacing medical diagnosers, educators, market researchers, design engineers, and a host of occupations which a decade ago seemed irreplaceable by "machine skills". It is clear that technological unemployment as well as technological underemployment* is likely to be a very big problem in the future.

Retraining and creation of new and meaningful jobs is the key. Unfortunately today's educational and training systems are not geared to the coming change. In most countries of the OECD, educational and training systems are now designed for about 3% to 4% of the total population, but it is likely that in coming years some 10% to 20% of the population will need some degree of mid-career educational assistance. The *Eurofutures* study which projected these needs to become serious in the next ten years also noted that the problem is already beginning to be encountered in parts of southern Europe. Where technological unemployment is occurring, there is particular pressure applied to women and minorities to surrender their jobs first.

The new Telepower technologies will affect more than just jobs. The scope, structure, and marketing strategies of high-technology corporations will also be greatly affected. It seems likely, based on current trends, that we will see the leveraged consolidation of many key technologies, particularly computers, robotics, artificial intelligence, telecommunications, advanced transportation, aerospace, and advanced energy systems. This leveraged combination of converging technologies is called, for a lack of a better name, Tele-Computer-Energetics. The parallels in technology that result from computer chips, solar cells, digital telecommunications techniques, and advanced software development creates a powerful incentive to create economies of scale, density, technology and scope in these increasingly interrelated fields. If you look at such diverse corporations as Mitsubishi, Toyota, TRW, General Motors, IBM, and ARCO one finds clear signs of Tele-Computer-Energetics in the making. General Motors with the acquisition of EDS, Hughes Aircraft and several other smaller robotics and software firms is not in a strong technology position with regard to computers, telecommunications, aerospace, robotics, and advanced energy and transportation systems. Although the silicon chip is the clearest connecting link in the move toward Tele-Computer-Energetics, it is likely that artificial intelligence will become the true "brain" from which all the other activities will derive in the 21st Century.

The key element in charting corporate and economic activity in the Age of Future Talk is that no important trend can or will be "local". Tele-Computer-Energetics, technological unemployment, and the 168-hour work week will be experienced around the world. The global electronic machine will serve to make these changes happen more quickly as the constraints of time are overcome. One trend will in fact happen as a direct result of the global machine. This is the creation of a new type of global worker—the "electronic immigrant".

This new worker will tele-commute to work over great distances, perhaps even many thousands of miles. People in "cheap labor markets" in Jamaica, Barbados, the Philippines, India and China will be recruited and trained to perform a variety of services that can be performed remotely, such as computer programming, word processing, inventory control and management or telephone sales. Since the cost of labor for services in Tokyo, New York, Toronto or Frankfurt is in the $15 to $25 per hour range, it is possible to recruit "electronic immigrants," train them, and pay $5 an hour for an international telephone line and still be well under the going market rate.

The ability to recruit and electronically import cheap professional services into the US, Japan and Europe could become the top international trade issue of the 21st Century. This should not be considered a theoretical possibility but an emerging Telepower reality. Several years ago American Airlines shifted its inventory control network from Tulsa, Oklahoma to Barbados. Local workers were easily recruited at less than half the previous US based wages, and the telephone charges were only marginally more. Many software programs to support Japanese industry are now being performed under contract in Korea, the Philippines, and elsewhere in the Southeast Asia region.

There is the issue that even goes beyond the trade and job-impact nature of "electronic immigrants," and that is the political impact. If a high percentage of all high paying jobs in a developing country are in fact electronically transported from say Jamaica to the United States, there could come a time where the economic ties begin to dictate political relationships. This is to suggest that if the "electronic immigrant" trend continues unchecked this could ultimately result in the creation of "Telecolonies" where true economic and political control flows from an overseas capital.

Tele-Education and Tele-Health

One might start to conclude that advanced Telepower technology only produces negative or hazardous results. This is certainly not the case. Without new advanced electronic services our lives could in fact be far worse and many important social problems would only deteriorate. Most people given a thoughtful choice would not go back to serfdom, the plague, starvation and worse. One of the areas where Telepower is helping to create a more beneficial world of Future Talk is that of Tele-Education as well as that of the closely related fields of Tele-Health and Tele-Medicine.

Many educational systems around the world are extremely dependent on advanced electronic technologies. One of these, rather surprisingly, is China. Here over one million students receive more than 150 hours of educational programming per month live via satellite from Beijing. This programming is locally produced by the Ministry of Education and by Central China TV. Eventually it is planned to train all 10 million Chinese teachers through expansion of their Tele-Education system started under Project Share only three years ago! Telepower can be incredibly swift even in very difficult areas like education.

In less ambitious ways Tele-Education projects that use only telephone, audioconferencing, facsimile, database sharing and slow-scan videoconferencing can accomplish much as has been shown by the University of the South Pacific and the University of the West Indies. They have demonstrated how to pool their educational resources and extension services over areas of millions of square miles and do so at a very modest cost. Progress in this field, of course, goes well beyond satellite Tele-Education. Computers have assumed a variety of teaching/training roles ranging from rote drills to advanced concepts and problem solving activities.

In developing countries where median ages are often 17 to 19, the school age population is larger than the available supply of trained teachers. Likewise in these countries the children far outnumber the adult workforce, which strains the ability of such societies to support education, health or other basic social services. It may well be that Tele-Education and Tele-Health may be the only hope for breaking the "vicious cycles" that go with exploring population, illiteracy, malnutrition, and lack of jobs. Scores of "real, live tests" carried out with Project Share have shown that these techniques can work in the developing world.

In the developed world of the OECD, millions of students and workers are also receiving training and formal education through such diverse techniques as computer assisted training, satellite Tele-Education, and even interactive video-disc. The level of sophistication is constantly rising. For instance, David Hon, President of IXXION, has just developed a teaching system involving a micro-computer, robotic sensors, and video-disc technologies that teach doctors how to perform orthoscopic surgery on joints.

Overall, Telepower techniques in education, health and medicine are very powerful and becoming more so. They are ideal for providing critical social services to rural and remote areas and can provide convenience and lower costs even in an urban environment. Unlike many other aspects of Telepower which frequently tend to concentrate and centralize power, these techniques can decentralize and distribute power. In some ways Telepower could even help democratize political practices in modern society.

The Global Brain

When Arthur C. Clarke was visiting friends in Washington, DC, as part of the World Communications Year celebrations a few years ago, he was asked what is the greatest invention of the 20th Century. As would be expected, Arthur Clarke gave the unexpected answer. "The greatest invention of the 20th Century," he replied, "is only starting to be created, but it will eventually change the course of history in important and unexpected ways." To end the riddle, Clarke explained that he meant, of course, Artificial Intelligence. To Arthur Clarke, artificial intelligence means far more than today's expert systems. It implies a whole new type of "machine" that "thinks" plans and then ultimately "recreates itself in improved form." This type of machine even has a name, the Von Neumann machine, in honor of the great mathematician and inventor of cybernetics and game theory. When we eventually invent such a "Von Neumann" machine, it will mark the start of an artificial and rapidly accelerating evolutionary path. Some believe that the greatest challenge of the 21st Century for humankind will be to keep up with machine-based evolution. It seems a remote issue today, but then the dinosaurs did not likely foresee their ultimate obsolescence either.

One thing is clear. Telepower technologies are doing more than creating a global economy or generating new Telecolonies to facilitate the electronic flow of work and labor into new markets. Likewise the trend is more than just speeded-up living and work patterns and phenomena like the 168-hour work week. Certainly Telepower implies good and bad, strength and weakness. Positive patterns such as electronic education, Tele-Health, Tele-commuting to convenient neighborhood work centers are likely to be offset by "negatives," such as loss of privacy, technological unemployment, information overload, and techno-terrorism. In short, it is of some importance to recognize and differentiate the positive from negative and to build on the desirable aspects and reduce or eliminate the undesirable.

With Telepower one should maintain a long term view, since we are ultimately creating not just a new technology but in effect designing a new fate for our species. We humans are beginning to evolve in new ways. Each time we extend our global electronic machine so that everyone is more linked to everyone else, we become different. Each time we invent a higher level of artificial intelligence, our own intelligence is challenged in new and different ways. As we create new and more intricate "smart" environments we are altering our future.

Biological evolution will no longer be in command as the forces of Telepower reign supreme. As radical as it may seem, Homo Sapiens may be replaced as the superior thinking being on planet Earth during the course of the 21st Century. What characteristics or skills the new species will possess is hard to say. The most likely key difference will be a brain of higher memory capacity, faster thinking skills, and improved communications skills with others. The true mystery is whether this new "species" will be derived from humans, from machines, or both. What will this interlinked species that communicates directly with all other beings be called? Perhaps it will be dubbed *Homo Electronicus*. Perhaps it will indeed mark the beginning of an interlocked consciousness that can be called quite simply—the Global Brain.

Conclusions

The new Age of Future Talk is coming with the 21st Century. It represents a time of incredible change as Telepower technology brings us super speed activity and a new type of time called "future compression." These are the areas of most significant change:

• *Globalism* - Increasingly there will be a global economy and a global market where remoteness largely disappears. Everyone, even in Burkina Faso and Borneo, will "plug-in" to the global electronic machine.

• *Pacific Dominance* - We will see a world where the Pacific Ocean rim countries take command. A curious new "coalition" called JA-CAN-US (Japan/Canada/US) will give a new meaning to Telepower and technological predominance of the world economy.

• *A Revolution at Work* - Both labor and patterns of work face a period of great turmoil. Changes to be faced include: perennial and life-long job retraining, technological unemployment, Telepower backlash aimed at women and minorities, 168-hour work week, Tele-commuting to work, and "electronic immigrants" from overseas territories competing for local service jobs.

• *Concerns about the Dark Side of Telepower* - The Age of Future Talk relates to a breakthrough in knowledge and capability for humankind, but the journey to this new frontier will be difficult, challenging and often dangerous. The abuse of Telepower is perhaps the greatest of dangers to be faced. The challenges posed by the dark side of Telepower include: invasion of privacy, information overload and super speed living, technology based terrorism, super lethal Tele-war, and electronic totalitarianism. Averting these misuses of Telepower must be a top priority if we are to achieve an enlightened and productive Age of Future Talk.

• *New Social Benefits of Telepower* - With the dark side is also the bright side of Telepower in such new guises as Tele-Education, new emergency and disaster warning and relief systems, remote health and medical services, etc.

• *The Global/Cosmic Brain* - The ultimate step toward the Age of Future Talk involves humankind's evolution to become a new, more intelligent, civilized and perhaps even wiser species—a species with more global consciousness, more emphatic links to the rest of the species, and a faster brain. This new species, perhaps arising from "artificial evolution" could be called *"Homo Electronicus"*. The name of course is not important. The purpose and mission of this species will be of great consequence, however, since this new species will be well adapted to a new role. This new being, if it can escape self destruction will undoubtedly colonize the Solar System and then, perhaps using the power of Von Neumann machines, seek over tens of thousands of years to reach out and perhaps provide order to the Galaxy. When this has been done and intelligent species in other star systems are in regular communications with planet Earth, then and only then, we will have truly reached the time of Future Talk.

*Technological underemployment results when a job is "deskilled" as a result of at least partial automation. Check-out clerks today largely need ears to hear 'beeps' of the machine readers of the Universal Product Code. Word processors with "spell check" no longer need to know how to spell. Thus many jobs don't disappear—they just become progressively deskilled.

THE GLOBAL CHALLENGE: CHANGING HABITS OR CHANGING CLIMATES

by

Claudine Schneider

The decade of the eighties has not been a good one for humanity. There are more malnourished people in the world today than ever before in the history of humankind. Famine and hunger-related diseases continue to claim the lives of over 50,000 individuals each and every day. Quality of life, as measured in infant mortality levels, lifespan, and literacy rates, remains desperately low for more than half of humanity. The 1980s is also witnessing the addition of nearly one billion individuals to the world's population, with an additional 90 million yearly births edging more and more developing countries beyond their carrying capacity.

The arms race has diverted over $6 trillion since 1980 from investments that could have spurred economic productivity and dramatically raised people's standard of living. For the past half decade, humans have lived with the frightening recognition that the release of just a few percent of the world's nuclear arsenal would trigger a global "nuclear winter," leaving surviving humans in stone age conditions. Biologists warn of another kind of nuclear winter slowly unfolding: the extinction of animal and plant species at a staggering rate not experienced since the disappearance of dinosaurs 60 million years ago.

The decade has become synonymous with debt and deficits. Growth and prosperity have receded from the economic horizons of most developing countries, as interest payments routinely surpass new credit levels. The United States entered the decade as a creditor nation with a trade surplus, went on an unprecedented spending spree, and closes the decade as the world's largest debtor nation with multi-hundred billion dollar budget and trade deficits.

Recent discovery of a Texas-size hole in the Antarctic's stratospheric ozone layer gives new urgency to the need to phase out ozone-destroying chlorofluorocarbons (CFCs). The ozone layer above the Antarctic has declined by 50 percent. North America has experienced a three percent decrease to date—triple the level predicted by scientific models. Scientists estimate that each percent decline in the ozone layer leads to a two percent increase in ultraviolet radiation, triggering a five percent increase in skin cancers.

Claudine Schneider *is a member of the US House of Representatives. She represents the second district of Rhode Island.*

Finally, this decade has experienced more years of record heat than any other decade over the past century. This trend conforms to what scientists anticipate occurring, given the rising atmospheric levels of CFCs, carbon-dioxide (CO_2), nitrous oxide, methane, and other infrared-trapping "greenhouse" gas emissions.

Nineteen Hundred and Eighty-Eight was not only one of the hottest years in recorded weather history, but the bearer of an unusual number of disasters. Drought withered away the crops and economic livelihoods of vast numbers of American farms, causing multi-billion dollar losses and farm bankruptcies before it ended. Raging forest fires spread uncontrollably through millions of acres of dry commercial timber and pristine wilderness areas. Hurricanes Gilbert and Helene ravaged the Caribbean and southeastern US shores, destroying property and leaving many homeless. A record heat wave gripped the nation and intensified the unhealthy effects of urban pollution. And the tragic flooding of Bangladesh left death, disease and starvation in its wake.

Scientists lack adequate data to say whether these costly incidents were caused by the global warming trend. But the scientific community is united in warning us that in the future such disasters will occur with increasing frequency and severity if the rise in greenhouse gas emissions goes unchecked. The National Academy of Sciences (NAS), the World Meteorological Organization (WMO), the United Nations Environment Program (UNEP), and the International Council of Scientific Unions (ICSU) are in agreement that a doubling of CO_2 concentrations over preindustrial levels would cause global temperatures to rise three to nine degrees Fahrenheit (1.5 to 4.5 degrees Centigrade). This could occur within the lifespan of middle-aged adults.

A recent report prepared for Congress by the Environmental Protection Agency (EPA) finds a rash of effects on the United States that may result from global climate change. Sea level rise would destroy one-fourth to two-thirds of coastal wetlands, jeopardizing US shellfish and finfish supplies. Significant dieback of southern forests could occur, which currently supply about half of the nation's softwood and hardwood timber.

An estimated $100 billion will have to be spent on sea walls and coast line protection against rising sea levels. This will still not prevent the loss of some 7000 square miles of shoreline. Farming would shift northward, as would agricultural pests and pathogens (many resistant to current pesticides) as temperatures and droughts increase. Some regions could suffer crop losses of up to 80 percent. Heat waves will drive up electricity demand, eventually leading to the need for upwards of 400,000 Megawatts of extra power plants at a cost of $325 billion. By 2055, utility bills could climb $30 to $75 billion per year beyond normal.

Global temperature increases would speed the reaction rates

among chemicals in the atmosphere and prolong their consequences as a result of a longer summer season. This will lead to
increased smog in many urban areas. According to the EPA study,
an area like the San Francisco Bay would experience a 20 percent
increase in ozone concentrations and a doubling of days exceeding
air quality standards, even if emissions did not increase from present levels.

The EPA did not study all possible consequences, and some
scientists believe that as global climate models become more sophisticated we are likely to discover more changes, including abrupt
ones. This was the message delivered by a number of prominent
ecologists and biologists at a recent World Wildlife Fund (WWF)
sponsored conference, "Global Warming Consequences on Biological Diversity." Profound and widespread biological disruption is
likely to occur in the coming decades.

Humans are in the process of changing the earth's atmosphere
10 to 40 times faster than natural climate changes have occurred
in the past, noted Dr. Stephen Schneider of the National Center
for Atmospheric Research. The annual rate of change is about 4
degrees F. in 1,000 years, while the forcing effect of rising
greenhouse gases could warm the global climate 4 to 9 degrees F.
in a century.

"Rapid change is the enemy of life," Dr. George Woodwell, director of the Woods Hole Research Center, pointed out. If the warming
is not stopped, the changes will be "open-ended, rapid and accelerating." Species extinction will be accelerated. Trees, for example, can only migrate tens of miles per century, whereas the changing climate will force their survival range hundreds of miles north-
ward. Even mobile species capable of shifting quickly are likely to
be blocked by cities and other impenetrable man-made barriers.

In worst case scenarios, where the polar ice caps melt and dramatically raise sea level, the lives and economic livelihoods of that
third of humanity residing near coastal areas would be jeopardized.
Some areas, like the Maldive Islands, could be entirely submerged
by the advancing sea.

This grim outlook on climate, combined with the seemingly
intractable problems noted at the outset of this article, have led
some individuals to resign themselves to a strategy of adaptation.
The harsh reality, it is argued, is that the world population will be
two to three times larger by the time it stabilizes in the next century.
If Gross World Product steadily climbs so as to provide everyone
with the same level of goods and services already achieved by
industrialized nations, then greenhouse gases will rise precipit-
ously. Some have suggested that adaptation will actually be promoted by northern tier countries like the Soviet Union, which stand
to profit from warmer climates.

Clearly some adaptation will be necessary. Industrial activity over the past century has already added hundreds of billions of tons of greenhouse gases into the atmosphere. More than five billion tons of carbon are currently being added each year. Even if there was a global moratorium on greenhouse gas emissions that went into effect tomorrow, it would take a century or more for the current volume of gases in the atmosphere to decline to safer levels. According to some estimates, the planet already faces a 2 to 4 degree F. warming.

Unfortunately, adaptation too readily lends itself to the crisis management mentality that pervades most policymaking. "Let's just wait and see what happens, then decide what to do," is an all-too-often heard refrain, as evidenced by the acid rain problem that has seen a decade of debate in Congress but no action.

A far preferable approach, one pioneered in this country by our founding statesman, Benjamin Franklin, is preventive management. Action is guided, in this case, by the familiar common sense maxim, "an ounce of prevention is worth a pound of cure." The WMO, UNEP, and ICSU all strongly advocate this position, jointly calling on all governments to take the necessary steps to prevent a worsening of the global warming trend. Minimum reductions of at least 20 percent from current CO_2 levels within the next 15 years was the recommendation issued at the 1988 Toronto World Conference on the Changing Atmosphere.

Considerable scientific uncertainty remains on a host of issues regarding the interaction of the geopshere and biosphere with rising greenhouse gases. For example, no one knows the capacity of the ocean to absorb rising levels of carbon-dioxide. A preventive strategy argued by a number of scientists is to seek 50 percent reductions in CO_2 emissions within the next several decades, along with a phaseout of the ozone-depleting chlorofluorocarbons. The Meteorological Society and the Physical Society of West Germany go much further. Their resolutions call for undertaking policy measures adequate to preventing the global temperature from rising more than 2 degrees Centigrade over the next 100 years.

Over the past two years, a series of congressional hearings have focused on the various preventive management options available for reducing greenhouse gas emissions. It is quite apparent, particularly in the case of CO_2 which accounts for nearly half of all greenhouse gases, that options can vary in cost by ten-fold or more. This makes it imperative that strategies and actions devised by governments in formulating global warming prevention policies avoid imposing needless and wasteful expenditures on taxpayers, ratepayers, and stockholders.

Indeed, given the range of severe global problems noted above, and the tight financial times in which we find ourselves, it is critical that we rank the options for cutting carbon emissions and other greenhouse gases in a cost-effective order. Clearly, the challenge before us is to identify and select the available choices that will spur economic prosperity without generating dangerous levels of greenhouse gases.

Ideally, each choice we make, each step we take, should spur multiple benefits that simultaneously alleviate or resolve the manifold problems noted above. Dr. Stephen Schneider calls this the "tie-in" strategy: take those actions that reduce greenhouse gases, and also tie-in with solving other problems.

Milking the Cash Cow

Fortunately, the scientific and engineering communities unwittingly took up this challenge in the wake of the 1973 Arab oil embargo and OPEC price hikes. Clearly the success story of the past 15 years has been the emergence of energy efficient technologies. The market has witnessed a steady flow of technical advancements for delivering energy services to buildings, factories, appliances, and vehicles at substantially lower cost and with significantly fewer pollutants.

Using energy more efficiently already has garnered a number of benefits. The United States now requires nearly one-third less energy to produce a dollar of Gross National Product. Carbon emissions are 40 percent lower than they otherwise would have been in the absence of efficiency improvements. Likewise, the nation's foreign oil imports are two-thirds lower than they would have been, reducing the trade deficit by more than $50 billion per year. The efficiency improvements worldwide have created a global oil glut, which has helped collapse world oil prices, reduce OPEC's power, and ease energy-fanned inflation rates. Moreover, these gains were achieved while saving Americans a whopping $160 billion per year on their energy bills.

Best of all, the pace of technological advancements shows no signs of abating. As one energy pundit has quipped, energy efficiency is America's, and world's, cash cow. We need to keep on milking it. If we do, we should be able to both cut greenhouse gases and energy bills for decades to come.

This is one of the conclusions put forward in *Energy for a Sustainable World*, a recently completed global energy study by the international team of Jose Goldemberg (Brazil), Thomas Johannson (Sweden), Amulya Reddy (India), and Robert Williams (USA). Goldemberg et al. analyzed the potential role of cost-effective efficiency improvements in meeting global energy demand over the next half century.

In order to accommodate a doubling of the world population and a quadrupling of Gross World Product, most conventional energy scenarios foresee a two- to four-fold increase in energy consumption during this period, up from the current level of 10 TeraWatt-years per year (TW). Serious problems are likely to result from these "business-as-usual" scenarios. The implied supply requirements are enormous. The equivalent of an Alaskan pipeline would have to be brought online every one to two months. A 1000 MegaWatt (MW) coal power plant would be needed every 1.5 to 2 days. A 1000 MW nuclear reactor would be needed every 4 to 6 days.

The strain on uranium resources would require breeder reactors using weapons-grade plutonium recycled from spent nuclear fuels. An estimated 2 to 4 million kilograms of plutonium would make its way into commercial transit each year; enough material to annually produce between 400,000 and 700,000 atomic bombs.

Production of OPEC oil would be pushed to maximum capacity. Historically, oil price hikes have occurred when OPEC capacity has exceeded 80 percent.

Carbon emissions from combusted fossil fuels would triple to more than 15 billion tons per year. Atmospheric levels of greenhouse gases would be nearly twice preindustrial levels by the early part of the next century.

Just to finance this massive energy growth would require prodigious sums of capital. Developing countries will need to increase their export earnings by a staggering, if not unrealistic, 15 percent per year beyond inflation. Nor is there any guarantee that this energy development will help satisfy basic human needs, which is imperative if population stabilization and the halting of tropical deforestation are to occur.

This is a scenario of multiple problems. In sharp contrast, Goldemberg et al. show that maintaining a three percent per year rise in energy efficiency (the US has achieved close to this rate over the past decade, Japan in excess of four percent) would reap multiple benefits. Most notably, oil consumption declines, as does dependence on OPEC. Carbon emissions decline from *today's* level, instead of climbing 300 percent. Nuclear power plateaus at 460,000 MW, five to 10 times lower than conventional forecasts. At this level, no breeders or recycling of plutonium is necessary.

Energy savings continue rising until they surpass a staggering $500 billion per year. These savings, for comparison, are roughly equal to world health expenditures in 1986. Energy savings become a key source of capital formation for meeting basic human needs and for developing the industrial infrastructure necessary for sustaining economic growth.

Basic human needs are more likely to be satisfied by this end-use-oriented, least-cost energy strategy, than in the "trickle-down" energy approach which typically ignores addressing this problem. By meeting basic human needs, incomes are likely to rise, fertility rates fall, and population stabilization occur more rapidly. Goldemberg et al. believe this scenario could prevent an estimated 700 million births over the next 50 years.

The combined effects of widespread efficiency gains and population decline would greatly diminish the rate of tropical deforestation, species extinction, and environmental destruction.

Some Bright Ideas

Specific examples of energy efficiency are highly instructive. Consider lighting, which provides one of the most dramatic illustrations of what can be achieved through low-cost efficiency gains. Lighting in the United States, along with the associated air conditioning required to offset the heat generated from inefficient lights, consumes the equivalent of roughly half of all coal burned by electric utilities. The market now offers several dozen kinds of highly efficient lighting products. It's been estimated that the full use of these various products could deliver the same lighting services, while reducing electrical consumption by more than 80 percent. This would save consumers over $25 billion per year, and prevent the combustion of tens to hundreds of millions of tons of coal per year.

Take the ubiquitous incandescent light bulb, a revolutionary advancement from the humble candle, which is itself succumbing to compact fluorescent lamps made with solid-state electronic chips and space-age materials.

Compact lamps come in various wattages, each displacing a light bulb consuming four or more times as much electricity to deliver similar levels of light. The compacts last 10 times longer (typically 10,000 hours vs. 1000). Each lamp saves a commercial building over $50 in electricity costs, demand charges, replacement bulbs, and labor savings in changing bulbs as frequently. The typical 15-watt compact also prevents the combustion of 400 pounds of carbon and 25 pounds of sulphur-dioxide (SO_2), an acid rain pollutant.

If one compact sounds impressive, consider the assembly line. Manufacturers like Sylvania, Osram (Siemens), General Electric, Phillips, and Panasonic each produce several million compacts per year. The combined output of two of these assembly lines would rank them as a top 50 coal producer in the United States. There is one essential difference: with the compact lamps consumers reap several hundred million dollars in savings, while three million tons of coal go uncombusted.

The 3M Company and other businesses have come up with another lighting advancement known as the "imaging specular reflector." This is a fancy word for creating a mirror-like surface that bounces more light out of fluorescent lighting fixtures. The shiny material makes two tubular lamps appear like four lamps, enabling office buildings to de-lamp half the tubes.

High-technology advancements in solid-state electronics are also revolutionizing lighting ballast technology. A ballast is a device necessary to start and maintain operation of fluorescent lamps. The electronic versions, which are replacing the less efficient electromagnetic types, have been shown to save electricity in a dozen different ways, including dimming lamps when daylight is available. According to an estimate by Amory Lovins and his associates at the Rocky Mountain Institute, full replacement of US ballasts with continuously dimmable electronic ballasts would save the output of 60,000 MW. That's equal to about 30 percent of the nation's current coal-fired electrical generation.

Architects are using dimmable electronic ballasts and photosensing systems to take advantage of skylight to obtain one-fourth or more of a building's daytime lighting needs. The Albany County Airport in Colonie, New York, is a good example. It gets 40% of the lighting and 20% of the heating from the skylit solar court. Southern California Edison, one of the nation's largest electric utilities, has helped scores of its customers implement daylighting designs, because it's cheaper than building new power plants. For example, the Mattel Toy Company warehouse and distribution centers totalling over one million square feet have not turned on their lights during daylight hours since installing skylights.

Windows of Opportunity

Windows offer another golden opportunity. The windows in American buildings are notoriously leaky, losing nearly the equivalent output of an Alaskan pipeline (1.8 million barrels of oil per day). However, as a result of a highly successful joint federal-private research and development effort begun in the 1970s, the market now offers super-efficient windows that are approaching the heat-retaining ability of insulated walls.

The windows are constructed with materials that let the light shine through, but block the infrared heat from passing through. The windows can be used to trap the heat inside the building in cold climates, or keep it from entering the building in hot climates. Looming on the horizon is even more sophisticated, "electrochromic" glass, that will regulate the entrance or exit of heat through the window. Within the next several decades windows will be acting as renewable energy collection devices. They will go from consuming an Alaskan pipeline to "producing" one, saving consumers several billion dollars per year on energy bills, and preventing the combustion of tens of millions of tons of carbon per year.

Cooling Food and the Global Greenhouse

Food-cooling consumes nearly one-fourth of US residential electricity—more than lighting and cooking combined. The refrigerator is another energy hog. The average US model consumes two to ten times more electricity than highly efficient models. It burns its volume in coal each year, while an efficient model reduces that volume to a vegetable bin's worth. Nationwide, refrigerators require the output of 25,000 megawatts. By replacing the current US stock with efficient models we could reduce the equivalent of seven to 13 percent of current coal fired electricity, preventing the combustion of between 30 and 60 million tons of coal per year.

Manufacturers like Whirlpool, Amana, and General Electric currently produce models that require half the electrical consumption of similar models, with the extra costs of the efficiency improvements paying back within several years from reduced utility bills. The return on investment is superior to after-tax returns on passbook savings accounts or stocks and bonds.

The Sunfrost refrigerator, marketed out of Northern California, is a cutting edge design. It consumes up to 90 percent less electricity than comparably sized models. Currently, it is marketed exclusively to rural households installing photovoltaic power systems. The refrigerator costs several times more than inefficient models, because it is hand-made, but it saves rural households $10,000 to $20,000 on photovoltaic arrays. When mass manufactured it is expected to cost no more than inefficient models.

All-Electric Efficient Homes With 80% Less Electricity

Technological advances have made it possible for virtually every energy-consuming device to produce more work and services with far less energy input and pollution output. For example, it's possible to operate an all-electric home with all modern conveniences using 80% less electricity, even in a highly efficient country like Sweden.

Fuel Efficient Vehicles

The US transportation sector consumes over 5 billion barrels of oil per year, nearly two-thirds of all oil used in the nation. Transportation is also responsible for one-third of the nation's carbon-dioxide emissions, as well as a significant fraction of other airborne pollutants that directly or indirectly worsen not only the global climate, but deteriorate local and regional air quality and public health.

Tremendous energy efficiency advances have been made to cars, trucks, buses, aircraft and trains in recent years, and many more opportunities remain available. Improving the efficiency of the all-pervasive car is imperative for reducing greenhouse gases, acid rain pollutants, and urban smog. America's 150 million light cars and trucks (constituting more than a third of world vehicles) each annually combust their weight in carbon.

An estimated 15 billion barrels of oil could be saved over the next 3 decades by gradually increasing the US vehicle fuel economy over the next decade. The national fuel standard would have to climb from the current level of 27 miles per gallon (mpg) to 45 mpg for cars, and from 20 mpg to 30 mpg for light trucks. An additional 7 billion barrels could be saved by steadily increasing the fuel economy standard through 2008 to 60 mpg and 45 mpg, respectively, for cars and light trucks. These modest improvements exceed the combined oil resources that could be extracted from the United States' Pacific Coast, Alaska, the Arctic National Wildlife Refuge, and the Atlantic Coast.

These cost-effective efficiency gains would prevent the combustion of between 1 and 2 billion tons of carbon (4 to 8 billion tons of CO_2), including numerous atmospheric pollutants like carbon monoxide, volatile organic compounds, and nitrogen oxides. This one action would greatly mitigate urban smog, regional acid rain threats, and global greenhouse warming. Fuel economy gains would also improve the nation's energy and economic security by reducing the need for several hundred billion dollars of foreign oil imports.

Vehicle efficiency opportunities in the US comprise a veritable Saudi oil field. The cost of improvements are about the same as a car radio, and pay back within several years from gas savings. Technological advancements looming on the horizon are even more impressive. Half a dozen auto companies have built and operated prototypes that get between 60 mpg and 135 mpg.

Volvo's LCP 2000 gets a combined city/highway mileage of 75 mpg and exceeds EPA crash tests. Volvo estimates that it will cost no more to mass produce than current models. The Toyota AXV, a 4 to 5 passenger car, has attained 98 mpg in combined city/highway driving. This high mileage was achieved through the systematic application of presently available technologies, including: the extensive use of light weight plastics and aluminum; lower aerodynamic drag design; a direct-injection engine; and, a continuously variable transmission.

Most of these prototypes were built specifically for fuel economy. Emission levels, safety, acceleration, roominess or other criteria were sometimes, but not always addressed. Technologically, however, the future looks extremely promising for achieving both high fuel economy and the broad range of consumer amenities and environmental concerns. This should result from increasing reliance on crash-resistant, space age composite plastics, the use of more durable, stronger and lighter metal alloys that are corrosion-resistant, more widespread use of heat-resistant ceramic materials, plus the use of dozens of innovative engine, transmission, and energy storage options.

Industrial Savings

The US industrial sector contributes about one-third of the nation's carbon emissions. Not surprisingly, enormous energy savings remain to be achieved, whether in processing steel, glass, plastics, aluminum, chemicals, or in fabricating and finishing manufactured goods.

A ton of US steel, for example, requires 75% more energy than Swedish techniques, and over 200% more than the emerging technologies like Plasma-smelt. Cement production requires 80 percent more heat and 45 percent more electricity than the best available technologies. Studies indicate tremendous potential for a wide range of industries to use efficiency improvements to simultaneously cut energy and other raw material inputs, hazardous waste outputs, and capital and labor requirements.

Increasing US recycling efforts is also essential. Not only does it cut a burgeoning waste stream and the cost of safely disposing of this trash, but remanufacturing recyclable wastes into reusable materials requires only a fraction of the energy used in the original manufacture of a product. Over 90 percent less energy is required for remanufacturing aluminum and plastics; 50 to 70 percent less for steel; 30 to 50 percent less for paper; and upwards of 30 percent less for glass.

Here, as well, multiple benefits accrue. Recycled wastes reduce air and water pollution: 95 and 97 percent, respectively, for aluminum; 85 and 76 percent for steel; 74 and 35 percent for paper; and 20 percent for glass. According to recent estimates by resources analysts Neil Seldman and Howard Geller, the US could realize energy savings equal to more than one billion barrels of oil and $30 billion in cumulative savings, by increasing the nation's rate of recycling by 10 percent above the projected level for 1992, and 30% above the projected level for 2008.

Summary of Efficiency Potential

Energy use in the United States has been emphasized for good reason: with only five percent of the world's population, the US consumes one-fourth of total world energy use, emits 25 percent of world carbon dioxide and nitrogen oxides, and emits about 15 percent of the world's sulfur dioxide. Energy efficiency has been singled out for equally good reason: its multiple benefits create wealth while cutting resource inputs and waste outputs. The US is so inefficient that it currently produces half as much GNP per unit of energy use than countries like Japan and West Germany. Energy efficiency comes in 57 varieties, and when broadly applied in the United States will result in upwards of $200 billion per year in energy savings and dramatic reductions in greenhouse gases and other airborne pollutants.

What About Solar and Renewable Resources?

Efficiency investments not only save money and cut emission, but they buy time to expand the pool of cost-effective, ecologically sustainable renewable resources. The sun, wind, falling water, geothermal energy, and biomass accumulated through photosynthesis, have been harnessed to provide nearly 10 percent of total US energy needs. Many developing countries derive half or more of their energy needs from solar and renewable resources. The prospects are outstanding for expanding the use of renewables in industrialized nations, and greatly increasing the more efficient use of renewables in developing countries.

Renewables comprise one of America's largest energy resource reserves, five to ten times larger than coal. According to a 1985 study by the US Department of Energy, maintaining a stable-funded research and development program over the next 25 years would enable 85 quads to be economically extracted from this 80,000 resource reserve. This would be enough to provide over three-fourths of total US energy needs at that time. Unfortunately, the federal government has slashed the renewables R&D budget by 75 percent, and abandoned all leadership on developing renewable resources.

Renewable options range from elegantly simple designs like daylighting and landscaping, to complex high technologies like aircraft-derived gas turbines and amorphous silicon photovoltaic cells. Selective tree-plantings around buildings make an incredibly cheap, passive solar-cooling system. Scientists at Lawrence Berkeley Laboratory have calculated that widespread use of this practice could diminish the "heat island effect" suffered by many urban areas. The trees reduce the need for air conditioning, reduce consumers' energy bills, and reduce the combustion of fossil fuels.

Amorphous silicon (a-Si) solar cells remain one of the most exciting technological advancements of this century. Unknown to theoretical physicists before 1975, a-Si cell efficiency gains have steadily climbed, while the price of production has steadily fallen since Sanyo first started using them to power calculators. Solar cells are made from one of the earth's most abundant materials, sand. One ton of sand used to fabricate a-Si cells can eliminate the need for 500,000 tons of coal!

Scientists Joan Ogden and Robert Williams at the Princeton Center for Energy and Environmental Studies, have shown that a-Si cells could be used to electrolyze water into hydrogen fuels, at prices roughly competitive to coal- and natural gas-derived liquid fuels. With hydrogen, however, all greenhouse gases, acid rain pollutants, and urban smog pollutants are avoided. It will take a commitment by this nation to promote this benign fuel option, but it is feasible to begin phasing in hydrogen as a vehicular fuel within the decade. US companies like Chronar, Amoco's Solarex, and Arco Solar are engaged in a fierce competition with Japanese and West German firms to market this technology worldwide.

Air Force Technology to the Rescue

With little fanfare, the US Air Force has spent $5 billion on R&D over the past decade on highly efficient, durable gas turbine engines for aircraft developed by General Electric and Pratt-Whitney. Only recently has it been realized that the turbines would make excellent electrical generators. Studies show that slight modification would make these "intercooled, steam-injected gas turbines" (ISTIGs) 40% more efficient than current powerplants, and cost less to build and operate than new coal or nuclear plants, even if gas prices triple.

Relative to current coal, oil or gas fired power plants, the ISTIG technology produces fewer greenhouse gases, and acid rain and urban ozone pollutants. Equally important, this technology has an immediate export opportunity. A US Agency for International Development (AID) study found a ready market for these aircraft-derived turbines in the 70 countries with sugar processing factories.

Used to cogenerate steam and electricity, this technology could meet 100 percent of the factories' processing needs, while generating an additional 50,000 Megawatts into utility grids. That amount is equal to one-fourth of all electricity currently generated in these countries. Moreover, the sugar wastes and other renewable resources like tree crops, can be used as the fuel source. This would reap enormous capital and fuel savings over the energy alternatives, imported oil or coal. Unlike the fossil fuels, the biomass crops do not add to global carbon emissions.

These biomass-gasified, steam-injected gas turbines (BSTIGs) would result in several other benefits. Debt-ridden, developing countries could reduce the export earnings necessary to expand energy and industrial development. Reliance on sustainably harvested, renewable resources would also be an abundant source of indigenous jobs.

Developing Countries Total Efficiency Potential

What about the total energy needs of developing countries? A pervasive misconception is that efficiency is great for the industrialized nations, but cannot be expected to offer much to developing countries. It is argued that: 1) developing countries consume 10 times less energy per capita than developed countries, hence have few, if any, savings opportunities available; 2) where available, efficiency investments would cost a lot of money, something in short supply in these debt-strapped countries; and, 3) efficiency technologies are mainly available from industrialized nations, and importing them would only worsen already disastrous trade deficits.

According to the detailed global energy study by Goldemberg et al., quite the contrary is true. Because developing countries are just beginning to build their factories, buildings, transport systems, etc., they have an opportunity to install the most efficient devices. For example, buildings using half as much energy or less can be built at no extra first cost.

Many of the efficiency technologies cited above are suitable in many parts of the developing world, most notably in the inefficient tourist hotels, government buildings, and commercial high rises being constructed. Many of the technologies are also being manufactured in developing countries—compact lamps in Mexico, high efficiency air conditioners in Brazil, high efficiency vehicles in India.

Most importantly, efficiency investments are five to ten times cheaper than conventional energy supply options. Developing countries, even more so than industrialized nations, will have to pursue these low-cost opportunities in order to free-up capital for non-energy sector investments.

As Goldemberg et al. show, the bottom line is that developing countries could raise their standard of living to that of West Europe in the 1970s, *while keeping energy consumption at the very low current levels*. How is this possible?

Firewood Crisis and Deforestation Rates

In addition to relying on the most efficient technologies available, developing countries possess considerable scope for squeezing more work out of currently used renewable resource. Take the stone fire, still used by over one billion people. It is only five percent efficient, compared to industrialized stoves at 80 percent efficiency. This highly wasteful use of wood is a major source of deforestation. The long term goal is to transition people to high efficiency gas stoves. The immediate goal is to quadruple the efficiency of current wood stoves.

Stove models four times more efficient than current ones are available, constructed by local people out of local materials, that pay back the investment within several months. Multiple benefits can accrue, including: saving women and children several hours per day of wood gathering; greatly reducing respiratory illnesses as smoke emissions sharply decline; and, freeing up the biomass resources for more efficient uses, as in the gas turbines mentioned above.

The potential savings garnered from more efficient wood stoves is enormous. Allocating just $1 billion per year for 10 years, would provide enough funds for loans to over one billion rural poor to build and purchase these more efficient stoves. In the process, enough renewable resources would be freed up to generate 160,000 megawatts of power! This is least-cost at its very best.

In short, by developing policies that encourage the purchase of the most efficient energy-consuming devices available, it is possible for even the poorest nations to spur economic development without massive energy growth. Conventional energy projections of 1000 percent increases or more are simply unnecessary. Quite the contrary, hundreds of billions of dollars would be saved, which may be the only source of capital for meeting basic human needs and developing the industrial infrastructure necessary to maintain economic development in an ecologically sustainable manner.

Market Barriers and Imperfections

Although efficiency and renewables have impressive track records, and present compelling reasons for increasing their use, they continue to face formidable barriers. Markets are distorted by subsidies to both energy producers and consumers. For example, US federal energy subsidies amounted to $45 billion in 1984, with over 90 percent going to promote fossil and nuclear power. In many developing countries the government subsidizes 50 percent or more of the price of electricity, dramatically reducing the incentive to use energy more efficiently.

Due to these and other market distortions, we need new policies that encourage reliance on these new low-cost, low-risk technology options. Recently, I introduced the Global Warming Prevention Act, along with several dozen of my colleagues in the House and the Senate, it proposes several dozen key policy measures to get us on the right track. In general terms, these measures include: adoption by the federal and state governments of "least-cost energy planning" practices; elimination of most energy subsidies; inclusion of the social and environmental costs of energy use, the externalities, in the cost of energy (e.g., factor in costs caused by acid rain, global warming, nuclear proliferation); spur, through vigorous public and private leadership, research, development, and commercialization of energy efficiency and renewable resource technologies; pursue steady increases in the fuel economy of vehicles; and focus foreign assistance on least-cost energy planning efforts.

Other Essential Actions

While this article has concentrated on energy policy, energy only comprises half to two-thirds of the global warming problem. Deforestation the size of Pennsylvania every year contributes an estimated 20 percent to greenhouse gas increases. Methane from expanding agriculture and livestock production, termites and wetlands, also contributes to a substantial degree to rising greenhouse gas emissions. And, of course, CFCs and other halocarbons are playing the dual role of destroying stratospheric ozone and heating up the atmosphere. Each of these areas will require preventive measures to slow or reduce the emissions, without curtailing basic human needs. My legislation proposes policy measures to address each of these problem areas. For example, it calls for the rapid phaseout of CFCs, which appears to be gaining international support.

Pursuing a global least-cost energy strategy will clearly, and unequivocally, gain us the dollars and buy us the time to tackle these other, less studied, and potentially more intractable areas of economic activity releasing enormous levels of greenhouse gases. Everything will have to be tried, from more aggressive land tenure reform and preserving tropical forests through debt swaps, to increasing family planning services to achieve population stabilization sooner than later.

Our future is not fated, but chosen. Mother Earth has a fever, and we ignore her symptoms at our own peril. Many positive steps are available to turn this looming adversity into a multi-faceted opportunity. The wildcard as we move into the future remains citizen concern and commitment to seeing the public policies pursue a preventive strategy rather than a crisis management one.

OFFWORLD DIVERSITY: THE BRANCHING OF LIFE IN SPACE

by

Brent Sherwood

Introduction

A pivotal accomplishment in the history of Earth life would be, through the agency of technological intelligence, its establishing ecologically independent extraterrestrial beachheads. Should this happen, Earth-based life would achieve an insurance, well beyond its evident tenacity, against periodic or unique planetary cataclysms. Distributed throughout the solar system, in fact, the special self-ordering, reproducing, growing phenomenon which is life could be safe from all but persistently willful disasters, or stellar or extrasolar catastrophes of an irrecoverable scale. Apart from simply insuring its survival, however, moving out into space will allow life to blossom in further variety as it adapts to the ecological niches available there.

We live in the age which, almost certainly, will bridge life's exclusively planetary past to a future of offworld opportunity. As executors of the spaceflight technology required to liberate life from the gravitational prison of its isolated birthplace, humans will determine the manner in which life expands off Earth. Primary in the human agenda, naturally, will be human life itself; other life will accompany and follow, and in some cases pave the way. In an effort to discern better how humans will inoculate space, this paper examines three linked issues: first, the reasons why free-space colonies will be an important component of human offworld expansion; second, some unavoidable conditions that will characterize life in such colonies; third, how those conditions will affect, and effect, offworld evolution.

Why Space Colonies?

The concept of large, manufactured colonies in free space, brought to public attention by Gerard K. O'Neill in 1974, immediately displaced older ideas and standards of space colonization. Since then however, despite a decade and a half of wide exposure in a rapidly changing technological society, despite the growth of dedicated advocacy groups, and despite stimulating and productive scientific and engineering work to develop tools to en-

---

Brent Sherwood *is senior engineer, future studies office, advanced civil space systems, Boeing.*

able space colonies, our collective image of such colonies and the civilization they embody has, like the older ideas before it, not changed much. But memes (ideas which replicate in human populations) must evolve in response to changing intellectual environments, or perish; it is time once again for the conceived image to mature.

That our image should change is important. As recent tragic US space history has demonstrated perfectly, long-term projects whose goals fail to evolve in step with their changing climate risk at best obsolescence and at worst parochial failure. Unfocused, nonadaptive or dusty images of goals make poor beacons to guide us into the future. While good work may emerge along wandering paths, great and inspiring collective work cannot, except in rare accident. Isolated technological discoveries, after all, often occur serendipitously, but real progress in ability and understanding requires a plan.

Large public works—be they wars or cathedrals or cities—certainly reflect, and may in turn inspire, the ethos of an age. For a society as steeped in the costly blessing of technology as ours is, space represents unequivocally the richest arena for exercising visible, public projects to reflect and inspire our values. Apropos to a media culture however, the space arena is for almost everyone only vicariously participatory. For everyone except the people directly involved in planning and mounting missions, it is not the detailed work itself but rather the *images* and *idea* of the work which can inspire. Ironically then, public perception (as distinct from real knowledge) both holds the financial key to progress in a democracy, and derives from information released by experts. Thus the images carrying that information, to portray the idea, must be critical.

We cannot avoid having some image of space society; the history of that image is eclectic but mainly dichotomous, and mirrors directly the American popular sensibilities of recent decades. In the 1950s and 60s, colonies in space were conceived to be complex planetary bases, where an endless bounty of scientific discovery sustained exuberant exploratory optimism. This limited utopia, populated somehow only by those able to challenge the secrets of Nature at the very edge of the abyss, grew naturally out of an expansionary America for which technology could answer anything. The population infected directly by this meme was, of course, those people who, albeit Earthbound, identified with the fortunate heroes. For them, there was much magic in the whole idea.

As the application of technology failed to solve society's problems at the end of the impatient 1960s, however, and as American popular interest shifted inward toward a more self-centered, materialistic social reconsolidation, the meme of space colonies donned a new, more accessible cloak. O'Neill's conceptual breakthrough was to realize that space industry could with extraterrestrial resources provide the means, in a technically foreseeable future, to house vast numbers of people in free space. Not tied gravitationally to planets, such societies would be free to live as they chose. That central conclusion remains as valid today as in 1974, and appears to represent unassailable logic.

A failure of foresight arose, though, in attempts to define details of the societies that would result, largely because no one understands well the economic setting of space civilization. Dispatching that context by inventing dependent connections to terrestrial economies (solar power satellites, for instance) is suspiciously circular and fragile logic, which fails to penetrate our ignorance of the motives of space dwellers. Laying out the architecture of space colony society is an enterprise far more involved than just outlining its feasibility. Vast voids in the concept have been filled with simple projections of the familiar. The lifestyle "choice" in published images of space colonies thus continues to reflect the dreams of bourgeois, suburban American culture. Jogging through Californian parks in space admittedly appeals to a wider (and incidentally more legislatively influential) popular base than the older "science hero" image, but is no less a utopian artifact of the time that produced it.

The "Island" colony concepts express directly an American 1970s and '80s longing for an Earth made new and clean, a society made prosperous and homogeneous. Its mannered extremes (a colony where Pennsylvania Dutch descendants regain the simple beauties of the rural 19th century replete with covered wooden bridges and horse-drawn carriages, according to one example published by a Sunday supplement in 1985) wax as romantically quaint—and impractical—to a modern view as did those of the "science hero" age. The "middle class in space" image risks foundering partly by leaving the world wondering just what the purpose of it all is supposed to be, and just what the enormous cost is supposed to be purchasing. Veneering space life with such a parochial slice of Earth culture, or even merely imagining that the veneer could be applied without being changed in the process, loses all the magic of new edges and new challenges, and all the potential of new growth, indeed of new life.

Another step in space colony concept evolution is needed now. As we prepare in the 1990s for increased human presence in space, a more careful joining between our knowledge of hard technical realities and of the irrepressible tendency of life to diversify can yield a fresh incarnation of the colony concept, and one with yet wider appeal. Lurking around the fringes of common colony images during their heydays has been a wealth of vignetted alternatives, framed primarily by the literature of speculative fiction. And from another quarter entirely have come such visionary urban planners as Paolo Soleri, with space colony designs as large as and no less sound technically than the island concepts, but yet utterly different in social sensibility. Some concepts nurture the delicacy of solitude; others glorify the darker, denser urban hive of the metropolis.

Apprehending the true range of possible geometries, populations, activities, and goals for free-space colonies—each as "feasible" as any other—can leave us numb. At the same time, the physical environment of space imposes a common set of constraints which cannot be avoided (although the "middle class in space" images tend to skirt them). Combining the real potential of unavoidably coarse—grained diversity with the real restrictions of equally unavoidable physical facts can be the theme of a new, more "open-hearted and tough-minded" generation of colony concepts. By exploring that theme, we can encourage a more mature dialog about space colonies, brightening and sharpening this important beacon to our future.

The Space Colony Environment

Space is necessarily a target-oriented place, where comparatively rare (if sometimes huge) mass concentrations move very quickly, separated by vast distances in a lethal void. That basic, if overly simplistic, structure characterizes all the scales of space, from planetary satellite systems to solar systems to stellar groups to galaxies to galactic clusters. The mass concentrations are where "all the action" is, and spaceflight is the essentially tedious activity of getting from one to another of them. The technical literature has proposed a range of interstellar travel concepts, which depending on their true feasibility and the advent of unpredictable breakthroughs might become possible even in futures beginning just generations from now. Before such time though, the targets available to us are those in our own solar system. And we have in hand some technologies (not the widest range, nor perhaps the best options yet) for reaching those places in our own time.

The attainable targets of our solar system are already essentially characterized. The planets are few, and mostly inimical to colonization. Earth's Moon and Mars present the most likely candidates for surface colonization, because they have natural environments apparently no worse than space itself. Fortunately they are both energetically close to Earth compared to other major solar system bodies, so an entire phase of planetary colonization will no doubt be focused on them. Self-sufficiency (essential for large-scale colonization) and modern technologies would allow a traditionally high "colonization" rate of population growth to be maintained, however. With a combined surface area of the same order as Earth's land, those two worlds would soon be rendered "finite" by even today's (non-colonizing) terrestrial population growth rate. Humans could occupy both of them completely and quickly, should they choose to. The number of generations that occupation might take is irrelevant to the familiar and invariant result: fully occupied worlds.

The many other moons and planetesimals distributed around the solar system are multifarious, providing at once a diverse range of settings and sources of retrievable raw materials for industry. Particularly with these bodies as catalysts, humans could create their own new places in space by manufacturing and populating them. O'Neill rationally pointed out that for a spacefaring industrial culture, planetary bases are an energetically expensive proposition. Operating transportation systems, as the basis of a material interplanetary economy, in planetary gravity wells incurs high propulsive costs beyond those of just moving from place to place in solar space. Basing operations instead at facilities in high planetary or heliocentric orbits avoids this additional penalty.

Rotation can approximately simulate normal gravity if needed, particularly for large colonies. Shielded from hard space radiation but admitting sunlight, such colonies could proffer the microcosmically earthlike environments common in the popular images—or intriguing settings weirdly unlike anything yet built by humans. Such worlds would close on themselves, generating their own universe of life within, while without would extend the void of space in all directions. We might expect many people, for deep resons, always to favor living environments on planetary surfaces, with solid ground below them and endless sky above. Still, the virtually unlimited and variegated living space available through manufacture just might make free-space colonies dominate a long-term space future featuring human species growth. Indeed, should Earth life eventually become able to consume the resources of our solar system, a Dyson sphere of swarmed free-space colonies could change, from a galactic viewpoint, the visage of our sun.

In the target-oriented expanse of our solar system, the cost of *physical* transportation is measured by both energy and time, which trade off inversely, in large numbers. For example, a carload of people can make a road trip on Earth of several hundred kilometers using chemical, airbreathing propulsion which consumes roughly 50 kg of fuel, taking as long as they like. But to send that same carload of people to Mars and back at an energetically favorable opportunity, using the most advanced technology we have, would take an order 500 metric tonnes of propellant and supplies, and two and a half years. That assumes they start from Earth orbit. A more costly opportunity would need twice as much mass, and take half as long from start to finish (ironically though, it would only let them stay at Mars one tenth as long). Even if Mars becomes a sustaining and refueling stop, the time required to make the trip remains the same, and the magnitude of the effort required is huge. Space is empty, and the targets in it worth catching up to move quite fast.

If high-leverage technologies like electric propulsion and auton-omus maintenance are applied, the proper infrastructure could be emplaced to supply steady cargo streams to almost any heliocentric orbit. Interplanetary commerce could become as regular and reliable as intercontinental shipping on Earth. Moving people throughout interplanetary space could in principle occur as regularly, but it is more difficult. Long trip times will always require multifunction life-support mechanisms that dominate populated-mission payloads. Thus no matter what the available interplanetary trans-portation capacity becomes at any time in our development, human transportation will be less efficient and more expensive than cargo shipping, and therefore limited by vessel manifesting.

Furthermore, human tolerance of extended spaceflight conspires with the cost of life-support to swing the energy-time tradeoff in favor of shorter, more propulsively expensive trips for populated flights. Even apart from the as-yet unresolved question of the need for artificial gravity, flights lasting many months and intended for large numbers of "business" or "leisure" travelers (rather than explorers) would require amenities yet more elaborate than those of modern cruise ships. Shortening the time allows simplifying the necessary "luxury." More advanced propulsion methods (such as nuclear thermal rockets) or truly breakthrough technologies (like mirror-matter-annihilation propulsion) would dramatically reduce interplanetary trip times, by releasing tremendous quantities of energy and converting it into useful work. For instance, constant acceleration equal to that of gravity at Earth's surface, applied to a space vehicle, could get it to Mars in several days (while supplying it with artificial gravity), but at an energy cost that would make sense only in the context of elaborate interplanetary commerce. Any way the problem is taken apart, and in almost any conceivable context, moving lots of people across the solar system is expensive.

The cost of *informational* transfer across space is measured by both link capacity and signal delay. The amount of information that can be transmitted is strikingly limited. Using the most ad-vanced technology available, an optical device smaller than a back-yard satellite dish could transmit a few stereo, color, realtime video channels from Earth to Mars. But lasers are not as widely tunable in frequency as radio signals; getting more than those few channels means using larger and much more complex equipment, and the limits for practical large systems are not yet known. However, physics dictates that moving the same equipment twice as far away reduces its link capacity fourfold, so high rates of information ex-change across interplanetary space come at a high price.

A firmer boundary is that electromagnetic carriers (optical, micro-wave, radio) are limited to the speed of light, the finiteness of which becomes appreciable over interplanetary distances. A signal sent from Earth to Mars, for instance, takes between a few and several minutes to get there, depending on the time of year (except for about 1% of the time when it cannot get there at all because the sun is in the way). Immediately reciprocal conversation is therefore impossible between widely separated places in space. The timescale of the message-response cycle, enforced by physical reality, is across space as it was on Earth for all of history before electrical technology: not immediate.

Because of these restrictive transportation and communication costs, free-space colonies will, unless clustered together intentionally, be extraordinarily isolated. Given adequate resources (and no true colony would be located without steady sources of energy and materials) it will always be cheaper for people to make more people where they are, than to move them around for the sake of repopulation. Interplanetary excursion travel will most likely be much less popular and available than is jet travel today. And the kind of world-spanning communications we presume today cannot exist when the "world" is the whole solar system. Thus in a future of many free-space colonies, a social isolation more characteristic of earlier centuries will return. This inescapable fact nevertheless also restores local freedom from "global" homogeneity. Depending on how a colony manages its access to the resources that sustain it, its economic independence from other colonies may be assurable; but its privacy and social autonomy almost certainly are. Long-lasting remote influence over colony affairs is unlikely, and even remote espionage impractical.

A colony in deep space is much more vulnerable to environmental disruption than is a planet. Its buffers of breathable air, drinkable water, comestible food, and finally available help, are all vanishingly small compared to those provided by an established planetary ecosystem like Earth's. The margins are thinner, and the balance finer; fluctuations even mildly outside the design range for a free-space colony could be irrecoverable. Colonies could never allow the kind of environmental degradation Earth has suffered in the last century, for instance. This situation is not surprising to farmers, aquarists or others who use technology to culture life where it otherwise would perish. Successfully culturing colonies in space will require the same type of empirical knowledge, careful monitoring, and exquisite control.

Heavily loaded life-support systems, such as those sustaining the urban population densities driven by spaceflight economics to be most prevalent in free-space colonies, run close to the hazardous edge of failure. Many sources of environmental catastrophe would be possible in space colonies: uncontrolled and devastating biological plague, physical destruction through technical accident, cosmic violence such as an obliterating impact, warfare arriving from outside or erupting from within, or willful, terrorist sabotage. Among these, the last seems the most realistic threat. Rigid control over critical environmental conditions, and of the potential for disruptive outside influences, would be literally vital to the entire colony. When death awaits forever just through the hull, attention to proper protocol can be no less imperative for enormous vessels than for our current tiny space ships. This hard fact of conformity is independent of the size, social complexity, or any individual motives among the vessel's population. But the strict need for such tight control over the total environment also makes every detail of every aspect of that environment a design variable.

The inhabitants of a free-space colony would get to, in fact would *have* to, choose *everything* about the way they lived. Isolated by the scale of space, they would have neither unwanted interference from, nor the opportunity for limitless exchange with, the rest of humanity. Focused connections to other colonies could be arranged if desired, however. Large colonies established in "cycler" orbits, or itinerant colonies equipped with efficient, low-thrust propulsion, could enjoy repeating or touring encounters with others. Such periodic meetings or revisitations could occur at frequencies spanning months to generations, supporting unique trade and cultural exchange rhythms at a grand scale unknown since the last century.

Thus within the constraints of comparative isolation, hazard, and time just outlined, life in space colonies could fulfill practically any agenda desired. The appeal of human expression freed from Earthly precedent can be as broad as the horizon of human imagination and aspiration. Therein lies the potency of space colonies as a beacon for human futures. The possibilities include, but clearly reach far beyond, colorless tableaux of science heroes and bourgeois parks. And the feasibility of free-space colonies then obligates us to attempt scoping the true range of possible futures they could usher in.

Spaceborne Evolution

It is fruitless to predict in detail what free-space colony societies will be like. We have, however, already outlined enough to discern some boundaries, and to see what they can *not* be like. Colony society will in general be nothing like middle America, partly because colonists' aspirations, freedoms and activities will be so different, and partly because their incontrovertible rules of conduct will generate a social milieu utterly foreign to us. Fierce independence and central self-interest will be no one's fundamental right in an isolated colony; the unforgiving hazards of space preclude it. A level of communality, with mutual respect, physical civility and civic duty for which no historical model exists (and which our modern Western sensibility can barely fathom) would seem strictly necessary. Truly dangerous behavior—that which could physically endanger the entire colony—would elicit stern prevention. Earlier, weaker versions of these features have recurred in most frontier societies; but the rigor imposed by the space frontier is the most severe that humans have ever encountered (the closest analog continues to be ships at sea). Furthermore, the rigor imposed by space will never abate for those who live there, because like the sea and unlike new shores, space will always be intrinsically hostile to *Homo sapiens*. Forever on the frontier, space colony life could enforce the development of exemplary urban order: freedom of opportunity within the boundaries of duty and interdependence.

Out of the internal consistency thus required of colony societies, focused by their limited outside contact and guided by their communal goals, will arise particular customs of civilization unique to each. In a future of far-flung free-space colonies, the paradox will inevitably develop that any single colony society must be homgeneous for the sake of its own survival, but that the sum of all colonies will display a range of diversity far exceeding any ethnic or nationalistic plurality we have yet seen. That is, fierce independence and central self-interest *can* be expected to characterize the motivations of whole colonies. Contemporary concepts have hinted at the potential for willful social diversity among separate colonies, but have stopped short either of recognizing its inevitability or of pursuing its evolutionary ramifications. If we take this extra step, some important conclusions are startling enough to recast reasonable projections about what human space colonization will lead us to.

About the most mild possible future is analogous to a social history like that of pre-European native North Americans living on the central plains. Nomadic by nature, these people achieved a stable social structure which, civilized by ritual behavior, lasted balanced in its natural environment for centuries. Bands of up to several hundred people grew and lived together, moving across the landscape according to its seasonal rhythms. Different bands were linked loosely by limited communication and genetic exchange through marriage, thus each developed its own customs and dialects. The regions overlapped by bands were crossed by their scouts, and periodically enormous festival gatherings of many bands would close and rejuvenate great cycles of social exchange.

Space colonies too can be expected to follow their own local rhythms and rituals, developing their own customs and characters in comparative isolation. Free-space colonies should be viable in virtually any size, from dozens to maybe millions of inhabitants. And the resources available in space, together with high procreative rates, will allow a virtually unlimited number of such colonies to orbit the sun. Choked communication channels, and occasional exchanges of small numbers of people, could link colonies culturally (and biologically) enough for them to feel some real allegiances to extended "nations." Their emissaries—scientists, athletes, and even tourists—would encounter each other when necessary or desirable, perhaps in locations remote to each home colony. And purposely itinerant colonies could periodically rendezvous for a time, fostering rich exchanges that would culminate heliocentric cycles taking perhaps generations to repeat.

A more adventurous future, not at all mutually exclusive with the "itinerant clan" scenario just outlined, would include renegade space colonies as well. Following their own agendas, some might choose complete isolation, giving them the freedom necessary to experiment with nature and with themselves, but without interference, exploring human futures as they wished. The result could go far beyond mere governmental self-determination. Gone would be media spyglasses trained upon their triumphs and traumas, motives and methods by the rest of humanity. The technological history of our species indicates that people do even potentially dangerous things, as soon as (and in fact because) they can, despite any proscription. The true freedom made possible by small directed groups in a large solar system would permit unprecedented expression of human ingenuity of all kinds, and incredible variety would result. In particular, a deeply technological species blowing wide the doors of opportunity in this way directly invites real, physical evolution.

Genetic evolution proceeds variously in species populations according to the frequency of mutations and the frequency of new niches opening up. In a large domain rich with opportunity, a starter species will diversify to fill all available niches, spawning distinct species which share the same environment but capitalize on different resources. The incredible branching of Cichlidae into hundreds of species over the last half million years in Lake Malawi exemplifies this sympatric speciation. And independent, isolated islands of life define the precondition for punctuated-equilibrium evolution. Given unique environments, abruptly isolated populations cannot avoid selective variation from their original mean as they optimize for different conditions. These processes of change will be every bit as valid in space as they have been on Earth. In time, biota descended from the life accompanying humans out into space will adapt to the spectrum of conditions there. Earth organisms have been found thriving in polar ice and scalding mineral springs; some forms can survive dessicated and encysted for decades, some metabolize sulphur around spreading vents under the crushing pressure of kilometers of overlying ocean, while others feed by corroding metals anaerobically inside reactor cooling systems. This tenaciousness leaves no doubt that the energy-rich vacuum of space itself would eventually stimulate variation among, and sustain, life forms once humans provided the substrate and the germ.

Within human populations, neither the subtlety of sympatric speciation nor the luxury of gradual adaptation over eons will most likely characterize evolution. If not already accepted and widely-applied by the time of space colonies, molecular engineering will certainly be a candidate exploratory activity for humans seeking to escape regulation of their curiosity. The isolation possible with free-space colonies would let those who wish to experiment do so. Humans with the nanotechnological ability to control individual atomic bonds, regardless of however or whenever they acquire that skill, will be able to design life to suit their goals. That includes tailoring organisms to work for them, to entertain them, and to inspire them, but it also includes remaking themselves. Humans will be able to apply their technology recursively, either to suppress the imperceptibly gradual biological changes brought naturally by isolation, or to accelerate their own evolution in directions they choose. Mere social variation among space colonies seems trivial by comparison.

Self-wrought genetic or somatic changes could signal the subtle beginning of true human adaptation to space. For example, black bears are the only hibernating mammals whose bone metabolism remains the same year-round, and which thus avoid excretion of calcium during the winter. The unique protection from osteoporosis thus conferred is thought to be regulated by specialized blood chemicals. Humans engineered to produce an analogous substance might be made naturally and permanently immune to one of the most debilitating, and limiting, effects of weightlessness. With this and other biochemical changes, humans could begin to make themselves into creatures native to space.

Or, changes in what defines humanness might be accomplished more drastically and with other ends in mind. The point is that once indpendent colonies are available, each benefitting from the accumulated knowledge of human history and technology, people intent upon setting their own course could not realistically be stopped. Given biological nanotechnology in an interplanetary future then, social variation in human goals may lead naturally to biological variation in human expression. The genus *Homo*, and other Earth life with it, would branch irrevocably into new species determined by the ingenuity of human will. A diaspora of proportions unknown since life first appeared on Earth, and proceeding at a rate never even approached before, could truly colonize space.

Far from just a means to transplant parochial, privileged pieces of modern Western culture intact to a capitalist "high frontier" of utopian opportunity, free-space colonies represent a powerful tool for determining the future of Earth life. Colonies will establish technologically habitable environments throughout the solar system. Through them and the freedoms they allow, humans will choose and apply a spectrum of conditions, methods and intentions unimaginable, impossible or impermissible heretofore. Restricting their inquiry will become unfeasible. By using advancing technology, life can evolve away from its old terrestrial limitations, expanding through diversity its presence in an infinite universe, as it branches to fill the new ecologies humans will find and make. An agent of change peerless in Earth's history then, free-space colonies may well guarantee that the boundless variety of inventive speciation defines both human destiny and the ultimate future of Earth-based life.

LEARNING FROM ONE LEVEL LOWER

by

Jan Tinbergen

1. The Necessity of Managing the Planet Earth

Global society is in a process of continual development. Population is growing quantitatively and qualitatively. Qualitative growth consists of a number of quality aspects, such as health and the resulting expectation of life, education and training and the resulting productive capabilities, cultural change such as philosophy of life, including religious and humanistic beliefs and so on.

Resources are changing, by external and internal processes. By external processes I understand those originating from outer space. An important source of energy is solar radiation, which is used in many different ways, directly and indirectly. For all practical purposes this source of energy is constant, but astronomically speaking it will change. Other processes originating from outer space may be collisions with other celestial objects, of which at least one is known with an asteroid or comet, 65 million years ago, (cf. L. and W. Alvarez, 1989).

Internal processes are numerous. Population growth tends to use resources and hence reduce the quantity of, among many others, oil and natural gas reserves. Qualitative changes in population and its production of durable goods may temporarily raise available resource reserves by digging more deeply in the earth. Reduction of resources again may be quantitative or qualitative. Some of today's serious problems originate from quality deterioration of the atmosphere, the oceans, the soil, and forests.

Alongside natural resources human-made resources are available as a consequence of the transformation of natural resources into the global infrastructure: capital goods of numerous types. Application of human resources such as scientific research has contributed to technological development resulting in higher productivity. With the aid of new technologies humankind succeeded in producing more goods and services per capita. Global productivity has risen between 1950 and 1977 by about six percent per annum (cf. Kravis, et al., 1982). This is productivity in the usual sense. We may also use a different productivity concept, the production of human welfare per capita or the production of human welfare per unit of natural resources. The latter concept is relevant for long-term planning in order to maintain the flow of welfare for an infinitely

Jan Tinbergen *is emeritus professor of development planning, Erasmus University, Rotterdam. In 1969 he shared the Nobel Prize in economics.*

long period, which is possible if technological development goes on.

Restricting ourselves to the next few decades we are confronted with three important problems, to be called the security problem, the environmental problem and the income distribution problem. The security problem is how to avoid nuclear or conventional war. Beyond a certain level of intensity conventional war means suicide, since the existence of nuclear power plants will change a conventional war also into a nuclear one. The environmental problem is the problem to stop environmental deterioration and preferably to improve the environment's quality. The income distribution or poverty problem is the problem to reduce worldwide income inequality, which has remained between 1950 and 1980 (and presumably 1989) at the same highly undesirable level (cf. Summers et al., 1984).

The solution of the three important problems is possible only by making a number of worldwide decisions and by implementing the decisions. This means that humanity is in need of really managing the planet Earth, at least to solve the problems mentioned, but presumably also a number of other related problems.

The present essay attempts to contribute to some of the measures necessary to arrive at a sound management of the Globe. It does so by learning from the organization of well-governed nations, which constitute "management at one level lower" if one aims at a well-managed planet Earth. Evidently this learning process is not the only method to discuss the feasibility of a sound management.

2. Management of Nations and of Enterprises

So far more or less successful management has been performed by national governments and by enterprises, transnational or national. Supranational public management only exists in very few cases, for instance in the European Coal and Steel Community, or in the distribution of loans and grants by the World Bank and the International Monetary Fund (IMF).

Global management, of which we are in need for the solution of at least the three important problems mentioned in Section 1, may learn from management one level lower, which, in the overwhelming majority of cases, is the national level. Before tackling the central problem of this essay we want to deal with the two cases of rather successful management just mentioned.

In some respects enterprises are managed more rigorously than governments. In order to learn from entrepreneurial success the tasks of a national government have sometimes been formulated by saying that the government should act as if it were a large enterprise: Great Britain Ltd., Nippon (Japan) KK, Sverige (Sweden) AB or Nederland NV. Such comparisons did lead to the "privatization" of a number of public services, especially in the 1980s, but occasionally earlier. Generally speaking it is useful indeed to check, from time to time, where the frontier between public and private responsibility has to be drawn. One of the greatest checks of this kind, with tremendous possibilities, is President Gorbachev's *perestroika* in the Soviet Union.

In the United States of America Professor James A. Yunker (1979) launched the idea that a regime he calls "pragmatic market socialism" is better than the other types of socialism in existence and better also than today's American "mixed order"—that is, a mixture of 1850 capitalism and socialism. Another American economist, Robert H. Haveman (1989) defends a mixed order which he recommends for immediate application by the Bush administration, and which, in my opinion, constitutes a form of socialism for the USA.

Whereas these comparisons and checks are very useful for improving the national social order as well as the international climate, it should not be overlooked that there remains one important difference between governments and enterprises: an enterprise is permitted to select its "population" that is, its employees, a government is not. This makes an enterprise's tasks considerably easier than a government's tasks.

3. Management as a Hierarchy

Both an enterprise and a government are managed by a hierarchy (and so are defense forces). A hierarchy consists of a configuration of individuals (or institutions) located at a number of levels. The number of individuals at the various levels is lowest at the highest level and increases downwards. Each individual controls a number of employees one level lower; that number is also called the span of control and need not be the same for all individuals or levels. The average span of control is a characteristic of a hierarchy, however; and a same total number of employees may be distributed over a larger number of levels if the span of control is low or over a smaller number of levels, if the span of control is high. The former hierarchy is steeper than the latter. It depends on the type of work done and of the technology used whether the hierarchy is steeper, but also on other causes; especially the number of individuals at the highest level. If this is small, there is a higher degree of centralization, if it is high, we have a more decentralized system of decision making.

There are also hierarchies of institutions. We may say that the machinery to govern a nation has as its top institution, or the upper level of authority, one or more parliaments; as the second, the government (the ministers); as the third the ministries; as the fourth level, a number of directorates-general; and a number of implementing organizations as the fifth level.

In various ways a distinction may be made between macro and micro tasks and corresponding institutions and decisions. Thus, we may, at the family level, think of a macro description indicating total income earned by productive activities of one or both of the parents and the micro aspect of the quantities of all sorts of goods and services consumed, and the micro decisions made while shopping. Similarly, at the level of a national government, we may describe its macro activities of taxation and loaning to finance total consumption and investment. The corresponding institutions are the Treasury, or Ministry of Finance and the Central Bank as macroinstitutions and the spending ministries which pay the expenditures for agricultural and fishing tasks, for industrial policy, for transportation, for education and scientific policies, justice and police, and so on. In a sense, the macro-institutions constitute one level higher than the spending institutions, to the extent that the total of expenditures are subject to the restriction set by financial resources. But the relationship may also be described as a negotiation by equals, within government as the all-embracing authority.

Individuals participate in numerous activities and these too are part of a micro description. An individual not only takes part in the government process by voting for a certain politician or party, but also takes part in professional associations, acting independently from the individual's workfloor, takes part in recreative associations, from stamp collecting to artistic activities. Here too a number of levels of decision making may exist. Each of the associations may be part of a national or even world organization, from which directives are given to the way of operating of local chapters. Political parties, but also churches, are organized internationally. Depending on the subject, professional associations or idealistic associations may play the roles of so-called Non-Governmental Organization (NGOs) as advisory institutions to governments, or to higher levels, such as the United Nations or the European Community.

4. Concrete Examples of Decision Making Within Nations

The lowest level of decision making is, of course, the level of individual citizens of the nation concerned. The task of governing the nation is delegated by the citizens with voting rights to the members of parliaments at various levels, the lowest level being the municipal "parliament." The same citizens also elect the members of provincial and national parliaments. The names given to the second level differ among nations. The United States calls them "states," Canada and the Netherlands call them "provinces," The Federal Republic of Germany calls them "Lander," Switzerland uses the name "cantons," and so on. In many cases, or for particular governmental tasks, intermediate levels exist. Thus, in large cities, district parliaments exist. In the Netherlands tasks such as protection against floods are the responsibility of a separate type of institutions ("waterstaat").

In many countries two parliaments exist, such as the House of

Representatives and the Senate. Often the Senate is elected in an indirect way: in the Netherlands the members of the Senate are elected by the Provincial parliaments.

With the aid of the theoretical and the concrete concepts developed we will now discuss an important thesis for our central subject. That thesis will be called the "principle of the optimum level of decision making." Its content is that the optimum level of decision making to solve a given problem must be as low as possible, but at a level where all whose welfare is affected are represented. This central proposition may be clarified by some examples, numbered (1) through (5).

(1) Decisions about municipal taxes may be made at the level of the municipality, since they do not affect the welfare of other municipalities and their inhabitants.

(2) So may choosing the names of new streets in any municipality or the addition or change of a tram route or bus route. If some citizens of other towns sometimes are affected, then they are in a negligible way.

(3) The colors used for the traffic lights in a city should not be decided upon by that city's government, however; such rules must be uniform and a particular choice (such as used in American cities in contrast to European cities, for instance) may affect traffic security, if done by one city. Higher levels of decision making are needed here.

(4) Decisions on the subjects taught and the levels of knowledge and insight required for a graduation exam cannot be made by individual municipalities either. There is enough migration between parts of most nations to create discrimination if the graduation exams were different in different cities. To most non-Swiss citizens it is somewhat amazing that such discrimination between different cantons exist for physicians and lawyers whose diplomas are not always recognized by other cantons than those where they graduated.

(5) Decisions against the pollution of the atmosphere or rivers must not be made at local or even at national levels, since citizens of other towns or even countries are affected. The pollution of the Rhine affects parts of all countries situated on the Rhine and anti-pollution policies cannot be made at national, let alone local levels (Basel or Strasbourg).

These examples hopefully suffice to clarify our proposition. It will be shown to be a useful instrument of analysis.

Within a well-governed nation the distribution of the decisions needed to carry out an efficient and equitable policy have been tried out by—in most cases—various generations of their citizens and been brought in accordance with our central thesis. This does not mean that all citizens agree, but, in democratic countries, a majority. Differences of opinion exist between the adherents of different political parties and there usually is a minority which differs in opinion about equity with the majority, for instance. Such ideas are developing over time and such development leads to changes in government institutions or in parties in power, or both. In such processes of change some citizens or parties are leading, whereas others may be lagging. So some time may elapse before decision-making becomes optimal in the sense described. There are also differences in educational level and alertness to new developments making for quality differences among countries. The present author thinks that Sweden, although not his native country, on many occasions, has shown itself to be a better-governed country than his own country, and also better governed than the superpowers. It goes without saying that elaboration on this opinion falls outside the space available in this essay.

5. Application to World Problems

After the introduction of the most important concepts we propose to use and our central thesis we are in a position to set out how, in order to find a solution to our main global problems, we may "learn from one level lower." In principle the solution of these problems requires a world decision-making structure satisfying our central thesis about the optimum level of decision making. As noted, this means that in devising an optimal world decision-making structure we must learn from well governed countries. On some occasions the national level is not exactly one level lower, because an intermediate level is under construction. That applies to Western Europe, where we are in the process of integration [the European community]. For the time being the realization of most structural changes has not been accomplished but we hope to have them take effect after 1992. Some lessons have been learned so far, which we shall mention.

Learning from well-governed nations may start with listing some characteristics of well-governed countries which deviate from our present world structure. A useful example to begin with refers to financial and monetary policies as part of general government policies. In most nations, apart from ordinary banks, three institutions in this field exist: the Treasury, the Central Bank and one or more investment banks. Of these the Treasury is by far the most important institution. Almost as important is the Central Bank, whereas the investment banks are much less important. Today's world institutions are the World Bank (WB) and the International Monetary Fund (IMF). In addition there are Regional Development Banks.

One conclusion is that the IMF should become the World's Central Bank. This statement has been made by many experts. The prospect that IMF will move in that direction seems likely in comparison with the other changes needed, and will not be elaborated upon.

A second conclusion will meet with much more opposition: the conclusion that a World Treasury is needed. Yet I submit that powerful arguments support this view. Today's world "order" (or rather world chaos) suffers from two main shortcomings in the way the financial means are collected for the United Nations institutions in existence. One is that this financing process is distributed over a large number of fund-collecting agencies, separately for each of the UN specialized agencies. This process can be much better organized by making it the task of one World Treasury. The costs of collection will be reduced considerably, to begin with. Secondly, care can be taken that the distribution of the revenue obtained over the various spending agencies corresponds to their relative importance for the world at large. More funds can be made available to urgent than to less urgent projects. With today's necessity of improving the quality of the environment this may imply considerable shifts in spending. A third important aspect is that the contributions by individual UN member countries will be in line with their income per capita and their population size, according to a tax system approved by the General Assembly. As a *quid pro quo* the voting system of the Assembly must be changed, however, in order also to reflect a modern system of representation.

The position of the third type of financial institutions, investment banks, is more favorable in the international community than in many countries. In several respects the World Bank and the Regional Development Banks already follow a coherent development financing policy. They are lacking, however, the power a treasury has: to require their contributions as they consider necessary and not as the donor countries prefer. This led to the far too low contributions made by the United States and Japan and some of the smaller industrialized nations. As I showed elsewhere (Tinbergen, 1989) the contributions should be much higher, if some real assistance is to be offered to the poverty-stricken countries, so as to create employment for their populations, assuming, however, that these countries will become more serious about population questions. At present the inequality of income distribution is hardly changing and there is no prospect that the gap between incomes of developed and developing countries will narrow. An appropriate goal would be to aim at a doubling of relative incomes in a period of twenty to thirty years—a period after which a sizeable part of the population will still be alive. I emphasize that I speak about relative incomes: in the long run it is relative incomes that will be the incentive for migration to the more prosperous countries. If the latter lack the feeling that ethically the tremendous welfare gap cannot be accepted, then let them understand that for their own internal political stability it is desirable that less immigrants from the poor continents enter their country and that the incentive to do so is visibly reduced.

A second broad field of policies and institutions concerns security, internal (police) and external (military forces). A most important feature of a well-governed nation does not permit its provinces to have military forces; only the nation has this right. There was a time when within the United States of America armies of individual states existed. We know that that made possible the Civil War in the 1860s and the final result was that only a national military force remained. Applied to the world at large we can and must learn the lesson of disarmament of national military forces. The existence of only one armed force is characteristic for all well-governed nations as we now know them: France and Great Britain for a long period already.

The dynamics of nation building has generally been one of integration into larger units. The nations mentioned came into existence through integration. There are some opposite cases. A well-known individual case is that, after World War I, the so-called Austrian-Hungarian Dual Monarchy disintegrated into Austria, Hungary, Czechoslovakia and parts of it were integrated into Yugoslavia, Poland and Russia. Apart from these individual cases there was the general process of decolonization which added an enormous number of new independent nations following World War II.

The first lesson to be learned for government at the world level from one level lower before anything else is the importance of disarmament. This is vital to any thought of an optimal management of the Earth. But quantum jumps are impossible in the process of international cooperation and so the process will consist of many steps. A few words about a first step will be added in Section 6.

Next to the security issue today an environmental policy has high priority. But here the existing nations themselves are confronted with a novel phenomenon and the organization of an effective environmental policy may best be based on an application of our central thesis. An effective policy against the pollution of the atmosphere and of the oceans requires a decision-making mechanism at the world level, because neither the atmosphere nor the oceans stop at national frontiers. For river pollution prevention or control continental decision making will suffice in most cases. For polluted soil, mostly national or even local decision-making is acceptable.

An income distribution policy, while largely a national affair, has an international aspect as well. We discussed the stagnant world income distribution and the desirability to reduce the incentive to emigrate from the Third World to the prosperous countries and emphasized its importance for the latter also. We offered recommendations with regard to the creation of a World Treasury and the increased effectiveness of the World Bank.

Trade policies are perhaps the oldest policies of an international character. Applying our central thesis we must conclude that supranational decision making is needed also here and the Havana conference briefly after World War II decided in the correct way: the creation of an International Trade Organization (ITO) was proposed. The proposal was not ratified by the United States Senate, however. This is evidently a lag in global thinking. The developing countries' leaders proposed the creation of the United Nations Conference on Trade and Development (UNCTAD), which got tasks more in line with our central thesis and so constituted a step forward.

It is not our purpose to offer a complete list of targets and instruments of a world socio-economic policy, but we trust that the examples given here are a set of clear lessons "to be learned from one level lower" and that the method of handling the problem has been clarified sufficiently. Instead of a complete description of an optimal international socio-economic policy we want to describe its character in a different way. We think it can be characterized as a need for a reorganization and strengthening of the system of institutions of the United Nations organization. Reorganization means, first of all, the redefinition of their competences and strengthening means giving more power to them, in order that their proposals, when accepted, are carried out. Reorganization also may imply different ways of voting in the decision-making process. Reorganization and strengthening the United Nations means the creation of a World Government.

A World Government does not mean—as is sometimes thought—a government replacing all national and lower governments, but supplementing them for the treatment of the subjects requiring a higher than national decision making. It means transferring national sovereignty on these issues to the new World Government.

6. First Steps Towards a World Order

The transformation process leading to a method of decision making more appropriate to the achievement of an optimal world order and world policy is a very complicated process, made more complicated than necessary because vested interests will oppose it. Following the proverb that a good beginning is half of the work, we will, in this last short section, suggest a beginning. Changes in the United Nations Charter can be effectuated only along the lines laid down in that Charter, that is, by meetings of the representatives of the member countries. Since not all representatives have familiarized themselves with the technical and specialized problems to be faced during these meetings it seems useful to make available to all a report which deals with these problems in a clear, concise and easily understood way. The composition of such a report may be sought from an "independent international commission" similar to studies already produced on some of the problems we have discussed. Thus, we had the Brandt Commission, dealing with the problems of developing countries and their cooperation with developed countries (Brandt, 1980, 1983). We also had the Palme Commission, dealing with the world security problem and disarmament (Palme, 1982). Finally we had the Brundtland Commission whose subject was the reduction of pollution of the environment (Brundtland, 1987). Because of their independence and their membership—always taken from different continents and political parties and thus reflecting many cultures and philosophies of life— these Commissions' reports have great authority and strive for objective information as well as a consideration of all shades of opinions among experts. The installation of such a Commission to report on the desirable reorganization and strengthening of the United Nations is the first step I propose.

References

Alvarez, L. W. and W. (1989), father and son, respectively, are mentioned in National (American) Academy of Sciences, Letter to Members, Vol. 18 No. 3, p. 33. The Alvarezes contributed to the understanding of this event.

Brundtland, G. H. (1987), Chairman, World Commission on Environment and Development, *Our Common Future*, Oxford/New York.

Haveman, R. H. (1988), *Starting Even*, A Twentieth Century Report, New York, London, Sydney, Tokyo, Toronto.

Kravis, I. B. et al. (1982), *World Product and Income*, published for the World Bank, Baltimore and London.

Palme, O. (1982), Chairman, The Independent Commission on Disarmament and Security Issues, Common Security, New York.

Summers, R. et al. (1984), "Changes in the World Income Distribution," *Journal on Policy Modeling*, Vol. G, No. 2, May, pp. 237-270.

Tinbergen, J. (1989), "The Optimum Amount of Development Assistance," in: H. W. Singer and J. Pickett, eds, *Economic Recovery in Sub-Saharan Africa*, Glasgow, forthcoming.

Yunker, J. A. (1979), "The Micro-economic Efficiency Argument for Socialism Revisited," *Journal of Economic Issues*, Vol. XIII no. 1, March, pp. 73 ff, and several later publications.

Applying Futures
Research

THE RISE OF FUTURES THINKING IN THE NEW STATES: THE DECISIONS OF NATIONHOOD

by

Wendell Bell

Purpose

The purpose of this paper is to examine the processes of state-formation since World War II as one source of the rise and spread of futures thinking. Such processes required new national leaders to make decisions on a broad range of issues in order to set the course of their new states. I aim (1) to show how the "decisions of nationhood" inherently required futures thinking, and (2) to give a few illustrations, especially from the new states of the Caribbean, of how such decisions were made and what role images of the future played in them.

The Creation of the New States

Depending on exactly what units are counted, in 1944 there were about 70 nation-states in existence. From 1943 to 1966, there was an average of about two-and-a-half new states added to this number each year, more than one new state being born every five months. As early as 1966, a total of 61 new states had entered the international system, and, by that time, Pearcy and Stoneman (1968) calculated that they already accounted for 24 percent of the total land surface of the earth (excluding Antarctica) and contained over one billion people which then constituted about a third of the Earth's population. From 1966 to 1989, about 40 additional new states were created, making a total of over 100 new states since 1944. Thus, within 45 years the number of nation-states grew by almost 250 percent to a total of 170.

State formation during this period included some of the most momentous events in human history: It resulted in wholesale—sometimes cataclysmic—change, not just of the international system, but also of the polities, economies, societies, and cultures of the new states themselves. And it culminated in the Age of the Nation-State: Today, nearly every person on Earth is a member of a modern state that claims priority over all other loyalties to groups, organizations, and institutions, from the family to the church.

Most of the new states were created from the former colonial

Wendell Bell *is professor and director of graduate studies, Department of Sociology, Yale University, New Haven, Connecticut.*

territories of Britain and France, but a few were political dependencies of Belgium, The Netherlands, Italy, Denmark, New Zealand, Japan, or the United States. They include territories from Asia (e.g., Indonesia, Malaysia, Singapore, the Philippines), the Middle East (e.g., Qatar, Libya, Tunisia, Algeria), Africa (e.g., Senegal, Nigeria, Zaire, Ghana), the Pacific (e.g., Nauru, Western Samoa, Fiji, Vanuatu), and the Caribbean (see Table 1).

Table 1
NEW STATES OF THE CARIBBEAN

New State	Date of Independence
Jamaica	6 August 1962
Trinidad and Tobago	31 August 1962
Guyana	26 May 1966
Barbados	30 November 1966
Bahamas	10 July 1973
Grenada	7 February 1974
Suriname	25 November 1975
Dominica	3 November 1978
St. Lucia	22 February 1979
St. Vincent and the Grenadines	26 October 1979
Belize	21 September 1981
Antigua and Barbuda	1 November 1981
St. Kitts-Nevis	19 September 1983

In the Caribbean, thirteen new states joined three independent states of an older period, Haiti (which achieved political independence in 1804), the Dominican Republic (in 1844), and Cuba (in 1901). The post-World War II period of state formation in the Caribbean began in 1944 when universal adult suffrage and limited self-government were introduced in Jamaica. After 18 years of periodic transitions toward self-government, Jamaica became fully independent politically on August 6, 1962. As can be seen from Table 1, Trinidad and Tobago also achieved nationhood in 1962, and eleven other Caribbean territories followed over the next twenty-one years, ending, at the time of writing, with the political independence of St. Kitts-Nevis in 1983. Formerly, all had been British colonies except one, Suriname, which had been Dutch.

Remaining in the Caribbean with various degrees of political integration with—and dependence on—metropolitan powers, and with varying amounts of internal self-governance short of nationhood, are Martinique and Guadeloupe (French); The Netherlands Antilles, including Aruba, Bonaire, Curaçao, St. Eustatius, part of St. Martin, and Saba; Puerto Rico (USA); the US and British Virgin Islands; and sundry other places such as Anguilla, the Cayman Islands, Montserrat, and the Turks and Caicos (British).

The spread of modern nationalism throughout Asia, the Middle

East, Africa, the Pacific, and the Caribbean in the 20th century continued what can be thought of as a single movement that began in Europe and North America in the latter part of the 18th century and that moved through Central and South America during the 19th (Palmer, 1959, 1964). It has just run its course, spreading over the rest of the globe, during the latter half of the 20th century. Only a few potential new states still wait in the wings, perhaps never to move onto the stage of independent statehood, such as the French Pacific territory of New Caledonia or the tiny British Caribbean island of Montserrat.

The Transition to Nationhood and Futures Thinking

The creation of the new states fostered futures thinking because it made problematic past and present political, economic, social, and cultural arrangements and because it invited the design of future alternatives to them. It did this in a number of ways:

First, the transition to political independence opened up real possibilities for social change that had been suppressed during the period of colonialism. Under colonial rule, the imperial masters had imposed to a greater or lesser degree forms of political, economic, and social organization that the bulk of the indigenous (local, Creole, or non-European) populations considered alien, that they sometimes saw as symbols of despised foreign domination. At best, there was an ambivalence toward colonial-produced structures and change, on the one hand an appreciation of some things British, French, Dutch, Belgian, Italian or American and on the other hand a smoldering anger at other things. Even though some aspects of modernization, for example, were approved by some local people, everywhere the inequalities and injustices based on class, race, and nationality were resented. They created invidious distinctions to the disadvantage of local people and they invariably were legitimated and enforced by colonial political and military domination.

In the Caribbean, where colonialism lasted nearly 500 years and included over 300 years of African slavery, this ambivalence between the attraction and rejection of metropolitan "civilization" is neatly summed up by a former British colonial subject, "the twin orbs of empire, the cricket ball and the black ball." Whatever the ambivalence of reaction, actual subjugation of the indigenous population—both of its traditional past and its present images of the future—was the norm. Even under "indirect rule" as in parts of colonial Africa, where foreign proconsuls ruled in part through local tribal chiefs and organizations, locally driven change led by indigenous people was often stifled.

With political independence, came the freedom for the new citizens to try to control more aspects of their own individual and collective futures. The reins of legitimate political power, whether through violent or peaceful change, were taken up by local leaders who used them, with a few exceptions, to lead their new states toward futures different from either their colonial or traditional pasts.

Second, the coming of nationhood raised the consciousness of local leaders and citizens to the fact that their future was, indeed, largely in their own hands. The transformation from colony to nation-state was accompanied nearly everywhere in the new states by the preparation for nationhood and a variety of consciousness-raising activities culminating in inaugural ceremonies designed to mark a momentous historical occasion. Here is one account of independence eve written by a student of Trinidadian nationalism:

> At midnight on August 30, 1962 one of the most familiar and significant political rituals of the present historical period was enacted within a flood-lighted area in front of Red House in Port of Spain, Trinidad & Tobago. Local notables and a representative of the British monarchy stood in readiness for a ceremony which had already been performed on numerous occasions throughout the Asian and African colonies. Just a few weeks before, an almost identical ritual had been staged for the first time in the Caribbean as Jamaica became an independent member of the Commonwealth. Now for the eleventh time since World War II, the Union Jack was slowly lowered in another outpost of empire and then the red, white and black flag of Trinidad & Tobago was run up the flagstaff.
>
> Up to that point in the proceedings, the enormous throng of black and brown people who had assembled in Woodford Square had stood quietly by, almost transfixed. But as the new national flag came into view and a band struck up the new national anthem the entire crowd hesitated a moment, and then—as if rehearsed to respond on cue—broke into an incredible, jubilant roar. The nearby Gulf of Paria reverberated with a droning and tooting chorus emanating from the ships docked in the harbor. Church bells throughout the city began to peal maniacally. For at least that stirring moment there was no doubt that the people of the islands had achieved a sense of national solidarity and destiny (Oxaal, 1968: 1).

But to their minds it was to be a "destiny" of their own choosing. I was living in Jamaica during 1961-62 and also traveling to other emergent nations of the Caribbean, leading a team of sociologists studying the political transitions. I can testify to the pervasive consciousness of anticipation among West Indian peoples at the time. Everywhere, nearly every day, the coming independence was a topic of conversation, in the newspapers, on the radio, at dinner parties, at tea, on the job, at home, and at play. It was a time of creative expectation. The formative years of the first new nation, the United States, must have been like that, too, alive with a spirit of openness and possibility.

In the West Indies during the transitional years, despite the limited economic resources, there was a sense of empowerment. Anyone might compose a prospective national song, propose a national motto, recommend what the national bird should be, comment on the new constitution being drafted, put forward an economic plan, or contribute something else to the founding and building of the new state. Led by the example of the local intellectuals, at that momentous occasion nearly every new citizen was concerned about what his or her new state's future should be. However much the subsequent realities may have betrayed the hopes in many of the new states, the transition to independence itself created an orientation to the future and spawned debates—sometimes, it must be noted, violent and bloody conflict—about alternative national futures.

Third, the goals of development and modernization also promoted an inherently future-oriented and instrumental approach to nation-building that had its own dynamics. Most new national leaders accepted the goals of social, cultural, and, especially, political and economic development. Thus, they set about manipulating the present in order to achieve future development. This effort was aided, of course, by the economically advanced countries and various international organizations that sent not only money and equipment to the developing areas but also experts bearing the gifts of economic models and planning methods. By the mid-1960s, nearly all of the new states then formed were looking at the future using the tools of economic forecasting, national development plans, and central planning units (Madge, 1968: 125).

Planning, as every futurist knows, directly involves futures thinking, even though the time horizon typically involved may be shorter than many futurists would recommend. Additionally, to have a goal dominating national thinking, such as economic growth (creating a bigger pie of national wealth), provides a framework to judge—and therefore to make problematic—everything else in the society that may bear on it. For example, is economic growth being enhanced by the way children are educated in schools (to make them capable workers or risk-taking entrepreneurs)? By the nature of kinship obligations (to keep managers from giving their unskilled or lazy relatives jobs)? By how many women are using contraceptive devices (to keep the birth rate down so income per capita will go up and so that, eventually, unemployment rates will go down)? Or by how newspapers report and comment on the news (to spread faith in the regime and encourage people to work hard)? The list of questions reached into every aspect of social life. Thus, modernizing national leaders, vigorously pursuing the goal of economic growth, made nearly every aspect of society problematic by asking, How could it be changed so as to maximize a positive contribution to economic growth? Using the yardstick of development as the criterion of the preferable, of course, they often crashed head first into the stone wall of the traditional ways of their people.

Fourth, the transition to nationhood itself raised questions about choices and decisions that had to be made; and decision-making,

in turn, fostered futures thinking. When the days of organizing nationalist political parties, leading independence movements, fighting wars of independence, establishing trade unions, raising money and political support abroad, buying arms and ammunition where violence was necessary, and giving fiery speeches against the imperial masters were over, there remained the "decisions of nationhood" (Bell, 1964; Bell and Oxaal, 1964). Everything from the name of the new state, its geographical boundaries, and its form of government to the nature of its economic system, its social system, its national symbols, and its international affairs in one new state or another became issues that had to be decided. Such decisions often were urgent, because transition time was sometimes very short. Since there was always some outcome on such issues, there was no such thing as "no decision". Rather, sometimes alternatives were considered more seriously and in greater detail than they were at other times.

The tasks involved in making and implementing the decisions of nationhood were staggering. They were especially staggering for small countries with limited resources, as most of the new states were. Furthermore, there were obvious limits which then-existing social realities placed on whether or not efforts toward deliberate change could succeed. Yet it was just such tasks that most of the new national leaders set for themselves. As new constitutions were written, as economic plans were constructed, as literacy and educational goals were set, and as designs for their future societies and cultures were made in the 100 or so new states, most of the world's leaders, like it or not, ready or not, became involved in futures thinking. In democratic and authoritarian states, in capitalist and socialist and mixed economies, in Asia, the Middle East, Africa, the Pacific, and the Caribbean, the future became a realm for which designs were made and historical action was taken. Images of the future held by new nationalist leaders increasingly came to cause present action and, to create the future itself, although, as Marx said, the results were not always—or even often—as the leaders intended.

There were several ways in which facing the decisions of nationhood led new national leaders to engage in futures thinking:

a. Since nation-founding and nation-building require decisions to act, new national leaders had to think about the results of their actions. It is impossible to make anything that passes for a conscious decision to act without considering the future consequences of acting one way versus others (Jouvenel, 1967: 26-27).

b. Deciding to act invites the study of present possibilities for the future, because decision-makers would like to know what alternative choices are really open to them before they act. That is, in order to make informed decisions, leaders urgently need to know not only the future consequences of different actions, but also what range of actions is possible.

c. Decision-making encourages viewing social realities as problematic, since such realities are partly contingent on what decisions are made and what actions are taken. "What is" and "What was," of course, must be studied in order to make informed decisions, but a decision-making perspective stresses that the social world is constantly being created and recreated. Knowledge of society is reflexive, that is, it both describes social realities and may be used to change them. Society, as it is, is not taken as written in concrete, as a reified given that always must be as it is. People's choices and decisions, their images of society, their anticipations and expectations as well as their memories, their negotiations, and, ultimately, their social actions construct the social world. Thus, decision-makers, because they are strategically placed where they can observe these mechanisms of social construction and their own role in them, are able, more than most people, to see the contingent and problematic becomingness of social realities.

d. Since decision-making fosters goal-thinking and value analysis, it leads to a future time orientation. Decision-makers must have some basis for judging which of their envisioned alternative futures are better, i.e., more desirable, than others. Thus, they tend to set explicit goals and to justify them with stated values. Such goals and values also provide a standard of judgment with which to contrast the imperfect realities of the past and present with the hoped for improvements of the ideal future for which they strive. Future orientations are encouraged because the future is the time when goals and values of the present will be attained.

e. Because decision-making for action encourages constant monitoring in order to evaluate the results of that action, it fosters a dynamic perspective. Ideally, actions are taken; actual results are observed, specified, and judged as to their desirability; new possible action is invented to achieve more desirable results, as necessary; decision-makers' beliefs about society and how it works, are revised as learning occurs; goals and values are re-examined and re-evaluated; new action is designed and taken; and subsequent actions and results—unintended and unanticipated as well as intended and anticipated—are constantly monitored and evaluated for both effectiveness of means and desirability of both means and ends, in an unending series of feedback cycles. Society, thus, is necessarily seen as moving through time.

Obviously, to claim that the circumstances of the creation of the new states fostered futures thinking, as I do, is not to say that it was necessarily done well. In fact, we now know that it was often done badly. Unintended and unanticipated consequences sometimes made a shambles of hopes for a better life. Some consequences of particular actions were not even recognized as such at first. Economic forecasts of consequences of particular policies often proved to be wrong. Possible political consequences of given policies were sometimes ignored or wrongly predicted. Alternative possibilities for the future were not usually fully explored. Basic values and specific goals were not always considered in their relationship to each other. Planning was too often short-sighted, i.e. on too near a time horizon. Implications of changing technology were sometimes ignored. Technologies inappropriate to particular situations were too often employed, often as a result of advice from foreign technical experts. Some intellectuals in the new states spent more of their creative energies laying blame for the atrocities of the colonial past rather than creating opportunities for a new nationalist future. In some new states, extremists of either the right or the left violated democratic procedures and human liberties. Individual corruption and greed sometimes made a mockery of the decision-making process. Even among honest men, ideology and ill-founded hopes sometimes substituted for grounded, realistic assessments of future consequences of action.

In sum, the future, even where there was a predominantly future orientation as among new national leaders, was not easily tamed. There was an obvious need for more reliable and valid, i.e., more "warranted," assertions about the future (Bell and Olick, 1989). There was a need for an action science of the future. Despite numerous false starts, many new national leaders, their advisers, ministry staffs, members of government research centers and institutes, university consultants, and others, in their efforts to cope with the decisions of nationhood, began in fact to create one.

Decisions of Nationhood: Some Illustrations

Geographical boundaries. Once the decision has been taken to strive for nationhood, many other questions must be decided. One concerns the geographical scale of the new state. What should its geographical boundaries be? Often, the colonial boundaries set by past agreements among European powers were basically adopted during the transition. That is, the colonial boundaries became the new national boundaries, as in Ghana and Nigeria. Sometimes, there were bloody conflicts about them, as in the partition of the British Indian Empire into the new states of India and Pakistan and the further subdivision of Pakistan with the creation of Bangladesh, the last occurring after West Pakistanis killed as many as one million Bengalis and forced another 10 million to take refuge in India.

In the Caribbean, there was an effort to create a West Indian nation that would have included ten island territories. For example, in 1958, an internally self-governing West Indies Federation was formed with British blessing and it was headed for independence. The separate territories, however, could not agree on a number of issues, including how much power to give to the Federal government, and in September of 1961, when a referendum held in Jamaica on the issue resulted in a Jamaican decision to "go-it-alone," the Federation was doomed. Most of the territories, since then, have reached independence on their own, but, of course, with a geographical scale much smaller than that of the once envisioned West Indian nation.

Relation of the state and the nation. A related question is, "Should the future state and the nation be coterminous?" That is, should the boundaries of the emergent state as defined by the political boundaries of the national government be the same as the boundaries of the nation as defined by some commonly shared cultural characteristics? The answer of the new nationalist leaders, for the most part, was YES. Yet, mostly, they also realized that they would have to tolerate considerable sub-cultural diversity since their societies were culturally plural as they became independent.

This decision is related to the decision about boundaries, because juggling the geographical boundaries of the state is one method of making the boundaries of the state and the nation conform. In the example given above, cultural homogeneity within each state was increased when Islamic Pakistan separated from Hindu India, and was increased again later when the Bengali-dominated East Pakistan seceded from the Punjabi-dominated West Pakistan and became the separate state of Bangladesh. Before independence in relatively tiny Trinidad, there was some speculation about its possible geographical partition into two states, separating Trinidadians of African from those of East Indian descent. Of course, such a split would have left in limbo a number of minority groups from Portuguese and French Creole to Chinese and Lebanese.

Mass migration, of course, is another method of increasing cultural homogeneity within state boundaries. Again, a major example is found in the mass movements about the time of independence of Muslims from India to Pakistan and of Hindus from Pakistan to India.

Genocide is a method, a reprehensible one obviously, that can reduce cultural diversity. In Burundi in the spring and summer of 1972, ten years after political independence, the Tutsis massacred some 200,000 Hutus. Fortunately, on this scale it is one of several deviant cases, although ethnic conflict on a lesser level has been— and remains—a constant threat in most of the new states.

In the mid-1960s, the Ibos of Nigeria illustrate all three of the above strategies. They were victims of mass killings at the hands of the Muslim Hausas, migrated by the thousands from the Northern to the Eastern Region where Ibos dominated, and in 1967 seceded from Nigeria and declared their territory an independent state, Biafra. After two and a half years of bloody civil war, the Biafrans were defeated and so, too, was any immediate chance they might have had of realizing their image of an independent Ibo-Biafran future.

Confronted with the facts of cultural diversity, the new national leaders generally adopted the strategy of promoting cultural unity on a countrywide level. That is, they accepted the geographical boundaries and set about to increase shared cultural traits of the people within them. They tried to establish a new national identity, a national culture, and national symbols in which all citizens could share, whatever their racial and ethnic subgroups.

Cultural traditions. The decision to create a nation of the same scale as the state by promoting national culture, of course, immediately raises another decision of nationhood: What should the new state's cultural traditions be? In some sense, this turns anthropology on its head. Instead of merely asking, as anthropologists usually have done, what were or are a people's cultural traditions, national decision-makers look to the future and also ask what such traditions could be and what they ought to be. That is, such decision-makers concern themselves with cultural management and policies (Marriott, 1963).

When formed, the new states had cultures in which the cup of custom had been broken by foreign domination. Nowhere was this more true than in the Caribbean with its long history of imported workers, plantation slavery and indentured labor. Sometimes by selecting from a rich and available cultural past, such as in India and Pakistan, and sometimes by rediscovering vaguely remembered historical roots or by creatively giving voice to the shared experiences of oppression and struggle, such as in the Caribbean diaspora of dislocated peoples, many new nationalist leaders set about building a cup of custom from which all of their new citizens could drink the meaning of existence (DeVos and Romanucii-Ross, 1975).

In Jamaica, for example, the national motto, "Out of Many, One People," symbolizes the ideal of a harmonious multi-racial society. Cultural festivals, National Heritage Week, National Heroes Day, place-namings, statue dedications, innumerable speeches, and other ceremonial activities since independence, have been designed to promote a Jamaican or West Indian identity. In music, dance, drama, and the arts, government, churches, and schools, for example, have promoted cultural unity. Special efforts have been made to incorporate people of African descent, by far the vast majority of the population. Even the University of the West Indies has offered workshops in traditional African wrap and hair braiding, African drumming, and traditional African dance. The aim was to change from a past when the "melody of Europe" dominated over the "rhythm of Africa," as Rex Nettleford (1972) has said, to a future of "West Indian harmony." The results have been dramatic. For example, from 1962, just prior to the independence, to 1974, twelve years afterwards, Jamaican leaders radically changed their cultural orientations from mostly Anglo-European to mostly

Jamaican and West Indian (Bell and Robinson, 1979).

Appeals to the traditional past were often used to legitimate new visions of the future, the past usually being drawn upon not as an end, but as a means to reinforce the future-oriented perspectives of the Western-educated elite. That is, the criteria of selection of past facts and the real purposes and aims of the leaders were to be found in their images of the future. Their use of the history of traditions of the local peoples was partly a strategy of argumentation to persuade people of the rightness of their images of the future and of their proposed actions to make such images become the social realities of the future.

Social structure and equity. Facing the coming of independence, the people of the emerging states were caught in the race and class inequalities and inequities of colonial social systems. Thus, it is understandable that they should ask, "What kind of social structure should the new state have?" Why should the social order of privilege erected by the European sahibs continue after local people came to power? What good is political freedom if the former foreign masters are merely replaced by new indigenous masters? What changes in the system of social stratification should be made?

When asked before independence, for example, nearly every genuine nationalist leader interviewed in the former British Caribbean expressed his or her hoped-for image of a more egalitarian future (Moskos, 1967). Nationalists professed "equality" as a major goal of political independence, by which they meant both equality as citizens of their own country compared with peoples of other countries and equality within the new state as well. In particular, the inequalities of class, race, and emergent nationality that separated the privileged representatives of the imperial power from the mostly underprivileged local peoples were to be destroyed after independence, but so, too, were the unfair inequalities among local peoples themselves. The leaders not only wanted economic growth so as to have a bigger pie, they also wanted social reforms so that every citizen would have a fair-sized piece of the pie.

As Jamaican leaders came to power, they did many things to create more equality. Racial discrimination in public places and by social clubs was made illegal. Literacy programs, minimum wages, workmen's compensation, pensions (modest though they were), tax reform, land-lease (renting unutilized agricultural land to landless peasants), free primary education for all, and other social legislation aimed to make egalitarian changes was passed (Cumper, 1972).

One notable example in Jamaica was the case of the "Bastardy Law." Its name was changed to the Affiliation Law, and the word, "bastard," deleted from its provisions. This was an important change toward more equality under the law, since in Jamaica about 70 percent of the children born were "illegitimate" and wealthy men sometimes had both legitimate and illegitimate children. Any change toward giving illegitimate children more legal protection and equality—in inheritance rights for example—meant a change toward a more equitable society. Changes such as this, of course, could be done at relatively little economic cost to the new national governments.

There was some success, too, in providing a primary-school education for all. The percentage of people in Jamaica with such schooling rose from 70.5 percent in 1943 (19 years before independence) to 76.9 percent in 1960 (near the end of the transition to independence) to 82.7 percent in 1970 (eight years after independence), although the 1970 figure may be an overstatement. The percentage of children age 5-14 enrolled in school rose too, from 66.4 in 1943, to 83.6 in 1960, to 92.0 in 1970, although actual attendance from 1964 to 1971 remained steady at about 65 percent of those enrolled (Bell, 1977).

In the cases of inequality of income and land distribution there was less success at creating equality. This was so despite an experiment with democratic socialism under the Manley regime from 1972 to 1980 that prominently included the goal of equality. (Editor's Note: Michael Manley was returned to office on February 9, 1989.) Some of the failures, however, were due to factors beyond Jamaica's control, such as the rising cost of oil, the poor world markets for bauxite and sugar, and the general downturn in the international economy in the mid-1970s. Although the experiment in democratic socialism ended in electoral defeat in 1980, it left permanent changes in Jamaica, such as a commitment to the basic needs of nutrition, health, housing, and employment; more local control over bauxite production; leadership among Third World countries; continuation of some of the land reforms; and the increased political and organizational mobilization of the lower classes (Stephens and Stephens, 1986).

Of course, we must not underestimate the difficulties faced by the new states in their efforts to change social realities to match their hopes. Resources are limited, compromises with ideals appear necessary, and knowledge of effective development strategies is problematic. Nonetheless, the Jamaican experience illustrates the importance of an image of a future of social justice, both during the drive for political independence itself and, after independence, in the design of a more equitable social structure.

Conclusion

Many other decisions of nationhood, of course, could be discussed, such as the options involved in deciding what form of government the new state should have, how much of a role the government should play in the economy, what relations with other nations should be entered into, and even what kind of people the new state should have. The last may be more difficult to imagine than the others, because we tend to think of the social psychology of a people largely as given by conditions beyond human control. But many of the new national leaders, in fact, aimed to shape even the character of their people in order to create a new national man and woman. At best, some aimed, as in most of the Caribbean new states, to make the people achievement oriented in their work, active participants in a democratic political system, committed to social justice in their behavior and judgments, dedicated to the principle of equality of opportunity for all citizens of their new state, and free of a "colonial mentality" of inferiority and dependence. At worst, corrupt or fanatical leaders—as in Uganda under Idi Amin or Kampuchea under Pol Pot—disregarded human dignity and appeared to value only power for themselves, obedience on the part of the populace, or adherence to an ideological program no matter what the human costs.

What I have tried to show here, however, whatever the successes or failures of the results, is how the transition from politically dependent colony to politically independent state created conditions that fostered futures-thinking. The unavoidable tasks of state-founding and state-building required that decisions be made; in turn, such decision-making required futures thinking. These political transformations in over 100 new states and the considerable involvement of the old states in the process helped shape current world perspectives on development, modernization, social engineering, the means and ends of social change, and, in particular, produced tons of forecasts and plans as well as numerous experienced forecasters and planners. Living through a period of deliberate change, the new national leaders tended to make political, economic, social, cultural, and psychological life in their new states problematic and often created approximations to what Campbell (1988) has called "experimenting societies."

Although the new national leaders may have had much to learn from the experience of the old states, there is much, too, that the old states today could learn from them. In the old states, people tend to accept their current social institutions as given, if not nearly sacred, handed down to them by giants rather than by fallible men and women like themselves. They could benefit from the contingent, problematic, decision-making perspective of the new national leaders which would enable them to see more alternatives for the future and to be more receptive to their possible realization. With proper guarantees for the safety and dignity of the individual, the old states, too, could benefit from becoming experimenting societies, promoting more far-reaching futures thinking, trying out a greater range of alternative possibilities, and breaking the chains that bind them to futures that are overly limited by the claims of the past.

References

Bell, Wendell. 1977. "Inequality in Independent Jamaica: A Preliminary Appraisal of Elite Performance." *Revista/Review Interamericana* 7 (Summer): 294-308.

Bell, Wendell. 1964. *Jamaican Leaders: Political Attitudes in a New Nation.* Berkeley and Los Angeles: University of California Press.

Bell, Wendell and Jeffrey K. Olick. 1989. "An Epistemology for the Futures Field: Problems and Possibilities of Prediction." *Futures,* 21 (April):115-135.

Bell, Wendell and Ivar Oxaal. 1964. *Decisions of Nationhood: Political and Social Development in the British Caribbean.* Denver, CO: Social Science Foundation, University of Denver.

Bell, Wendell and Robert V. Robinson. 1979. "European Melody, African Rhythm, or West Indian Harmony? Changing Cultural Identity Among Leaders in a New State." *Social Forces* 58 (September): 249-279.

Campbell, Donald T. 1988. *Methodology and Epistemology for Social Science.* Chicago: The University of Chicago Press. Chapter 11, "The Experimenting Society," pp. 290-314.

Cumper, Gloria. 1972. *Survey of Social Legislation in Jamaica.* Jamaica: Institute of Social and Economic Research, University of the West Indies.

DeVos, G. and L. Romanucci-Ross. 1975. "Ethnicity: Vessel of Meaning and Emblem of Contrast." pp. 363-390 in George DeVos and Lola Romanucci-Ross (eds.), *Ethnic Identity: Cultural Continuities and Change.* Palo Alto: Mayfield.

Jouvenel, Bertrand de. (1964) 1967. *The Art of Conjecture.* New York: Basic Books.

Madge, Charles. 1968. "Planning, Social: Introduction." pp. 125-129 in David L. Sills (ed.), *International Encyclopedia of the Social Sciences.* Vol. 12. New York: Macmillan & The Free Press.

Marriott, McKim. 1963. "Cultural Policy in the New States." pp. 27-56 in Clifford Geertz (ed.), *Old Societies and New States.* New York: Free Press.

Moskos, Charles C., Jr. 1967, *The Sociology of Political Independence.* Cambridge, MA: Schenkman.

Nettleford, Rex M. 1972. *Identity, Race, and Protest in Jamaica.* New York: Morrow.

Oxaal, Ivar. 1968. *Black Intellectuals Come to Power: The Rise of Creole Nationalism in Trinidad & Tobago.* Cambridge, MA: Schenkman.

Palmer, R. R. 1959. *The Age of the Democratic Revolution: A Political History of Europe and America, 1760-1800,* "The Challenge," and 1964, "The Struggle." Princeton, NJ: Princeton University Press.

Pearcy, G. Etzel and Elvyn A. Stoneman, 1968. *A Handbook of New Nations.* New York: Crowell.

Stephens, Evelyne Huber and John D. Stephens. 1986. *Democratic Socialism in Jamaica.* Princeton, NJ: Princeton University Press.

EXPLAINING AND IMPLEMENTING FUTURES RESEARCH: PART I—A DEVELOPMENT PERSPECTIVE

by

O. W. Markley

Introduction[1]

What are the major problems faced by practitioners of the professional futures field? Both from my own experience and from what I hear from others, two concerns stand out in importance: 1. How to explain the futures field to those who are unfamiliar with its unique outlook, assumptions and methods—debunking preconceived notions and setting realistic expectations for what it entails; and 2. How to achieve successful implementation of forecasts and other futures research results, especially in organizational cultures in which decision-making based on credible foresight is not readily supported.

The purpose of this position paper is to share several approaches for making futures research more "used and useful." These include the incorporation of proven "change management" methods from the field of organization development, and the use of new ways to describe the field of futures research itself. They are meant to be "user-friendly" strategies through which to help business executives, community leaders, and other potential clients visualize the nature of futures research for themselves, and to more easily imagine how they might use futures methods for their own purposes. This essay is thus meant to complement, not to supplant, other published treatments of the futures field and its tools.

Explaining Futures Research

At an introductory level, futures work can usefully be explained by distinguishing three common ways of treating social changes and the future—*reactive, responsive,* and *creative.*

The first and certainly the most common way of dealing with various aspects of social change and the future is to ignore them, essentially assuming that although change is always occurring, the future will be like the past, only more so. Things that are getting big will get bigger; things that are getting tiny will get tinier; and

O. W. Markley *is chairman of the Graduate Program in Studies of the Future at the University of Houston-Clear Lake, Houston, Texas. Previously he directed futures research projects at the Center for Study of Social Policy, Management and Social Systems Group, SRI International, where for 10 years he was a senior policy analyst.*

so on. The population of growing regions like California and the microcomputers which its "Silicon Valley" has spawned upon the world are two cases in point. This approach involves waiting until external changes occur before dealing with them, and *reacting* to them as necessary, even though it may require the well-known mode of crisis management to do so.

The second way of treating the future is to pay attention to possible changes that will have an impact before it is too late to do anything about them, seeking foresight about the types of future conditions that are most likely. It then becomes feasible to antici-pate, and proactively *respond* to ways in which the future is likely to differ from the past, rather than reacting to these changes after they have already occurred. Although this helps avoid the crisis-reaction mode, it does not necessarily help you get what you really want. As Yogi Berra, the great US baseball catcher and master of the one-line quip used to say, "If you don't know where you want to go, you can bet on the fact that you'll end up somewhere else."

In contrast to the second mode, which is to anticipate what is probable and to respond to that outlook proactively, the third mode for dealing with the future is to be *creative*, envisioning what is desired. This involves clarifying your hopes and fears for the future, and then working to promote the former but prevent the latter. Successful use of the creative approach, however, usually requires the responsive approach as well. After all, many things are chang-ing which we cannot much influence or control. And finally, since we can't pay attention to all that is happening around us, the reactive approach is unavoidable as well.

It is thus important to use each of these three modes strategically and with effectiveness; and a central purpose of futures research is to help understand how to do so.

Evolution of the Modern Futures Research Movement

Another way to help explain the nature and function of modern futures research is briefly to review several particularly important historical "benchmarks" that shed light on how the futures field was shaped into what it is today. (This brief overview will necessar-ily leave out many things that would also be informative if space allowed, and it emphasizes the development of the field as practiced in the US. For a more detailed, albeit less up to date account, see writings by Jones.[2])

As a first cultural underpinning of what is now called "futures" work, I point to the Old Testament tradition of the prophets. Most people think of the word "prophecy" as dealing only with things to come, as in forecasting. But a close reading reveals this to be the second, and less important, of two major meanings of the word. The first definition can be paraphrased as "truth seer and truth teller." In the Hans Christian Andersen story, "The Emperor's New

Clothes," the naive youth who told the truth that nobody else would admit, was in this sense, acting as a prophet.

Only when both definitions come together, however, as in the oft quoted phrase, "Look at the handwriting on the wall, see what will happen to us if we don't change our ways," is the essence of the futures field revealed. By identifying key threats and opportunities that face us, and by assessing our strengths and weaknesses for treating them, futures research is clearly a prophetic profession.

The second major advance came in the mid-1930s. In order to prevent a re-occurrence of the catastrophic stock market crash and subsequent economic depression, the US Government began what has become a powerful system for defining, monitoring, modelling, analyzing and forecasting economic indicators, such as the gross national product. These indicators and their projection have been of fundamental importance ever since, both in the US and worldwide.

A third "great leap forward" in futures research came after the Second World War. The combination of the USA's "Cold War" with the USSR and its allies, and the US national will never again to be caught unprepared as with Pearl Harbor, led to the phenomenon of future-oriented "think tanks," such as the RAND corporation and the Stanford Research Institute. These, in turn, created a new battery of methods and tools for long-range forecasting and planning, systems analysis and management. The professional prophets of this era asked such questions as "What type of war might be fought in 20 years—who, where, why and with what kinds of weapons?" In responding, they invented scenarios and the Delphi technique as two of a range of methods and tools to think about *possible, probable* and *preferable* futures—and to derive implications for R&D as well as other types of strategic policy.

A fourth advance came with the liberal reformist movements of the 1960s which focused on civil rights, environmental protection and other concerns. The so-called "War on Poverty," the Peace Corps, and a new breed of think-tanks contributed participatory methods through which agencies in all sectors of society (public, private, and voluntary) could become involved in efforts to create the better society. These contributions ranged from complex methodologies for doing environmental impact assessments of technology, to relatively simple, but effective tools such as the Nominal Group Technique.

In 1973-74 the OPEC blockade wrought havoc throughout the economy. This event was an unanticipated but utterly significant source of serious cross-impacts, rapidly affecting the breadth and depth of national and international political and socio-economic systems. It has become a prototype illustration of what is often called "a wild-card scenario"—future possibilities that are not feasible to forecast at all reliably, even though they are quite obviously important if and when they happen.

The consternation among serious futures researchers regarding how best to deal with such events and the socio-techno-politico-economic turbulence associated thereto, led to the fifth and final advance in the field, I would cite, namely the creation and adaptation of *strategic intelligence* methods for application in both business corporations and public agencies. This aspect of futures research has as its central mission: *the promotion of management effectiveness in spite of a turbulent environment*.

Terms such as **strategic planning** and **issues management** came from this last advance. Together with **technology assessment,** they have become the major methodologies of futures research as it is known and practiced today.

And tomorrow? If I were to be a bit prophetic myself, and to conjecture about the *future* of futures research, I would focus on the issue of implementation, and how to treat resistance to it.

Resistance to Implementation: A Central Challenge for Futures Researchers

It is unfortunately the case that strategic forecasting and futures research methods often do not work according to the textbooks. Let me illustrate one reason why by means of a case example. In 1975 I was working in a small futures research "think tank" at the Stanford Research Institute (now SRI International). SRI's president called to make a special request. He said that he had just had an urgent call from a friend of his—the president of one of the big three US automobile companies, who wanted a quick turnaround forecast on consumer demand preferences for cars during the coming decade. He wanted to know if we could do such a study within a month and be confident of our results, but do it under conditions of total secrecy. We said we could and we did—drawing a number of conclusions a few weeks later. Our main forecast was that *because of the interaction of several key trends* —principally the increase in fuel prices and the increase in conservationist values and consumer lifestyles—there would almost surely be a significantly *decreasing* market for the traditionally large US cars and a corresponding *increase* in demand for smaller and fuel-efficient, but nevertheless classy models, such as the Japanese were already starting to produce. Our recommendations followed suit.

We sent our results on, still not even knowing who the client was (although we had our suspicions). Years later, when the secrecy no longer needed to be as tightly kept, I mentioned our study to a senior planning executive at a large energy and petrochemical corporation in Houston, who filled in the rest of the story. He revealed that he had been a planner at a particular car company in Detroit at the time; and that he and his colleagues had made essentially the same forecast. Their CEO, however, would not buy the reasoned vision of the future which they produced, so he sent to the West Coast for a second opinion. He did not believe SRI either and overrode both forecasts by ordering a continuation of the style known in the trade as "Big Detroit Iron," which brings in a far greater profit per car than do smaller, more sophisticated and fuel efficient models. The resulting debacle and its impact on the US economy is well known. Less well known is that although this company (and other US car companies as well) missed the chance to be proactively *responsive* to credible forecasts of change, it made a significant recovery only when it *reactively* imitated Japanese styles, but by then it also had to import the technology necessary for rapid retooling and efficient production. Similar examples exist in other sectors.

There are many understandable reasons why resistance to anticipatory management and planned change occur so frequently. One reason is that they tend to alter well-established patterns of power, communication and control. Another is that doing new things in new ways brings out feelings of uncertainty and the fear of failure. At least a dozen other factors could also be listed, not the least of which is the one operative in the above example: if forecasts or other futures research conclusions disagree with the personal outlook of the top executives for whom they were made, they will often be rejected or ignored. At the bottom line, it seems that we all resist the need to *change the boundaries of our ideas and our organizations to fit the changing "shape" of significant environmental forces all around us.*[3]

What can we do with the dilemma of having better tools than are often feasible to implement? Do we need to find better ways of communicating the nature of our methods and assumptions and why they are vital to good management? Or might it be that our future-oriented tools are insufficient by themselves?

I think that both are true, and that neither is sufficient by itself. We who are future-oriented professionals *do* need to add other tools to our menu of standard approaches, especially those that are more well-suited to the task of fostering implementation. And we *also* need to do a better job of communicating the essence of the tools we rely on, so that able leaders can *adapt* them as best suits their purpose, rather than *adopting* them in the form and with the terminology that futures researchers tend to prefer.

"Flawless Consulting" Tools—A Needed Addition to the Futures Field

The most direct way I know to increase the likelihood of successful implementation is to make use of a recently emerged professional field whose *raison d'etre* is the fostering of theories, tools, and skills for managing change. It is an applied behavioral science methodology usually called "organization development," but more

187

frequently referred to among its practitioners simply as "OD." For purposes of promoting implementation, the version of OD apt to be most useful to futures researchers may be a little handbook with the provocative title, *Flawless Consulting: A Guide to Getting Your Expertise Used.*[4] Its author, Peter Block, defines a manager as anyone who calls the shots which really matter in any given situation; every one else is a consultant, whether or not they are called that. Thus defined, it is clear that *most of us and most of our clients necessarily act as consultants most of the time,* even though we may have a title such as Manager or Director, Chairman or President. Derivatively, flawless consulting is not defined as getting the results we want all the time, but as a continuing consensual process of engagement, negotiation, and renegotiation as may be needed as the vicissitudes of organizational turbulence are treated.

Block's book and several related writings[5] set forth practical guidelines that help avoid the trap of trying to *overcome* people's resistance; and to instead do what is necessary to enlist them in the process of helping to establish such things as: 1. A revitalized sense of purposefulness, vision and mission for the organization—one that acknowledges rather than suppresses gaps between "is" and "ought"; and 2. A sense of alignment as to what is worth doing, and how it should be done, so that people naturally tend to do what is needed, even when not explicitly directed to do so.

To help envision practical ways in which this type of anticipatory leadership can be fostered, the following sections describe: 1) the essential nature of futures research; 2) how implementation-oriented OD methods can be effectively integrated with those of futures research; and 3) how the resulting synthesis can be visually portrayed for clients.

Futures Research as Applied Strategic Intelligence: An Analytic Model

As the historical overview sketched above suggests, the central objective of the futures field has shifted over the years, and has now taken on many of the characteristics of the intelligence field in order to promote the effectiveness of management in spite of environmental turbulence.

To see this analytically, rather than historically, consider the question, *"What are the minimum requirements for good management?"* Although something of an oversimplification, a good answer might be: 1. The ability either to *control* all variables having make-or-break significance for one's mission, or to *forecast* the behavior of those that cannot be controlled accurately enough to anticipate and control for their effects to the extent that is feasible; and 2. The ability to discern situations where neither control nor forecasting can be done satisfactorily and to substitute *intelligence-based strategic methods* in their stead.

Exhibit 1
SITUATIONAL INTELLIGENCE: MATCHING THE TYPE OF MANAGEMENT INFORMATION STRATEGY TO THE CHARACTERISTICS OF THE SITUATION

Ability to *control* the issue being considered

		HIGH	LOW
Planning time horizon, relative to degree of environmental turbulence (that is, *forecasting accuracy*)	NEAR (high)	I	II
	FAR (low)	III	IV

SITUATION I: *MANAGEMENT INFORMATION SYSTEMS*
Indicators of the status quo

SITUATION II: *PREDICTIVE FORECASTING*
Expectations of the "most likely" future

SITUATION III: *LONG-RANGE PLANNING*
Longer-term projections of influences, activities, and accomplishments

SITUATION IV: *STRATEGIC METHODS*
Alternative forecasts, contingency plans, scenarios, and situational management strategies

---

The framework shown in Exhibit 1 is based on this insight.[6] Arraying the two dimensions of controllability and forecastability against each other makes it easier to see the "situational relevance" of four important tools for management intelligence. The first three are frequently taught in business schools: 1. *Management information systems* —Collection, storage, summary reporting, and selective retrieval of historical, pragmatic data for short-range forecasting, planning, management, and assessment of activities and accomplishments. Frequently updated, the data provide *indicators of the status quo*. 2. *Predictive forecasting* —Anticipation of trends, trend discontinuities, and other projected occurrences expected to influence current plans and activities in significant ways. Revised periodically or when necessary, predictive forecasts yield *indicators of the expected or "most likely" future*. 3. *Long-range planning* —Coordination and alignment of long-range plans and operational programs with corporate budgets at all levels. Updated infrequently and requiring high commitment if implementation is to be more than rhetorical, long-range plans produce *longer-term projections of influences, activities, and accomplishments.*

The fourth "methodology" is the focus of modern futures research. Traditionally it was something that good managers and executives had to learn gradually in the school of hard knocks; it has emerged only within the past decade or so as a flexible set of concepts, methods, and tools for dealing with environmental turbulence and uncertainty: 4. *Strategic intelligence* —Identification and assessment of critical planning issues; advance formulation of alternative strategies for proactively responding to anticipated challenges that otherwise would eventually have to be dealt with on a "crisis reaction" basis; and development of the organizational capacity for responding in creative ways to the challenges of emergent conditions. Done on a regular basis or when needed because of "emerging issues," it provides management with a workable approach for *strategic intelligence and shared foresight.*

Especially when used with historical examples such as the OPEC blockade and the subsequent roller-coaster series of oil price fluctuations, the analytic model shown on Exhibit 1 is useful as a way to communicate why the methods of the modern futures field are so essential for managing in turbulent times. But models of this type do not do much to help the executive see *how* to actually employ such tools, especially in light of the resistance that usually attends their use.

A Methodological Synthesis for Improved Implementation[7]

Exhibits 2 and 3 pull together most of what has been said thus far. They portray the essential elements of an integrated model which organizational leaders usually find easy to grasp—both as an overall policy strategy for becoming more proactive in their approach to executive decision-making, and as a more detailed set of specific processes to use at different times for different purposes.

The left hand side of this model incorporates most of the strategic tools which comprise the field of futures research: **environmental scanning, issue identification and monitoring; forecasting and projection of alternative futures; contingent impact assessment and policy analysis; planning and evaluation.** The right hand side incorporates specific OD tools that develop the capabilities needed for successful implementation. For purposes of anticipatory management, the act of doing one side without the other may be compared to trying to walk with only one leg.

Depending on what you want to do and how you want to do it, this overall approach can be begun with virtually any of the major blocks of activity shown on Exhibits 2 and 3. Personally, I like to start with the **"plan to plan"** phase of the Strategic Direction block, doing it as the type of activity which Albert Einstein called *Gedanken* (literally, "thought experiments")—a way of thinking in which the doing of all the other blocks is visualized in various ways, resulting in agreement on how to proceed. The check-list shown on Exhibit 4 makes this type of thinking (sometimes characterized as "back of the envelope" planning) easier to do.[8]

To Dig Deeper

To further elaborate the above ideas would go beyond the scope of this essay. Specific references which provide detailed information for implementing each of the blocks on Exhibits 2 and 3 are as follows.

Strategic Assessment is a broad category which can be done in many ways. For guidance on **Environmental Assessment,** see *A Guidebook for Technology Assessment and Impact Analysis,*[9] and *Issues Management: How You Can Plan, Organize and Manage for the Future.*[10] For guidance on **Organizational Assessment** in the general context of OD, see Chapters Two and Nine of *Organization Development: Principles and Practices;*[11] especially discussion of the "Weisbord Six-Box Model" (pp. 169 ff), which was the principal point of departure for the list of items in this box of Exhibit 3. Or, see Weisbord's own formulation in "Organizational Diagnosis: Six Places to Look for Trouble With or Without a Theory."[12] An important approach to strategic assessment which is *not* reflected in the version of the model shown on Exhibits 2 and 3, but which is particularly important in many business applications is that of *Competitive Analysis.*[13]

Recognizing that strategic methods need to be tailored to the needs of different audiences, it may be helpful to cite books on **Strategic Direction** and **Strategic Planning** that are oriented toward different sectors of society:

- *Strategic Planning: What Every Manager Must Know* [14]
- *Strategic Planning for Public and Nonprofit Organizations: A Guide to Strengthening and Sustaining Organizational Achievement* [15]
- *Guide to Strategic Planning for Educators* [16]
- *Strategic Management and the United Way—A Guideline Series.* [17]

(The United Way is one of the largest charitable organizations in the US; this loose-leaf bound series comprises: 1. *Strategic Management;* 2. *Environmental Analysis,* 3. *Organizational Assessment,* 4. *Strategic Direction,* 5. *Strategic Plan,* 6. *Implementation,* and 7. *Performance Evaluation.* The conceptual model on which this guideline series is based served as a point of departure for the model shown here on Exhibits 2 and 3.)

Among the best methodological works on planning with multiple scenarios (primarily for business applications, but relevant to any type of organization) are:

- *Planning Under Uncertainty: Multiple Scenarios and Contingency Planning* [18]

EXHIBIT 2

Overview Schematic of
A Strategic Development Methodology
for
Anticipatory Management

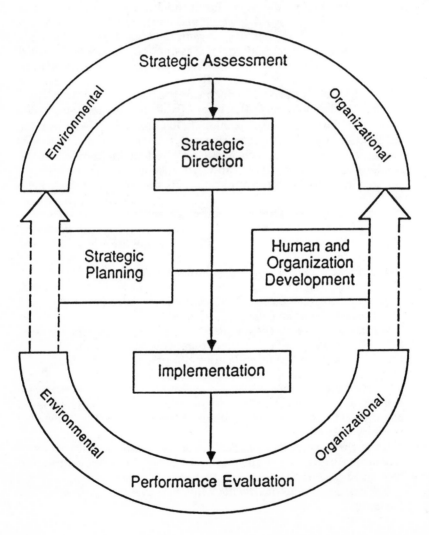

EXHIBIT 3

Detailed Phases of
a Strategic Development Methodology
for Anticipatory Management

Strategic Assessment

Environmental:

Social
Technological
Economic
Ecological
Political
Client/Project-Specific

Organizational:

Vision
Motivation
Leadership
Structure
Relationships
Mechanisms

Strategic Direction

Mission
Strategic thinking about
   alternatives
Goals
"Plan to plan"

Strategic Planning

Objectives
Strategies
Scenarios and Trigger
   Points
Strategic and Operational
   Plans

Human and Organizational
Development

Entry/Contracting
Diagnosis
Feedback/Decision
Implementation
Recycle/Extend/Terminate

Implementation

Who?
How?
When? (both start and finish)
With what?
To accomplish what
   "evaluatable" objectives?

Performance Evaluation

Environmental:

What happened by way of results?
(Both for us and for competitors.)

Organizational:

Did we do what we said we
planned to do, and did we
do it satisfactorily?
(If not, why not?)

NOTE: In the above model, the term "implementation" is used in two different but overlapping ways. As a phase of activity within Human and Organization Development, it refers primarily to the doing of whatever is necessary to ensure that a given organizational unit has the capacity to resolve pressing problems and to successfully implement its part of the strategic plan for the organization as a whole. In other words, what might be called "developmental implementation" is different from "operational implementation."

EXHIBIT 4

A CHECKLIST OF QUESTIONS

FOR ADVANCED "BACK OF THE ENVELOPE" PLANNING

1. **Vision**. What are my (my group's) predominant $\left\langle \begin{array}{l} \text{. hopes} \\ \text{. fears} \\ \text{. expectations} \end{array} \right\rangle$ regarding the future of "X"?

2. **Direction**. What do I (we) particularly want to $\left\langle \begin{array}{l} \text{. protect} \\ \text{. maintain} \\ \text{. achieve} \\ \text{. change} \\ \text{. create} \end{array} \right\rangle$

   in the $\left\langle \begin{array}{l} \text{. short} \\ \text{. medium} \\ \text{. long} \end{array} \right\rangle$ range?

3. **SWOT**. What are the main $\left\langle \begin{array}{l} \text{. strengths} \\ \text{. weaknesses} \\ \text{. opportunities} \\ \text{. threats} \\ \text{. other factors} \end{array} \right\rangle$ that need to be

   considered? In particular, what obstacles would prevent success if not overcome or otherwise addressed?

4. **Networking and Huddling**. How, and with whom, do I want to plan for action? What are their considerations about "X?"

5. **Technology**. What methods, tools, or strategies look promising? How rigorously might we want to use each?

6. **Commitment**. How much time and effort am I (and others I can count on) willing to dedicate to this, and for how long? What other resources are likely to be available if needed?

7. **Payoff/Costs/Tradeoffs**. Assuming that adequate time and effort is expended to implement the plans within likely resource constraints, what outcomes can realistically be expected, and when? What costs are likely? If not done, what different costs must be borne? I.e., what are the tradeoffs?

8. **Go/No Go.** Given whatever answers you have to the above questions, is the venture really worth doing? If so, who should do what? When? What are the first steps? If not, is there anything else that makes sense to do?

- *Scenarios: Uncharted Waters Ahead,* and *Scenarios: Shooting the Rapids* [19]

In the next block the word **human** was added to **organization development** in order to emphasize the need for training, team building, and other people-intensive aspects of OD work which, for reasons that were detailed above, I hypothesize as being essential concommitants of applied futures research in most settings. The five item list shown on Exhibit 3 are the specific steps described in the *Flawless Consulting* book described above. They are particularly useful for getting managers of various organizational units to "buy in" to the process of futures-oriented strategic management. By way of comparison, another model which I find quite useful for conceptualizing this entire process, but difficult to implement in most "real-world" organizations, is Gordon Lippitt's Organization Renewal Model. It is shown here as Exhibit 5. [20]

Good detailed guidance on **implementation** and on **performance evaluation** is hard to come by. Many titles exist, but none I would cite here. Instead I recommend that the "how" of intended implementation and evaluation be concretely visualized during the "planning to plan" stage, and that a specific individual or team accept the responsibility for monitoring compliance with whatever ends up being agreed upon, so that non-compliance does not—*as is so typically the case* —end up being ignored. The simple questions listed at the bottom of Exhibit 3 were framed with this *"realpolitik"* approach to implementation and evaluation in mind.

Summary and Conclusion

The foregoing essay introduces an easy to understand methodology for describing essential elements of futures research and of promoting their successful implementation. But it is only an introduction. The practitioner must still develop and adapt this methodology to the needs of particular situations if these ideas are to serve as an "appropriate technology" for anticipatory leadership.

In OD work, it is sometimes said that "the fundamental instrument is the consultant." [21] The same may be said for *applied* futures research.

Notes for Part I

1. Beginning in the fall of 1989, the required core curriculum of the graduate program in studies of the future at the University of Houston-Clear Lake will be changed from that described in "Preparing for the Professional Futures Field: Views from the UHCLC Futures Program," by O.W. Markley (*Futures,* February 1983, pages 47-64). The single research methods course previously required of all students will be divided into two: one emphasizing qualitative methods, to be taught in the fall; and a more advanced and quantitatively oriented course for the spring semester. Additionally, the

EXHIBIT 5

SYSTEMS RENEWAL MODEL

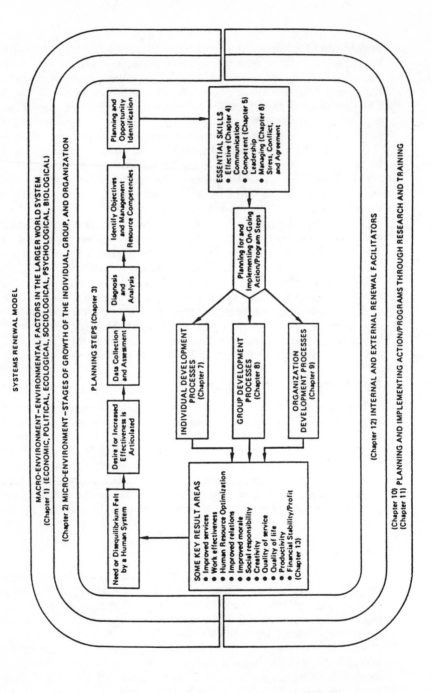

MACRO-ENVIRONMENT—ENVIRONMENTAL FACTORS IN THE LARGER WORLD SYSTEM
(Chapter 1) (ECONOMIC, POLITICAL, ECOLOGICAL, SOCIOLOGICAL, PSYCHOLOGICAL, BIOLOGICAL)

(Chapter 2) MICRO-ENVIRONMENT—STAGES OF GROWTH OF THE INDIVIDUAL, GROUP, AND ORGANIZATION

PLANNING STEPS (Chapter 3)

Need or Disequilibrium Felt by a Human System

Desire for Increased Effectiveness is Articulated

Data Collection and Assessment

Diagnosis and Analysis

Identify Objectives and Management Resource Competencies

Planning and Opportunity Identification

ESSENTIAL SKILLS
● Effective (Chapter 4) Communication
● Competent (Chapter 5) Leadership
● Managing (Chapter 6) Stress, Conflict, and Agreement

Planning for and Implementing On-Going Action/Program Steps

INDIVIDUAL DEVELOPMENT PROCESSES (Chapter 7)

GROUP DEVELOPMENT PROCESSES (Chapter 8)

ORGANIZATION DEVELOPMENT PROCESSES (Chapter 9)

SOME KEY RESULT AREAS
● Improved services
● Work effectiveness
● Human Resource Optimization
● Improved relations
● Improved morale
● Social responsibility
● Creativity
● Quality of service
● Quality of life
● Productivity
● Financial Stability/Profit
(Chapter 13)

(Chapter 12) INTERNAL AND EXTERNAL RENEWAL FACILITATORS

(Chapter 10)
(Chapter 11) PLANNING AND IMPLEMENTING ACTION/PROGRAMS THROUGH RESEARCH AND TRAINING

196

core course entitled, "Using Systems Approaches" will be moved from the spring to the fall semester. Together, these changes will give students a better methodological preparation before completing this masters degree program.

This methodological position paper was written as one of several curricular materials being developed for the new introductory core course, *Qualitative Futures Research Methods*. In addition to the sources cited herein, it is based on research done by the author at SRI International, the NASA Johnson Space Center, and the Institute for Strategic Innovation; and it incorporates several approaches for explaining the nature and function of futures research developed for a graduation address to members and guests of Class Five of the futures-oriented executive training program of the California Law Enforcement Command College, January 29, 1988. Constructive comments by Clare Degenhardt, Ken Hamik, Tim Sullivan and Cissy Yoes are gratefully acknowledged.

2. Thomas Jones, "The Futurist Movement: A Brief History," *World Future Society Bulletin*, July-August, 1979, pages 13-25. A more in-depth treatment can be found in Thomas Jones, *Options for the Future: A Comparative Analysis of Policy-Oriented Forecasts* (New York: Praeger, 1980).

3. Donald N. Michael, *On Learning to Plan—and Planning to Learn: The Social Psychology of Changing Toward Future-Responsive Societal Learning* (San Francisco, Jossey-Bass, 1973).

4. Peter Block, *Flawless Consulting: A Guide to Getting Your Expertise Used* (Austin, TX, Learning Concepts, 1981. Distributed by University Associates, Inc., San Diego, CA.)

5. Garth Morgan, "Cybernetics and Organization Theory: Epistemology or Technique?" *Human Relations*, Vol. 35, No. 7, pages 521-537, 1982; Charles Kiefer and Peter Senge, "Metanoic Organizations in the Transition to a Sustainable Society," *Technological Forecasting and Social Change*, Vol. 22, No. 2, 1982; A. Levy, "Second-Order Planned Change: Definition and Conceptualization," *Organizational Dynamics*, Vol. 15, No. 1, pages 5-20, 1986; Peter Block, *The Empowered Manager: Positive Political Skills at Work*, (San Francisco, CA, Jossey Bass, 1987); James M. Kouzes and Barry Z. Posner, *The Leadership Challenge: How to Get Extraordinary Things Done in Organizations*, (San Francisco, CA, Jossey-Bass, 1987); and O. W. Markley, "Using Depth Intuition in Creative Problem Solving and Strategic Innovation," *Journal of Creative Behavior*, Vol. 22, No. 2, 1988.

6. This framework was first published in O. W. Markley, "Conducting a Situation Audit: A Case Study," Chapter 5 in Robert L. Heath and Associates (eds.), *Strategic Issues Management: How Organizations Influence and Respond to Public Interests and Policies* (San Francisco, Jossey-Bass, 1988).

7. The synthesis shown on Exhibits 2 and 3 is based on a model developed by the author as a project of the Institute for Strategic Innovation. Karla M. Back first suggested the need for such a model.

8. This checklist was first published in "Planning to Use Emerging Instructional Technologies: Some Useful Methods and Guidelines," by O. W. Markley, Chris J. Dede, and Karla M. Back (Chapter 5 in *Preparing for the Future of the Workplace—Vol. III: Planning Materials for Educators*, Clear Lake Shores, TX, Institute for Strategic Innovation, 1988). For other related ideas that make it easier to implement the model shown on Exhibits 2 and 3, see the "Methodological Guidelines for Interesting Times," pages 58 ff of O. W. Markley, "Preparing for the Professional Futures Field," *Futures*, February, 1983; the "Snowball Survey" methodology used in O. W. Markley, "Conducting a Situation Audit: A Case Study," Chapter 5 in Robert L. Heath and Associates, *Strategic Issues Management: How Organizations Influence and Respond to Public Interests and Policies* (San Francisco, Jossey-Bass, 1988); and the "Strategic Intelligence Cycle" and "Social Intelligence Architecture" designs described below in Part II of this position paper.

9. Alan Porter, Frederick Rossini, Stanley Carpenter, with Ronald Larson and Jeffrey Tiller, *A Guidebook for Technology Assessment and Impact Analysis* (New York, North Holland, 1980).

10. Joseph F. Coates and the staff of J.F. Coates, Inc., *Issues Management: How You Can Plan, Organize, and Manage for the Future* (Mt. Airy, MD, Lomond Publications, 1986).

11. W. Warner Burke, *Organization Development: Principles and Practices* (Boston, Little, Brown and Co., 1982).

12. Marvin R. Weisbord, "Organizational Diagnosis: Six Places to Look for Trouble With or Without a Theory," *Group and Organization Studies I*, 1976, pages 430-447.

13. Michael E. Porter, *Competitive Strategy: Techniques for Analyzing Industries and Competitors* (New York, The Free Press, 1980).

14. Gary Steiner, *Strategic Planning: What Every Manager Must Know* (New York, The Free Press, 1979).

15. John M. Bryson, *Strategic Planning for Public and Nonprofit Organizations: A Guide to Strengthening and Sustaining Organizational Achievement* (San Francisco, Jossey-Bass, 1988).

16. Shirley McCune, *Guide to Strategic Planning for Educators.* (Alexandria, VA, Association for Supervision and Curriculum Development, 1986).

17. United Way of America, *Strategic Management and the United Way Guideline Series* (Alexandria VA: Strategic Planning Division, United Way of America, 1985).

18. Rochelle O'Conner, *Planning Under Uncertainty: Multiple Scenarios and Contingency Planning* (New York, The Conference Board, Report No. 741, 1978).

19. Pierre Wack, "Scenarios: Uncharted Waters Ahead," and "Scenarios: Shooting the Rapids," *Harvard Business Review*, Sep-

tember/October 1985, pages 73-89; and November/December 1985, pages 139-150.

20. Gordon L. Lippitt, *Organization Renewal: A Holistic Approach to Organization Development*, 2nd ed. (Englewood Cliffs, NJ, Prentice-Hall, 1982).

21. Burke, ibid, page 212.

Exhibit Sources

Exhibit 1: O.W. Markley, "Conducting a Situation Audit: A Case Study," Chapter 5 of *Strategic Issues Management: How Organizations Influence and Respond to Public Interests and Policies*, edited by Robert L. Heath and Associates, Jossey-Bass, San Francisco, CA, 1988. Reprinted with permission.

Exhibits 2-4: Institute for Strategic Innovation, ©1989 O.W. Markley. Reprinted with permission.

Exhibit 5: Gordon L. Lippitt, *Organizational Renewal: A Holistic Approach to Organization Development*, 2nd ed. 1982. Reprinted by permission of Prentice-Hall, Inc., Englewood Cliffs, NJ.

EXPLAINING AND IMPLEMENTING FUTURES RESEARCH: PART II—MORE ARCHITECTURES FOR ANTICIPATING MANAGEMENT

by

O.W. Markley

Introduction

In Part I, futures research was described as a relatively recent methodology for *strategic intelligence and shared foresight,* especially useful in times of *environmental turbulence* —i.e., times in which it is neither feasible to predict nor to control the behavior of variables essential to the fulfillment of mission, due to the number and intensity of changes occurring in various sectors of importance.

Part II is somewhat more technical, and is of necessity quite abbreviated due to space constraints, relying extensively on graphical rather than textual exposition. Its purpose is to convey several process "architectures" which are especially appropriate for anticipating and detecting what was defined in Part I as "Type IV" (high turbulence) environments, a hitherto left out aspect of most issues management methodologies.

To introduce these architectures, it is useful to first consider a distinction made in cybernetic systems theory between what has come to be called "1st order" change and "2nd order" or "systemic" change.

1st and 2nd Order Change

Jokes and cartoons, although not customarily used to communicate technical concepts, are sometimes better than lots of words to help an audience "jump-step" away from conventional thinking and into a new and radically different way of viewing things. A cartoon which has this potential when considering futures research and the management of complex change is shown on Exhibit 1.

I have found this cartoon to be of significant assistance in helping organizational leaders to not only appreciate the difference between 1st and 2nd order change, but to also recognize the importance of developing the *organizational capacity* for creating and implementing appropriate 2nd order change strategies when significant shifts in the "sea state" of the organizational environment require it.[1]

Exhibit 1

1st order change: Playing the game as you find it but moving the
                   pieces into a new arrangement
2nd order change: Seeing the game itself in a new way and creating
                   new types of moves

Architectures for 2nd Order Change and Anticipatory Management

In information systems work, the term "architecture" nowadays often refers not only to "bricks and mortar" buildings, but also to specifically designed configurations of hardware, software, and procedural management policies through which information is gathered, processed, retrieved and used.

As an example of the systemic nature of change which high technology management architectures may have to undergo if they are to be responsive to the potentials and needs brought by emerg-

EXHIBIT 2

Fifth Generation Management for Fifth Generation Technology

First:	Small/Entrepreneurial
Second:	Hierarchical/Functional/Divisional
Third:	Matrix
Fourth:	CIM I - Computer Interfaced Manufacturing
	Smith/Taylor Bottleneck
Fifth:	CIM II—Computer Integrative Manufacturing of the Manufacturing Enterprise

Figure 2. Generations of enterprise management.

First:	Electronic Vacuum Tube
Second:	Transistor
Third:	Integrated Circuit
Fourth:	Very Large Scale Integration
	von Neumann Bottleneck
Fifth:	Parallel Networked Process Units and Symbolic Processing

Figure 1. Generations of computer technology.

EXHIBIT 3

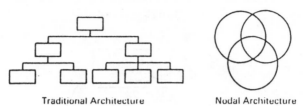

Traditional Architecture   Nodal Architecture

Figure 15. **Shifting management architectures.**

SECOND-TO-FOURTH GENERATION MANAGEMENT	FIFTH GENERATION MANAGEMENT
Functional Departments	Knowledge Centers
Jobs	Careers
Training	Education
Management by Variance	Nodal Project Management
Informational Amnesia	Informational Memory
Disposable Data	Data as an Asset

Figure 19. **Contrasting characteristics of FGM.**

---

ing "fifth generation" computer technologies, consider several illustrations developed by the Technical Council of the Computer and Automated Systems Association of the Society of Manufacturing Engineers (CAS/SME) in 1988.[2] These are shown on Exhibits 2 and 3.

The "Strategic Development Methodology" introduced earlier (please see Exhibits 2 and 3 of Part I) is, by the above definition, an architecture for 2nd order change and anticipatory management. A major advantage of this first model is that it uses state of the art tools that are widely practiced in major organizations. As such, it is feasible to implement in organizations as they now exist, and builds the organizational capacity for next generation applications.

A strength of this first architecture is thus its implementability. But a corresponding weakness is that it is usually implemented in an episodic fashion, and is thereby unable on an ongoing basis to systematically anticipate, detect and proactively respond to "Type IV" environmental "sea states" with respect to key issues which have make or break significance for the achievement of organizational mission.

A more advanced architecture, designed with this requirement in mind, is shown below on Exhibits 4, 5, and 6. Note the structural similarity of this architecture with that portrayed on Exhibit 3. They were developed independently.

EXHIBIT 4

A Generic Social Intelligence Architecture for Proactive Management

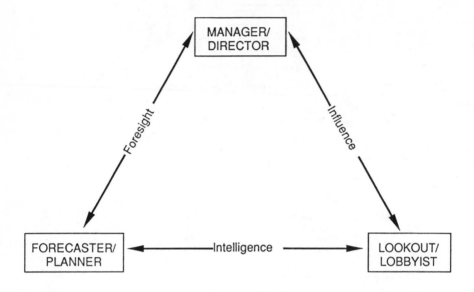

By way of review, the first architecture introduced here (Part I, Exhibits 2 and 3) emphasized specific *methods and tools* which are familiar in the field. Its main point of novelty is the way in which these methods are integrated in order: a) to increase the implementability of the left hand side; b) to increase the proactive responsiveness of the right hand side; and c) to thereby build the capacity for 2nd order, anticipatory change management by integrating both. The second architecture (Part II, Exhibits 4, 5, and 6) emphasizes a specific *organizational structure* which can be implemented both within a given organization, or within a network of organizations which have a common mission. Its main point of novelty is that it provides an ongoing basis for systematically anticipating, detecting and proactively responding to "Type IV" environmental "sea states" with respect to key issues which have make or break significance for the achievement of organizational mission. Thus, where the first architecture represents a way to increase the capacity for 2nd order change; the second architecture represents an actual 2nd order *change* that organizations can make to bring this capability into actual practice.

EXHIBIT 5

Social Intelligence and Proactive Management
Within a Formal Organization

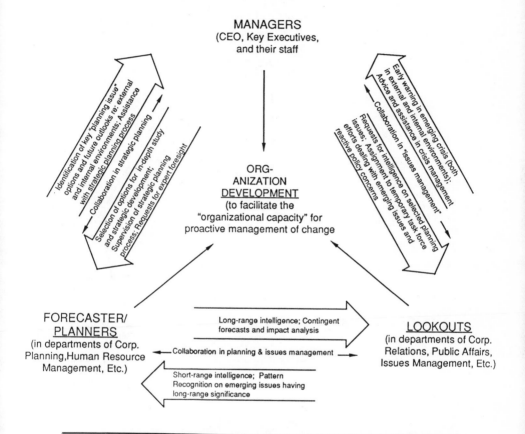

MANAGERS
(CEO, Key Executives,
and their staff

ORG-
ANIZATION
DEVELOPMENT
(to facilitate the
"organizational capacity" for
proactive management of change

FORECASTER/
PLANNERS
(in departments of Corp.
Planning,Human Resource
Management, Etc.)

LOOKOUTS
(in departments of Corp.
Relations, Public Affairs,
Issues Management, Etc.)

Long-range intelligence; Contingent
forecasts and impact analysis

Collaboration in planning & issues management

Short-range intelligence; Pattern
Recognition on emerging issues having
long-range significance

Identification of key "planning issue" options and future outlooks re: external and internal environments; Assistance with strategic planning process

Collaboration in strategic planning

Selection of options for in-depth study and strategic development; Supervision of strategic planning process; Requests for expert foresight

Early warning in emerging crisis (both in external and internal environments); Advice and assistance in crisis management

Collaboration in "issues management"

Requests for intelligence on selected planning issues; Assignment to temporary task force efforts dealing with emerging issues and reactive policy concerns

The third architecture, to be introduced next, represents closely sequenced series of questions, which when answered, increase not only the implementability, but also the political effectiveness, of whatever strategies come to be chosen.

A Political Process Architecture for Anticipatory Management

Exhibit 7 provides an overview of another process architecture, this one more associated with the practice of issues management, and designed in large part to resolve two seemingly opposite problems that often afflict applied futures research:

1) most people who are practical "movers and shakers" in man-

EXHIBIT 6

Social Intelligence and Proactive Management
Within a Community or Network of Organizations

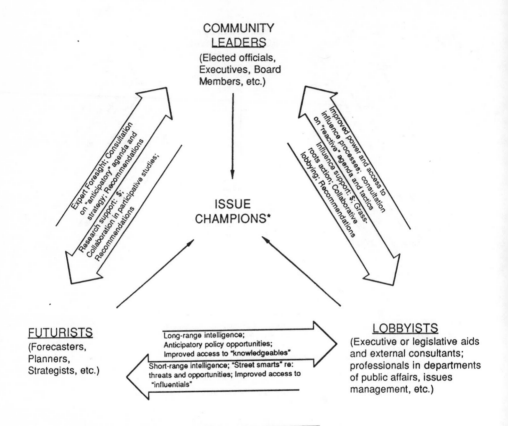

COMMUNITY
LEADERS
(Elected officials,
Executives, Board
Members, etc.)

ISSUE
CHAMPIONS*

FUTURISTS
(Forecasters,
Planners,
Strategists, etc.)

Long-range intelligence;
Anticipatory policy opportunities;
Improved access to "knowledgeables"

Short-range intelligence; "Street smarts" re:
threats and opportunities; Improved access to
"influentials"

LOBBYISTS
(Executive or legislative aids
and external consultants;
professionals in departments
of public affairs, issues
management, etc.)

*Sometimes called a "networker" or "point man", the "issue champion"
(like the "product champion" described by Peters and Waterman in
In Search of Excellence) provides the legitimacy, inspiration, and coordination necessary for successful collaborative action.

agerial or political settings tend to ignore the fact that there is much
information available that could illuminate their actions;

2) most people who are "researchers and analysts" in academic
or administrative staff settings tend to ignore that there are a variety
of political customs that must be reflected if information is to be
effectively used by practical leaders.

Dubbed "The Strategic Intelligence Cycle," its purpose is to give
an organization the capability to realistically envision:

- The nature of important cause and effect relationships and cross-cutting factors which influence a given issue strongly;
- How the issue and related factors are perceived by important interest groups;
- The workings of different social institutions and systems in which the issue is embedded.

The Strategic Intelligence Cycle represents a practical method of approach through which these difficult understandings can be developed within realistic time and resource constraints. It embodies the methods and styles that good lobbyists, regional development leaders, and other successful social change agents tend to use in their day to day work. Originally introduced in the book *Information and the Future: A Handbook of Sources and Strategies,* [3] this architecture was created by an informal "knowledge engineering" research process which led to the synthesis of three essential types of expertise for knowledgeably influencing the future:

- *Information research* (as practiced by reference librarians)
- *Forecasting and strategic planning* (as practiced by futures researchers)
- *Public relations and issues management* (as practiced by political lobbyists).

A central characteristic of the Strategic Intelligence Cycle is that in addition to helping select preferred strategies for directly influencing change, it also emphasizes the *refinement* of information seeking, once it is clear what action-oriented strategies the information is intended to support, so that the theoretical assumptions of "2nd order cybernetics" involving the "learning to learn" process sometimes called "double loop learning" can be honored in practice.[4] Toward this end, the "80-20 rule" is often useful to invoke. Simply stated, it is to go fast and get 80% of the results you want in 20% of the total time you think you have. Then sit down and figure out what to do next. You may or may not want to spend the remaining 80% of the time you budgeted to get the final 20% of information or accomplishment you initially envisioned. Based on what you just learned, something else may now appear much more important.

Exhibits 8, 9, 10, and 11 depict the essential details of each phase of the model. For more information on each, please see pages 124-135 of *Information and the Future,* where this methodology was first published. Experienced practitioners will recognize that the elements shown in each phase, although moderately detailed, represent a vast simplification of matters that are highly complex and often ambiguous. They are presented this way, not with the idea that they will rigorously fit all situations for which they may be applied, but with the knowledge that, when combined with the other architectures introduced above, it is feasible to learn whatever is necessary to adapt them successfully to the needs of the specific situation.

EXHIBIT 7

An Overview of the Strategic Intelligence Cycle

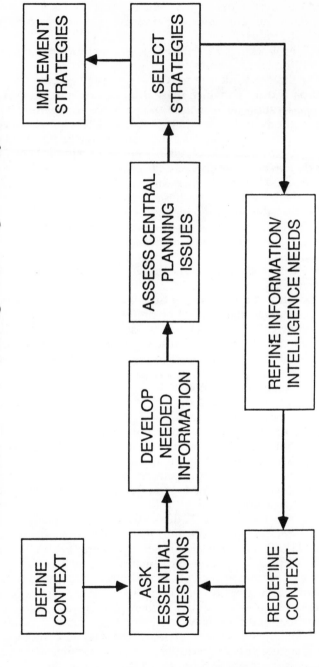

EXHIBIT 8

The Strategic Intelligence Cycle

Phase 1: Get Underway

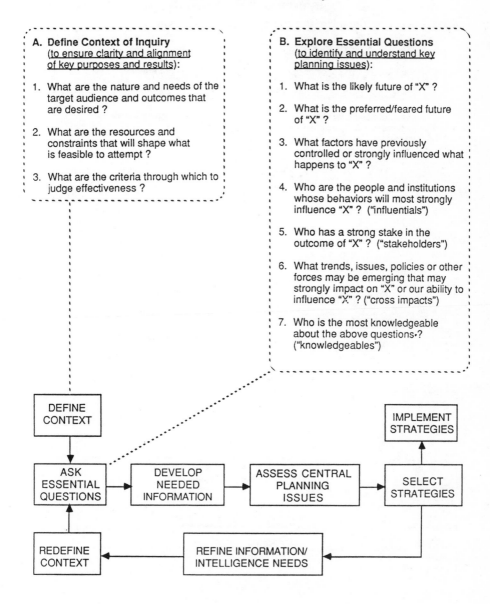

A. **Define Context of Inquiry**
(to ensure clarity and alignment
of key purposes and results):

1. What are the nature and needs of the target audience and outcomes that are desired ?

2. What are the resources and constraints that will shape what is feasible to attempt ?

3. What are the criteria through which to judge effectiveness ?

B. **Explore Essential Questions**
(to identify and understand key
planning issues):

1. What is the likely future of "X" ?

2. What is the preferred/feared future of "X" ?

3. What factors have previously controlled or strongly influenced what happens to "X" ?

4. Who are the people and institutions whose behaviors will most strongly influence "X" ? ("influentials")

5. Who has a strong stake in the outcome of "X" ? ("stakeholders")

6. What trends, issues, policies or other forces may be emerging that may strongly impact on "X" or our ability to influence "X" ? ("cross impacts")

7. Who is the most knowledgeable about the above questions·? ("knowledgeables")

DEFINE CONTEXT

IMPLEMENT STRATEGIES

ASK ESSENTIAL QUESTIONS → DEVELOP NEEDED INFORMATION → ASSESS CENTRAL PLANNING ISSUES → SELECT STRATEGIES

REDEFINE CONTEXT ← REFINE INFORMATION/ INTELLIGENCE NEEDS

EXHIBIT 9

The Strategic Intelligence Cycle

Phase 2: Develop a Change Oriented Information Framework
(to organize and manage needed information)

a. Historical Context of "X"

- Past writings of importance

- Legislative and/or judicial history

- Other historical factors of importance (e.g., key vested interests)

b. Key Actors and Agenda

- Influentials

- Stakeholders

- Knowledgeables

c. Key types of Information

- Documents

- Contacts

- Messages

d. Alternative Approaches

- Ideologies

- Schools of thought

- Policy proposals

- Possible coalitions

e. Things to Monitor

- Media coverage

- Movement in key policy proposals

- Changes in "story" of key actors

- Changes in other key factors

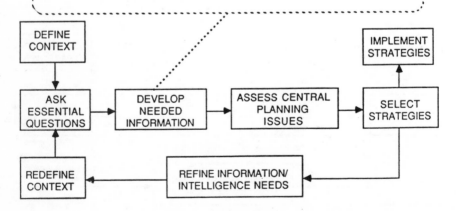

EXHIBIT 10 |

The Strategic Intelligence Cycle

PHASE 3. Assess Central Planning Issues
(to develop appropriate strategies)

a. <u>Identify critical factors, obstacles and incentives</u>

What factors must be influenced if the future of "X" is to become what we want it to be ?

What obstacles are likely to prevent us from influencing things as we would like ?

What incentives can be brought to bear to overcome obstacles ?

b. <u>Estimate critical timing relationships</u>

Are any key factors likely to become "acute" and require a crisis-reaction strategy that would be less effective or more costly than a proactive response ?

What is the likely sequence and timing of events that will most strongly influence "X" assuming that we do not intervene "proactively" ?

c. <u>Identify Probable and Desirable Roles</u>

Who are the relevant players ?

What is the range of roles that each is likely to play, assuming either that we do, or that we do not act proactively ?

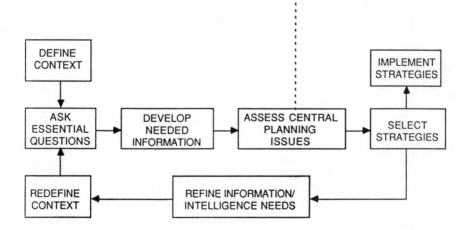

EXHIBIT 11

The Strategic Intelligence Cycle

Phase 4. Select Strategies
(to successfully influence the future of "X")

- Take direct action

- Engage in single-issue lobbying

- Collaborate with coalition networks to develop a broad range of proactive agenda

- Publicize selected issues or points of view

- Develop needed information to answer critical questions

Phase 5. Refine Information/ Intelligence Needs

a. Type of Information

- Statistical data

- Authoritative reports

- Knowledgeable experts

b. Immediacy of Source

- Primary sources (personal communication or original writing)

- Secondary Sources (popular literature, news media, trade/professional working papers, etc.

- Tertiary sources (summaries, abstracts, indexes, etc.)

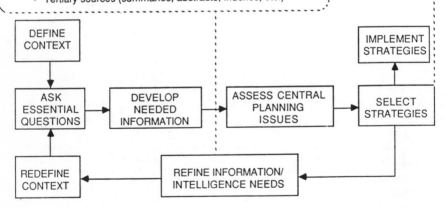

Summary and Conclusion

The architectures and other guidelines presented in this two-part methodological position paper are the result of a decade-long search for efficient and effective approaches through which to explain and to implement the poorly understood field of futures research. An important by-product of this search is the recognition that the organizational capacity to implement forecasts, strategic plans, and other change-demanding results of futures research doesn't just happen. It must be created.

If futures research tools are to contribute all they are intended to and capable of, therefore, the "field" of futures research may itself have to be envisioned and practiced in new ways. Some possible directions of new growth are described herein.

Notes for Part II

1. Readers wanting a theoretical and/or practical discussion of the distinction between 1st and 2nd order change may find the following two references particularly useful: A. Levy, "Second-Order Planned Change: Definition and Conceptualization," *Organizational Dynamics*, pages 5-20, Summer 1986; and L. Hoffman, "Beyond Power and Control: Toward a 'Second Order' Family Systems Therapy," *Family Systems Medicine*, Vol. 3, No. 4, pages 381-396, 1985. Also see O. Markley, "Conducting a Situation Audit," Chapter 5 in R. L. Heath and Associates, *Strategic Issues Management: How Organizations Influence and Respond to Public Interests and Policies* (San Francisco, Jossey-Bass, 1988).

In general, 1st order (change) theories, tools and practices tend to be more suitable for what are defined in Part I as Type I, II, and III Environments, whereas environments having Type IV characteristics tend to require second-order approaches.

2. C. Savage, "CIM and Fifth Generation Management: Reflections Inspired by the CASA/SME Round Table on Fifth Generation Management" (P.O. Box 93, Dearborn, MI, Society of Manufacturing Engineers, Reference Publications Division, 1988).

3. A. Wygant and O. Markley, *Information and the Future: A Handbook of Sources and Strategies* (Greenwood Press, 1988).

4. See G. Morgan, "Cybernetics and Organization Theory: Epistemology or Technique?" *Human Relations*, Vol. 35, No. 7, pages 521-537, 1982.

Exhibit Sources

Exhibit 1: Adapted from various sources by the author.
Exhibits 2 and 3: Charles M. Savage, *Fifth Generation Management for Fifth Generation Technology*, Society of Manufacturing Engineers, Dearborn, MI, 1988. Reprinted with permission.
Exhibits 4-11: Alice Chambers Wygant and O.W. Markley, *Information and the Future*, Greenwood Press, Westport, CT, 1988. Reprinted with permission.

New Mental Attitudes

CREATIVITY AND INNOVATION IN THE HIGH-TECHNOLOGY ERA

by

S.C. Kitsopoulos

Introduction

In parallel with extraordinarily rapid technological developments, one can observe today social changes in the direction of more independence and more responsibility of the individual as well as a democratization and humanization of the enterprise. This in turn results in a flattening of the traditionally hierarchical organization and an improvement of the quality of work life. These internal organizational developments proceed at a much slower pace than the technological progress. Outside the technological enterprises, we observe a globalization of markets, an intensification of competition on an international level, and highly differentiated needs and quality demands by customers.

If the commercial enterprise wants to remain successful, even to survive, it must change its corporate culture accordingly. This is especially true, and especially important, for the high-technology firm, because it tends to be driven by technology rather than human social values. At the heart of these new considerations is the realization that people, all employees of a firm, come first; finance, marketing, manufacturing, development, etc. are only the results of human activities. Leadership may no longer be expected only at the top but throughout the organization. The wide diversity of people must thereby be taken into consideration. The creativity of the individual as well as the team must be consciously fostered in order to ensure continuous innovation. The *sine qua non* of such endeavors is an open and honest interpersonal communication. Obstacles to communication and the creative development of all workers must be eliminated.[1]

In order to foster creativity, it is important to understand how people differ from each other in their psychological functioning. We shall explore this subject next, on the basis of C. G. Jung's theory of psychological types.[2] We shall then describe the process of creativity and discuss how blocks to creativity can be recognized and eliminated.

People Diversity

Jung has defined four psychological types, based on four different cognitive styles or psychological functions. These functions are: *sensation* or the input of the senses, which tells us that something exists; *thinking*, which tells us what it is; *intuition*, which tells us

---

S.C. Kitsopoulos *is founder and senior partner of InterConsult.*

whence it comes and where it is going; and *feeling*, which tells us whether it is agreeable or not. These are only four of many criteria of human behavior, such as will, temperament, introversion, extraversion, imagination, etc. Their fundamental nature recommends them as simple and appropriate categories for a psychological typology.

The pronounced sensation types react to the world primarily through their sense perception. In order to believe something they want to have heard, seen or touched it themselves. They are oriented towards a practical, common-sense approach and live in the here and now. They will process patiently and methodically large amounts of facts and data, without getting bored. They show little interest in the global view and the meaning of these data. That is the domain of the pronounced intuitive types who simply know without being aware that they have perceived. They are fascinated by theories, complex interrelations, gestalts and future possibilities. They find details boring. Like the proverbial absent-minded professor, they seem unaware of their surroundings and the present. They are imaginative and creative but not very much interested in the practical implications of their many ideas. The pronounced thinking types make decisions on a rational basis, objectively, analytically and dispassionately. Their feelings can get in their way though, and they do not like it. We all know such types who can lose control when their feelings—love for example—overcome their personality with elemental force. The pronounced feeling types on the other hand, let subjective values color their decision making and act with personal conviction. They judge the situation at hand on the basis of its feeling value. Their objective thinking can be faulty, because they do not like to take all factors into account and subject them to rational analysis. Naturally, such extreme types are as rare as those who partake equally of all four functions. Most of us fall somewhere in between and also change type as a function of time and accumulated life experience.

Various studies[3] have revealed that three quarters of young engineers are thinking types, while other studies suggest that the most successful executives are rather intuitive and feeling types[4]. The high-technology company, which is dominated and often led by engineers, also runs the risk of becoming one sided. These managers have the all too human tendency to recruit and promote others who are in their own image. Despite short-term advantages, an inbreeding situation can develop in the long run, whereby the organization can no longer keep up with the rapidly changing competitive environment. As in natural evolution, this contains the germ of an eventual demise of the firm despite its technical excellence. In order to prevent such events, it is imperative to understand not only that all psychological types are of equal importance but also that all four cognitive styles are necessary for the success of the enterprise, as they are for every human endeavor.

But let us now return to the individual. The key to our growth, to realizing all our potentialities, lies in our own unconscious (in the Jungian sense). This is a difficult, life-long process. It can not be taught, it can only be lived. But the first step is to acknowledge and understand this process. In this way we also learn how to accept others as the different people they really are.

The most creative individuals combine the four functions into a transcendent whole. Science and technology do not feed only on rational method, specialized knowledge and hard work. They are at their best when their practitioners do not lose the awe before the unknown and the great secrets of nature, and the pleasures of the imaginative insight which relies on inspiration rather than calculation. The most creative scientists share these attributes with the great artists. It is the humanity of an Andrej Sakharov, the humility of an Albert Einstein, the prophetic insights of a Sigmund Freud, the life of a Leonardo da Vinci—artist and engineer at one and the same time—that bridge the gaps of the opposing functions.

Think of the painter who has the wonderful ability to perceive even the minutest details of an object or scene, in order to transfer them to the canvas. At the same time he or she conveys a message which transcends by far the sum total of these sense perceptions and which can not be expressed in any other way except by the work of art itself. The detailed perception is pure sensation; the undescribable message is pure intuition: the gap has been bridged.

Let us see how the act of creation comes about, whether it results in a poem, a symphony, a painting, a scientific discovery or a technological invention. The creator delivers himself or herself to the inner impulse, is frustrated, restless, moody. But when the basic idea surfaces, he or she feels great joy, happiness, elation. Then comes the systematic, painstaking, rational work that helps the implementation of the opus: calculating, grooming, refining, polishing. Thinking and feeling merge; the opposites are united.

Great talent is certainly inborn, and very rare indeed. Very, very few of us will ever attain the creative heights of a Mozart or a Newton. But there is no doubt that the discovery and development of the innate potentialities hidden in every individual will promote his or her creativity. These potentialities are in every one of us: in every engineer there is a poet and in every artist hides a scientist.

Team creativity will also be fostered, if the team members become aware of their diversity and learn how to value it. We experience our differences and our similarities very strongly, when we enjoy our diversity, when we communicate and celebrate it. Opening the communication channels, which are blocked by our differing cognitive styles, offers us new opportunities to lead a more creative life whether at work or in our community.

The Process of Creativity

When we think of creativity, we usually think of someone who does something useful, beautiful or pleasant, which was not obvious before it was done.

In the arts, creativity is the work of a single individual in most cases. The work of art obtains its aesthetic value through communication. The artist delves into the unconscious and brings up from it a message of universal value. The beholder lets this message sink into his or her own unconscious. The connection, true communication, occurs in the realm of the collective unconscious. This explains the substantial effect great works of art have on so many different people and over such long periods of time.

The scientist on the other hand, coaxes nature through theory and experiment into revealing its secrets. We call this discovery but its process is similar to the artistic creation. Scientific discoveries are also more often than not the work of single individuals. However, scientific collaboration in teams is becoming more and more important, as in high-energy physics for example.

In engineering, applied science and technology, creativity finds its expression in inventions. Scientific discoveries are used to create products or processes which are economically or socially useful. Although many inventions are produced by single individuals, their reduction to practice necessitates the collaboration of many individuals. The entire process from discovery through invention to implementation is called innovation.

For good measure, the process of creativity is also applicable in our daily lives. New ideas and their reduction to practice are useful not only in industry and commerce; they are also of great value in all human interactions.

Arthur Koestler said: "Every creative act involves . . . a new innocence of perception, liberated from the cataract of accepted belief." And Janos Starker, the cellist, said: "Creativity is the obsessive drive for reducing chaos and finding beauty."

Creation entails the risk of leaving the beaten path, of questioning conventional beliefs. It thrives in chaotic, ambiguous situations out of which it crystallizes a new order. It involves obsessive hard work and pain as well as beauty, elegance and the pleasures of sudden illumination. It proceeds by analogy, metaphor, paradox and the use of opposites. It is thereby very much related to humor and puzzles. The psychological mechanism of projection is also at work in the act of creation. The starry night sky for example is a very good, seemingly chaotic screen upon which we project the contents of the unconscious; this is how both astronomy and astrology were born. Sensory deprivation and its opposite, sensory overload, provide propitious conditions for such projections: Many of us have had new ideas and have come up with unexpected solutions to problems while showering: with eyes closed and the random noise of the water hitting our head, thereby overloading our sense of hearing. Meditation, hypnagogic states (i.e., when we are about to fall asleep), fantasies and dreams are often bearers of creative illuminations.

There are four stages to the process of creativity. *Preparation* involves learning the methods and techniques of one's craft, whether it is engineering, farming, poetry or painting. It also includes the definition of the task at hand or the problem to be solved. It is based mostly on our *thinking* function which is what we use predominantly in college or apprenticeship. Pasteur said: "Chance favors the prepared mind." The stage is *incubation,* letting things descend and simmer in the *intuitive* function. Incubation leads to the next stage, *illumination.* This is the aha! experience with its accompanying joy and pleasure, which belong in the realm of *feeling.* In the final stage, *verification,* one confirms the creative idea by using all the senses to collect and validate the pertinent facts, thus using the *sensing* function.

We already talked about one barrier to creativity, which is based on our differing cognitive styles. It reveals itself as an internal block if the individual does not make use of the opposite functions within. We have also seen that it can be an external obstacle to team creativity when it blocks communication between opposite types.

Another barrier to creativity is our inability to break out of our habitual reference systems. Humor is very much related to creativity because it often succeeds in bursting this frame of reference. Through paradox and metaphor it leads us to expect the unexpected. Here is a joke that illustrates the point. A very fat man stepped on a scale to check his weight. It was one of these scales with a large round dial and a pointer that indicates the weight. The man was so heavy that the pointer turned all the way around and stopped at zero again. A young boy happened to look at just that moment at the man, scale and pointer. He turned to his friend and said excitedly: "Look, the man is empty!" This shows how children lack the limits to open thinking which education and experience impose on us adults. Nietsche was right saying: "In every grown up a child is hidden; it wants to play!" Play also fosters creativity.

Puzzles and riddles are good examples of creative problem solving because they often illustrate how one can overcome or bypass barriers. Riddles can often be solved elegantly in unconventional ways. In order to solve problems we make use of different cognitive "languages" such as natural language, logic, mathematics or imagery. If we limit ourselves only to the one of these languages which seems most appropriate at first, we may not be able to solve the problem at all. Let us illustrate with the following example. What is the next term of the following series and what is the formula describing the general term?
O,T,T,F,F, . . .
Many people, but especially engineers and scientists, have difficulty solving this problem because they choose and stay with the mathematical approach, which turns out to be utterly inappropriate in this case.

The next term is S and the "formula" is to use the initials of the names of the numerals: One, Two, Three, Four, Five, Six, etc.

Another set of blocks to creativity are of an environmental nature. Few things stifle creativity more effectively for example, than a boss who is always very judgmental, as some are. Here are examples from a long list of subtle obstacles which are often thrown prematurely into the path of new ideas:

We tried that before and it did not work

It costs too much

We have always done it this way

That is not our job

It is against company policy

That is not our problem

The big boss will not like that

Write me a note about it

Let us form a committee to look into this

etc., etc.

Several techniques have been developed over the years to stimulate creativity by making it possible to avoid or overcome these hurdles. They include using analogies, metaphors, and opposites; morphological analysis; a questioning but not judgmental attitude (what if . . .); brainstorming; the odd man in; and others.

In conclusion, our capacity for creative endeavor is very much underutilized. If we become aware of the diversity in people, of the creative process and of the many obstacles to creativity, we can foster an attitude and a climate which stimulates it in the individual as well as the team. It is imperative that the high-technology enterprise, with its large investment in research and development, learn how to better utilize its creative human resources, if it wants to ensure its success in today's global competitive environment.

Notes

1. Kitsopoulos, S.C. et al. "Communication and Corporate Culture in the High-Tech Enterprise," *Information Technology for Organizational Systems,* H. J. Bullinger et al. (eds.), pp. 259-263, Elsevier Science Publishers B.V. (North Holland) 1988.

2. Jung, C. G. "Psychological Types," *Collected Works,* Vol. 6, Bollingen Series XX, Princeton University Press 1971.

3. McCaulley, M. H. et al. "Myers-Briggs Type Indicator and Retention in Engineering," *Int. J. Appl. Engng. Ed.,* Vol. 3, No. 2, pp. 99-109, Great Britain 1987.

4. Howard, A. "Can Engineers Succeed in General Management?" IEEE Careers Conference, Conference Record, pp. 76-80, USA, 1983.

COMPUTER PARTNERS IN OUR FUTURE

by

Ted Slovin and Beverly Woolf

Intelligent Tutors and Consultants

Expert systems have been shown to encode the knowledge of an expert and even to outperform humans in domains that require reasoning and problem-solving (Feigenbaum et al., 1988). Successful systems have been built for medical diagnosis, e.g., MYCIN, computer configuration, e.g. DEC's XCON system, and chess playing, e.g., systems with Master's ratings are on the market for around $250. However, intelligent systems that work with humans as colleagues and partners have just begun to emerge and they have the potential to perform even better than expert systems.

Potentially powerful and significant personal and societal transformations are now underway partially as a result of Artificial Intelligence and the potential of the computer (Ambron and Hooper, 1988; Brand, 1987; Levy, 1984; McCorduck, 1985; Nelson, 1987; Schank, 1984; Shafer, 1986; Winograd and Flores, 1986; Turkle, 1984; Zuboff, 1988). For example, Turkle says, "Technology catalyzes changes not only in what we do but in how we think. It changes people's awareness of themselves, of one another, of their relationship with the world. The new machine that stands behind the flashing digital signal, unlike the clock, the telescope or the train, is a machine that thinks. It challenges our notions not only of time and distance but of mind . . . I look at the computer . . . not in terms of its nature as an 'analytical engine', but in terms of its 'second nature' as an evocative object, an object that fascinates, disturbs equanimity, and precipitates thought . . . Computers call up strong feelings, even for those who are not in direct contact with them. People sense the presence of something new and exciting. But they fear the machine as powerful and threatening" (Turkle, p. 13).

Nelson suggests that "Computing has always been personal. By this I mean that if you weren't intensely involved in it, sometimes with every fiber in your mind atwitch, you weren't doing computers, you were just a user. If you get involved, it involves all of you, your heart and mind and way of doing things and your image of yourself. A whole way of life" (Nelson, 1987, Computer Lib, p. 3).

Ted Slovin, *Counseling and Academic Development, University of Massachusetts, Amherst.* Beverly Woolf, *Computing and Information Science, University of Massachusetts, Amherst.*

"We are indeed in the early stages of a major technological transformation, one that is far more sweeping than the most ecstatic of the 'futurologists' yet realize, greater even than Megatrends or Future Shock" (Drucker, quoted in Brand, 1987, p. xiv).

We have built systems that begin to demonstrate the kind of interactivity and pedagogy suggested in these predictions. Computers can now take on at least four roles: "trusted consultant", "benevolent mentor", "cognizant tool" and "problem-solving partner" (Peelle and Riseman, 1975). Each of these roles is discussed below along with examples that provide evidence of the machine's increasing ability to function as a partner and a colleague. The social transformations of the future will take place as such systems become more proficient working with and assisting users, clients, and students.

We encourage the reader to begin to reflect upon and imagine the kinds of intelligent systems that would be most personally useful to him or her. What areas of daily life would benefit from consultation with a computer system using Artificial Intelligence (AI) to assist in increasing personal effectiveness, enjoyment, learning and general sense of fulfillment?

The Computer as Trusted Consultant

In the role of trusted consultant, the computer acts as a sensitive and concerned advisor. The system is designed to improve a user's attitude, knowledge and skills. The system should facilitate personal exploration, self-reflection and increased self-knowledge, essential aspects of expert personal/psychological consultation. Possibilities exist for humanistic, productive, and skillful partnerships between people and computer systems.

A consultant system differs from a tutoring system in that its primary goal is not to teach a particular content area and differs from an expert system in that its primary goal is not to solve a problem. Though a consultant system might teach and might solve problems, content is less important than how the system facilitates the process of self reflection and personal empowerment. Thus a consultant system spends little computational power on reasoning about the domain or on error diagnosis. Its goal is to "join with" the client, to allow the client's input to direct the flow of discourse while still pursuing instructional goals. For example, if the client is avoiding expressing his or her feelings by refusing to answer questions, the consultant might move to a dialogue intended to make the client feel more comfortable with the consultation. A consultant requires more flexibility to perform instructional planning and discourse management than does a traditional tutor.

The client is presented with a series of statements which focus on attitudes, knowledge, and skills related to time perspective (Stanford Time Perspective Inventory, Gonzales and Zimbardo,

Figure 1
PHASES IN THE CONSULTATION

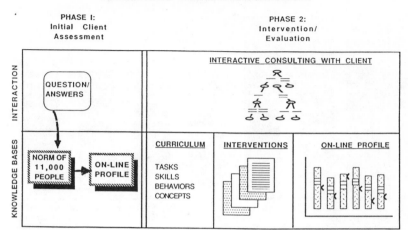

PHASE I:
Initial Client
Assessment

PHASE 2:
Intervention/
Evaluation

INTERACTION

KNOWLEDGE BASES

INTERACTIVE CONSULTING WITH CLIENT

QUESTION/
ANSWERS

NORM OF 11,000 PEOPLE → ON-LINE PROFILE

CURRICULUM

TASKS
SKILLS
BEHAVIORS
CONCEPTS

INTERVENTIONS

ON-LINE PROFILE

1985). For each statement the client is given a choice of five ratings ranging from very characteristic to very uncharacteristic and is asked to indicate "How characteristic is this of you?" Example statements include the following:

- Thinking about the future is pleasant to me.
- If things don't get done on time, I don't worry about them.
- I do things impulsively, making decisions on the spur of the moment.
- I try to live one day at a time.

Responses are evaluated according to the established interpretation of the instrument and then used in two ways. First they are shown to the client in a graph which reflects the client's rating among his age-group peers, see Figure 2. Then an explanation of the results is provided along with an opportunity for the client to react. The evaluation and the client's response are used as the initial database to form an internal client profile. The profile is used to help determine the future direction of the consultation and to generate expectations about client responses. Future machine response is based on reasoning about this profile and about prior student responses. The profile becomes the primary determining knowledge base for designing the consultation and is constantly updated to provide a moment-to-moment view of the client.

The second phase uses the profile to begin the consultation process. Here the goal is to create an ongoing dialogue which leads the client to form and hold a more balanced time perspective. A second goal is to improve the client's repertoire of useful time management behaviors. These goals are achieved through dialogue

225

Figure 2
ACTUAL EVALUATION OF A CLIENT WHO PRESENTED A PRESENT-ORIENTED TIME PERSPECTIVE

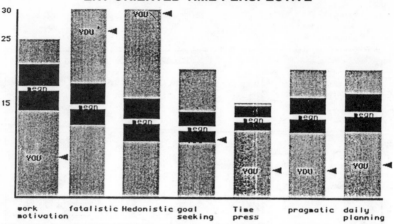

consultation, specifically through the use of interventions, which are exercises or presentations designed to facilitate awareness of time perspectives or to provide learning or practice of skills. Example interventions which might be suggested to the client are "Learning to Say No", "Life Goals", and "Time Wasters". Dialogue strategies are derived from a repertoire of similar activities used in one-on-one and group consultation over the last 15 years by the first author, a counseling psychologist (see dialogue below).

Tutor: Your scores indicate that you have a basically present-oriented time perspective. Do you agree? *Person A:* No, I think I also consider the future in my life. *Tutor:* Well, let's look more closely at your scores, and see where you think they are wrong. *Person A:* OK. *Tutor:* Your score on the hedonism scale indicates that you may be extremely similar to people who are primarily interested in having a good time, taking risks, and who often act impulsively. Does that sound like you? *Person A:* Mostly, but it sounds a little extreme. *Tutor:* OK, let's look now at the fatalism scale; it indicates that you may be very similar to people who live one day at a time in order to avoid planning for a future they believe is determined by fate. Is that what you do? *Person A:* Yes, I guess so. *Tutor:* Let's look at one more scale, Goal-seeking. Your score here shows that you may not be similar to people who plan for the future and get satisfaction from setting and achieving their goals. Do you agree? *Person A:* It is true that I don't do much goal setting. *Tutor:* It was mainly your scores on these scales that led me to view you as basically a present-oriented person. Since you disagree with the hedonism score slightly, why don't we say slightly present-oriented? *Person A:* Yes, that sounds more like me? (Actual

226

Dialogue with TEV about the Evaluation of Figure 2.)

The dialogue is not generated through natural language processing, rather through menu input and canned text output. This is a limitation of the system. However, prior work in the area of computer-based therapy (Servan-Schreiber, 1986) shows that clinically significant therapy can be achieved in spite of this limitation.

The Computer as Benevolent Mentor

In the role of benevolent mentor the computer acts as a sensitive and flexible tutor. Such a system is capable of describing a problem or problem-solving procedure to a student and of answering questions. The student can influence many factors of instruction in such systems, including mode of interaction and level of difficulty. Either computer or student can ask questions or focus control on specific issues or problems (Peelle & Riseman, 1975).

As an example of this type of computer, we describe the Recovery Boiler Tutor, RBT, a system for teaching a complex industrial process (Woolf et al., 1987; Woolf & Cunningham, 1987). This system is now being used for training in nearly 60 industrial sites across America. It provides multiple explanations and tutoring facilities tempered to the individual user (a control room operator). The tutor is based on a mathematically accurate formulation of a boiler and provides an interactive simulation complete with help, hints, explanations, and tutoring (see Figure 3).

Figure 3
A SECTIONAL VIEW OF THE RECOVER BOILER

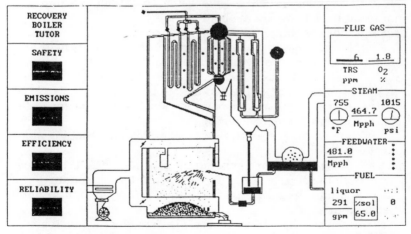

Students can initiate any of 20 training situations, emergencies, and operating conditions—or they can ask that an emergency be chosen for them. Students can also inadvertently trigger an emergency as a result of their actions. Once an emergency has been initiated, students are encouraged to adjust meters and perform actions on the simulated boiler to solve the emergency. The system challenges student operators to solve new problems while it monitors and advises those operators. RBT can recognize optimal, less than optimal, and clearly irrelevant actions. Students can continue their freewheeling or purposeful problem-solving behavior while the tutor offers help, hints, and explanations—plus provides tutoring advice when needed or requested. Operators are expected to observe the impact of their actions of the simulated boiler and to react before the tutor advises them regarding potential problems.

An example dialogue. In the example interaction below a partial blackout is in progress that will lead to combustion process deterioration if no action is taken. As students change set-point controllers and request information about the boiler, the tutor selectively discusses the optimality of their actions and suggests how they might better focus their actions or utilize their data. An important feature to note about this dialogue is that at any point during the simulated emergency there are many actions that operators might take and, as the problem worsens, an increasing number of actions that they *should* take to correct the operating conditions. Thus, an immediate and correct response might require only one action, such as rodding the primary air ports. But a delayed response causes the situation to worsen, requiring the addition of auxiliary fuel.

Meters indicate that CO, SO_2, and O_2 readings are abnormally high. An alarm buzzer sounds, beginning the following dialogue:

Tutor: What action are you going to take?

Student: Check smelt spout cooling water (The student's action does not result in a change in the boiler.)

Tutor: It looks as though the liquor isn't burning . . .

Student: Help. What is going on? (The student requests help.)

Tutor: A partial blackout is occurring and this causes TRS, CO, SO_2, and O_2 to increase. Steam flow and steam temperature are dropping. I think part of the bed is not burning.

Student: Rod the primary air ports. (A small improvement in the boiler readings can be observed.)

Tutor: Your action is correct; however, at this time rodding alone is not effective . . .

Student: Raise the liquor temperature. (The student's action does not reverse the emergency and a new alarm buzzer sounds.)

Tutor: Rodding the air port apparently was not enough to undo the blackout.

Student: Increase the oil fuel supply. (The student's action reverses the emergency.)

Tutor: That solved the problem all right. Good thinking.

Analysis of the problem: You had a partial blackout caused by plugged primary air ports and a cold bed. Partial blackouts can be effectively treated through a combination of rodding the primary air ports and adding more heat. The problem can be avoided by keeping the air ports clean.

This dialogue was not actually produced in natural language; student input was handled through menus and tutor output produced by cutting text from emergency-specific text files loaded when the emergency was invoked.

While the simulation of the recovery boiler is running, operators can view the boiler from many directions and can focus on several components. The tutor provides assistance through visual clues such as a darkened smelt bed, acoustic clues, ringing alarm buzzers, textual help, explanations, and dialogues.

The Computer as Cognizant Tool

In the role of cognizant tool, the computer provides the student with a set of tools to amplify his or her own problem-solving powers. Such tools are designed to allow the student to explore and analyze the situation upon which he or she is focused. Different tools provide feedback on the utility of various strategies for solving the problem. The tool is "cognizant" to the extent that it informs the student about how the tool is being used. The tutor can tell the student if the tool is used incorrectly or ineffectively (Peelle & Riseman, 1975).

RBT offers several such tools. Operators can request up to 30 process parameters on the complete panel board, view an alarm board (not shown), change 20 set points, and ask menu questions such as "What is the problem?" "How do I get out of it?" "What caused it?" and "What can I do to prevent it?"

In addition, RBT provides tools designed to aid students in reasoning about implicit processes in the boiler. One such tool is composite meters (shown on the left side of Figure 4) recording the state of the boiler using synthetic measures for *safety, emissions, efficiency,* and *reliability* of the boiler. The meter readings are calculated from complex mathematical formulas that would rarely (if ever) be used by operators to evaluate the boiler.

Other reasoning tools include trend analyses (see Figure 4) and animated graphics. Animated graphics provide realistic and dynamic drawings of the several boiler components such as steam, fire, smoke, black liquor, and fuel. Trend analyses show how essential process variables interact in real time by allowing operators to select up to 10 variables including liquor flow, oil flow, and air flow—and to plot each against the others and against time.

Each student action, be it a set-point adjustment or a proposed solution, is recorded in an accumulated response value reflecting overall operator scores and how successful (or unsuccessful) operator actions have been and whether actions were performed in sequence with other relevant or irrelevant actions.

Figure 4

TRENDS SELECTED BY THE OPERATOR

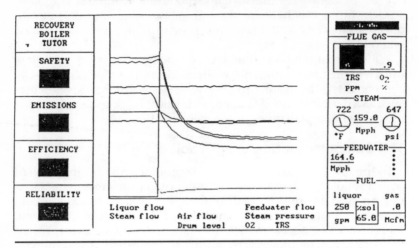

The Computer as Problem-Solving Partner

In the role of partner the computer collaborates with the user. Both user and machine jointly engage in problem-solving and each supplies the ability in which she/he/it excels (Peele and Riseman, 1975). For example, humans are particularly good at high level cognitive strategies, including the use of intuition, decoding noisy data messages, deciphering cultural clues and recognizing analogies. Machines are more powerful at storing alternative solutions, planning or organizing tasks, and performing low-level actions (including computation).

The RBT tutor is on the threshold of behaving as a problem-solving partner. A new version of the tutor has been designed to know only what the student knows. Unlike the original RBT tutor, it does not have information about the simulation from which it can make judgments about the state of the boiler. Thus it does not know the cause of emergency or inefficient operating condition. Without such inside information, its role is one of an equivalent problem-solving partner with the student, rather than a tutor.

In addition, the system performs problem diagnosis. It uses sophisticated models to teach operators to identify problems and how to best gather more information in order to decide which of several things might be wrong. This type of joint problem-solving ensures that the advanced student continues to be challenged.

Insights, Prescriptions and Predictions

Intelligent tutoring or consultant systems such as described above are rare—fewer than half a dozen of them have reached the market;

less than two dozen have reached classroom or training sites. In this section we provide glimpses of why these systems are so difficult to build and describe some of the barriers, predictions, prescriptions and insights we have experienced or evolved while developing our own systems.

Insights

One observation about building these systems, is that a large number of people are needed to do the research and development for each new system. Interdisciplinary teams of several experts are essential (Bobrow et al., 1986; Mittal & Dym, 1985). Much of the knowledge used to build the system is subjective, unorganized and misunderstood. No one person, whether computer scientist, domain expert or instructional designer, can supply the wide variety of knowledge required. Thus, an important part of building an intelligent consulting or tutoring system includes development of a community memory in which multiple experts contribute their knowledge to the project. For example, Woolf et al., (1987) incorporated knowledge from experts with more than 30 years of experience working with boiler operations before building the Recovery Boiler Tutor. The consultant system, TEV, is based upon 15 years experience of an expert psychological consultant, workshop designer and teacher at the university and as well as extensive research findings of other experts on time perspective (Gonzalez and Zimbardo, 1985). A language tutor, CALEB, was developed by a person who holds two graduate degrees, one in teaching English as a second language and one more than seven years using the Silent Way to teach intensive language courses for people living in foreign countries, before building the language tutor. Such "in-house" domain experts are critical for building these systems. By in-house we mean that the domain expert must be part of the project team (available weekly) for anywhere from six weeks to several years while domain knowledge is acquired. Less commitment or a less active role would provide a less than adequate transfer of domain knowledge.

Prescriptions

Woolf (forthcoming) has formulated a comprehensive approach to the design and construction of knowledge-based, (i.e., intelligent) systems in the field of education. A summary of some of her major recommendations for building new systems includes:

- *Make sure that a large set of users* exists and build systems in areas where an ongoing need for training exists.
- *Focus of information* initially on several small topics, processes, or laws. The systems will be built in a modular way so that topics can be added during the construction stage.
- *Do not underestimate the impact of hardware and software* costs.

These costs will ultimately come down, but currently they are very high. Acquiring adequate resources may take several months lead time.

• *Teams of experts* are required to build these systems. At least four experts are needed to participate in each project including, a domain, cognitive, teaching, and interface expert. Long-distance experts, can be linked by phone, network mail, and jet plane.

• *Industries, military, and academic management* will need to commit resources and have already shown interest in doing so. Building such systems will be a separate research and development project for the organization which will need to be integrated into the direction of the organization.

• *Visibly positive practical benefits* will have to be demonstrated to potential managers and administrators in organizational settings, before large scale production is established.

Predictions

The following predictions regarding future development of intelligent systems and their impact in education and the workplace are offered in the hope that they provide some direction and guidance for individuals concerned about possible future scenarios in the field of information and computer technology.

Some breakthroughs and continuing developments in hardware and software will enable development of knowledge-based educational systems (Dede, 1988). These include:

• *The memory and speed of computer systems* should continue to increase and their size and cost continue to dramatically decrease. Processing speed should increase by more than two orders of magnitude (to the equivalent of current supercomputers) and conventional computers should be outfitted with workstation quality graphics (e.g, flexible window managers, buttonable icons, menus, etc.) and be capable of networking. The powerful systems should be reduced to desk or lap top size and their cost per student for ten hours/week usage reduced to around $1,000 per year.

• *Implementation of intelligent systems* will continue to be limited by time-consuming AI instructional problems, such as the lack of domain independent natural language processing systems or effective learning systems.

• *Progress in discourse responses* should continue to include improving a machine's explanatory capabilities, its theories of hints, rhetorical strategies, interfaces, and its understanding of human-machine interaction.

• *Ability to represent qualitative causal reasoning* in the domain should continue to advance and ultimately be expressible in a clear and simple way.

• *Cognitive processes* of teaching and learning should continue to be made expressible and ultimately to be representable in the student model.

• *Improved transfer of expertise* between humans and computers will develop as the numbers and background of researchers continue to expand into related fields such as psychology, cognitive science, linguistics, education, philosophy, and instructional design.

• Increased emphasis on understanding effective teaching and learning will become increasingly important for construction of these systems. Greater understanding of the role of acknowledgement, rewards and visibility of 'master teachers' is important to the development of responsive partner-based systems.

• *Collaboration between researchers* in Artificial Intelligence and people in training and education is critical to the development of new training and decision support systems.

Educational Breakthroughs

Several breakthroughs in education will be needed in order to complement the advances taking place in Artificial Intelligence and hardware development. These include but are not limited to:

• Distributed Teaching: Education should continue to move outward and to be disseminated equally in school, home, community, and workplace. Families now spend two to ten times the amount of money spent by schools on computer education programs (Wakefield, 1986) and many industries contribute large sums to develop primary and secondary education, e.g., General Electric and Exxon have spent up to 10 million dollars to improve pre-college education (Teltsch, 1988).

• Cooperative Teaching: Education will involve groups of people, working on problems in concert with tutoring systems. It will focus on the dialectic form of teaching which stresses the individual's responsibility for his or her own learning progress through self-study in ungraded schools, with help from machines, peers, parents, and teacher counselors.

• Constructive Education: Both students and teachers will learn by doing; our world has become far too complex for any other possibility and what students learn must be relevant to what they do in life.

Changes in Education

Here we propose four phases of evolutionary changes that might occur as a result of the introduction of knowledge-based systems (modified from Dede, 1988):

• *Phase One:* Knowledge-based systems, such as intelligent tutors, are adopted by schools and training sites. The systems carry on limited one-on-one tutoring sessions with a limited number of students. This phase is underway (Anderson, 1985; Johnson &

Soloway, 1985; Woolf, et al., 1987 and Postka, 1988).

• *Phase Two:* Schools begin to change internally to take better advantage of these tools. More networked systems, distributed at a distance, learning, and non-school sites become basic to the school curriculum. This phase has also begun e.g., see (Tinker, 1987; Southworth, 1988).

• *Phase Three:* Schools develop new functions and activities enabled by knowledge-based systems. For example, classrooms might be reorganized to include tutors in the classroom. This phase is just years away and thus planning and policy analysis should begin now.

• *Phase Four:* The original role of schools may become radically transformed, displaced or obsolete as new goals dominate education. This phase is possibly a decade away and again should be planned for.

The future of electronic teaching and guidance will serve learners and clients in all kinds of educational settings (classrooms, boardrooms, libraries, community centers, shopping malls and prisons) working with multi-media environments, containing computers, displays, videodiscs and network connections. The teacher's role will change based on Artificial Intelligence and the information explosion. The teacher will cease being the person who "holds" the information and "pumps" it into the student. Rather, the teacher in conjunction with the technology, will manage instructional resources, integrate knowledge, and motivate and consult with students (Hoyle and Johnson, 1987). The teacher may lead the student to use the technology, but ultimately the technology will provide the stimulation for self-direction and motivation among learners (Ambron and Hooper, 1988).

Education will no longer be the responsibility of educators alone; it has already moved beyond the classroom. Industries bear the responsibility for educating workers, not only for on the job related subjects but also in basic literacy. Communities supply teaching programs and services in areas such as drug and alcohol counseling, literacy, and educational training.

Impact of Technology on the Workplace

A new role for humans is evolving in the workplace. Humans and machines are beginning to work together as partners. Machines already replace people in complex but well structured tasks, such as scheduling factory tasks, monitoring, diagnosing, and summarizing events in an electric power plant, trouble shooting electronic equipment, and designing new copier machines (Bruno et al., 1986, Feigenbaum et al., 1988; Talukdar et al., 1986, Mittal et al., 1986, Zuboff, 1988).

On the other hand, people are more adept at recognizing and learning from analogical situations, at solving unusual problems, and in reasoning from incomplete and imperfect data. Using these complementary intellectual strengths, both computers and humans could work together in a partnership which emhasizes the strengths of each (Peelle & Riseman, 1975).

A knowledge-based workplace, where humans and computers share the learning and performance tasks, requires *more*, not less, human-worker intelligence (Clarendon, 1986). Humans will need machine intelligence to augment their own thinking; as a result, the human's job will become more complex. Controlling sophisticated machinery requires sophisticated skills. Complex jobs require both structured and unstructured decision making (Holtzman, 1989). Humans will still supply sophisticated reasoning such as creativity, flexibility, decision making, evaluation synthesis, and holistic thinking. The cooperation of humans and machines in the workplace requires that machine intelligence employ models of skilled activities, intelligent tutors, and expert decision-aids in order to communicate with humans. AI systems are beginning to demonstrate these basic cognitive skills; systems are already successful at pattern matching, designing, and planning.

Education now needs to shift its emphasis from lower level skills, such as the steps for double-entry bookkeeping, towards high order cognitive skills, such as training for creativity and decision making. To continue to train people on lower level skills would be as effective as "grooming John Henry to compete with the steam engine" (Dede, 1988). People will need a foundation of lower order concepts, i.e., to know the algorithm for long division, but they should not be drilled on the computational skill itself, such as addition and multiplication, or how to update columns of numbers, which can be better performed by calculators and computers. Training should evolve towards helping humans understand how sophisticated problems are solved, how unusual cases are recognized and how to communicate with humans or machines. Thus educational assessment should shift from evaluation of memorized topics to evaluation of higher order cognitive skills.

To create this scenario, workers will also have to be educated in affective abilities, such as cooperation, compromise, and group decision-making. This is necessary because industries that become decentralized and democratic, as a result of knowledge-based tools, require more human communication and more in-depth understanding of management (Dede, 1988). Affective and interpersonal abilities will become an important measure of educational effectiveness in a future which includes person/tools partnership.

Barriers to Development of the Knowledge-Based Society

The knowledge-based society described above may not happen if recent advances in AI bog down or if barriers to improving the power/cost ratio are not overcome (physical constraints associated with quantum mechanical effects and the speed of light). Even if AI proceeds rapidly, but development of knowledge-based systems stagnates due to insufficient funding, lack of skilled human resources, or a failure to implement research initiatives, the goal will not be met.

Another possible deterrent to the development of a knowledge-based society is rejection of computer technology by the educational community, including schools, universities, parents, and communities. Inertia, self-interest, and resistance to change have been known to undermine educational reforms in the past. To create a shift to a new instructional mode requires massive external presssure, extensive teacher training and community awareness programs. The present dissension about proper goals, methods, responsibilities, and funding for education makes such a coordinated transformation very difficult (Dede, 1988).

Moral Issues

Ethical and moral issues must be considered as they relate to the use of technology in education, the private consulting room and the workplace (Weizenbaum, 1976; McCorduck, 1979, 1985; Turkle, 1984; Dreyfus and Dreyfus, 1986; Winograd and Flores, 1986; Zerzan and Carnes, 1988; and Zuboff, 1988). Concern for the responsible use of "computer power" should play a significant role in the development of the scenarios presented here. It is important to consider value issues related to the use of technology in general and AI in particular. Discussions of the social and ethical responsibilities encumbered upon individuals involved in the construction of high impact technology should be encouraged. Questions of goals, motives, purposes and values are embedded in the design of intelligent systems and should be made explicit by knowledge engineers and domain experts. Perhaps some statement regarding ethical considerations in design should be required of developers.

Weizenbaum has been outspoken about the matter: "The point is . . . that there are some human functions for which computers ought not to be substituted. It has nothing to do with what computers can or cannot be made to do. Respect, understanding, and love are not technical problems. . . . Scientists and technologists have, because of their power, an especially heavy responsibility, one that is not to be sluffed off behind a facade of slogans such as that of technological inevitability." (Weizenbaum, 1976, p. 270 and 272). Winograd and Flores (1986) offer the following understandings: "Computers like every technology, are vehicles for the transformation of tradition . . . We can let our awareness of the potentials for transformation guide our actions in creating and applying technology. In ontological designing, we are doing more than asking what can be built. We are engaging in a philosophical discourse about the self—about what we can do and what can be. Tools are fundamental to action, and through our actions we generate the world" (1986, p. 179).

Future collaboration with intelligent computer systems will generate new problems and new possibilities in education, training and consulting. We need to continually clarify the roles and improve the competencies of each of the partners. The unfolding process will provide guidance for further innovation in the design and development of a promising partnership.

References

Ambron, S. and Hooper, K. 1988. *Interactive Multimedia.* Redmond, Washington: Microsoft Press.

Anderson, J.R., Boyle, C., Yost, G. 1985. "The Geometry Tutor." Proceedings of the International Joint Conference on Artificial Intelligence. Los Angeles, CA, p. 17.

Blau, L., Woolf, B., and Slovin, T. Joining with the client in a Consultant Tutor. COINS Technical Report to appear (no date).

Bloom, B., 1984. "The 2 Sigma Problem: The Search for Methods of Group Instruction as Effective as One-to-One Tutoring." *Educational Researcher,* (June/July).

Bruno, G., Elia, A., and Laface, P. 1986. "A Rule-Based System to Schedule Production." *IEEE Computer* 19, no. 7, Los Almitos, CA.

Bobrow, D., Mittal, S., Stefik, M. 1986. "Expert Systems: Perils and Promise." *Communication ACM*, September.

Brand, Stewart. 1987. *The Media Lab.* New York: Viking Penguin.

Clancey, W. 1987. Knowledge-based Tutoring: The GUIDON Program, Cambridge: MIT Press.

Claredon, A. 1986. Elit New Technology at Work 3. New York: Oxford University Press.

Cunningham, P., Iberall, T., and Woolf, B. 1986. Caleb: An Intelligent Second Language Tutor. In *Proceedings of the IEEE International Conference on Systems, Man, and Cybernetics.* Atlanta, GA, pp. 1210-1215.

Dede, C. 1988. Probable Evolution of Artificial Intelligence Based on Educational Devices. Technological Forecasting & Social Change, 34, pp. 111-133.

Dreyfus, Hubert, and Dreyfus, Stuart. 1986. Mind Over Machine. New York: The Free Press.

Feigenbaum, E., McCorduck, P., and Nii, P. 1988. The Rise of the Expert Company. New York: Time Books.

Gonzalez, A., and Zimbardo, P. 1985. "Time in Perspective." *Psychology Today* pp. 21-26, (March).

Holtzman, Samuel. 1989. Intelligent Decision Systems. Reading, MA: Addison-Wesley.

Hoyle, G. R., and Johnson, J.R. 1987. "The 21st Century Professor-Bailing Out of the Ivory Tower." *The Futurist.* 21:6, pp. 26-27, (November-December).

Jastrow, Robert. 1981. The Enchanted Loom. New York: Simon and Schuster.

Johnson, L., and Soloway, E.M. 1985. "PROUST: An Automatic Debugger for Pascal Programs." *BYTE*, 10, no. 4, pp. 170-190.

Kearsley, Greg P. 1987. Artificial Intelligence Instruction. Reading, MA: Addison-Wesley.

McCorduck, Pamela. 1979. *Machines Who Think*. W. H. Freeman: New York.

McCorduck, Pamela. 1985. *The Universal Machine*. New York: McGraw Hill.

Mittal, S., and Dym, C. 1985. "Knowledge Acquisition from Multiple Experts." In *AI Magazine*, 6(2), (Summer).

Minsky, Marvin. 1986. *The Society of Mind*. New York: Simon and Schuster.

Nelson, Ted. 1987. *Computer Lib/Dream Machines*. Redmond, Washington: Tempus Books.

Peelle, H., and Riseman, E., 1975. The Four Faces of Hal: A Framework for Using Artificial Intelligence Techniques in Computer-Assisted Instruction. *IEEE Transactions on Systems, Man, and Cybernetics* (May).

Psotka, J. 1988. (eds.) *Intelligent Tutoring Systems: Lessons Learned*. Lawrence Erlbaum.

Schank, Roger C. 1984. *The Cognitive Computer*. Reading, MA: Addison Schreiber Wesley.

Servan-Scrieber, D. 1986. *From Intelligent Tutoring to Computerized Psychotherapy*. Proceedings of the Sixth National Conference on Artificial Intelligence (AAAI 86). Los Altos: Morgan Kaufmann.

Shafer, Dan. 1986. Silicon Visions. New York: Prentice Hall.

Slovin, T., and Woolf, B. 1988. *A Consultant Tutor for Personal Development*, Proceedings of the International Conference on Intelligent Tutoring Systems. University of Montreal.

Southworth, J. 1988. *Hawaii Distance Learning—Technology Project Computer Education and Children*. Published by the Association of Computer Based Systems ADCIS.

Talukdar, S., Cardozo, E., and Lea, L. 1986. Toast: The Power System's Assistant. *IEEE Computer*. Los Alamitos, CA.

Teltsch, K. 1988. "Business Sees Aid to Schools as a Net Gain." *New York Times*. p. 1 (December 4).

Tinker, R. 1987. "Network Science Arrives." In *Hands ON!* . A Newsletter produced by Technical Education Research Centers (TERC) 10, no. 1 (Winter).

Turkle, Sherry. 1984. The Second Self. New York: Simon & Schuster.

Wakefield, R. 1986. "Home Computers and Families: The Empowerment Revolution." *The Futurist* 20:5. pp. 18-22, (September-October).

Weizenbaum, Joseph. 1976. *Computer Power and Human Reason*. San Francisco, CA: W. H. Freeman.

Winograd, Terry, and Flores, Fernando. 1986. *Understanding Com-*

puters and Cognition. Norwood, NJ: Ablex Publishing.

Woolf, B., et al. 1987. "Tutoring a Complex Industrial Process," In *Learning Environments and Tutoring Systems.* Norwood, NJ: Ablex Publishing.

Woolf, Beverly P. 1989. *Knowledge-Based Tutors: Applying Artificial Intelligence in Education.* (Forthcoming).

Woolf, B., and Cunningham, R. 1987. "Multiple Knowledge Scores in Intelligent Tutoring Systems." *IEEE Expert* (Summer).

Zerzan, J. and Carnes, A. (eds.) 1988. *Questioning Technology.* London: Freedom Press.

Zuboff, S. 1988. *In the Age of the Smart Machine.* New York: Basic Books.

THEOLOGY, SCIENCE, AND MANAGEMENT: PAST, PRESENT, FUTURE

by

Frederick C. Thayer

Introduction

This essay argues the following propositions:

I. Management principles and practices have been the same throughout the few thousand years of civilization, as long as written language has been available to spell them out. The principles and practices are global.

II. The legitimate authority to issue orders is based upon the assumption that a boss has knowledge (derived from God or Science) that subordinates do not have, i.e., what values (objectives) are to be pursued and how. Religion and management, therefore, are a single theory. The only change in the history of civilization has been a shift from certain knowledge (God) to uncertain knowledge (Science), but this shift remains unrecognized in some organizations and has not been implemented in the others.

III. Hierarchy and obedience remains a global theory of religion and management, and also of knowledge (objectivity), economics (competition and consumer sovereignty) and politics (winners and losers).

IV. There can be no viable planetary future so long as we believe this single theory of religion, management, science, ideology and values can be retained. Only the creation of yet another civilization holds out any hope but some optimism is possible.

As an academic, I am used to hearing and reading phrases that are considered absolutely fundamental to the jobs academics allegedly perform. One such phrase (there are many versions) is "we live in a turbulent and dynamic environment that is more complex than any the world has ever seen, with complexity increasing all the time." Another such phrase is "we must be ever aware that many variables are involved in every problem we study." Keeping in mind that academics can be said to have a vested interest in "complexity" (the more "variables" the better), I have been exploring for some time the possibility that the world, and especially the *social* world, is much *less* "complex" than we claim it to be. The more I think about it, the more convinced I am that the social world

Frederick C. Thayer *is with the Graduate School of Public and International Affairs, University of Pittsburgh, Pennsylvania.*

must be simpler than we declare it to be, for at least three overlapping reasons:

● The design and operation of large-scale human organizations, whether "communities," "churches," "families," "armies and navies," "corporations," "schools," "bureaucracies" or "nation-states" must be based upon a relatively few basic and simple rules if large numbers of people are to be "mobilized" in pursuit of designated objectives. And the objectives themselves must be relatively similar to each other ("win" or "be number 1") if humans are to change organizational memberships.

● Because these types of organizations have been around for a long time, at least since the dawn of civilization and the invention of writing, the most important factors in our history are not a "multitude of variables" but rather the *constants* that have persisted throughout that history.

● If we are serious about *change* because we believe that *change* is needed for planetary survival, we must search for a handful of *constants* rather than a million "variables" because reorganizing the world is otherwise impossible.

This quest has led me to the conclusion that the history of civilization is based upon *one* basic constant, and perhaps *one* corollary mode of behavior that is sometimes viewed as an antidote to the constant because most humans are not happy with the situation produced by that constant. The constant is that combination of *domination* and *obedience* that can be labeled as "hierarchy" (any one of several labels will do). It is nothing more than the belief that humans cannot take effective action (whether in a two-person family or a nation-state) unless there is first established a clear relationship between a *superior* (who gives the commands) and *subordinates* (who carries them out). *Dis*obedience is not to be tolerated, whether it be labeled "blasphemy," "dissidence" or "insubordination." These three words cover only the most obvious versions that can be encountered by single individuals, and they include religion, the acts that Americans designate as "political" events in the Soviet Union, and mere "administrative" events in this country. The "infidel," "dissident" and "malcontent" are punished for the same category of violation within the same type of organizational framework. The categories remain formally combined in states where "church" and "state" still are united, and are only superficially separated elsewhere ("moral" behavior is expected at the workplace).

The corollary "semi-constant," accepted in some parts of the world as an *escape* from an allegedly unacceptable form of hierarchy (monopoly economic authority), but also accepted throughout the world as the only available method for determining who shall be dominant is *competition*. We revere it in this country as the best way to serve the needs of consumers in a "free" and "peaceful" marketplace, but we subscribe to it along with everyone else in the world as the only available way to decide who shall win and who shall lose, who shall dominate and who shall obey. In this country, we don't even attempt to reconcile these totally opposite "ideals" of competition, preferring to believe that competition can be kept wholly peaceful and serene when history suggests that international competition moves quite easily from peace to war.

A theory of *management,* a theory of *religion,* a political and/or economic *ideology,* a theory of *knowledge* itself, and a theory of *values* are, in history and in fact, very probably *identical,* and the principles and practices associated with each category vary only by labels that are otherwise interchangeable. We all are the victims of this single theory, for practical purposes a global theory, and the "we" obviously includes all of humanity, but not humanity alone. Our combined theory commands humans to dominate *nature,* and nature is displaying blasphemous behavior by telling us, as best it can, that it no longer will quietly submit to whatever *humans* do in carrying out the instructions given them. As to the immediate problems facing humans and the interactions among them, only a few examples need be briefly outlined here:

1. If war is no longer possible because of the obvious destruction it will visit upon the planet, including perhaps extinction for the human and many other species, then the principal function of nation-states and especially their leaders is called into question. Many such leaders seem very fearful that to acknowledge as much except in vague abstractions will cause "peace to break out" and leave them with no important responsibilities. This should be familiar to us because we routinely list our "greatest" presidents as those who brought us victory in the three most important and "successful" wars in our national history. Unfortunately, we like to forget that the management theory designated as Christianity first became a powerful force in the world as the official justification for the bloody activities of emperors and kings.

2. We cannot request the people of the Middle East to end their age-old struggles against each other unless we acknowledge that they must renounce the management principles that are considered beyond change because they are embodied in the religious versions of those theories; it is unnecessary to distinguish between a management theory that instructs one people that it is "chosen," and a management theory that instructs one people to hate the other. We can only request that they renounce *their* creeds while admitting that *ours* is (or are) no better.

3. The immediate issue that produces demonstration after demonstration in this country at the moment is abortion, but the issue has yet to be articulated as it must be if we are to understand it, let alone address it. The issue demonstrates that giving women the right to vote more than a half-century ago did not give them what

they need to become full-fledged citizens, even though voting is the most important "right" any citizen can be given to participate in government. The issue demonstrates that we as a society and as a world are not yet ready to think about inventing a *social duty to restrict population growth* to replace the thousands-of-years old *social duty to increase population*. Individual duty and responsibility to one's self is a much less fulfilling argument than *social* duty and responsibility, but individualism seems the best women can do at the moment, and they are generally left to raise the question by and for themselves.

We cannot understand the amount of *change* that is needed for a viable future unless we stop using history as a form of kitty litter that is used to keep out of sight the issues we would prefer to avoid. What we need is nothing less than the invention of a new form of human society that is as different from the one of the past 6000 years or so (agriculture and urbanism) as the 6000 years have been from a vastly different prehistory (gathering/hunting). I sketch out herein, by way of expanding upon a few general propositions, why there is only *one* theory and set of management principles, and that only *one* civilization must change. For those who might be concerned about the future of *Western* civilization, it may help to consider the *possibility* that there is no such thing as a separate and distinct *Western* civilization, whether we date it from the time of the Romans and Greeks or from the "enlightenment" and such associated events as the Protestant Reformation and the invention of modern science. What we have called "change" and "progress" has not been truly fundamental change but only relatively trivial revisions.

I. Management principles and practices have been the same throughout the few thousand years of civilization, as long as written language has been available to spell them out. The principles and practices are global.

Because management principles and practices are applicable to *all* organizations, not just modern corporations and "capitalist" or "socialist" government agencies, it is necessary to discard the distinctions we have come to use in the contemporary world, largely textbook distinctions that at least in part, are designed to turn our eyes away from such tough questions as the direct relationship between religious and management concepts. In everyday life, of course, the distinctions aren't all that clear anyway. Routinely, parents *manage* their children, constantly searching for the best available forms of *motivation* so as to elicit from those children (via the promise of reward or the threat of punishment) the behavior the parents want. Just as routinely, the head of a corporation or government agency may announce to *his* employees that "We are a family!" while saying softly to himself that "I am the head of the family." The child is being reminded ("50 cents if you take out the garbage") of what it will be like in the impersonal workplace, just as employees are asked to look upon their bosses as benevolent patriarchs.

The overarching management principle of the past several thousand years can be simply stated: *no organization (family, church, corporation, public agency, nation-state) can achieve its social purposes other than through the interaction of those designated "superiors" and those labeled "subordinates."* This principle, assumption or belief is thus far wholly independent of changes in ideology, form of government or whatever, and wholly consistent from religion to religion, society to society, culture to culture. We have tried in the modern West, the "democratic" West, to hide this consistency from ourselves, a form of collective self-deception to which I will soon return. A brief survey of the historical record is in order at this point; it is crystal clear.

The Egyptians recognized the need for planning, organizing and controlling at least as far back as 4000 BC. The Hebrews, Chinese and Greeks developed such concepts as layers of management supervision, staff advice, specialization, centralization, motion study, materials handling and job descriptions between that time and 100 years BC. Obviously, the guidelines for managing relatively small organizations, e.g., families, must be compatible with those for managing larger entities because even if families are no longer the most important organizations for economic production (though many still are, in agriculture), families must *train* children (a management function) to be productive in other organizations (schools, workplaces).[1] The historical record could be set forth, century by century or even year by year, for the period from 4000 BC to 1989, but two modern examples can be used to make the important corollary point that ideology does not affect management theory and practice.

Woodrow Wilson who, before becoming President of the US had been a political scientist and actually had written about the administration of public affairs, made the case in 1887[2]:

> . . . So far as administrative functions are concerned, all governments have a strong structural likeness; more than that, if they are to be uniformly useful and efficient, they *must* have a strong structural likeness. A free man has the same bodily organs, the same executive parts, as the slave, however different may be his motives, his services, his energies. Monarchies and democracies, radically different as they are in other respects, have in reality much the same business to look to.
>
> . . . That man is blindly astray who denounces attempts to transplant foreign systems into this country . . . why should we not use such parts of foreign contrivances as we want, if they be in any way serviceable? . . .
>
> . . . When we study the administrative systems of France and Germany, knowing that we are not in search of *political* principles, we need not care a peppercorn for the constitutional or political

reasons which Frenchmen or Germans give for their practices when explaining them to us. If I see a murderous fellow sharpening a knife cleverly, I can borrow his way of sharpening the knife without borrowing his probable intention . . . if I see a monarchist dyed in the wool managing a public bureau well, I can learn his business methods without changing one of my republican spots. He may serve his king; I will continue to serve the people; but I should like to serve my sovereign as well as he serves his . . . (emphasis in original).

Lenin came to power in the Soviet Union while Wilson was serving as US President, but Lenin did not turn to Wilson's version of universal management doctrine. He turned instead to the published works of Frederick W. Taylor, the acknowledged "father" of what was then the latest version of "scientific management." According to Lenin[3]:

> . . . the Taylor system—without its initiators knowing or wishing it—is preparing the time when the proletariat will take over all social production and appoint its workers' committees for the purpose of properly distributing and rationalizing all social labor. Large-scale production, machinery, railways, telephone—all provide thousands of opportunities to cut by three-fourths the working time of the organized workers and make them four times better off than they are today.

According to the author of an approved 1972 Soviet management text, Lenin "believed that a distinction should be made between [Taylorism's] scientific achievements, reflecting the actual nature of large-scale social production, and those of its standards that were conditioned by the needs of capitalist exploitation."[4] Lenin, the first organizer of the Soviet Union, understandably appears 47 times in the index of that text; Taylor's name is cited 42 times, while Marx is a distant third-place finisher with only 29 citations.

Because this brief survey cannot be instantly plausible to a reader long accustomed to believing that societies are more different than similar, it can be fleshed out a bit by using the device of responding to anticipated questions:

1. *If a different set of principles and practices existed in pre-history, what were they, and what evidence suggests that current approaches are only as old as civilizations?* If the human species must invent new management concepts if it and the planet are to survive, it is unnecessary to argue that we can find support for a necessary future in the record of the distant past. Yet it can be suggested that civilized hierarchy is not the only social design that humans have used, even though our prehistoric ancestors did not write books. We owe something in this regard to those who study the oldest human fossils and their surrounding environments, women who are not content to accept subordination as the only role ever acted out by women, and even those who study the function of the human brain (but seldom with reference to management).

Richard Leakey is among those who suggest that before the basic design of human society shifted from gathering and hunting to farming and urbanism, there may have been no recognizable form of hierarchy at all. It is possible that nomadic bands reached agreement whenever decisions had to be made; in the absence of permanent property ownership, they had no reason to insist upon clear identification of parentage. The changeover from one social design to another was swift, more "revolutionary" than "evolutionary" according to Leakey, and occurred between five and ten thousand years ago, a time span that seems very long to us but is relatively brief in planetary time.[5] Leakey, in addition to a few books, has produced a television series outlining his thesis, one that is worth attention no matter what one's reactions to it.

Women have been one of the groups most affected by hierarchy and its subsidiary principles but, of course, they do not comprise the only such group. In order to have an operating hierarchy, it is necessary to specify who leads and who follows, and the easiest way to do this is to use some rule of *difference* such as sex or race, with the members of a "boss" sex or race designating themselves as "superior" to the others. In a homogeneous situation, it is necessary to find another rule, e.g., intelligence or brute strength. Elizabeth Fisher is just one example of women who suggest that *Woman's Creation*[6] as a social inferior is a by-product of the invention of civilization.

Studies of left- and right-brain hemisphere functioning are so relatively new (beginning only about 25 years ago) that little has yet been done to integrate these developments with management questions, especially given the limitations inherent to modern Western psychology, on which more later. But I support the view that the solidification of social hierarchies involved the development of left-hemisphere consciousness, along with its invention and mastery of written language (so that administrators could produce written regulations, especially with the arrival of simplified alphabets about 3000 years ago), linear and analytical thinking (to enable one to calculate how best to carry out instructions) and conscious memory (so as to immediately recall what pleased a boss in similar situations, a regular part of our child-indoctrination).[7] In this context, a previous *management change* may well have initiated a *mind change* (beginning in the world's northern temperate zone and ultimately spreading throughout the world), just as it is now argued that a livable future calls for a *Global Mind Change.* [8]

It is admittedly possible to become too entranced with bits of historical speculation, but one apparently minor item is both fascinating and potentially significant. It appears that with the spread of civilization came a widespread insistence that humans be encouraged or compelled to be *right-handed*, and that left-handedness be almost universally condemned or scorned. The *right-hand*, repeatedly given Biblical prominence (a worry for left-handed members of some churches, who now seek to remove anti-left-handedness from church rituals), has long been an important aspect of child management. The deeper reasons for this, generally ignored by psychologists trained to believe that right-handedness is "natural" for 90 percent of the human species, may be that as hierarchy and written commands took over, it was discovered through trial and error that right-handers were easier to control at that time (the right side of the body is directly controlled by the language-oriented left brain hemisphere).[9] To managers seeking to ensure obedience on the part of subordinates, indoctrination in right-handedness may have been attractive, and some readers may even have had their hands slapped by teachers determined to prevent left-handed writing.

Finally, it is well to introduce here the most obvious connection of all, but one that is seldom spelled out. The world's great religions appear in our history just as the shift from gathering and hunting to farming and urbanism was really taking hold in the north temperate zone. In management terms, the social shift included the idea of monotheism (a form of centralization) and the disappearance of *visible* gods (including totems and idols) in favor of the *invisible (male) God* whose instructions are in written form. It is as though the new idea of a single invisible male God and his holy written commands were the *culmination* of a massive social change rather than the *initiation* of one. This is why I believe such a change did occur; if the arrival of sedentary urban communities, written language and a single male God were not connected, if the social forms of prehistory simply moved forward in an evolutionary and gradual way, then the great religions have no social significance. It makes more sense to intimately connect them with a change so massive that it even awakened the left side of the human brain.

2. *What about the "national," "cultural" and "ideological" differences that are so important in the way we look at the world, even the differences in "management styles" that make contemporary headlines, as in the case of Japan?* In a word, all of this is hogwash, even though much of it is extraordinarily well intended, as in the image of the "enlightened" citizen who "respects" cultural differences. The primary reason throughout history for building theories around these alleged "differences" is to make the important and immediately necessary argument that *one* "nation," "culture," "ideology," "management style," "sex" or "race" is *superior* to others. It is the superior/inferior distinction that has justified oppression, domination, war and genocide. If a theory *appears* to be necessary, it gains enormous staying power, even when five minutes of calm thinking will highlight its absurdities.

Throughout civilized history, "differences" and "similarities" have not been determining social factors. Christians war on each other as well as on those of other religions. Capitalists war on each other as well as on socialists. In an oft-used phrase, "nations do not have permanent friends or enemies, only permanent interests." When Americans loudly insist that children in school "must learn about *Western* culture," the underlying premise is one of Western superiority. In other words, the concept of "difference" is a part of the struggle to determine who will be boss and who will be subordinate.

The idea of "different management styles" fits the same pattern. We currently envy the Japanese because they appear to have invented some new form of "management magic" that has enabled them to replace us, or almost replace us, as the world's leading economic power. This has caused Americans to vacillate between intense self-criticism for "falling behind," and widespread screaming that "the Japanese are using unfair trade tactics!" The alternative explanations are easy to come by. The current Japanese production advantage lies in cheaper labor, including very low-paid women who do industrial work at home. If the national differences were all that different, Japanese firms could not set up Japanese-operated subsidiaries in the US. And it should be remembered that it has been only a few years since Americans were gaping at the "German industrial miracle," one that quickly has fallen victim to cheaper-labor countries. In a world of all-out competition, the lead changes hands from time to time, and the reasons are not mysterious, no matter how much we try to avoid facing them. The US was economically successful in the 1950s and 1960s, for example, because most of the world's industry was destroyed during World War II, not because of any home-grown "management magic."

3. Well, what about such unique inventions of the modern Western world as "individualism," "free will" and "democracy?"

The answer here is so simple that I am ashamed it took me so many years to realize it. There is indeed *one* aspect of modern Western thinking that is unique, *but we have not yet put it to use.* This is the scientific doctrine that *all knowledge is uncertain,* a notion I return to later. "Individualism" is a classic example of false advertising; it purports to offer an escape from oppressive authority, but it really is a reinforcement of hierarchy and its dominant-submissive relationships.

Suppose, for example, that one individual (A) makes a decision that affects at least one other individual (B). If B must accept the decision because A has the right, the authority or the strength to enforce it, then B must obey; as A's subordinate, B's individualism is destroyed. If, on the other hand, we set up a new rule that requires A and B to reach agreement in noncoercive conditions, then any decision becomes a *joint* or *collective* decision, not an individual decision. [10] This rather abstract model can be fleshed out by the use of more concrete examples in the context of the global traditions of hierarchy:

• The doctrine of "free will" was not intended to apply to women, for it was assumed that their *job* was to carry out the instructions of their husbands, including instructions (and some delegation of authority) for household management and child-rearing. Their primary *social* duty was to produce children, not necessarily because they *wanted* to do so, and also at considerable risk to their well-being. These overlapping duties were to go on 24 hours per day, with allowances for sleeping but not for personal leisure time.

• The doctrine of "free will" was not intended to apply to children, whose every activity was and is presumed to be carried out according to instructions or authorizations from parents or their surrogates (teachers). While we still celebrate the joys of "play," it is a form of training, not self-directed leisure.

• The doctrine of "free will" was not intended to apply to slaves, unless one can image Thomas Jefferson and George Washington, not to mention Aristotle, offering "free will" seminars to slaves. This is not to condemn those historic leaders, but simply to emphasize the limits of the doctrine.

• The doctrine of "free will" was not and is not intended to apply to *employees at work,* who are expected and required (under threat of firing) to carry out the instructions of their employers. It must be assumed that all such activities are carried out under duress because of the conditions of employment.

When these constraints are taken into account, it turns out that the doctrine of "free will" never was intended to apply to anything except the *leisure time* of *white males,* and that the doctrine could have no real meaning even to white males unless their jobs and salaries permitted them to enjoy a satisfactory quality of life on their "leisure" time. Neither the struggling farmer nor the factory worker laboring for poverty wages has ever gotten all that much out of "leisure" time other than the generally protected authority to take out his frustrations on those who are expected to obey him (families).

"Free will," therefore, is a doctrine really applicable only to *rich* white males, and that is its history. The best that can be said for the doctrine is that it included for a long time, and still does to some extent, the concept that rich white males should repay society for their good fortune by managing public affairs (running the government) as an avocation, even if they lose a fraction of their wealth while doing so. The assumption was, and is, that a very rich individual is not tempted to use his position in government to enrich himself still further, and such beliefs did indeed drive Washington and Jefferson, and to some extent the members of wealthy families who today opt for public service while living on inherited wealth.

The correct title should be "free will leisure doctrine," and the traditional notion was and is that the affluent white male is able to enjoy his leisure in large part because he has some combination of slaves, servants, subordinate family members and invited guests (paid off with food, drink and social activities) to expand his enjoyment. In economic terms, the objective of leisure time is maximum consumption, as Adam Smith informed us[11]:

> . . . Consumption is the sole end purpose of all production; and the interest of the producer ought to be attended to only so far as it may be necessary for promoting that of the consumer. The maxim is so perfectly self-evident that it would be absurd to attempt to prove it.

Small wonder that our Western intellectual disciplines, all dedicated to helping the rich enjoy their leisure, have provided a base for economic "consumerism" and political "utilitarianism" as the most laudable of earthly pursuits.

To a considerable extent, the "free will at leisure" doctrine is an important byproduct of Protestantism, which presumably freed individuals of any requirement to obey secular bosses, including priests and governments, on matters of moral conscience. Promises of "freedom" always are alluring to the repressed, but popularity often is gained by misrepresentation, intended or not. Being released from priestly authority had no effect on employer-employee relationships (remember that wives and children are employees), and even "freedom of conscience" implies that orders issued by employers or secular governments are wholly legitimate. For those most concerned with the future and global survival, modern Western philosophy holds a special irony.

Reduced to essentials, Western doctrine suggests that while salvation in eternal life after death can remain an ultimate goal, the immediate objective is to consume as much of this world's resources as possible before moving on to the next world. Employers and governments are thus under pressure to help *all* citizens consume more, by whatever means of support are necessary. As Arnold Toynbee reminded us in 1971, all the "democracies" we have known about have been tyrannical in many ways, and we should think about inventing meanings that move beyond "direct" or "representative" democracy.[12] Maximum consumption of resources means not only that the resources are to be depleted as quickly as possible but that governments are expected to "acquire" or "appropriate" whatever seems available for the taking. The modern West, to include European Russia, has developed expansionism to the maximum, to include the bloodiest of wars.

4. *Am I trying to argue that the "freedom" doctrines of the modern democratic West cannot be distinguished in any meaningful way from Marxism, at a time when some are celebrating the global collapse of communism?* In a word, yes, but one word obviously is not enough. Marxism has been an inviting target and still is, but it is only a minor revision of standard Western doctrine that was launched and became a bit attractive for a time because it built upon the

loophole in this Western doctrine. In emphasizing "consumerism," the West separated "consumers" from "workers." In the age of slavery that gave birth to free market theories, this was a reflection of reality; consumption among the affluent is helped along by the use of slave labor and subsistence wages. Because the industrializing West never explained how *poor* workers would ever become *rich* consumers, Marxism stepped in to champion the cause of *workers* who, obviously, would have to earn money at work if they were to enjoy their leisure. As exemplified in the passage from Lenin quoted earlier, the Marxist objective was and is the same as any other, i.e., to make it possible for citizens to increase consumption. Marxism merely gave *worker* interests first priority. If this is all Marxism ever amounted to, what has all the fuss been about?

In raising the specter of "atheism," Marx took on the status of a "false prophet" or an illegitimate "secular God." While the direct connection between monotheistic religion and management theory has yet to be widely understood (and I have yet to clearly show it here), the notion of God as *some* sort of legitimate authority was indeed widely accepted. In this context, Marx fulfilled the role of a traditional infidel who deserved neither continued life nor attention. The issue was and is the legitimacy of authority, not the doctrine itself. As to the "collapse" of Marxism, who can know what this means?

Since there is nothing unusual in Marxism except for the "false prophet" problem, its alleged "collapse" is a non-event. More concretely, the Soviet Union has been officially in existence since 1917, a period of 72 years. At age 72, the US was a long way from filling out its present geographical boundaries, was two decades away from a terrible Civil War, and had several truly major depressions and two huge international wars ahead. All the "different" cultures and societies tend to look upon their histories as steady marches toward perfection, a typical example being the recent re-release of the completely refurbished motion picture, "Gone With the Wind," with "color more beautiful than ever!" To turn the miserable experience of the Civil War into a glorified soap opera ("Dynasty" in period dress) shows only how easy it is to create a mythical history of perfection, and to do this *first*, in the midst of a Great Depression (the 1930s), and *second*, in 1989, at a time when the unemployment record of the past 14 years is the *third worst in the past century* (exceeded only by the depressions of the 1890s and 1930s). Marx is neither a God nor hero; as a conventional Westerner who was politically stupid to make God an issue, how could he be? If we are witnessing a *real* collapse of the Soviet Union, the operating question is whether other societies (China and the West) will follow the traditional path of seeking to appropriate its gas and oil reserves.

The next step is to make a more convincing case that what we know as religion is inextricably intertwined with what we label "management theory," and also with the *operational* meaning of that most important of words, "values." As usual, we have hidden the obvious from ourselves; "Lord" and "King" are words that are well-known in both religion and government.

II. The legitimate authority to issue orders is based upon the assumption that a boss has knowledge (derived from God or Science) that subordinates do not have, i.e., what values (objectives) are to be pursued and how. Religion and management, therefore, are a single theory. The only change in the history of civilization has been a shift from certain knowledge (God) to uncertain knowledge (Science), but this shift remains unrecognized in some organizations and has not been implemented in the others.

Written principles of management appeared about 6000 years ago, and the great religions appeared some time later. In management terms, God is a symbol of *all* knowledge and wisdom, but an invisible one. The concrete question is not "Does God exist?" but rather, "Who speaks for God?" and, if one believes that Scripture speaks for God, whose interpretation of Scripture is valid? Debating the existence or non-existence of God, therefore, is foolish; at best, the issue is what God wants us to do or, in historical terms, *what values has He commanded our leaders to pursue?*

What in the world are "values" anyway? Philosophically and concretely, the definitions are identical[13]:

> A value is a conception, explicit or implicit, of an individual or characteristic of a group, of the desirable which influences the selection from available modes, means, and ends of action.

Reframed in ordinary management language, the meaning remains the same:

> A value is a statement of an objective (goal, end, purpose, mission) which influences the choice from alternative means that are available.

We tend to hide this simple meaning from ourselves because we prefer not to suggest that we *want* to do some of the things we feel we *must* do. Thus, *peace* is desirable, but we do not enjoy dropping atomic bombs. The good behavior of a child is "desirable," but we do not relish spanking. There is absolutely no question, however, that if we decide to drop bombs, we *want* them to hit the target and, if we smack our children, we want them to feel it. Our *immediate values* can indeed be murder and punishment, even though we prefer to think about peace and goodness. The corollary operational question is *who* decides on the objectives (values) a family, firm, agency or nation is to achieve? This, of course, is the function of those holding legitimate authority.

As Kenneth Clark put it in his television series on "Civilization," the enlightenment marked the shift from the certainty of "divine authority" to the uncertainty of "experience, experiment and observation," or the shift from God to Science. In the old view, God was[14]:

> . . . the source of all authority, the maker and master of all that there

is, the author of the world and its laws both physical and moral . . .
The authority of parents, of priests and kings, of teachers, and of
executives [came] from God. Each [played] a role in the divine scheme
of things . . .

The associated belief was that because God's knowledge was all-encompassing, His instructions were beyond question; it was absolutely certain that if He was obeyed, His objectives would be
achieved. Disagreement with a leader instructed by God could not
be tolerated because those who disagreed were disputing God's
word; as infidels, they did not deserve to live.

The combination of Protestant and scientific revolutions brought
with it a hidden struggle, yet to be resolved because it cannot be
resolved, over the question of what kind of knowledge will bosses
use if they cannot claim they are instructed by God? Science has
come to fill that role, an unsatisfactory solution because the doctrines of science do not allow for the immediate transformation of
scientific "knowledge" into a basis for authority. The contrast between God and Science has been clearly spelled out[15]:

> The quest for scientific knowledge is . . . regulated by standards
> formulated in the form of ideals to be approximated . . . What is
> . . . involved is . . . the requirement that the knowledge claims of
> science be in principle capable of test (confirmation or disconfirma-
> tion, at the least indirectly and to some degree) on the part of any
> person properly equipped with intelligence and the technical devices
> [needed]. The term *intersubjective* stresses the social nature of the
> scientific enterprise. If there be any "truths" that are accessible only
> to privileged individuals, such as mystics or visionaries—that is,
> knowledge-claims which by their very nature cannot independently
> be checked by anyone else—then such "truths" are not of the kind
> that we seek in the sciences. The criterion of intersubjective testability
> thus delimits the scientific from the nonscientific activities of man . . .
>
> Religious ecstasy, the elations of love, the inspiration of the artist,
> yes, even the flash of insight on the part of a scientific genius are
> not in themselves scientific activities . . . they do not validate knowl-
> edge-claims. Beliefs transcending all possible tests for observation,
> experiment, measurement, or statistical analysis are recognized as
> theological or metaphysical . . . the sort of significance with which
> the . . . assertions of transcendent theology and metaphysics impress
> so many people is largely emotive.

While these words do not immediately suggest that even "management scientists" are managers in the normal sense, the tasks are
identical. *Any* decision made by *any* administrator (including even
the decision to make war) is the test of the hypothesis that the
decision will achieve the desired value or objective. To recommend
a course of action to one's boss is to formulate and present the
hypothesis; to make the decision is to conduct an experiment.[16]
All managers are experimental scientists, and their subordinates
are the *subjects* of their experiments. The accumulated *interpretations*

of the "successes" or "failures" of those experiments constitute the body of managerial knowledge,[17] just as they comprise what we label "history."

The record will show a manager how often a given decision has produced what outcomes in similar situations in the past, thereby enabling the manager to assess the *probability* that the next decision will produce desired outcomes, but the manager cannot *know for sure* what will happen. Obviously, any number of experiments do not turn out well, e.g., Vietnam.

The *greatest contribution* of Western philosophy is the doctrine of uncertain knowledge; the *greatest failure* of the modern world is to put the doctrine to work as an ideal basis for initiating social change. If a manager does not know precisely what to do and how to do it, the manager is incompetent to exercise unilateral authority. The West has dodged this profound problem by a combination of sweeping it under the rug and relying upon such mystical formulations as "leadership skills" (especially if leaders are "charismatic") and, in the case of government, the "public interest" or "people's will" as a guideline for those elected to office. Contemporary philosophers have done so much sweeping as anyone else.

Philosopher Richard Sennett, for example, provides these confusing guidelines[18]:

> . . . The need for authority is basic. Children need authorities to guide and reassure them. Adults fill an essential part of themselves in being authorities; it is one way of expressing care for others. There is a persistent fear that we will be deprived of this experience . . . Today, there is another fear of authority when it exists. We have come to fear the influence of authority as a threat to our liberties, in the family and in society at large. The very need for authority redoubles this modern fear; will we give up our liberties, become abjectly dependent, because we want so much for someone to take care of us?

Even though nobody in charge can know what he or she is doing, it appears, there must be a boss, although Sennett follows the conventional escape route by highlighting parent-child relationships instead of those at the workplace. In our world of organizations, very few people issue instructions to very many, so that most humans cannot even hope to satisfy that "essential part of themselves" that thirsts for authority because "caring" is presumably some sort of inner drive. And even the surrender to commands of others can be wished away as an instinct to be "abjectly dependent." Virtually all of us who work for a living are dependent upon our employers for continued support.

To a careful reader, Sennett's words vaguely highlight one of the great tragedies of the modern West, the US included. The "free will" doctrine, based only upon leisure activities of a small part of the population, has been used to hide both the concept of uncertainty and the continuation of unilateral authority. Philosophers have treated the uncertainty doctrine as something applicable only to officially designated "scientists," thereby absolving even scientists of responsibility for what they do. While scientists are urged to reach "intersubjective" (collegial, cooperative) agreements on how to build atomic bombs and create energy from nuclear fusion, they leave it completely to government to decide what *values* should be served by their inventions (the slaughter of Japanese civilians? limitless industrial growth?). Even though we cannot expect philosophers of science to attack the political constitutions that affect their lives, there is a special irony in these government-science relationships. Our *management* concepts do indeed hold that those in charge of administrative activities *should* possess knowledge (experience) relevant to their positions. In our *political* theories and in our *political* constitutions, however, there is not the slightest suggestion that those elected to manage our affairs either *should know* or *do know* anything at all about what they are to do. Depending upon given situations, they are able to experiment at will with the future of the planet. If, on the other hand, scientists create innovations only with the help of funds supplied by government and other donors, this is not really "free will" activity at all, but obedience to authority. Philosophers have been hiding the meaning of authority and obedience from themselves, and the rest of us have been too willing to believe that workers *want* to work in unsafe factories and that women *want* to be abused and raped. In the 1980s, of all things, psychologists still debate the question of whether women are *innately* masochistic!

We are blindly stumbling around in the modern West because we have convinced ourselves that we invented something "new," when the invention is only pretense. This minor-league invention, only a by-product of Protestanism, has merely nibbled at the edges of the older design of authority. In the modern era, we are often reminded (but notice less often than we should) that the philosophy of the modern West is so inevitably lacking clarity that concepts from the older design are called into play:

• Leaders routinely invoke God and piousness when they are looking for ways to justify their acts. President William McKinley told a Methodist group that after earnest prayers, a revelation had come to him that "there was nothing left to do but to . . . educate the Filipinos, and uplift and civilize them, and by God's grace do the very best we could by them as our fellow-men for whom Christ also died.[19] Franklin Roosevelt vowed to defeat Japan with divine help ("So help us God"), Ferdinand Marcos imposed martial law in the Philippines and then announced that God had used "signs" to tell him to do so,[20] and Jimmy Carter instructed an auditorium full of government employees to "get married if you are living in sin," and [if] you have left your spouses, go back home—I'm very serious about this."[21] More recently, the Protestant denomination presumably most dedicated to retaining a separation of church and state has been producing ministers who want to be extremely influential in politics and even run for president. More than ever, God is being invoked as a source of immediate knowledge and authority.

• The search for "leadership" is running amok. Humans, it is argued, universally "hunger" for the type of "compelling and creative leadership" that can inspire them to "march," "fight" and sometimes "die," as though the response to commands in war can be labeled acts of "free will."[22]

• As John Gardner reminds us, the word "charisma" has come to refer to[23]:

> . . . Speakers who hold their audiences spellbound, show business celebrities who leave their fans weak-kneed, and almost any variety of magniloquent blowhard . . .

Gardner adds that "St. Paul would find it all quite puzzling," and with good reason. Max Weber, the German sociologist remembered for his study of bureaucracy, borrowed the word from a church historian who, in turn, had borrowed it from St. Paul. Originally, the word referred to "gifts or powers that were manifestations of God's grace." If we can discard our single-vision cultural and religious blinders, it is obvious that the word initially made sense only for such figures as Jesus, Mohammad and Moses, as well as others granted similar status if in slightly different ways, e.g., Gautama Buddha, Confucius. Weber was correct in linking *charisma* with *authority*, in the sense that these individuals are believed by countless numbers of people to have *transmitted to humans the absolutely correct instructions on how to manage things on earth*. If there is a "test" for charisma, it can be answered only after the individuals involved are long gone from earth, but whose instructions are believed wholly legitimate by the multitudes who follow those instructions or, even if they do not follow them to the letter, believe that their own actions are within the boundaries of what the original charismatics intended to convey.

Neither the older nor the newer concepts of legitimate authority can pass muster. Some still accept the notion that managers should make decisions on the basis of "God's word," as relayed to His designated lieutenants (prophets), and then to present-day managers (or rulers), and all consequences of all decisions should be accepted as part of "God's Plan." The "successful" overthrow of a manager (no matter the human misery involved) can be labeled part of the "Plan," but so can successful *resistance* to overthrow efforts; even the concept of "consent of the governed" refers only to the ability to defeat revolution by whatever means are handy.

The newer idea is that even though scientific knowledge *can never be proven, only disproven*,[24] it is something of a legitimate basis for authority, but not over "personal" activities that remain to be decided in direct communication between God and a "universal priesthood of all believers." The latter is uncomfortably connected with a vague notion of "free will leisure time," a sort of male-dominated anarchy, and we all are supposed to obey our bosses at work and in government, even though they cannot know what they are doing. In operational terms, *hierarchy* and *obedience* remain the simple but all-encompassing management theory. Because it is not widely understood that *all* theories involving social decision and action are derived from this single relationship of hierarchy to obedience, I include brief mention of three other theories that really are derived from the single theory of management/religion.

III. Hierarchy and obedience remains a global theory of religion and management, and also of knowledge (objectivity), economics (competition and consumer sovereignty) and politics (winners and losers).

The cases for economic and political theories are not quite as clear as for epistemology (knowledge theory) because we have been deluged with misleading propaganda about economics and politics, principally by kidding ourselves about who is really in charge.

A theory of knowledge can be no more or less than a legitimized decision-making process for deciding what is *true* for a given community, organization, family or state. Thus, a theory of knowledge, in common with a theory of religion, is a management theory. The theory of knowledge and the theory of management must emerge simultaneously, even if they are not consciously observed and written down at the same time.

As already argued, hierarchy is the prevailing management theory (except, perhaps, for a few "uncivilized" peoples who still occupy some areas). A management theory of hierarchy is a knowledge theory of *objectivity*, and no other theory of knowledge can exist so long as hierarchies are operational. *The theory of objectivity is necessary to justify the position of any superior (Proposition II), and to prescribe and explain what subordinates do (take action on the basis of knowledge external to them).* If hierarchy is accepted and in use, debates about alternative theories of knowledge (subjectivity, intersubjectivity, positivism, phenomenology, etc.) are meaningless because it cannot be otherwise.

In the modern scientific view, "scientists observe 'givens' in the world which are not yet affected by judgments."[25] "Reality," that is to say, is independent of the scientific observer who "discovers" it, a concept of "distance" that by separating the thinker from the thought, is itself alienating, just as hierarchy is itself probably the cause of what we label "alienation."[26] The doctrine of objectivity compels scientists to describe many of their discoveries as those processes *ought* to have occurred rather than as they *did* occur, a method known as "rational reconstruction."[27] A good bit of double-talk within scientific communities is necessary because scientists give lip service to a vague ideal of "intersubjectivity" while living and working in hierarchies. As one observer reminds us, "The Galileos of today are not likely to be kneeling before cardinals and muttering the truth under their breath, but kneeling before professors with tenure."[28] In the operational world, of course, subordinates (including members of presidential cabinets) are expected to *pretend* they agree with the decisions of their bosses regardless of their personal views.

To abruptly condense an argument made at greater length elsewhere,[29] scientists are compelled to deal uncomfortably with a *neutral* doctrine of *intersubjectivity* while functioning in a world of *objectivity*. Their own *values* (the organizational and societal objectives they would prefer to see achieved) must be kept out of their endeavors because they are expected to produce only the knowledge that is sought by legitimate authority. A consistent doctrine of intersubjectivity would take account of the values of scientists (and all other humans) but could be operationalized only as a *replacement* for hierarchy/objectivity. The knowledge and truth transmitted by a supreme being, of course, can be thought of as a form of *subjectivity* created by a single self, but even God could not transmit His truth without the assistance of a second, or at least an additional and identifiable, being. *Inter*subjectivity is incompatible with hierarchy, just as Willis Harman's quest for the "transpersonal" requires the abandonment of objectivity in favor of intersubjectivity.[30]

I turn only briefly to the problems of economic theory, lengthier analyses for which can be found in other volumes of the *World Future Society* and elsewhere.[31] It is important to emphasize a few major points because many in the US are now celebrating not only the presumed demise of "socialism" and/or Marxism, but wildly applauding yet another round of glorifying *competition*. This free market ideology is only the economic equivalent of pure unadulterated anarchy, a false front if there ever was one. A *political* anarchist is a symbol of chaos and social disintegration, but an *economic* anarchist is always welcome in policy-making circles as an "expert" in the science of transforming total self-interest (with no thought to equity or social consequences at all) into peace, equilibrium and unceasing "progress."

Contrary to what often is portrayed as a theory of "mutual and voluntary exchange," free market theory actually seeks to transfer authority *from* a monopoly producer who can control price and supply, *to* the individual "consumer" who will be able to satisfy "demands" by paying the lowest possible price for the highest possible quality. The consumer, it is argued, will best be able to do this if *many* producers are seeking his or her favors. *Competition*, therefore, means that a *limitless duplication of goods and services* will leave producers at the mercy of consumers who will be able to exercise *their* "freedom" (Milton Friedman) and "sovereignty" (Paul

Samuelson) by choosing one producer and rejecting all others at the time of each purchase. The ideal of "perfect competition" calls for *unregulated and unrestricted* duplication in the service of the consumer, and the closer we come to attaining this "perfection" (maximum duplication, lowest prices), the closer we come to repetitions of the primary consequence of competition—*depression*. History and our most recent depression presidents (Herbert Hoover, Franklin Roosevelt) have so informed us, but we collectively refuse to listen because the lure of "freedom to consume" sweeps away all doubt. Nor is this an ideological matter; if every nation were dedicated to "socialism," the competition, depression and trade wars have led to wars in the past.

At its ancient *best*, "democracy" was only a system of rotating leadership every so often among the rich males who dominated their communities. The Greek tradition was that of the "exclusive club" that simply excluded the many ineligibles from deliberations.[32] It has been transformed over time into an ongoing series of bitter struggles to "win," with campaigns that center on alleged "issues" that often are forgotten after elections. The only legitimate form of citizen participation in government that is provided by the Constitution and interpretations of it is *voting* —an isolated, lonely and antisocial act that must be hidden behind a curtain so that voters cannot be attacked by those they voted against. Hiding behind a curtain does not really provide much in the way of "citizen participation," and it is small wonder that people often choose not to vote. Yet we glorify voting, and we in the US constantly suggest to others in the world that they will "fail" the test of "democracy" unless they follow our lead. While it is reasonable to argue that this system is not the *worst* in the world, our own history does not suggest that our 200-year record should be looked upon as a form of perfection to which the rest of the world should aspire. "Honest" campaigns are logically impossible.

Because all political ideologies are trapped within a single managerial concept, the function of all *national* leaders is to act as the heads of quasi-religious organizations (the "nation" is often seen as a community existing by virtue of a franchise granted by God), and nationalism has driven many countries to ruin.[33] At the national level, the preparation for, and the fighting and winning of wars, has been the primary value, along with the promotion of expansion into other areas and the appropriation of the resources found there, so that citizens can gorge themselves on the goods so procured. Nationalism is only another expression of cultural, ideological or religious superiority, and religion, nationalism and war have been constant partners. There can be no solution to this mess so long as any nation, religion or culture considers itself "different" than all the others.

IV. There can be no viable planetary future so long as we believe this single theory of religion, management, science, ideology and values can be retained. Only the creation of yet another civilization holds out any hope but some optimism is possible.

The logic of history seems to lead inexorably to the conclusion that the great religions were the solidifying and codifying of a massive social change that had largely been completed before the religions appeared. The great religions and their prophets provided an explanation that justified the new management structure and the fundamental rules for conducting its affairs. Indeed, who can know what might have happened to Christianity if Emperor Constantine had not made it the official religion of the Roman Empire?[34]

As Arnold Toynbee once observed, "The *Genesis* of Pollution" is to be found in Book I in the Holy Bible.[35]

> And God said, Let us make man in our image, after our likeness; and let them have dominion over the fish of the sea, and over the fowl of the air, and over the cattle, and over all the earth, and over every creeping thing that creepeth upon the earth.
>
> So God created man in his own image, in the image of God created he him; male and female created he them.
>
> And God blessed them, and God said unto them, Be fruitful, and multiply, and replenish the earth, and subdue it; and have dominion over the fish of the sea, and the fowl of the air, and over every living thing that moveth upon the earth.

The logic of history suggests that the management concepts in the holy books of the great religions were those that already were being implemented because they seemed necessary at the time. If more humans seemed necessary so that land could be farmed and armies and navies filled with soldiers and sailors, then it was desirable to spell this out in an authoritative handbook of rules and regulations. All of this is more easily understood in the *concrete* context of management than in the often *abstract* context of *some* religions. *The Holy Quran* provides a contrast that serves to make the point:

• *The Holy Quran* serves today as a day-to-day book of rules for managers. President Anwar Sadat referred to it as the current constitution of Egypt. Managers in some parts of the world, therefore, are accustomed to turning directly to the *Quran* for guidance, not to presumably "secular" laws that have replaced it.

• *The Holy Quran* also provides a quick answer to an old question; despite the most intense of disputes over the years, why do Moslems attribute more legitimacy to Jesus and Moses, for example, as prophets of God than Christians accord to Muhammad? Because Muhammad came after the other prophets in calendar time, the Word of God transmitted to him as the last Word of God and, therefore, included all necessary corrections and improved instructions. The concept of the *last* Word is operationally identical to the standard management directive that "this regulation supersedes all previous regulations on the same subject." If Christians and

Jews accorded Muhammad the highest status, they would have to acknowledge the supremacy of the *Quran*.

This does not trivialize religion, as suggested earlier, but elevates it to a position of prominence *within* a massive social change that may have gone so far as to completely change the way humans used their brains and, of course, the way they reached decisions and carried them out. It seems possible that this social change was so profound for human behavior that it amounted to the *Creation* of a new species, a species that appeared the same as its predecessors but was, and is, different. In the most functional ways imaginable, social change created a wholly new definition of *literacy*, the definition we use today.

The modern compromise has not worked, and may have been the catalyst for making things worse. The combination of the Protestant Reformation, and the scientific, political and industrial "revolutions" that followed it, may be seen in hindsight as relatively minor in conceptual terms, but in operational terms as well. We have created an array of *impersonal* and *machine-like* organizations in which humans are expected to behave as nonpersons because their inner selves and consciences are not the property of those organizations. But we also have told those same humans that a supreme being remains a fundamental source of the *rules* that should govern their behavior, especially at home, where holy rules still prescribe that women are to obey men and produce many children. And, while we have glorified "progress," we now come close to realizing that it is the "progress" of the modern age that most threatens its viability.

The needs of the future cannot be spelled out in detail, but *if* the problems now gaining more and more attention in the world are *real* problems, the basis for facing them can be stated with all necessary bluntness. Unless we are prepared to assume that gross overpopulation, extinction of innumerable species, the smothering of the planet by greenhouse gases, nuclear war, destruction of the ozone layer, depletion of water, massive deforestation, and all sorts of other catastrophes that need not be listed are parts of His plan for the world, then we must *repeal* those guidelines, not merely look for ways to violate them without admitting the basic lack of validity in all such guidelines. If humans have been on earth for more than 1,000,000 years, there is no reason to believe that this particular version of the species, now a mere 6000 or so years of age, is the *final* version and humans, we must remember, are *social* animals whose decisions and actions are responses to their situations, not the outcomes of purely "inner" motivations and "instincts."

The compromise reached after the Protestant Reformation entailed the invention of an unwieldy combination; we retained existing management structures *after* producing a logical social doctrine that anyone exercising unilateral authority was incompetent to do so. This prevented the modern West from becoming a global *social* innovator, thereby killing off the most promising aspect of the Enlightenment while reinforcing the worst aspects of the design it claimed to replace. We have little choice but to admit without holding back that *the management manuals we look upon as "holy books" are obsolete and must be discarded on behalf of the planet and the universe, emphasizing as we detail the nature of the obsolescence that the "holy books" are more similar to each other than different.* Wrenching as it may be, the idea of the all-knowing God must go.

The real issue, of course, is not God, but rather hierarchy, obedience and, to a huge extent, the corollaries of competition, nationalism and war. There is not a single major "futures" problem before us that can be dealt with on anything but a *global* basis. Not a one of them can be solved by a single "independent" or "sovereign" nation. Admittedly, a *cooperative* management theory may be impossible to articulate and implement (even our language is a by-product of hierarchy and obedience). This essay, however, is not about the *possible,* only the *necessary.*

When Pope John Paul II visited the US in 1979, a headline in *The Washington Post* proclaimed, "Pontiff Urges Commitment to Human Values." The Pope, asserting that "human values are strengthened when power and authority are exercised in full respect for all the fundamental rights of the human person," merely outlined our 6000-year old trap. So long as those in authority can make unilateral decisions about *values,* there cannot be any. Nor can a prayer often attributed to Reinhold Niebuhr be accepted any longer, for it will not do to say, "O God, give us serenity to accept what cannot be changed . . . " We cannot afford serenity.

There is nevertheless a very *optimistic* way of looking at what has been happening, and is happening, provided we do not hesitate to examine the meaning of the trends. It is well that we have learned that giving the vote to previously unvoting citizens (the poor, minorities, women) does not make it more probable that they will be content with this right of citizenship. We are more uncertain than before that this basic Constitutional right is significant; the first to have the right, the rich who were running things, did not need the vote. And, since other rights, including those in the Bill of Rights, were parts of a larger theory that related only to the leisure time of rich white males, we shall have to ask more questions about "rights." The issues of this era seem increasingly to involve the unlisted rights of citizens while they are at the workplace.

A century is a long time to those of us now living but, in planetary time, it is nothing. The change from gathering and hunting to farming and urbanism was very sudden in planetary time but perhaps hardly noticeable in day-to-day living, especially since rather sudden change is easily forgotten. It is much less than a century since the standard view among white Western intellectuals was that black people were subhuman. Some still do, and black citizens in this country are far from convinced that their situation has really changed. The common-sense view, of course, is that some of the most important changes are underrated because we do make the obvious comparison. Herewith a brief statement of how that comparison looks.

We may very well have to conclude that what we are coming to regard as *social* progress is very often a direct rejection of our 6000-year past, most especially its codification in the great religions a few millennia later, and also a rejection of the minor Western revision launched a few centuries ago. Increasingly what is "right" is in that category precisely because it is "wrong." We may have to stop pretending that the changes we adopt are consistent with the management/religion theory of civilization. Dropping the pretense would accelerate both thought and action. If we are unafraid of the issue's ramifications, abortion may serve as an example; we have yet to face the real questions.

An Endnote: The Real Abortion Issue

As at the beginning, a major problem affecting women (but the rest of us as well) makes the point. The abortion debate has yet to be joined because the opposing positions cannot meet as the current jargon, is a lineal descendant of the old proposition that women have a *social duty to bear children,* and that they must *obey* the regulations that set forth this duty. The "pro-choice" position holds in general that women should have "control" over the uses to which their bodies are put, and that the decision in each case is properly one to be made by the individual woman, as she sees fit.

The debate will only be joined if and when it is acknowledged that there is a *social duty, on a global scale,* to "manage" population. The acknowledgement will have to be accompanied by the invention of decision mechanisms to do this and, hopefully, they will not include forced abortions late in pregnancies. As it stands now, the "pro-choice" argument is a variant of consumer economics that assumes that the world can accommodate itself to *any* combination of decisions, the matter made individually by every woman in the world, with no considerations of social consequences being a part of the decision process.

Once the door is open to fundamental questions, change may begin to accelerate. Even a Supreme Court Justice or two hinted at the fundamentals in the recent hearing on an abortion law before the Court. Attorneys were asked about the "right" to procreate; if the state can insist that a woman bear a child she does not wish to bear, can the state also insist that a woman *not* have a child she wishes to have? While these questions were not widely noted or analyzed in the media, they were linked briefly in the Court itself to future population issues. If it becomes necessary to ensure that many people do *not* reproduce themselves, how shall we act on that necessity? How shall it be decided who is to have children and who is not to have them?

The residual *political* strength of those who oppose population management is traceable to the traditional concept of a social duty (and national need) to expand population. These national policies (still embodied in such corollaries as extra tax deductions) have held sway because increases in population have been seen as important elements of national power (especially bigger armies), but also because the policies have echoed the "Word of God," often an unassailable rule. If we are to admit to the social desirability of managing population growth and setting limits on that growth, we shall obviously have to declare the "Word of God" obsolete.

This is not to argue that upon further study and consideration, humans will agree to manage population growth in the planetary interest. If humans so decide, they will not be sure this is the correct decision, only that they will have weighed one *uncertain* future against another *uncertain* future, choosing "limits" over "no limits." It will do for now to suggest that the concept that *all knowledge [truth] is uncertain* should be considered equally applicable to theology, science, ideology and management. These are, and can only be, a single theory.

Notes

1. Claude S. George, Jr., *The History of Management Thought* (Englewood Cliffs, NJ: Prentice-Hall, 1972), esp. Preface and Ch. 1; Henry Jacoby, *The Bureaucratization of the World* (translated from the German by Eveline Kanes) Berkeley: California Press, 1973, esp. Introduction.

2. Woodrow Wilson, "The Study of Administration," *Political Science Quarterly* 2 (1887), reprinted in Jay M. Shafritz and Albert C. Hyde (eds.), *Classics of Public Administration* (Chicago: Dorsey Press, 2nd edition, 1987), pp. 10-26.

3. D. Gvishiani, *Organisation and Management* (Moscow: Progress Publishers, 1972), p. 27.

4. Ibid.

5. Richard E. Leakey and Roger Lewin, *People of the Lake: Mankind and its Beginnings* (Garden City, NY: Anchor/Doubleday, 1978).

6. Elizabeth Fisher, *Woman's Creation: Sexual Evolution and the Shaping of Society* (New York: McGraw-Hill, 1979).

7. Julian Jaynes, *The Origin of Consciousness in the Breakdown of the Bicameral Mind* (Boston: Houghton Miffly, 1976).

8. Willis Harman, *Global Mind Change: The Promise of the Last Years of the Twentieth Century* (Indianapolis: Knowledge Systems, 1988).

9. For an expanded argument, see my *An End to Hierarchy and Competition: Administration in the Post-Affluent World* (New York:

Franklin Watts, 2nd edition, 1981), Introduction to 2nd Edition.

10. Ibid.

11. Adam Smith, *The Wealth of Nations*, edited by Edwin Cannan (New York: Random House, 1937), p. 625.

12. Arnold Toynbee, *Surviving the Future* (New York: Oxford, 1971), pp. 15, 106.

13. Christopher Hodgkinson, *Towards a Philosophy of Administration* (New York: St. Martin's, 1978), p. 121.

14. Richard T. DeGeorge, *The Nature and Limits of Authority* (Lawrence: University Press of Kansas, 1985), p. 93.

15. H. Feigl, "The Scientific Outlook: Naturalism and Humanism," in Feigl and May Brodbeck (eds.), *Readings in the Philosophy of Science* (New York: Appleton-Century-Crofts, 1953), pp. 9-11.

16. Martin Landau, "On the Concept of a Self-Correcting Organization," *Public Administration Review* 33, 6 (November/December 1972), 533-42.

17. Herbert A. Simon, *Administrative Behavior* (New York: Free Press, 2nd edition, 1957), p. 49.

18. Richard Sennett, *Authority* (New York: Knopf, 1980), p. 15.

19. Julius W. Pratt, *A History of United States Foreign Policy* (Englewood Cliffs, NJ: Prentice-Hall, 1955), p. 386.

20. *The New York Times*, Dec. 4, 1972.

21. *The Washington Post*, Feb. 11, 1977.

22. James MacGregor Burns, *Leadership* (New York: Harper & Row, 1978).

23. John W. Gardner, *The Heart of the Matter: Leader-Constituent Interaction* (Washington: Independent Sector, 1986), pp. 20-22.

24. Karl R. Popper, *The Logic of Scientific Discovery* (New York: Harper Torchbooks, 1968).

25. E. F. Miller, "Positivism, Historicism and Political Inquiry," *American Political Science Review*, 66 (September, 1972), 798.

26. "Alienation" is not logically attributable either to the Industrial Revolution or capitalism, since neither changed the design of social organizations. Thayer, *An End to Hierarchy*, Ch. 2.

27. I. Scheffler, *Science and Subjectivity* (Indianapolis: Bobbs-Merrill, 1967), p. 70.

28. William A. Thompson, *At the Edge of History* (New York: Knopf, 1970), pp. 128-32.

29. See my "Organization Theory as Epistemology," in Carl J. Bellone (ed.), *Organization Theory and the New Public Administration* (Boston: Allyn Bacon, 1980), pp. 113-39.

30. This is my conclusion, not necessarily Harman's. *Global Mind Change*, pp. 69-71.

31. See my "The Crisis of Industrial Overcapacity: Avoiding Another Great Depression," in Howard F. Didsbury, Jr., *The Global Economy: Today, Tomorrow and the Transition* (World Future Society,

1985), pp. 353-90; my "Avoiding a Crash: Public Investment, Private Regulation," in Didsbury (ed.) *Challenges and Opportunities: From Now to 2001* (World Future Society, 1986), p.. 215-43 (also in *World Policy Journal*, Summer 1985); and my *Rebuilding America: The Case for Economic Regulation* (New York: Praeger, 1984).

32. Dwight Waldo, *The Enterprise of Public Administration* (Novato, CA: Chandler & Sharp, 1980), pp. 84-5.

33. Toynbee, *Surviving the Future*, p. 66.

34. See summary in Riane Eisler, *The Chalice & The Blade: Our History, Our Future* (New York: Harper & Row, 1987) pp. 130-31.

35. *Horizon*, Summer 1974 (emphasis added); *The Holy Bible*, Genesis, Verses 26-28.

Humanist Views
of the Future

ENDTIME AND BEYOND

by

Bruce Brander

> . . . if the West is to go under, it will have had the pleasure of reading its own obituary, the most erudite and voluminous obituary ever penned. And no Westerner can protest that he was not warned.
> — Toynbee scholar, Professor Kenneth Winetrout

Almost everyone living in the 20th century has witnessed more world-shaping change than anyone since the European Renaissance and probably since the fall of ancient Rome. Seen from a historical perspective, the spectacle is breathtaking.

Changes in technology and its effects—both positive and negative—are immense. Influencing our lives considerably more are changes in ethics, ideals, aspirations and the arts, in social relationships and world political boundaries. Change is shaking to their very foundations not only single countries but all the nations of the West, while its tremors spread outward to every corner of the earth. Rarely in history have changes loomed so large and so many.

This raises a question of immense significance: Exactly what does the floodtide of change mean? Does it signify no more than a temporary upset, a passing aberration in an otherwise steady line of endless social progress? Or do the massive changes rumbling through the culture signify a major cultural transformation?

Any age of sweeping social change stimulates a surge of social thought. This was true in the time of Plato as the culture of Greece declined. It proved equally so in the waning days of ancient Rome. The twilight of Europe's Gothic Age and the dawning of Renaissance brought still another great wave of social thinking.

Now as a new age of massive change unfolds matching or exceeding such ages of the past, perceptive observers once again have been striving to comprehend the nature of their time. Noted more by historians and sociologists than by the general public, seers of the modern age began recording their views long before the birth of the 20th century. They continue in significant numbers to this day.

For members of a more or less unified school of thought, the civilization-watchers show remarkable diversity. In their ranks are Russians, Germans, Frenchmen, Britons and Americans. Among them are historians, social scientists, literary figures, political and religious thinkers, and humanitarians.

Many of them have worked alone, unaware of each other's efforts in the same direction. Yet they all have one thing in common. They

---

Bruce Brander *is international editor of* World Vision, *Monrovia, CA.*

agree that the Western world is experiencing no mere temporary upset. Rather, they say we are witnessing an upheaval of the greatest historic magnitude—a grand tidal transformation from one form of culture to another that involves the decline and ultimate disappearance of our present civilization.

Some of the earlier observers to come to this conclusion began sounding the alarm in the mid-19th century. The poet Charles Baudelaire proclaimed in 1851 that "we shall perish by the very thing by which we fancy that we live"—namely, technocracy and progress—which he believed would starve mankind's spirituality and lead to governments of "sweeping brutality . . . which will make us, who already are callous, shudder."[1]

A few years later Tolstoy, journeying through a rapidly progressing Western Europe, saw the society already sinking into spiritual atrophy, its great material advances serving only to shore up its sagging structure in a temporary way. The technological culture, he forecast, rather than redeeming the world, would corrupt the world then burn itself out in self-destruction.

Two decades later, Dostoyevsky saw the modernizing world in similar terms. He warned that Russia's ambition to catch up with the West was absurd, since the whole civilization was hurtling toward terrible collapse.

In 1897, with Western society triumphant worldwide and wildly optimistic for its future, the English writer Rudyard Kipling published a poem called "Recessional" to mark Queen Victoria's Diamond Jubilee. Warning against trusting human strength rather than the "God of our fathers," it conjured up grim visions of the culture's mighty splendors vanishing like once-great cities of the ancient world.

In 1902, Henry Adams, a leading American historian and intellectual and descendant of two presidents, declared, as had Tolstoy, that modern technology has nothing to do with genuine progress. Through its devices, people draw unprecedented energy from sources outside themselves. But this only testifies to the rapid exhaustion of their own energies and resources, and their growing dependence on nature's reserves to keep them going. Thus, technology merely masks human decline and speeds it along. In a private letter Adams predicted that the coming century would witness an "ultimate, colossal, cosmic collapse."[2]

Other voices sounding early warnings included Alfred Nobel, the Swedish inventor of dynamite. A millionaire industrialist, he founded the Nobel Peace Prize in the hope of halting the civilization's march into a dark age of violence and barbarism. "One hears in the distance its hollow rumble already,"[3] he wrote to an aristocratic friend.

Jacob Burckhardt, one of the most eminent historians of the 19th century, likened Europe of his time to ancient Rome in decay, a topic on which he was a specialist. The Swiss scholar predicted a future of economic depressions and great wars, a Europe united economically and militarily, the end of democracy and the rise of totalitarianism.

With the outbreak of World War I, the humanitarian doctor and philosopher Albert Schweitzer warned that, "We are living today under the sign of the collapse of civilization."[4] He went on to urge a renewal of humane ethics, based upon reverence for life, as a way to reverse the society's skid toward disaster.

Similar warnings have continued through the 20th century: in the writings of Jack London, H. G. Wells, Aldous Huxley and George Orwell; in studies by sociologist Max Weber, psychoanalyst Erich Fromm and other behavioral scientists; in works by economists and diplomats; in poems, essays and short stories. They have been widely heard, then more or less dismissed from mind.

This reaction, though seemingly contradictory makes a fair amount of sense. Warnings hold a limited value. They alert, they alarm, but rarely do they explain. Lacking thorough comprehension of a problem, people are inclined to let it slip from their attention.

That changed completely with the studies of three intellectual giants of the present century. The German philosopher-historian Oswald Spengler, the English historian Arnold Toynbee and the Russian-American sociologist Pitirim Sorokin carried investigations of the culture far beyond simple warnings.[5] The trio of scholars made exhaustive studies of modern Western civilization as a whole. Their investigations covered graphic arts and architecture, music and literature, religion, science and philosophical thought, ethics and law, economics and social relationships, and other principal fields of human endeavor that make up civilized culture. They went on to examine other cultures as diverse as the Roman, Egyptian, Chinese and Aztec. In the centuries-long arcs of growth and decay followed by the other civilizations, they found intriguingly similar patterns. All high cultures seem to follow the same basic course as they climb, then at some point stall, then decline and eventually collapse.

Taking these patterns and weaving them together with brilliant flashes of personal insight, they produced a curve-line that shows where Western culture has been, where it stands now and where it is likely to be going.

The earliest of the panoramic scholars was Spengler. He spent the culturally cataclysmic years of the First World War writing his classic thousand-page study, *The Decline of the West*.

The historian Toynbee came close on his heels. With access to the rich resources of modern historical and archaeological research and an almost super-human memory, he is by far the most learned scholar ever to work in his field. For four decades he applied his vast erudition to the task of examining every known civilization of past and present—more than a score of them. The result was the largest book written in this century, his monumental 12-volume, three-million-word masterwork, *A Study of History.*

The Russian-born Sorokin also did things in a grand manner. The founder of sociology departments at first Leningrad then Harvard Universities, Sorokin enlisted whole teams of academic specialists in Europe and America to systematically investigate all 2,500 years of historic civilization in the West.

His international team catalogued every known work of art (scores of thousands), every significant philosophy and scientific discovery, every important movement in every major field of culture from the days of ancient Greece to the present century. The study—probably the largest sociological research project ever undertaken—took 10 years. It filled nearly 3,000 pages in a four-volume work titled *Social and Cultural Dynamics.*

Viewed together, the studies present a sweeping panorama of all the world's civilizations passing through their lifespans. The focus then narrows to modern Western culture moving down its own path through history and into a predictable future.

Civilizations begin, according to Toynbee, not in conditions of lotus-eating ease, as some theorists have imagined. Rather, they arise from the stimulation of extreme challenge followed by successful response.

Primitive pre-Egyptians, threatened by climate changes that were drying up their Sahara grassland habitat, slashed into tangled swamps along the Nile River and created a new homeland. The pioneering triumph propelled their culture from complacent primitivism to the civilized state of high and growing human achievement.

So goes the birth of every civilization, with people first challenged mightily then responding triumphantly. A civilization's growth continues with more challenges and successful responses, each cycle bringing greater human strength.

A culture's growth, Toynbee pointed out, need have nothing to do with geographic expansion or improved technology. Rather, civilization grows through a struggle for greater self-determination. Gradually the challenges that arise to be met shift from external to internal, from working on the environment to working out higher ethical standards and improved political relations within the body social.

All civilized cultures begin with a religion. This serves as a focus for awareness and endeavor. People living in the growth stage hold a distinctly religious view of reality. They conceive of it not as something material to be grasped by the senses. Rather, the real is spiritual: Brahma, Tao, Nirvana, Almighty God. The main human concerns at such times are good and evil, conscience and consciousness, soul and salvation. Riches and power are unimportant, as are fame, status, prestige, comfort, pleasure, happiness. If anything, these values are seen as a threat to peace of mind and health of soul.

Material life during a civilization's growth remains simple. People dwell close to nature, their economy agricultural, their government local and feudal. Their existence is ascetic and morally sound. They revel in personal strength and hardihood. With people living in this manner, the civilization accumulates a great fund of inner human strength.

Yet any age of growth inevitably must end. The reason for this lies in human misjudgment. People tend to carry their habits too far.

A phase of growth, like Western civilization's medieval age of faith, attempts to expand its ways into a monopoly. An excess of religious restrictions suppress the flesh more than most people can bear. That spurs rebellion. Then a cultural pendulum that Sorokin found in history begins to swing the other way. Indomitably the weight of human sympathy moves away from things of the spirit toward the opposite mode of existence. To describe the other side of the pendulum swing Sorokin used the word sensate: a way of life that finds its expression mainly in the human senses.

A culture changing from spiritual to sensate begins with people still full of inner strength. Richly endowed in a spiritual sense, it produces superb art and brilliant formal thought: the Parthenon of Periclean Athens; the philosophies of Socrates, Plato and Aristotle; the reasoned theological works of St. Thomas Aquinas and his fellow scholastics around the 13th century; the painting and sculpture of the Renaissance.

But after a time, the culture realizes fairly fully its creative possibilities and ideals. Then, with energy and ambition largely spent, it slumps into the decline of ever-increasing exhaustion.

A Russian social thinker named Nikolai Berdyaev saw the 20th century as the bitter end of the Renaissance, a time when the great spiritual accumulation of the middle ages finally is used up. Other observers, Spengler among them, believed Western culture entered decline as early as the French Revolution of 1789. Though material progress soared from that time forward, the advances in knowledge and technique, as Henry Adams also pointed out, served less to add to the sum of human character and moral stature than to compensate for steady human atrophy.

During the 19th century many serious thinkers noted severe malaise in the culture. And as the 20th century approached, an apprehensive mood of *fin-de-siecle* spread everywhere—the French phrase standing for not merely end-of-century but a whole symptomatology of social deterioration and decay.

At the same time, paradoxically, much of the society flaunted ferocious optimism. Celebrating the achievements of science and technology, less conscious of inward human values and well-being, many people believed that paradise on earth awaited just around the corner of the next centennial.

Machines would eliminate poverty, providing wealth and leisure for all. Immunization and sanitation would put an end to disease. Education would enlighten and ennoble the masses. The age of progress would even speed human evolution, with man advancing toward an angelic future as the fittest who survived also turned out to be the morally strongest and best.

War, people generally felt, already was a thing of the past. Humanity had grown too rational, too intelligent, and too humane to allow for further armed strife between civilized nations.

World War I shattered the culture's humanist dream of man's march toward perfection. Many social observers consider this catastrophic conflict as the first clear sign of Western culture's breakdown. In any case, the war sent the West's industrial monopoly into decline, along with its global political hegemony, its supreme confidence, its system of morality and values and its faith in endless upward progress.

Both Spengler and Toynbee saw the enormity of the First World War as perfectly normal. All through history, spells of suicidal statecraft provide the most gruesome symptom of high cultures entering their age of disintegration.

The West's "time of troubles," as Toynbee calls the bloodstained evening of civilizations, began with the Napoleonic Wars around the start of the 19th century. If patterns of history serve to predict, the modern siege of maddog militarism might not be over yet. Usually in a decline time a succession of wars eats away at the margins of ordinary life until the society lies prostrate and exhausted under its own wanton and savage destruction. Then a final great war strikes a knockout blow, leaving a single surviving power in control of the culture's world.

Just as fratricidal wars hurl brother states at each other in frenzies of mutual destruction, so do other schisms gape open in disintegrating cultures.

An enormous split occurs when the ruling class is sundered from the ruled. Both Toynbee and Sorokin pointed out that societies are led by only a few of their members. Out of the billions of people who have inhabited the earth since history began, Sorokin tallied no more than 200,000 of any lasting significance. Toynbee calls the leaders of a growing culture the creative minority. The common folk follow them because they radiate charisma and creative inspiration.

In a declining civilization, the leaders have lost their way. They have ceased to meet the civilization's challenges with successful responses. The rulers of ancient Greece, for example, at a time of population growth and economic squeeze, failed to merge competing city-states into a cooperative nation, which would have solved their problems. Instead, they waged war upon each other, which weakened and destroyed the culture. Toynbee sees countries of the modern West facing a similar challenge and failing similarly to meet it.

Yet, even while a ruling class is losing its ability to lead, rarely will it consent to losing its power and privilege. So the onetime group of inspiring guides turns into an uninspiring dominant minority of masters. They lead their people no longer by charm but by force and fraud. The greater their failure, the worse their abusiveness grows.

The masses, meanwhile, feel their civilization turning strange and alien. No longer do they sense any real share in its future. Increasingly in bondage to bankrupt rulers, they begin to revolt against their servitude. Thus class conflict erupts alongside fratricidal war as a second major schism in the disintegrating body social.

A third split common to declining civilizations cleaves the very souls of people. In every civilization on the wane, most people abandon creative living, turning to one of two alternatives. Some cast off moral law, flinging themselves into momentary pleasures. Others struggle for strict self-control, fighting passions, striving for ascetic modes of living.

The former habit of following the culture's leaders also gives way to two alternatives. Some people drop out of the society, feeling that the cause they are given to serve no longer is worth their service. Others wrest free from social stagnation by pursuing lofty ideals. These are the stoic philosophers and the spiritually potent religious devotees.

Most people also suffer a passive sense of drift as they feel their lives running out of control. This is one of the most painful tribulations in an age of decline. Others, shocked by seeing their social structure caving in around them, are reawakened to a sense of sin. Blaming the social troubles not on forces beyond their control but on the malfeasance of themselves and their fellows, they seek God's will and open their souls to grace.

Meanwhile, the general breakdown in the civilization's style—in its manners, arts, language, philosophy, religion—pushes many people into cultural promiscuity. The arts pick up bizarre styles randomly from distant corners of the world. Leaders mimic lower classes in dress, speech, behavior. The civilization's people begin to imitate barbarians and savages. Exotic religions thrive. At the same time, the breakdown of cultural style leads stronger souls to a sense of human unity. This gives rise to exalted new visions of the brotherhood of man. It also makes way spiritually for a universal state, a one-world government for the culture, like the Roman Imperium.

As the culture's wars of annihilation come to a close, the universal state draws together the fragments of the battered and weary civilization. Usually people, yearning for order and peace, welcome the world government. They welcome too its Caesar, or dictator, or master, often raising him to the status of a saving god.

The universal state never becomes more than a temporary shelter in the wilderness of decline. Its goal is strictly conservative: to hold ground, to fight a rearguard action. It is dull and anticreative, negative in every regard. Yet it does slow deterioration. The spell of unity provides the pale warmth of a peaceful Indian summer. Many people living at such a time believe their civilization has been saved—unaware of a dark age approaching with the roar of vast disasters, ghastly calamities and irremediable ruin.

Meanwhile, the waning culture performs prodigies of sterilization upon its people. Weighed down by its anti-creative influence, they find normal human growth in a free, wholesome, satisfying way virtually impossible. Its debilitating atmosphere bars almost everyone from developing talents unimpaired. In its later stages, only the most extraordinary people are capable of anything more than following a routine.

At the same time, the civilization's great style in all things has dissipated almost completely. Grand courtesy is long gone. Languages of fine expression turn coarse, even barbaric. Philosophy fades into a mere history of philosophy, or so much sterile academic thought that has little to do with people and their lives.

The arts follow suit, turning undisciplined, arbitrary, falsely creative. Often they substitute gigantic size for grace of form and proportion, especially in sculpture and architecture. They also become dully imitative and crassly commercial, artists turning into industrious cobblers producing only for the marketplace.

Cities in decline times swell to super size. They sprawl and soar as monstrous symbols of soulless intellect, with arrow-straight streets and artificial chessboard design. Fascinating, seductive, they suck populations off the land, using up the best and most talented, exhausting the countryside of human vitality.

Citizens of the decline-time megalopolis dwell amid a decadent blend of refinement and brutality, without tradition, without roots, without religion, parasitical and sterile. In their stone and concrete deserts, they are caught up in an endless vortex of nerve tensions—tense work, tense play, tense relationships.

Marriage ceases to be a creative union for producing offspring, becoming a quest for companionship, a craft-art for the achievement of mutual understanding, a problem of mentalities. Women, who once longed only to be mothers, now seek emancipation. By choice they belong not to husband and family but to themselves, and they are unfruitful. They have soul conflicts rather than children.

The number of children decreases mainly because people no longer see reason for having them. First the society prudently limits births. Then limitation gets out of hand and general depopulation begins. In time, the demographic shrinkage threatens military defense and the production of necessities. Rulers strive to promote higher birthrates. But life itself has fallen into question, and nothing serves to restore fruitfulness.

As depopulation continues, provincial communities empty out, then the great metropolises. Classical writers tell of renowned cities where crumbling buildings lined the streets, cattle grazed in shopping centers and amphitheaters were sown as fields.

As life in a decline time turns increasingly meaningless and joyless, many people look for escape from its burdens.

Some retreat, by one means or another, into the past, which beckons like a cozy home from which the society has strayed. Others try to overleap the present, living for future utopias. Still others, feeling trapped in a drab, mechanical, vulgar existence, withdraw into the fortress of themselves—the choice of Greco-Roman Stoics and disciplines of India's Gautama Buddha, who sought detachment, invulnerability, annihilation of self. Yet all these escapes are life-negating and sterile. In the end, none of them works.

That leaves only one more avenue of flight: what Toynbee called "transfiguration." People who choose this route move into a radically new and invigorating spiritual clime. First they withdraw, like the Stoics of the ancient world. But unlike the Stoics, they do not stay detached. Once rested and renewed, they give up their comfort, and, in compassion and love, return to the confused and turbulent world to aid their fellow men. Instead of trying to exclude the world, they transcend the world, then try to rescue others from it.

This kind of transfiguration in waning high cultures gives rise to history's major religions. Thus life is served evenamid death as a low point for civilization stimulates a high point for spiritual renewal.

Ordinarily a dying civilization produces not only a universal world-state but also a universal church. Religion deals best with the psychic storms battering the landscape of decline. A church also can absorb an avalanche of bright and wasted talent that drops away from the culture's dreary establishment.

Rarely, if ever, does the universal religion bring restoration to the culture around it. Ancient Romans hoped that Christianity would save the Imperium. But the growing church could only watch while the weary and dying culture collapsed of its own accumulating dead weight. Yet the new faith can provide a seedbed for the next high culture in history's procession, as Christianity arising in a dying Rome became the soil for Western civilization.

Western culture's prophets of decline differ greatly in their estimates of when the civilization will collapse. Some, like Dostoyevsky and Henry Adams, saw the endtime coming soon. Others, like

Spengler and Toynbee, believed the cultural winter is only now setting in, and generations, perhaps centuries, might pass before a dark and stormy age of barbarism wipes away its final traces.

Both of the latter thinkers expected world government and totalitarian rule around the year 2000. Both also saw the possibility of cultural petrifaction, the effete civilization being preserved indefinitely within a bureaucratic iron cage. This has happened to other dying cultures, Egypt and China as cases in point. In Western culture, science and technology could give its masters virtually unlimited power to freeze all things in place.

Material science and its sister art, technology, are by far the strongest elements of modern culture. As ancient Greece raised the ideal of beauty to heights never surpassed, as ancient Rome excelled in political organization and law, as Semitic civilizations lifted religious creativity to soaring levels, so the main achievement of Western civilization is unparalleled development of the physical sciences.

Yet it seems that science also has peaked and started down the slope of decline. Once its priests prided themselves on finding absolute truth and reducing nature to a set of fixed laws. Now the certainties of yesterday are melting away.

The growing use of statistics has displaced scientific necessity with probability and chance. The atom, once seen as the ultimate irreducible particle of matter, solid as a billiard ball, has dissolved into a complex and mysterious universe of intra-atomic forces. Likewise, the theory of relativity, the elimination of mass, the abandonment of absolute time and space, the uncertainty principle of quantum mechanics and especially the concept of entropy in the second law of thermodynamics—all contradict basic scientific surities of former times, signifying that dissolution has begun.

Some scholars of civilizations regard science as a product of earlier religion—the intellectual leavings of a soul-feeling gone dead. According to Spengler, scientific interest within a culture runs its course within two centuries or so. Then people grow weary of its steel-bright concepts, wander into skepticism and long to return to its spiritual home of faith.

Modern Western culture will endure as long as science and technology hold it together. But sooner or later, scientists and technologists will grow weary of it too. Overwhelmed by a sense of satanism in the tyranny of wheels, cables and circuits, they will lay aside their tools and seek salvation of their souls. Then machine industry will flicker out.

Whether disintegration proceeds slowly under a universal state or quickly in the conflagration of warfare, a dark age of barbarism is almost certain to follow. Barbarians serve a definite purpose. They are human culture's negative agencies. Raging through the bleak landscape of decline like historical tornados, they help a failing civilization to die. They pick its carcass clean like vultures. Then, when their task is done, they too disappear.

But where will the future find its new barbarians? The great hordes of Visigoths and Ostrogoths, Vandals and Huns that menaced Europe for 3,000 years were absorbed into Christendom or wiped off the earth by the end of the 14th century. Some commentators have suggested that the barbarians to come will arise from the culture itself. As one put it: "Ancient civilizations were destroyed by imported barbarians; we breed our own."[6]

Finally, after the whole predictable procession of events—annihilative wars, the universal state, divine rulers, a universal church and barbarian threats—within a few centuries at most, as Spengler wrote, "there will no more be a Western culture, no more be German, English, or French than there were Romans in the time of Justinian."[7]

And what of the West's technological splendors? They "will lie in fragments, *forgotten*—our railways and steamships as dead as the Roman roads and Chinese wall, our giant cities and skyscrapers in ruins like old Memphis and Babylon."[8]

Spengler was an uncompromising doomsayer. Yet not all the observers of the civilization's malaise believed the West was absolutely doomed to die and go to archaeology.

The Swiss historian Burckhardt, even while he accurately forecast the 20th century's ghastliest miseries, held that fresh creativity welling up unexpectedly never should be ruled out as a means of bringing new life to a society.

Toynbee was certain that the West's world leadership is passing away. But he refused to declare the culture's conclusion foregone. While the Western civilization is in no way immune to the fate of every previous high culture, it still can rise to meet the challenge of the present with a successful response, and in doing so come back to vibrant life.

Toynbee defined this challenge as overcoming outdated nationalism, a modern idolatry promoting mass suicide in an age of supersonic jets, instant communications and superbombs within a global village. The creative response that would save us from this challenge is voluntary world government.

Yet salvation ultimately is no matter of political engineering. What is needed, Toynbee affirmed, is a spiritual redemption of souls. A society's decline, after all, is nothing but a symptom of spiritual decline among its people.

So the fate of the West will be decided not only by the course of man's relationship with his fellows, but also by his relationship with himself and, above all, with his God. Though Toynbee spent much of his working years as a declared agnostic, he nonetheless urged modern people to pray to God "in a humble spirit and with a contrite heart"[9] for a reprieve from continued warfare and self-annihilation.

Sorokin concluded that the present sensate culture must burn itself out in a conflagration of excesses before anything better can arise. Sensate art presses realism to its limits in photography then hits a dead end. It can proceed no further, and a pendulum-swing to symbolic spiritual art is the only direction open to the future. Likewise, sensate pleasures increase until they sate, enervate and kill. A rediscovery of the austere but deeply satisfying pleasures of spiritual growth is the only way left to go.

So it is with every other facet of culture, whether economics, science, ethics or social relations. All must rush ahead into sensate absurdity then perish. New life awaits only in a fresh revelation of spiritual alternatives.

Meanwhile, for our immediate future, Sorokin predicted hard times. The humanist dream of orderly progress leading to a terrestrial paradise—a future with prosperity and leisure for all, with crime, sickness and ignorance vanishing, with cooperation and goodwill blossoming between nations while guns are beaten into golf clubs and electric toasters—will not come to pass. In its place Sorokin foresaw a desperate period of bloodshed, cruelty and misery, with much of mankind violated and uprooted.

Yet the sociologist, though very much a doomsayer for modern Western civilization as it stands, or teeters today, in no way lacked hope for humanity. He regarded present and coming miseries as only a a process of clearing away the debris of the old so new life can blossom. In the modern West, the overripe and rotting sensate system and its adherents will rush on to self-destruction. But the very ordeal of their passing will bring about a cleansing transformation. The agony of the dying culture will force people to open their eyes to the increasing hollowness of their values. Then a great moral awakening will occur.

Several of the social philosophers speculated that the new culture might include an unprecedented meeting and merging of the earth's eastern and western hemispheres. Oriental peoples would awake from a centuries-long torpor to rejoin the torrent of history. Meanwhile a planetary way of looking at the world is arising everywhere.

But who will preside over the union? Not the West, they declared. Russia and the Slavic nations are positioned geographically to provide an intra-hemispheric bridge. They also might give birth to the next great civilization.

Slavic peoples never have built a civilization of their own. They have ridden through history in the procession of other high cultures. Today they continue to lack a native structure for their society, hitchhiking on the West, copying ideas, ideals and forms that originated in Western Europe and America. Some civilization-watchers believe they possess what now is lacking in the weary West—the raw spiritual energy to build a new high culture.

Ideally, the West and the Slavic peoples might combine assets. The aged culture, decaying from the inside out, is left with a structure empty of content: form without life. Russia and its brother nations have life without form. Conceivably, the two regions can merge on a cooperative basis.

Such a union, however, comes with no guarantee of being peaceful. The dying Roman world and the Germanic tribes that eventually merged to create Western civilization often battled their way to mutual understanding. Similarly, the West and Russia might use war as one means among many for joint interpenetration.

Meanwhile, any high culture created by the Slavs, the social observers insist, will look nothing like their present nation-states. The Marxist Communism that governs them now is one more Western import overlaid upon Slavic populations and ill-fitting to their nature. The oppressive grayness of the Soviet period must pass before a true Slavic epoch can arise.

If this or any other new culture blossoms into being, it will be radically different from the dominant civilization of the past five or six hundred years. Rather than developing the material environment, it will develop human beings. It will grow as a spiritual culture, thoroughly religious, tenderly humane, full of Messianic promise.

The time is ripe for that kind of civilization. Many people already are gagging on the excesses of modern materialism, losing faith in dry reason and brittle science, longing for inner certitudes, eager to recapture life's joy and sweetness. The next millennium will belong to a civilization better measured for holistic human needs.

But what about us? How should we live in the interesting, eventful and fearsome here and now? Until the endtime itself comes to an end, how can we manage our lives to maximum effect? How can we abide with good sense and fulfillment in the midst of growing social crises?

Spengler offered a few recommendations for the young. Since the arts are dead, he wrote, "I can only hope that men of the new generation may be moved by [his] book to devote themselves to technics instead of lyrics, [transportation] instead of the paintbrush, and politics instead of epistemology. Better they could not do."[10]

Since freedom and democracy will wither and vanish, according to all the social thinkers, politically-minded people are well advised not to burn themselves out fighting for civil liberty or against totalitarian masters. Collectives will arise as a refuge in which a weary people can lean upon each other. Modern Caesars will be born from the womb of mass insecurity. To battle either is to defy the public yearning. Future freedom fighters would do better to build inner spiritual freedom and let politics pursue its inevitable downward path.

Sorokin saw no point in trying to save the sinking culture and its society. Rather, he recommended that conscientious and concerned people save themselves by abandoning the foundering ship of sensate values and swimming toward spiritual values as the only island of safety they shall see. Only thus would they also aid the grand social transformation from death to new life.

Toynbee believed the coming spiritual age might evolve into a social order unprecedented in all history—a form of culture higher than civilization. As freshly inspired religions regularly have given birth to new civilizations, so the historian saw the possibility of civilization being replaced completely by religion.

In his view, this is a logical and natural leap of human progress. Primitive societies—of which, by one count, 650 exist today—represent mankind's first great ascent above animal level. Civilization, a second species of human society, rests on a far higher ledge up the cliff of human progress. Religion, Toynbee speculated, might constitute a third social species, as distinct from civilization as civilization is from primitivism, and resting on a loftier ledge still.

Conceivably, mankind, in a massive upward struggle, might leave civilization behind, coming to dwell in the higher society of religion. This society is higher not only because it upholds loftier ethics, but also because it includes as its principal member Almighty God.

Notes

1. Charles Baudelaire wrote this in one of his many unfinished works which was to be titled "The End of the World." It is quoted by Karl Lowith in *Meaning in History*, pp. 97-98.

2. Henry Adams, quoted by Timothy Paul Donovan in *Henry Adams and Brooks Adams*, p. 118.

3. Alfred Nobel, quoted by Barbara W. Tuchman in *The Proud Tower*, p. 233.

4. Albert Schweitzer, *The Philosophy of Civilization*, p. 1.

5. The balance of this chapter integrates the writings of Spengler, Toynbee and Sorokin where they agree and supplement each other.

6. William Ralph Inge in *The Idea of Progress*, quoted by Arnold Toynbee in *A Study of History*, abridged version, vol. 1, p. 419.

7. Oswald Spengler, *The Decline of the West*, vol. I, p. 167.

8. Oswald Spengler, *Man and Technics*, p. 103.

9. Arnold Toynbee, *A Study of History*, abridged version, vol. 1, p. 554.

10. Oswald Spengler, *Decline of the West*, vol. I, p. 40-41.

FAITH AND THE FUTURE: THE ROLE OF BELIEF IN SHAPING EVENTS

by

Michael J.G. Gray-Fow

To know the future we must understand the past; to grasp the role of belief in forming the future we must examine how it has worked in the past. Truly *tempora mutantur et nos, mutamur in illis,* [times change and we change with them], but unless humanity changes dramatically it will be swayed as much by beliefs in times to come as in former ages. To understand what lies ahead, therefore, we need to examine how belief has operated on human history in the past. To explain this I propose a conceptual framework of eight pages: 1) we must distinguish between initiators of belief and followers, 2) followers are essential, 3) the *ultimate* impact of a belief owes nothing to the initiator's temporal authority, 4) followers organize, and the organization may affect the future in its own right, 5) organizations generate authority, and that authority, *qua* authority, can powerfully influence events, 6) a belief may fortuitously alter the future without regard to the nature of the belief, 7) the force of belief relates to conviction, not verifiability, and 8) all beliefs can be explained equally by Divine Providence, irresistible social forces, or random chance. We will consider each equally, but one example illustrates all. The modern Druses of Lebanon believe in the divinity of the Fatimid Khalif Al-Hakim Beamrillah (otherwise Hakim the Mad), murdered by his sister's orders in February 1021. His friend Darazi (hence *Darazians,* hence *Druses*) had proclaimed his divinity, and had attracted adherents. Here we have initiator and followers. Hakim's status had given the new religion its impetus, but it survived persecuting centuries as a Moslem heresy, preserved against Moslem orthodoxy through its organization and from internal strains through its own calcifying authority, the final and unpredicted result being a modern para-military Lebanese movement (far removed from the dreams of Hakim and Darazi), with unshakeable beliefs fervently held against all counter-argument, the whole phenomenon equally explicable in terms of God, human progress, and sheer luck.

The example indicates a historian's dilemma: belief is in people and causes, but the causes are persuasive through influential or eloquent figures. These are famous, and fame is elitist; either that or we follow social historians into the land of statistics. Even statis-

Michael J. G. Gray-Fow *is director of studies, Northwestern Military and Naval Academy, Lake Geneva, WI.*

tics show only those that were convinced, and we ask who convinced them; for people are convinced by people, whether immediately and directly, or through influences ultimately traceable to individuals. The famous are not disqualified by their fame from representing an age, nor the unknown and unsung transmitters of their views. Believers argue that truth prevails without eloquent intermediaries; this argues that one *should* believe, not whether one *does* believe. In the end, we *choose* to believe in people or ideas, and in the latter case because we have been persuaded by people also, whether immediately or through their thoughts and writings. Given this, we turn to the eight pegs of our framework and their exemplars.

Our first peg is that of initiators of belief. Their authority was either personal (self-claimed or asserted for them) or derivative; they usually proclaimed their message first and themselves second (if at all), and they announced either a new truth or the restoration of an old neglected one. Our knowledge of belief initiators comes largely from the records of believers, which are as much doctrinal as historical, and for believers the initiator himself becomes part of the message. We see this with Christ, Buddha, and Mahavira. Jesus spoke with authority. The earliest gospel (Mark's) shows him reticent about its nature; the last gospel (John's) declares it clearly divine. Jesus himself proclaimed the Kingdom of God; his followers proclaimed him as inaugurating the Kingdom, and the later creeds omit the Kingdom entirely. Matthew's gospel emphasizes Jesus' fulfillment of Hebrew prophecy, but a century later the Church was mainly Gentile.[1] ??? Gautama Buddha taught the Four Noble Truths and the Noble Eight-fold Path; his followers preached a transcendental Buddha. Even in the primitive Hinayana Buddhism Gautama was already quasi-divine; in developed Mahayana Buddhism his discipline has become a religion, with himself at the center. We see the same phenomenon with Mahavira Vardhamana and Jainism.[2] Christ, Buddha, and Mahavira spoke on their own authority; Moses and Mohammed spoke as messengers, but with a unique authority for their followers. Moses identified himself as sent by the god of Abraham; Mohammed asserted he was restoring the religion of Ibrahim. For Jews Moses links patriarchal prehistory with later Judaism, a beleaguered continuum centering around the Torah and Israel, yet Moses always remains human, even fallible. Moslems have tended to make Mohammed perfect, and the Sufis ascribed miracles to him. The Sikhs have similarly elevated their founder Guru Nanak.[3]

The initiator can be forgotten, while the belief survives. The Persian Mani (d. c. AD 275) claimed to be a divine messenger, asserting a cosmic dualism of good and evil, light and dark. After briefly enjoying royal favor, Manichaeism entered on centuries of persecution. It spread widely nevertheless, cropping up in many guises, among the Bogomils of Bulgaria (10th century) and the Cathari of southern France (c. 1100). The Bulgarian connection gave believers the nickname *Bougres,* with a connotation of sexual irregularity, but despite repeated official condemnation the Manichaeans survived. Manichaeism underlies modern Satanism, but Mani himself is long forgotten.[4]

Despite Mohammed's claim about the religion of Ibrahim, all of these initiators in fact consciously set out to bring a new belief to men. Others have consciously tried to go back, and have really gone forwards. Confucius called for a return to ancient values but actually introduced the new idea of ethical government. His thinking dominated China to 1949. Charlemagne (d. 814) tried to revive classical civilization at his court but the Carolingian Renaissance laid the foundations of the Middle Ages.[5]

Reformers *within* belief systems have initiated beliefs that shaped the future while intending only to purify what existed. Christianity has had many such. Arius (d. 336) questioned Christ's divinity, and his views prevailed among the barbarian tribes on Rome's frontier. When the barbarians overran the western Empire their heresy hindered assimilation with the local population, hampering their rule. Those barbarians who switched to Catholicism survived, the Arian kingdoms perished. Nestorius (d. 451) doubted the union of divine and human in Christ. Driven from the Roman Empire, Nestorianism survived intermittent oppression in Asia and flowered in odd places, as at the court of the Great Khans. One Nestorian community held out in Kurdistan until this century. Eutyches (d. 454) was so anxious to correct the errors of Nestorius that he asserted only one nature in Christ. This belief, Monophysitism, was widely popular in Syria and Egypt, despite persecution by the Byzantine government. When the Arabs invaded in the 640s Byzantine defenses were weakened by Monophysite disaffection, and Syria and Egypt became Arab and Moslem. The Monophysites survive still, and constituted the state Church of Ethiopia until Haile Selasie's fall in 1974.[6]

More recent reformer-initiators would include Luther, Calvin, and Wesley. The first shattered the unity of western Christendom, and he and Calvin through the limits of their success inadvertently created a world where religious toleration would become inevitable. Calvin's influence diffused through curious channels, and in the Dutch Reformed Church of the Afrikaners underpins the theology behind apartheid. Wesley's stimulation of popular activism in 18th century England contributed to the cooperative movements in the next century, and thus to the birth of trade unions and socialism.[7]

Equally unintended and even more important had been St. Benedict's contribution centuries before in founding western monasticism (6th century). Fleeing from the world, generations of monks preserved, copied, and transmitted classical learning. The medieval university took over the job, bolstered by a flood of translations emanating from Toledo, where Bishop Raymund I (d. 1151) and Archdeacon Domingo Gundisalvo had founded a great translating school where Christian, Jewish, and Moslem scholars exchanged ideas.[8] Benedict and Raymund take us from religious to intellectual initiators of belief, which raises the question of derivation. Tracing actual lines of influence by stages shows connections, not necessarily cause and effect. The influence of even great ideas is often erratic and unpredictable; we need to be cautious of our own ingenuity as detectives, and beware of imposing our own preferred order on events. Even so, some initiators of ideas are of undisputed importance. Plato and Aristotle dominated western thought for hundreds of years. Through St. Augustine (d. 430) Platonism colored Christian theology, until the Toledo translators released Aristotle on the West. Through Aquinas (d. 1274) and the Council of Trent (1545-63 int.) Aristotleianism became and remains the philosophical substratum of much Roman Catholic thinking.[9]

Reviewing other initiators of great ideas that influenced the future a kaleidoscope of images presents itself: Charles Darwin aboard the *Beagle*, Karl Marx scribbling away in the British Museum, a deaf Beethoven bridging classical and romantic music, Pasteur with his dishes, and so on. The list is *not* endless, but drawing the line is hard, and cultural elitism can mislead us. We unhesitatingly acknowledge a Newton and an Einstein, give a nod to Galileo, recognize Harvey and Jenner, Rontgen and Freud, but only briefly touch on a James Watt, a George Stephenson, a Bessemer, and even an Edison or Marconi. With all of these, as with the great religious initiators, there were people who *believed* in them or their work, who gave it value, if not immediately then later.

The second peg of our framework, the need for followers, is evident from our knowledge of the foregoing. Without followers, or people who carried on their work, they would have been interesting but without lasting influence. A brief further illustration comes from two failed initiators. The Roman Lucretius (d. c. 55 BC) tried to convert his friends to Epicureanism through the verses. They liked his poetry and ignored his advice. He did have an accidental influence; through him we largely know Epicurus, and through Epicurus, Democritus, Leucippus, and the Greek atomists. A meandering line links them all through Lucretius to Rutherford and Oppenheimer. Another proselytizer without followers was Mazdak (d. 528), who briefly persuaded the Persian court to accept an odd mixture of communism and animal rights. A reaction of Church and Property ended this aberration. Lucretius and Mazdak had their fleeting admirers, but with no committed following and none to pick up the torch later, they proved ephemeral voices. Prophets without followers are effectively mute.[10]

Our third propositional peg is the ultimate irrelevancy of an initiator's temporary authority in promoting the belief. We have three dimensions here: those with authority whose beliefs did not survive, those with authority whose beliefs did, and those without authority whose beliefs flourished and lasted. In the first group the Pharaoh Akhenaton (d. 1350 BC) failed despite a god-king's powers to win his people to monotheism; the usurping Emperor Wang Mang (d. AD 23) failed to sway the Chinese toward social levelling; the Roman Emperor Marcus Aurelius (d. 180) gained few imitators for his espousal of Stoicism; the Khmer conqueror Jayavarman VII (d. c. 1218) dismally failed to convert his Hindu subjects to Buddhism; and the attempts of the Moghul Akbar (d. 1605) to unite his wrangling Hindu and Moslem millions in a new "Divine Faith" perished with him.[11] We should mention, however, the Indian Emperor Asoka (d. 232 BC), whose promotion of Buddhism did give it a powerful impetus, though its survival for some centuries in India was due to believers' devotion to Buddha, not to Asoka's vanished dynasty.[12] Those who had authority and used it successfully to promote their beliefs include King Tissa of Ceylon (d. 210 BC), whose adoption of Buddhism was followed by his people, and whose country remains a bastion of Theravada Buddhism. Constantine the Great (d. 337) effectively made Rome Christian, and the barbarian kings Clovis, Aethelberht, and Edwin ordained the same religion for the Franks and Saxons (6th-7th centuries).[13] After some initial uncertainties these conversions held good. Why did they succeed where others failed? We can posit these factors: a) dissatisfaction with the existing order, b) existing support for new ideas, c) enfeeblement of likely opponents, and d) indifference (at least) among the masses. These are local, temporary factors, leaving aside broader theories of history, which we turn to later. They explain the success of political as well as religious beliefs. The first pharaoh and the first Chinese Emperor ended years of chaos after destroying all likely opponents, so did the first Roman Emperor, Augustus.[14] It is always dangerous to say that people yearned for peace and stability since our knowledge of the popular will comes from partisan sources, but the general desire of mankind for peace (along with the desire of rulers for glory) has been a potent force at times in shaping the future. A feeling rather than an idea, it has nevertheless moulded events.

So have those without any authority in their day. Seemingly just an itinerant rabbi killed by the Romans, Jesus Christ influenced the future through his ideas and those of his followers more than any other historical figure. Nearly two millennia later his followers outnumber all others, and most of the world numbers its years from his birth. He is too extraordinary to be typical, so we pass to Florence Nightingale and Henri Dunant, the reformer of nursing and the founder of the Red Cross, to educators like Jean-Jacques Rousseau, and Arnold of Rugby. There was also Galen (d. 199), the gladiators' doctor whose works dominated medicine to the Age of Science, the monk Copernicus (d. 1543) who altered the heavens for us, the naturalist Darwin (d. 1882) whose ideas still agitate our schools and courts, and Einstein (d. 1955)—whom Bertrand Russell claimed only ten people ever really understood,[15] but whose name is bandied about to justify a relativism that has as little connection with relativity as Social Darwinism has with Darwin. (Even so, misrepresentation and misapplication *is* an influence on the future, and has ever been so.)

We pass to the fourth propositional peg: believers organize, and organization itself influences the future. The Christian Church in Europe, the Theban priesthood in Egypt, the Babylonian priest-hood, the Buddhist Church in Ceylon, all provide examples. The organization of the Christian Church enabled it to withstand official persecution before Constantine, and after that in the West allowed it to oppose the encroachments of the Christian state. It remained and remains a power rising above nationalism and the passing ethos. More united than divided by a common sacred literature, holy calendar, and liturgical customs, it survives abuse and misuse to proclaim in every age an appeal to different standards. The priesthood of Amun-Re at Thebes achieved importance under the 12th Dynasty (1991-1786 BC), assumed sacerdotal preeminence under the great 18th Dynasty (1570-1320 BC), gobbled up a status next to Pharaoh's own under the increasingly feeble 20th Dynasty (1200-1085 BC), and ruled southern Egypt in its own right under the powerless 21st Dynasty (1085-945 BC). Put back in its political place by the 22nd Dynasty, it retained enormous wealth and influence, became the nationalist focus after the loss of Egyptian independence (like the Roman Catholic Church in Communist eastern Europe), and only declined with the decline of Thebes itself. The Babylonian priests of Bel-Marduk never aspired so high, but from the days of Hammurabi (d. 1750 BC) regulated a curious ceremony, the "taking of the hand of Bel", which alone conferred legitimacy on the rulers of that part of the world. Like the Delphic Oracle, they were doubtless politically astute, but as an order had influence and power. The Buddhist Church in Ceylon was so endowed by the enduring devotion of pious rulers that by the 19th century it controlled one-third of all cultivated land. As with medieval Europe, the monk was poor, his monastery was not; vows pertain to individuals, not corporations.[16]

We should note in passing that the power of organization can be grass-roots, not hierarchical. The opposition of Byzantine monks to iconoclasm in the 8th and 9th centuries (with mixed general popular reaction) was not centrally organized but effective nonethe-less.[17] It was a successful *conservative* response to changes (unlike the fate of the "Old Believers" in Russia), but differs only in point of origin from such anti-conservative movements as the Civil Rights momentum in the United States in the 1960s. Historians are always suspicious of "grass-roots" movements; they assume a charismatic leader. Reality *and* their suspicions both have force. Governments *and* people can sway the future. They have never been synonymous, and probably never will be; politics is the art of reconciling the two.

Our fifth propositional peg is that organizations generate their own internal authority, and these in turn can acquire a life of their own that shapes and influences the future. It is impossible to resist the Papacy as an obvious example. Whatever its theological justifications, as a historical phenomenon it has dominated post-classical Europe, and through Europe the World. It also affords a strange and wondrous example of how to influence the future through ideas and beliefs. Pope Gregory I (d. 604) sent monks to convert the heathen English. The newly Christian English in due course became an eccentric nation of travellers and colonizers, and one of their colonial offshoots transmogrified itself into a new Republic, "One Nation, Under God, Indivisible", while others became the Commonwealth countries, all with established churches. In their medieval heyday the popes deposed monarchs and allocated kingdoms, they launched crusades and carved up continents. The Eastern Church had broken away by 1054; northern Europe repudiated the Papacy at the Reformation, and the popes went into a political decline that also affected their spiritual dominion. In the last century their spiritual authority has grown again, and their influence in the world.[18] In a smaller compass than the Papacy, the Dalai Lamas also represent the way in which an organization-generated authority can influence events in its own right. They progressed over 250 years from being leaders of a Buddhist reform sect to being rulers of Tibet.[19] Today, the current Dalai Lama, even in exile, can command international attention.

Such religious or ideological authorities have often shaped the future as guardians of orthodoxy. The Spanish Grand-Inquisitors stifled Spanish literature for years; in Sassanian Iran (AD 226-652) the chief mobads obliterated the rich Hellenistic heritage of the previous era, and in the communist world the Party Secretaries and Chairmen have promoted (until Gorbachev in Russia at least) a rigid control over all expressions of creative thought. We should remember that the future can be shaped as much by what is prevented or frustrated, as by what is fostered or encouraged.

Our sixth peg is that future changes brought about by a belief may have little or no connection with the nature of the original belief. The relationship between the modern Lebanese Druses and the Khalif Hakim, the connection between medieval civilization and Charlemagne's efforts to revive classical culture are cases in point. Another illustration is afforded by the Pirenne Thesis: that the Moslem conquest of the north African coast in the 7th century ended the ancient trading security of the Mediterranean and forced western Europe back on to a land-based, non-monetary economy, leading to the rise of feudalism. The Moslem motivation was religious, directly attributable to the teachings of Mohammed; the consequences, at the other end of the Mediterranean, were economic and political. We could add further long-term ramifications: from feudalism came much of western class consciousness (the ambiguity of terms like 'noble'), and even, in the English-speaking world, the idea of the 'gentleman'.[20] Despite Pirenne, probably the most famous example of unexpected changes and consequences flowing from a belief was the discovery (or rediscovery) of America as a result of Columbus' mistaken notions about a shorter route to the Indies.[21]

Turning to the last two pegs in our propositional framework, I recognize that I move on to thorny ground. The premise that belief has to do with certainty of conviction and not necessarily verifiable truth, and the proposition that the influence of beliefs on the future can equally well be ascribed to Divine Providence, *inevitable* socioeconomic forces, or to mere chance touches on the assumptions most people take for granted—and are unhappy to see questioned. Emotional involvements notwithstanding, we progress—with respect and humility.

Verifiable truth is itself a thorny issue, and the truth of a proposition or belief is independent of the adduceable evidence. *That* relates only to the right to command assent,[22] but that in its turn hinges on popular assumptions. We lack evidence for the truth of the Aztec belief that a "New Fire" ceremony was necessary every 52 years to keep Life and Nature going, though thousands were slaughtered at the time for this theory. The Aztec need to find an ongoing supply of victims for their bloody deities every year drained their manpower, hindered progress, and curtailed population growth;[23] these were *real* impacts of their ideas on the immediate future. The same was true of the Carthaginian sacrifice of their brightest and best children to Baal Hammon in times of crisis. The Romans were suitably appalled, as they were by Druid human sacrifice, but were not above being rushed into it themselves in moments of panic.[24] We are dealing here with Magic, where surety of conviction bears little connection with either acceptable evidence or objective truth. If we dismiss it all as primitive superstition, we should remember our own world is replete with horoscopes and astrologers.

We come finally to our last propositional peg, that all changes and influences on the future resulting from belief can be attributed equally well to Divine Providence, irresistible social and economic forces, or random chance. There are similarities between the first two alternatives. They both assume a broad interpretation of history, with incidents interpreted in this light after the event. They both involve accepting incidents as currently inexplicable, given the general premise, but which are presumed to be explicable ultimately, at some future date. The last alternative by definition rules out a broad interpretation, at least a coherent one; in terms of Divine Providence, a number of examples come to mind. When the Goths sacked Rome in AD 410 the pagans blamed it on the official defection to Christianity. St. Augustine wrote *The City of God* to refute the charge, and explain Roman history in the context of God's eternal plan. Both Augustine and the pagan writers assumed history reflected divine ordinance. On a grander scale, within the last half century, Pierre Teilhard de Chardin has set out to explain the whole of evolution and human progress from its remotest ancestry as part of God's plan for the universe. To the skeptic both Augustine and Fr. Teilhard are just rationalizations after the event; to the believer they offer wonderful insights into the sublime grandeur of the Creator's purposes.[25] Lastly, there is sheer chance as an explanation of how beliefs affect the future. As a hypothesis it represents the tip of a veritable iceberg of other assumptions, ultimately resting on the proposition that there is no purpose in or to the Universe. In effect, it presupposes a kind of cosmic anarchism, and as a theory has historically appealed only to a number of jaundiced intellectuals. This is not a comment on its viability as a hypothesis, and as a hypothesis it is just as tenable as any other, but it does suggest that the explanation of random chance as that which governs history, past, present, and future, lacks the kind of criteria that make it amenable to assessment or validation.

We can now review the pegs of our framework. We have asserted that we need to distinguish between initiators of belief and followers, and that there must indeed be followers. We have claimed that the impact of a belief is ultimately independent of the temporal authority of the belief's initiator. We have said that followers organize and that such organizations can exert an influence on the future simply as organizations, and that such organizations tend to throw up internal authorities which themselves, in their own right, can shape the future. We have noted that beliefs may produce unforeseen consequences in the future, totally unrelated to the nature of the original belief, and that the *force* of any belief is related to surety of conviction, not to verifiable truth. Finally, we have observed that all changes due to belief may be explicable in the light of a number of different causes, including the hand of Divine Providence, hypothetical blind and irresistible social and/or economic forces, or simply the haphazard of mere luck.

Our original purpose was to examine the role of belief in creating or influencing history. We have not tried to provide a definitive answer. However, it appears to be an inescapable conclusion that unless the nature of humanity is to change dramatically in the next century or so, we must seek to understand what is likely to influence and govern our future in the light of what kind of ideas have dominated our past. We are not condemned to repeat our mistakes, nor are we consigned to following blindly the errors of former ages. Equally, we must force ourselves to assess our present wisdom with humility, our projections and assumptions with some prudence, and our visions with some caution. I would suggest in passing to futurists that historians may yet prove the surest guides to what lies before us, based on what lies behind us.

Notes

1. A. Farrer *A Study in St. Mark* (London 1951) p. 221f; R. Fuller *A Critical Introduction to the New Testament* (London 1971) p. 109f; O. Cullmann *The Christology of the New Testament* (London 1973) p. 109f; J. Jeremias *New Testament Theology* (London 1971) Vol. 1 p. 96f; J. N. D. Kelly *Early Christian Doctrines* (London 1968) p. 138f; M. Simon & A. Benoit *Le Judaisme et le Christianisme Antique* (Paris 1968) p. 99f.

2. S. Cave *An Introduction to the Study of Some Living Religions of the East* (London 1952) p. 104f; C. Humphries *Buddhism* (Harmondsworth 1958) pp. 90f, 108f; R. C. Majumdar et al. *An Advanced History of India* (Delhi 1974) Vol. 1 p. 80f.

3. I. Epstein *Judaism* (Harmondsworth 1959) p. 16f; H. Ringgren *Israelite Religion* (London 1966) p. 28f; Cave *Religions* pp. 194, 213f; W. Durant *The Age of Faith* (New York 1950) p. 211f; A.C. Bouquet *Comparative Religion* (Harmondsworth 1954) p. 142f.

4. R. Ghirshman *Iran* (Harmondsworth 1954) p. 315f; H. Chadwick *The Early Church* (New York 1986) p. 169f; C. Previte-Orton *The Shorter Cambridge Medieval History* (Cambridge 1952) Vol. 2 p. 660f.

5. E. Reischaur & J. Fairbank *East Asia: The Great Tradition* (Boston 1960) pp. 69f, 80f; Cave *Religions* p. 157f; C. Dawson *The Making of Europe* (New York 1966) p. 193f; M. Deanesley *A History of Early Medieval Europe 476-911* (London 1956) p. 525f.

6. Previte-Orton *Medieval History* Vol. 1 p. 129f; J. W. C. Wand *A History of the Early Church to AD 500* (London 1965) p. 219f; R. Grousset *The Empire of the Steppes* (New Brunswick 1970) pp. 255, 270f, 300f; D. Mathew *Ethiopia* (London 1947) p. 11f; Chadwick *Early Church* p. 200f.

7. F. Cross *The Oxford Dictionary of the Christian Church* (London 1958) pp. 219f, 831f; R. Oliver & J.D. Fage *A Short History of Africa* (Harmondsworth 1965) p. 162; J. Moorman *A History of the Church in England* (London 1967) p. 72f; A. Briggs *The Age of Improvement* (London 1964) p. 66f.

8. Previte-Orton *Medieval History* Vol. 1 p. 283f; R.H.C. Davis *A History of Medieval Europe* (London 1961) p. 74f; F. Heer *The Medieval World* (London 1962) p. 39f.

9. Bertrand Russell *A History of Western Philosophy* (London 1961)

pp. 125f, 173f, 212; Heer *Medieval World* p. 38f; H. von Campenhausen *The Fathers of the Latin Church* (London 1964) p. 250f; G. Leff *Medieval Thought* (Harmondsworth 1962) p. 46f.

10. R. E. Latham *Lucretius: The Nature of the Universe* (Harmondsworth 1960) p. 8f; W. E. Leonard & S.B. Smith *T. Lucreti Cari: De Rerum Natura* (Madison 1942) p. 41f; R. Frye *The Heritage of Persia* (London 1962) p. 221f; A. Bausani *The Persians* (London 1975) p. 62f.

11. A. Gardiner *Egypt of the Pharaohs* (Oxford 1961) p. 228f; Reischaur & Fairbank *Great Tradition* p. 120f; M. Cary & H.H. Scullard *A History of Rome Down to the Reign of Constantine* (New York 1983) p. 482f; D.G.E. Hall *A History of South-East Asia* (London 1964) p. 110f; W. Haig "Akbar, Mystic & Prophet" *Cambridge History of India* (Delhi 1971) Vol. 4 p. 119f.

12. Majumdar *India* p. 95f.

13. Humphries *Buddhism* p. 63f; M. Grant *The Climax of Rome* (Boston 1968) p. 236f; Deanesley *Medieval Europe* p. 59; J. Godfrey *The Church in Anglo-Saxon England* (Cambridge 1962) p. 73f.

14. W. Emery *Archaic Egypt* (Harmondsworth 1961) pp. 38f, 105f; Reischaur & Fairbank *Great Tradition* p. 86f; Cary & Scullard *Rome* pp. 229, 237f; T. Mommsen *History of Rome* (London 1930 ed.) Vol. 3 p. 250.

15. L. Strachey *Eminent Victorians* (Harmondsworth 1948) p. 129f; A. Rusk *Doctrines of the Great Educators* (New York 1965) p. 157f; H.C. Barnard *A History of English Education from 1760* (London 1968) p. 79f; *Oxford Classical Dictionary* N.G.L. Hammond & H.H. Scullard ed. (Oxford 1979) p. 454f; D. Boorstin *The Discoverers* (New York 1983) pp. 296f, 465f.

16. T.D. Barnes "Legislation Against the Christians" *Jnl. Rom. Stud.* 58 (1968) p. 32f; Simon & Benoit *Christianisme* p. 125f; Gardiner *Pharaohs* pp. 126f, 177, 298f, 328; G. Roux *Ancient Iraq* (London 1964) pp. 168, 257, 329f, cf. J. Pritchard *The Ancient Near East* (Princeton 1973) Vol. 1 p. 206f; W. Tennent *Ceylon* (London 1860) Vol. 1 pp. 355f, 375f, 391f.

17. G. Ostrogorsky *History of the Byzantine State* (New Brunswick 1957) p. 154f.

18. Cf. passim W. Ulhmann *The Growth of Papal Government in the Middle Ages* (London 1955); H. Kuhner *Encyclopedia of the Papacy* (London 1959).

19. Reischaur & Fairbank *Great Tradition* p. 360f; Grousset *Steppes* p. 513f.

20. H. Pirenne *Mahomet and Charlemagne* (London 1939) passim; *Economic and Social History of Medieval Europe* (London 1961) p. 3f; cf. J.M. Abun-Nasir *A History of the Maghrib* (Cambridge 1975) p. 67f.

21. Boorstin *Discoverers* p. 224f; S. Clissold *The Seven Cities of Cibola* (London 1961) p. 13f.

22. Cf. M. Singer *Generalization in Ethics* (New York 1971) p. 53;

293

C.E.M. Joad *A Critique of Logical Positivism* (London 1950) p. 43f; J. Kupperman *Ethical Knowledge* (London 1970) p. 50f.

23. G.C. Vaillant *The Aztecs of Mexico* (Harmondsworth 1960) p. 195f (cf. pl. 29).

24. B. Warmington *Carthage* (New York 1969) p. 148f; H.H. Scullard *Roman Britain: Outpost of Empire* (London 1986) p. 20 (cf. Caes. *Bell. Gall.* 6.16); Livy *Ab Urbe Cond.* 22.57.2f; W. Warde Fowler *The Religious Experience of the Roman People* (London 1922) pp. 33f, 44f, 107, 112.

25. Von Campenhausen *Latin Church* p. 241f; Russell *Western Philosophy* p. 353f; P. Teilhard de Chardin *The Phenomenon of Man* (London 1966) passim.

HISTORIES OF THE FUTURE

by

W. Warren Wagar

The conventional wisdom—with which in this case I have no quarrel—argues that modern utopias differ from traditional utopias in three significant ways. First, the modern utopia is a world order, or a model for one, not an oasis of perfection in some cunningly concealed cranny of the earth. Second, the modern utopia is dynamic, in process of ceaseless ameliorative change through the machinations of human reason. And third, the modern utopia flourishes not in some mysterious neverwhen but in the future, our own future, often in some specific year. The same may be said for most modern dystopias—for example, the baleful world order imagined by George Orwell, set in the year 1984, and in process of ceaseless pejorative change.

Of course there are plenty of exceptions to one or more of these criteria for the modern utopia, if by "modern" we mean pertaining to the last few centuries. James Hilton's Shangri-la is an oasis of perfection in a cunningly concealed cranny of the earth. The future England of William Morris's *News from Nowhere* is not undergoing ceaseless change of any kind; on the contrary, Morris finds it warmly nestled in an "epoch of rest." Far from belonging to some adventuresome future, the insular utopia imagined by Aldous Huxley in his last novel, *Island*, was founded in the nineteenth century and at the end of the story, set in the present, it faces occupation and destruction by a ruthless dictatorship.

But we can always say that these are not typical modern utopias, or better still, that they are throwbacks to premodern utopian sensibilities. Hilton, Morris, and Huxley are not, after all, textbook examples of the modernizing mentality. In many respects, they belong to what might be called the neo-romantic counterculture, a large and powerful force in modern times, but clearly anti-modern in many of its values and beliefs.

The quintessentially modern utopia (using "modern" in the sense it enjoys among historians as opposed to literary critics) is the utopia of science, technology, reason, progress, and world order, a secular utopia, the vision of a planet living in peace, prosperity, and harmony under a rational star. The tradition begins, somewhat tentatively and ambiguously, with Francis Bacon in *The New Atlantis* and descends through St. Pierre, Condorcet, Comte, Cabet, and Marx to Edward Bellamy, H. G. Wells, and B. F. Skinner. Essentially

W. Warren Wagar *is a professor of history at the State University of New York at Binghamton.*

the representative modern utopia is a technocracy, or perhaps even a "scientocracy," a society governed by the steel logic of science and technique.

But it is not a static utopia. If only because science and technique are endlessly self-correcting and self-fructifying, the "perfect" society imagined by writers of the modernist-rationalist persuasion is a society that is never quite perfect. It keeps changing and evolving into something still higher, so that it cannot be torn out of time and viewed *sub specie aeternitatis*. It is a society locked into history, with a past, a present, and a future.

To some extent, then, all authentic modern utopias elude description. The structure of the classic utopian tale, in which one or more wide-eyed visitors receive a guided tour of an ideal society thriving in some exotic clime (like Voltaire's Eldorado in *Candide*), does not quite work for a modern utopia, because modern utopias must be *told*, as one would narrate a series of events in history. The utopographer may focus on present-day conditions in his or her modern utopia, but its origins and destiny are implicitly no less important.

On rare occasions, modern utopias are even cast in the form of history texts, works that draw freely on the utopian tradition, but adopt the conventions of the historical narrative, rather than of so-called imaginative literature.

Obviously many important utopian texts down through the centuries have been non-fictional, such as Fourier's *Theory of the Four Movements* or Comte's *System of Positive Polity* or *The Communist Manifesto* of Marx and Engels. In others, like Bacon's *The New Atlantis*, or for that matter More's *Utopia*, the mantle of fiction rests lightly on the shoulders, like the abbreviated gown of an Oxford don.

But the theme of this paper is a sub-genre that lies exactly midway, in a kind of literary no-man's-land, between fiction and non-fiction: that is, the imaginary history of the future, the work that reads as if it were a textbook miraculously snatched from the cabin of a time machine, a book such as H. G. Wells's *The Shape of Things to Come*, first published in 1933, and later scavenged by Wells himself to furnish the screenplay of his film, *Things to Come*.

What a strange hybrid volume like *The Shape of Things to Come* achieves, among other things, is a fleshing-out of all three premises of the modern utopia. As defined above, a modern utopia is typically a world order, in process of dynamic ameliorative change, set in a specific future time. All of this, especially the second premise, implies a chronology, a future history. If utopia is no longer perceived as a static ideal but rather as a process, then it must be expected to unfold by degrees through future time. It must have a history: and what better way to convey its historical dimension than by emulating the style and methods of the historian?

Unfortunately, many readers have trouble coping with imaginary histories of times to come. People like things clearly labeled: music must be either classical or non-classical, words must be either prose or poetry, and, for most readers, a vision of the future must be either unambiguously fictional (like a novel) or non-fictional (like a sociological treatise). Hypothetical scholarship, imaginary science, and fictitious history may leave them confused and uneasy.

For all that, writers do sometimes try their hand, and readers do sometimes respond. To my mind the best parts of Orwell's *Nineteen Eighty-Four* are the two chapters from the imaginary sociological tract by Emmanuel Goldstein, entitled "The Theory and Practice of Oligarchical Collectivism," together with the bone-chilling appendix, "The Principles of Newspeak." Orwell's American publishers wanted to leave out these items, but Orwell (even on his deathbed) stubbornly refused to comply.

Among my other favorite hypothetical works are Dougal Dixon's *After Man*, a zoologist's illustrated guide to the fauna of the earth after *Homo sapiens* becomes extinct, and two volumes by Stanislaw Lem, *Imaginary Magnitude* and *A Perfect Vacuum*, the first of which contains a collection of introductions by Lem to imaginary books, and the second, reviews by Lem of imaginary books, including Lem's fictional review of his own reviews!

So all kinds of intriguing possibilities exist in the realm of hypothetical scholarship. But what of imaginary histories that embody visions of utopia?

First, a brief list. I do not pretend to have scoured the world for my examples, as, for example, Lyman Tower Sargent has done with utopias of all kinds or Paul Brians with tales of nuclear war. But I have started collecting them casually, as one might collect sea shells. In the collection are two books by Wells, *The Shape of Things to Come* and an earlier work, *The World Set Free*, which dates from 1914 and contains his uncanny forecast of atomic energy and atomic bombs. Most of my examples are more recent, like Robert Prehoda's *Your Next Fifty Years*; Paul Hawken and colleagues, *Seven Tomorrows*; Norman Macrae's *The 2025 Report*; Gerard K. O'Neill's *2081*; and Peter Jay and Michael Stewart's *Apocalypse 2000*.

In addition, there are quite a few novels that oscillate back and forth between the methods of scholarship and the conventions of imaginative fiction, notably Olaf Stapledon's *Last and First Men* and *Starmaker*, and others in a Stapledonian vein, such as George Zebrowski's *Macrolife*. Nor should we forget the fragments of future history routinely embedded in many modern, and anti-modern, utopias: for example, the brief lectures on history given by Dr. Leete in chapters 5 and 24 of Bellamy's *Looking Backward*, or the history chapter, "How the Change Came," in *News from Nowhere*.

Of still greater interest are writers who have gone the whole way, constructing literal histories of the future. Apart from Wells's archetypical *Shape of Things to Come*, the model text is *The Third*

Millennium: A History of the World, AD 2000-3000, by two English writers of science fiction, the sociologist Brian Stableford and the physicist David Langford, which appeared in the fall of 1985 in a glossy format, replete with a hologram on the cover and many trick photographs and paintings inside, from the illustrious house of Alfred A. Knopf.

One wonders just how many Americans have read or at least heard of *The Third Millennium*. According to Stableford, in a letter to me, the book "sank almost without a trace" in the States, despite the Knopf imprint; but it has done rather well elsewhere. The original London edition from Sidgwick and Jackson was a modest success, and there is a new paperbound edition in the UK from Paladin Books. *The Third Millennium* also sold briskly in French and Japanese translations.

The four parts of the book narrate four epochs of future history, from the Period of Crisis (2000 to 2180), when all the gathering woes of the 20th century culminate in various disasters, through periods of Recovery and Transformation, to the fourth epoch, entitled "The Creation of the New World," from 2650 to 3000. As the titles suggest, the history of the future according to Stableford and Langford is a history of accelerating progress after a longish time of troubles, which is also, by the way, the plot of *The Shape of Things to Come*.

But Stableford and Langford's troubles are less apocalyptic than Wells's. In 1933 Wells foresaw a second world war starting as a conflict between Germany and Poland that spreads until it devastates civilization. In *The Third Millennium* we have only local wars, spot famines, business depressions, coastal flooding from the greenhouse effect, earthquakes, and mysterious outbreaks of guerrilla war waged with bacteriological weapons by unknown aggressors. But toward the end of the 21st century, the health of the planet begins gradually to improve. After disarmament talks in 2080, the nations wind down the arms race, and, in concert with an enlightened confederacy of global corporations, bring an end to the military phase of human history. Fusion power solves the energy problem, biotechnology eliminates world hunger, mass reversible sterilization defuses the population bomb, and poverty disappears.

The scene is then set for more or less continuous progress, thanks largely to technology. Gerontologists prolong the life span to three hundred years. New human species are engineered, as earthlings fling into space and populate the galaxy. Thanks to unlimited abundance, politics loses its desperate quality, and peace reigns supreme. Stableford and Langford's imaginary historian muses that at long last "progress has brought us to the goal for which we were always aiming." It all sounds very much like utopia!

Reviewing *The Third Millennium* in *The Bulletin of the Science Fiction*

Writers of America, I found only one flaw in the book: its political naivete, which allows the authors to imagine that technology is a cornucopia capable of depoliticizing the human animal and that corporations will work with bureaucrats to contrive a wise, harmonious world order with liberty and justice for all.

But this twofold hope, in the rationality of commerce and the capacity of science and technology to solve all social problems, distills the modern faith in progress handed down from Francis Bacon and Adam Smith. It is the dominant myth of modern culture, and one shared, in most respects, by the man whose utopian novel *Looking Backward* celebrated its one hundredth birthday in 1988, Edward Bellamy. Bellamy would have scoffed at Stableford and Langford's qualified endorsement of private capital, but the technocratic state capitalism he preached is not so very different.

Nor does it take a keen imagination to figure out what Karl Marx would have had to say about both books. Marx, too, harbored a vision of the future that owes much to the modernizing impulse, although he declined to enter into any of the pertinent details. He and Engels shared a mortal fear of falling into the mind-trap of utopian wishful thinking, the kind of mind-trap that converts potential hard-headed revolutionists into harmless eccentrics.

Nevertheless, the Marxian vision of the future, which peeps out from between the lines of many texts by Engels and Marx alike, commands a wide following around the world. They foresaw a distant future, after the workers' overthrow of the regime of the bourgeoisie, when no man or woman would exploit another, when classes and even class consciousness had disappeared from the face of the earth, and when all use of coercive force—in short, all government—had been abolished, and replaced by public administration. Then, and only then, would the real history of the human race commence, a history of freedom from the miserliness of nature and the plutocratic tyranny of greed. Every citizen would be free to actualize all of his or her potentialities, in a commonwealth of sociable joys and limitless progress. Even anti-Marxists may be willing to see in this vision a plausible secular version of Paradise. So why doesn't someone write a history of the future that embodies the Marxian idea of utopia?

I asked myself that question several years ago and my answer is *A Short History of the Future* (which the University of Chicago Press will publish later this year). Since the manuscript weighs in at just over 100,000 words, the adjective "short" is perhaps misleading. *A Medium-Length History of the Future* might be more appropriate.

In any case, the text is an imaginary history of the next 200 years. My alter ego, a Danish-American historian named Peter Jensen, takes the human race from a coming nightmare of technocratic monopoly capital through the catharsis of world war and armed revolution to a socialist commonwealth of the survivors and finally, in the mid-22nd century, to a decentralized world society of autonomous ecotopian communities. This final vision corresponds roughly to Marx's forecast in his "Critique of the Gotha Program" of a second, higher stage of communism after the total extirpation of private capital. The three sections of the book are entitled, respectively, "Earth, Inc.," "Red Earth," and "The House of Earth."

Most of the text consists of a narrative history, in twelve chapters not unlike those in a schoolbook, although (necessarily!) the events described are fictional. Sandwiched between the chapters are "interludes," featuring letters, diary entries, book reviews, newspaper articles, and other documents of future life drawn from the family archive of Peter Jensen.

My aim in writing this book has been not to predict the future—I have no illusions about my ability, or anyone else's to do that—but to explore a variety of futuribles in the manner of the practicing historian, to bring a sequence of conceivable future events to life as only narration can do. Knowledge of the real future is denied to us. But we must never lose sight of the one thing we *can* know about the future: that it will happen, piece by piece, hour by hour, in a relentless procession of causes and effects. No act is without consequences, and no consequences are without further consequences, unscrolling in the forward flow of time.

I also hope that my *Short History* and all the other histories of the future that have appeared in recent years will help turn the writing of utopias in a new direction. Just like the future itself, any utopian society that we ever succeed in building will be the outcome of historical processes. The imaginary future history is a useful device for anticipating—and designing—the roads we may travel to reach our destination. Because there are many credible futures, and also many imaginable destinations, we need such scenarios not by the ones and twos, but by the bushel. As I say in the Foreword to my own version, if you don't like it, write a better one. Nothing would please me more!

Histories of the Future: A Select List

Note: Some of these works are not, by any definition, utopias, but all of them make use of the historian's technique of nonfictional narrative.

Hackett, Sir John, *The Third World War: August 1985* (New York: Macmillan Publishing Co., 1979)

Hackett, Sir John, *The Third World War: The Untold Story* (New York: Macmillan Publishing Co., 1982)

Hawken, Paul, James Ogilvy, and Peter Schwartz, *Seven Tomorrows: Toward a Voluntary History* (New York: Bantam Books, 1982)

Jay, Peter, and Michael Stewart, *Apocalypse 2000: Economic Breakdown and the Suicide of Democracy 1989-2000* (New York: Prentice Hall Press, 1987)

Macrae, Norman, *The 2025 Report* (New York: Macmillan Publishing Co., 1984)

O'Neill, Gerard K., *2081: A Hopeful View of the Human Future* (New York: Simon & Schuster, 1981)

Prehoda, Robert W., *Your Next Fifty Years* (New York: Grosset & Dunlap, 1980)

Stableford, Brian, and David Langford, *The Third Millennium: A History of the World, AD 2000-3000* (New York: Alfred A. Knopf, 1985)

Stapledon, Olaf, *Last and First Men* (London: Methuen & Co., 1930)

Theobald, Robert, and J. M. Scott, *Teg's 1994: An Anticipation of the Near Future* (2nd ed., Chicago: Swallow Press, 1972)

Wagar, W. Warren, *A Short History of the Future* (Chicago: University of Chicago Press, 1989)

Wells, H. G., *The Shape of Things to Come* (New York: The Macmillan Company, 1933)

Wells, H. G., *The World Set Free: A Story of Mankind* (New York: E. P. Dutton, 1914)

About the World Future Society

The World Future Society is an independent, nonprofit, scientific and educational organization concerned with how people will live in the coming decades.

Founded in 1966, the Society currently has over 25,000 members worldwide. Individuals and groups from all nations are eligible to join the Society and participate in its programs and activities.

The Society publishes a number of periodicals and books, sponsors local chapters, and holds conferences and assemblies.

The publications include THE FUTURIST, a bimonthly magazine reporting trends, forecasts, and ideas about the future; FUTURE SURVEY, a monthly digest of abstracts of futures-relevant literature; and FUTURES RESEARCH QUARTERLY, a professional journal providing information on more technical future-oriented topics.

The Society also maintains a unique bookstore that enables members to purchase future-related books, cassette recordings of Society conference sessions, videocassettes, and more, all at special member prices.

Chapters of the World Future Society are active in both the United States and abroad. Chapters offer speakers, educational courses, seminars, and other opportunities for members in local areas to meet and work together.

World Future Society conferences and general assemblies provide opportunities to hear and meet many outstanding thinkers such as the Society's Sixth General Assembly, "Future View: The 1990s & Beyond," held in Washington, D.C., July 16-20, 1989.

For additional information about Society membership or publications, write:

World Future Society
4916 Saint Elmo Avenue
Bethesda, Maryland 20814
U.S.A.